NO STONE
UNTURNED

NO STONE UNTURNED

The Story of NecroSearch International

STEVE JACKSON

KENSINGTON BOOKS
http://www.kensingtonbooks.com

Some names have been changed to protect the privacy of individuals connected to this story.

KENSINGTON BOOKS are published by

Kensington Publishing Corp.
850 Third Avenue
New York, NY 10022

Library of Congress Card Catalogue Number: 2001090401
ISBN: 1-57566-456-9

First Printing: January 2002
10 9 8 7 6 5 4 3 2 1

Printed in the United States of America

Designed by Leonard Telesca

This book is dedicated to the memory of Dick C. Hopkins.
Hoppy, Holmes would have been proud.

CONTENTS

FOREWORD

In 1988, several criminalists and other scientists sat down in a Denver-area restaurant and came up with the idea of burying pigs to study changes to the environment caused by the graves and their contents. Disturbed by what they'd witnessed of outdated techniques for locating clandestine burial sites and the recovery of the remains of murder victims, their idea was to "find a better way" through the application of a variety of scientific disciplines and good old-fashioned detective work. As their successes and reputation mounted, they became known affectionately to law enforcement agencies as "the Pig People," a name that stuck long after they officially incorporated as a nonprofit organization, NecroSearch International.

When the idea for this book was broached in 1997, the members of NecroSearch pointed out that their involvement in their most dramatic cases often came at the end of what had been years of work by law enforcement officers. If those investigators had not gone above and beyond the call of duty, if they had not been driven to seek justice for the victims despite the emotional and physical wear and tear on them personally, there would have been no need for NecroSearch's involvement. The victims would have remained lost to their loved ones, the killers not held accountable.

This, then, is the story of those in law enforcement and the members of NecroSearch who, when all seemed lost, or one last push was needed to tip the scales of justice, loaned their expertise, hearts, and minds to the cause.

PROLOGUE

I shall be as secret as the grave.
—Miguel de Cervantes, *Don Quixote.*

August 4, 1990, The Missouri River

The two men worked quickly in the dark around the beat-up two-door sedan perched on a boat ramp facing the river. The night air was as thick and muggy as a sauna. Quiet except for the whine of a million insects, the gentle lapping of the river, and the muted voices of the men.

Alone among the shadows that haunted the heavily wooded bank 45 miles northwest of Maryville, Missouri, the pair fixed a tree branch between the steering wheel and the front seat to keep the car from veering. They took another stick and wedged it between the gas pedal and the driver's-side seat, the pedal pressed to the floor.

One of the men leaned in and turned the key in the ignition. The car roared to life; the engine screamed to hurry and get it over with. The man threw the transmission into drive and stepped back, closing the door as the maroon Oldsmobile lurched forward, down the ramp, and into the river.

The water quickly drowned the engine, but it had served its purpose. Momentum carried the car out into the current, which grabbed the vehicle—still afloat even with the driver's-side window open—and dragged it downstream.

Tony Emery and his childhood pal, Ron Coy, watched the car slip deeper into the water. That's when Emery noticed the woman's purse lying on the boat ramp. "Shit!" he exclaimed. He'd meant to put it in the car. He picked it up and tossed it as far as he could toward the water.

Coy didn't say anything, but he was thinking that tossing the purse into the river was a dumb move. No telling if a fisherman would find it hung up on some bushes along a bank and report it to the police. Someone might come looking here. But saying that to Tony Emery, even if they were friends, wasn't a smart idea either.

"No witness, no case." Emery shrugged and grinned. He was a big guy—barrel-chested, weightlifter arms—and good-looking, with a head of thick, dark hair. But he was as mean as he was handsome, the town bully of tiny Maryville, eighty miles due north of Kansas City.

With a population of about 20,000, Maryville was a quaint little town: courthouse in the middle of town square, the home of Northwest Missouri State University. Everybody in town and for miles around knew Emery, and many feared him and his "enforcer," Coy, who, though only five-feet-eight, was a walking 200-pound muscle with a crewcut, beady eyes, and a nasty attitude. Bad things tended to happen when someone crossed Emery or his family. He considered himself beyond the reach of the law, treating it and its sworn officers with disdain.

The Maryville Department of Public Safety, the Nodaway County Sheriff, and the Missouri State Highway Patrol had been after Emery for years, but they could never make much of anything stick. In 1979, he was convicted on a penny-ante charge for possession of burglary tools, and he spent two years in the state penitentiary.

Upon his release, he swore he'd never go back. But that didn't stop him from expanding his criminal activities into dealing methamphetamine. It only made him more determined to stay one step ahead of the law.

With its penchant for guns and violence, the meth trade was perfect for a guy like Tony Emery. Anywhere he went, he went armed, and if he needed a little extra muscle to intimidate the locals, he called on his good friend Ron Coy.

By 1987, Emery had decided to take over the region's methamphetamine distribution, first in Maryville and then expanding to include all of northwest Missouri and southwest Iowa. It was a lucrative enough business to build a home, buy others for rentals, purchase an $18,000 truck and a $40,000 sports car, plus have enough cash on hand to buy pounds of meth at $10,000 a pop. The police believed the whole family was involved, including his mother, who they discovered had plunked down $40,000 in a single year toward the principal on her mortgage. All of it—the houses, the vehicles, the mortgages—paid for in cash.

With so much at stake, Emery let it be known that he would fight to keep what he viewed as his. He carried a huge .44 magnum handgun, purchased for him by his mother because he was a felon and not legally allowed to buy or own firearms. He also kept an assault rifle close at hand in his home.

Capitalizing on his reputation for violence, he moved quickly against threats to his monopoly. When one lowlife tried to set himself up in the methamphetamine business in Maryville, Emery sent him a message. With his henchmen, Coy, Emery went to the young man's home, stood outside on the street, and shot the walls and windows full of holes. The young man quickly left town.

Cold and calculating, Tony Emery was smart enough not to use meth himself. "It'll screw you up," he told his associates. But while he didn't use it, many of Emery's distributors were addicts, such as Christine Elkins, the 32-year-old girlfriend of one of his drug-dealing pals, Bob Clark.

It was through Christine that the police tried to get him again. Along with agents of the U.S. Bureau of Alcohol, Tobacco and Firearms, they used her to nail him on drug and weapons charges. With her testimony at Emery's upcoming trial in September, they thought they would have enough to put him behind the walls of the penitentiary for a long, long time. However, that night as he watched the Oldsmobile drift out into the current and at last sink beneath the swift, dark waters of the Missouri, Emery knew he wasn't going to have to worry about Christine Elkins testifying. Her whereabouts would be as secret as the grave. And if the cops didn't have a witness, they wouldn't have a case. But then, Emery had never heard of the Pig People.

I

A Brief History of Forensic Science

The Lord said to Cain, "Where is Abel your brother?" And Cain said, "I do not know. Am I my brother's keeper?" And He said, "What have you done? The voice of your brother's blood cries out to Me from the ground."

It may have been the first murder. The shepherd Cain killing his farmer brother Abel in a fit of jealousy and envy. And ever since that initial homicide, the blood of murder victims has cried out for justice from the ground, as well as from attics and basements, the bottoms of rivers, and the trunks of automobiles.

However, man, lacking the omnipotence of God, has had to rely on his brain to catch killers when the answer wasn't as obvious as a smoking gun. He accomplished that through a marriage of science and law enforcement known as forensic science.

Forensic means "applied to law" and entails a variety of enterprises from gathering and testing evidence to "expert testimony" in a court of law. In today's world, forensic experts cover a wide variety of scientific specialties, including anthropology, botany, entomology, chemistry, serology, psychology, and geophysics. They work for government agencies and colleges and universities, and as private consultants.

No one can say exactly when science first entered the realm of law enforcement, but certainly before it was recognized as a field of study. For a long time, working for the police was considered beneath the dignity of the serious scientist.

Indeed, science's early contributions to law enforcement were often unintentional or coincidental, such as when Anton van Leeuwenhoek of Holland invented the first simple microscope in the 1670s. He certainly wasn't trying to solve crimes, but without the descendants of that first microscope such forensic techniques as blood stain and fiber analysis, ballistic comparisons, and DNA testing would be impossible.

It wasn't until 1810 that the world's first purely investigative agency, the French Surete, was created. (The term *detective,* as a police specialty, wasn't actually used until Charles Dickens wrote *Bleak*

House in 1856.) The formation of the Surete was also notable in that the police recognized that an "expert" from outside their ranks might be of some assistance. Its first director, Francois Vidocq, was a notorious criminal before he tired of always being on the run and volunteered to assist the overwhelmed Paris police in exchange for a clean slate.

Vidocq is credited with creating the first police files, by recording the physical appearance of apprehended criminals. He was also a pioneer in the field of those who would someday be known as criminal behaviorists. He noted that professional criminals tended to work in consistent patterns. Thieves generally remained thieves. Bank robbers robbed banks using certain phrases or in a particular manner. One killer may like to strangle his victims; another may use a knife.

Understanding the criminal's mind, Vidocq knew, might lead to capture. So when a crime was committed in Paris, he and his men—many of them also former criminals—looked in the files and attempted to match physical description and modus operandi, Latin for *method of operation,* to narrow down the list of potential suspects.

His methods were eventually adopted by every major police force in the world. The continuation and expansion of his work can be seen in today's FBI's Behavioral Sciences Unit and its famed criminal profilers.

In 1840, Marie Lafarge, the pretty young widow of old Charles Lafarge, hardly waited for his body to grow cold before she was off to see the family attorney about the will. She thought she had nothing to worry about. After all, her husband had exhibited all the symptoms of cholera, a common enough disease of the time.

At the dead man's bedside, however, a Dr. Lespinasse told Charles's mother that he believed her son had been poisoned. He interviewed the house servants, who told him that they had seen Marie sprinkle a white powder over the dead man's meals, including the cup of eggnog she'd given him just hours before his death. The gardener claimed she'd sent him to buy arsenic to rid the home of rats a few weeks earlier.

The good doctor directed the police to seize the glass of eggnog Charles Lafarge had been drinking, and to transport his body for an autopsy. But whatever Lespinasse's suspicions, proving it would be another matter. Up to that time, there was no way to test for arsenic—a colorless, odorless poison—or for many other poisons.

Marie Lafarge was certainly aware of this. But what she didn't know was the existence of a new alliance between science and law enforcement called toxicology, the study of poisons.

Two years earlier, a French scientist, Dr. Mathieu Orfila, had begun working on a test for arsenic. But he was beaten to it by the English scientist James Marsh, who invented a process that could detect the presence of the gas arsine, which is produced when arsenic is heated at the correct temperature.

The trial of the beautiful Marie Lafarge captured worldwide attention through newspaper accounts. Readers were divided over her guilt or innocence.

All the prosecutors had were the accounts of the house servants, which had other plausible explanations—after all, arsenic was a common means of ridding a house of rats. However, midway through the trial, Orfila was asked by the prosecution to test for arsenic using Marsh's process. He was quickly able to establish that arsenic, "enough to kill ten people," was in the eggnog given to Charles Lafarge. But he also needed to prove that Lafarge had ingested the poison.

Orfila obtained fluid from Charles's stomach, which when tested also revealed the presence of arsenic. He reported his findings to the court, and Marie Lafarge, confronted by the irrefutable evidence of science, was convicted of murder and spent the rest of her life in prison.

In the era before television, the stories of notorious criminals, sensational crimes, and the exploits of detectives were followed avidly by newspaper readers. The general public got its first taste of forensic chemistry during the trial of Marie Lafarge.

However, a fictional character did the most, beginning in 1886, to popularize the concept of science and law enforcement working together to solve crimes. Sherlock Holmes, the pipe-smoking London detective who, with his companion Dr. John Watson, solved what appeared to be inexplicable murders through observation, deductive logic, and experimentation, was a character invented by a young medical doctor, Arthur Conan Doyle. Holmes wasn't strictly a product of Doyle's imagination, but a composite of his medical school professors.

Chief among them was Doyle's mentor, Dr. Joe Bell. Holmes's abilities to reach conclusions through simple observation and attention to details that others missed was modeled after what Doyle called "Bell's method." For instance, Bell once perplexed Doyle by observing that a patient must have walked over the local golf course to reach their office. Bell had noted that it was a rainy day and that the man's boots bore small stains of red clay, which could only be found locally on bare spots on the links and nowhere else in that part of the country.

Holmes blended the man of science with the specialist in crime, becoming the predecessor of the criminalist in today's crime laboratories. Real-life detectives adopted Holmes's method of deductive logic, defined in *Webster's* as "reasoning from a known principle to an unknown, from the general to the specific, or from a premise to a logical conclusion"—common to the scientist trying to prove or disprove a theory. However, even as readers devoured the adventures of Holmes and Watson, advances in forensic science were outstripping even the foresight of the legendary detective and his creator.

Again, some advances were made due to purposes other than crime solving. For instance, in 1888, George Eastman of the United States invented the first handheld camera. It was portable and used roll film rather than the bulky and cumbersome equipment and glass plates of its predecessors. Thus, it became the first practical means of recording a crime scene, making it possible for a jury to be shown dozens of photographs.

Other advances in forensic applications were made simply out of curiosity. Such was the case with dactylography—the study of fingerprints—the single most important means of human identification.

In the 1860s, an Englishman in India, William James Herschel, noticed that the imprints his fingers left on a glass matched the collection of lines of his fingertips. He began studying his own and those of his family, noting that even among people closely related by blood, fingerprints were markedly different. The imprints seen on Herschel's glass were actually the residue left over from millions of sweat pores scrunched together along the ridges on the fingertips.

These pores are constantly pumping out a mixture of 99-percent water and 1-percent fatty acid. More is produced when a person is nervous, as in the act of committing a crime. Left on a surface, the water evaporates, but the fatty acid remains.

About the same time, another Englishman, Dr. Henry Faulds, who lived in Japan and had read about the ancient use of thumbprints by China's emperors to "sign" official papers, was conducting a study of his own. Faulds wrote an article for *Nature* magazine in 1880 about his study and how he had used it to help solve a Japanese burglary case. Most police agencies ignored the report, believing, as did the general population, that fingerprints would change with time and that more than one person was likely to have the same prints.

However, not all police detectives were as indifferent. In 1892, the bodies of two young children were found bludgeoned to death in their beds in Argentina. No one had witnessed the murders, but the children's mother blamed a spurned boyfriend, saying he must have done the deed because she had taken a new lover.

A detective, who happened to have read the Faulds article, saw a bloody print where the murderer had opened the door to leave. He sent officers to fetch the accused, as well as an ink pad, paper, and a magnifying glass. When that was done, he compared the man's prints to those in the now-dry blood. They did not match. But he had another idea.

The detective asked the mother to go through the same process. Her prints matched, and, frightened by this magic, she quickly confessed that she had killed her own children to keep her new lover from leaving her.

It was the first recorded instance of fingerprints being used to solve a murder. However, the new science also created a problem. Police departments realized that they would soon have thousands of fingerprints on file, but no way to go through them quickly.

The difficulty was partially solved by an English biologist, Francis Galton, who devised a basic means of classifying fingerprints into different types based on the locations of five basic patterns found on fingerprints: whorls, radial loops, ulnar loops, arches, and tented arches. His method was soon expanded upon and incorporated into the practices of Scotland Yard by its director, Sir Edward R. Henry. No two people have ever been found to have identical fingerprints. And the work of Henry, though refined and computerized and its five patterns condensed to three (whorls, loops, and arches), remains in use a century later.

Throughout the past hundred years, the worlds of science and law enforcement continued to intersect like grapevines, meeting and diverging only to meet again farther up the trellis of history. The farther up, the more frequently their paths crossed.

One of the most important intertwinings occured at the turn of the century. It involved the one substance that, more than any other, spells murder: B-L-O-O-D.

Abel's cried out from the ground to accuse his killer. Pontius Pilate and MacBeth both tried to wash the guilt of it from their hands. It carries nutrients and oxygen to the muscles and organs of the body; without it, they shut down and we die. Yet through the nineteenth century, little was known about blood.

There was no way of identifying blood, especially dried blood, from other substances. Or differentiating between animal and human blood. Or what blood belonged to which individual. The first two of those issues were resolved in time to catch one of the most frightening and brutal killers of any era.

In September 1898, two 9-year-old girls disappeared from the German village of Lechtingen while on their way to school. The girls' butchered bodies were found the next day in the woods.

A man named Ludwig Tessnow, who had been seen talking to the girls the morning they disappeared, was immediately suspected of the crime, but it wasn't just because of the witness's report. Tessnow was an odd sort. He was not a native of the village, and walked around carrying on a quiet conversation with himself and smirking, as if in possession of some deep, amusing secret.

Tessnow was arrested, and the police discovered clothing in his hut that appeared to be smeared with a dried brown liquid that they thought might be blood. However, pointing to a container of liquid, he claimed the discolorations were caused by a wood stain he was using in his work as a carpenter. With no way to prove their suspicions and no other evidence, the police had to let him go.

Smirking and mumbling, Tessnow left the village. What he did for the next three years is unknown, and only terrifying to imagine. But in the summer of 1901, he again fell under suspicion for horrific violence. It started with the slaughter of six sheep near another small

German town. The animals had been hacked to pieces and their body parts strewn about the pasture. A man was seen running away.

A few weeks later, two young brothers disappeared from the town. A search was launched, but they weren't discovered until the next morning—their bodies cut up and the pieces tossed here and there in the woods. A witness came forward to say he had seen that odd man, Tessnow, in the area with dark stains on his clothing that, on reflection, may have been blood.

Tessnow was again arrested and his clothing confiscated. But again, he claimed the brown smears were nothing more than wood stain. He might again have gone free but for an accident of science.

Two years earlier, a young German doctor named Paul Uhlenhuth, working at the Berlin Institute of Infectious Diseases, was trying to find a way to immunize cattle against foot-and-mouth disease. As a byproduct, he discovered that the blood serum from a rabbit would react with, and thus identify, human blood. Uhlenhuth published his findings in 1901, and it happened that the prosecutor assigned to making a case against Tessnow read the report. He sent Tessnow's stained clothing to the doctor for testing.

Soaking the dried stains in salt water and then using his serum, Uhlenhuth located human blood on Tessnow's clothing in twenty-two different places. As an added measure, he used another serum to locate nine spots of sheep's blood. It was enough to convict Tessnow, who went to his execution still murmuring and smiling, with the blood of God only knows how many victims on his hands and clothes.

A child killer was stopped because a scientist was trying to save cattle, not solve crimes. Nor did the next giant leap forward in forensic serology owe its genesis to a member of the law enforcement community.

At the time Uhlenhuth was publishing his report, physicians were trying to find out why blood transfusions worked for some patients but killed others. The answer came when Dr. Karl Landsteiner, also of Germany, led a team that classified human blood into four major groups: A, B, O, and AB. They discovered that blood transfusions worked only when the blood group of the giver matched the blood group of the recipient.

Their work would save uncounted lives. But it also had immediate implications for law enforcement. Not only could police scientists now distinguish human blood from the blood of animals or unidentified stains; they could narrow the possible owners of blood stains found at a crime scene or on a suspect.

Over the remaining years of his life, Landsteiner developed an interest in the forensic applications of his work. Another of his contributions was the discovery that most people are "secretors," meaning that their other body fluids—saliva, sweat, urine, and semen—could also be classified into the four major blood groups. Only a small number of people in the population were nonsecretors.

Unfortunately, Landsteiner was practically laughed out of the courtroom the first time he tried to testify about secretors as an expert witness. The police investigating the bludgeoning death of a elderly man found a cigarette butt apparently left at the scene by his killer. Identifying a suspect, they had followed the man until he dropped another cigarette butt.

Both butts were sent to Landsteiner, who tested the residue of the saliva left on them. He noted that not only did the smoker of both cigarettes have the same blood type, but that the blood type, AB, only occured in about five percent of the population. The suspect had AB blood.

In the courtroom, however, the defense attorney mocked Landsteiner, effectively labeling him a fraud and his science bunk. How could anyone believe that a man's spit could identify him from another man? the defense lawyer laughed and the jury laughed with him.

The defendant was acquitted and set free. A few days later, the suspect confessed the murder. Of course, by then it was too late—in Germany, as in the United States, a man could not be tried a second time for the same crime.

Landsteiner's work was confirmed by other scientists and gradually accepted into courts of law. But it was typical of the roadblocks science has had to get past to make its contributions to the cause of justice. Even when the science was proven, it wasn't always the defense attorneys who stood in the way. Sometimes it has been the prosecutors or police, who either didn't understand what they were being told, or resented others walking about on their turf. And frequently, it was the fault of scientists who were unwilling or unable to explain what they were doing in order to get law enforcement on their side.

For these and other reasons, the use of forensic science has at times been disjointed and sporadic. For instance, in 1903, the New York City police were the first major police department to fingerprint every person arrested for a crime. But it wasn't until 1911, nineteen years after the murder case in Argentina, that fingerprints were accepted as evidence in a United States courtroom.

During the latter half of the nineteenth century, most of the significant advances in forensic science were accomplished in Europe. However, in 1915, a New Yorker was one of two men, working on opposite sides of the globe, who came up with the next major breakthrough. And he first made use of it to reverse a terrible miscarriage of justice by overzealous police investigators.

In 1915, a mildly retarded man was arrested for the murder of a neighbor. Early on in the police interview, he had admitted owning a gun of the same caliber used to shoot the man, but he steadfastly denied committing the murder. Only after three sleepless days of interrogation and threats, did he finally confess.

In court, the defendant recanted his confession, saying he had just wanted to be left alone. But the prosecution introduced an "expert witness," a doctor who claimed to have expertise in several fields dealing with criminal matters. This "scientist" had enlarged photographs of bullets taken from the dead man's body and several shot from the defendant's gun for comparison purposes. He noted for the jury a similar scratch on both. The man was not really a doctor, nor an expert in anything, and the enlarged photographs of the bullets were of poor quality. However, despite other evidence that indicated the defendant wasn't the killer, he was convicted. The accused was sentenced to die and taken to death row.

Fortunately, before he could be strapped into the electric chair, another man confessed to the killing. Still, the new confession wasn't enough to free the first suspect. The governor of New York appointed a commission to look into the matter.

One of its members, Charles Waite, took the bullets removed from the dead man to an optical company to be examined under a microscope. The technician there said there was no scratch on the bullets; indeed, the scratch on the photographs was due to the way the film had been processed. However, the technician did show Waite that the bullets had spiraling lines etched into the metal, lines almost too fine to be seen by the unaided eye.

Continuing his investigation, Waite talked to gunsmiths who explained that when the barrel of a gun is drilled, the cutting edge of the machine was designed to carve small, spiraling ridges, which they called lands, with grooves between them, into the bore. The reason was to cause a bullet to spin as it passed through the barrel on its way to the target, making it fly straighter and farther.

These were the lines the optical technician had shown Waite. He also learned that the lands and grooves differed from one gun manufacturer to the next. Some spiraled to the right, some to the left; some had more lands; some had tighter spirals. Therefore, a bullet fired from a .22-caliber Colt would not have the same spiraling lines as a bullet fired from a .22-caliber Smith & Wesson.

Comparing the lands and grooves on the bullets taken from the victim to those taken from the defendant's gun, Waite could see that they were markedly different. The scientist took this evidence to the commission and from there to the governor, who pardoned the innocent man three years after his conviction.

Waite continued his research into the new realm of firearms identification, visiting nearly every gun manufacturer in the United States and Europe and learning the characteristics of their weapons. When he finished, he could look at a bullet and tell which manufacturer produced the gun it had been fired from, and sometimes even the years in which that particular model was made. He also learned another important fact. With each barrel that is bored, the cutting blade is changed microscopically. Therefore, each barrel is slightly different than those made before and after it. That meant that every barrel, and thus every bullet shot through it, was nearly as unique as a set of fingerprints.

Amazingly, Waite was not alone in his work. At the same time that he was conducting his initial research to free an innocent man, Dr. Sydney Smith, a forensic expert with the British colonial government in Eygpt, was trying to catch members of a cult who were assassinating British and Eygptian officials. He noticed that some of the bullets taken from different shootings had a similar "scratch," which he correctly theorized was caused by some imperfection in the gun's barrel.

The police had an idea who the assassins were, but the suspects were crafty and kept their guns hidden. Smith came up with the idea of having an informant "warn" the assassins that they were about to be arrested. The men tried to flee the country, taking their guns with them, and were apprehended. One of the guns turned out to be one that Smith was looking for, and the men were convicted based on that small scratch.

Like Waite, Smith continued to be fascinated by firearms identification, and would be responsible for two more major contributions. One was the invention of the comparison microscope, which allowed two bullets to be viewed at the same time. The second was also an excellent example of how good old-fashioned detective work, as ancient as the first homicide, and new science could work together.

It began when a man was shot in the desert. Nomad Bedouin trackers were brought in. They first backtracked the killer's footsteps from the body (he had apparently come to view his victim) to where he had waited in ambush. There they found the spent cartridges from the rifle used in the murder.

They then followed the killer's tracks to an army outpost several miles away. At Smith's insistence, the commander of the post had his men march across the parade grounds. Incredibly, the trackers were able to pick one man's tracks from many and contended that he was the assassin they had followed.

As a test, the suspect was removed from the ranks when the trackers were otherwise occupied. The soldiers were again marched across the parade grounds; the trackers weren't fooled and said the man's tracks were not there.

Still, it was doubtful that the man could be convicted of murder because of the trackers. So Smith confiscated a couple of dozen rifles from the soldiers, including that of the suspect. However, he faced a new problem; the bullet had passed through the victim and wasn't recovered.

But using a microscope, Smith discovered that individual guns also left unique marks on cartridges—such as those from the firing pin, and scratches on the side from the ejector of a bolt-action rifle. Scratches on test cartridges ejected from the suspect's rifle matched those on the cartridges found at the murder scene. Once again, old-fashioned detective work and science had combined to convict a killer who otherwise would not have been caught.

* * *

The evolution of forensic science was often spurred on by fields not generally thought of as being even remotely connected with law enforcement. One of the first such fields to gain much public notoriety for crime solving was botany, the science of plants: their life, structure, growth, and classification. It involved what was called—long before O. J. Simpson and JonBenet Ramsey—the "crime of the century."

In March 1932, the 20-month-old son of aviation hero Charles Lindbergh was kidnapped from his second-story bedroom in the family's rural New Jersey home. Every newspaper in the country carried the story under huge headlines.

Unfortunately, much of the initial police work involved a lot of bungling. Potential fingerprints and foot impressions were wiped out by overeager investigators, the press, and even sympathetic members of the public who swarmed the place. However, a crude ladder made of boards was discovered in the yard, apparently used by the kidnapper to reach the child's bedroom.

A $50,000 ransom was paid to the kidnapper in April, but efforts to locate the baby from directions left on a note were unsuccessful. Tragically, the child's body was discovered in a shallow grave that May, just a few miles from his home. His skull had been crushed apparently during, or shortly after, the kidnapping.

All the police knew was that the kidnapper spoke with a German accent and was seen once by a go-between. It was two years before they had a suspect. With considerably better detective work than was initially done, the police were able to follow a trail of the ransom money, which had been marked, to the Bronx and a German immigrant named Bruno Richard Hauptmann.

The police believed that they had their man. But Hauptmann had his explanations ready. The money, some of which was found beneath the floor of his garage, he said he had found in a box that had been left in his care by a former business partner who had died in Germany. The go-between who identified him in a lineup was mistaken, Hauptmann contended, and his wife swore that he had not left their home on the night in question. Some handwriting experts contended the ransom notes were written by Hauptmann, but others said they weren't.

The crime of the century was headed for the trial of the century, its outcome anything but certain. But help for the prosecution came from an unexpected direction.

Early in the investigation, a U.S. Forest Service scientist named Arthur Koehler, who had read the newspaper accounts of the kidnapping, wrote to Lindbergh saying he might be able to help trace the lumber used to make the ladder. Koehler was a xylotomist, a specialty in the field of botany. Specifically, he studied the growth patterns and cellular structure of wood.

At first he was ignored. But a year after the kidnapping and murder, and before the money was traced to Hauptmann, the stymied New Jersey police asked him to help.

Koehler, a short, plump little man who looked like anything except a detective, painstakingly traced the lumber from the ladder to the Southern mill that had produced it. From there, he tracked it to a lumberyard in the Bronx. Shortly thereafter, Hauptmann was arrested.

The trial began with enormous press coverage. Hauptmann's lawyers were absolutely convinced that their client would walk out of the courtroom a free man. But then the prosecution called Koehler to the stand. The little scientist recounted how he had traced the wood from the ladder to the Bronx lumberyard—a lumberyard where, the police had since ascertained, Hauptmann had once worked. But there was more.

Koehler and a detective had gone to Hauptmann's house in the Bronx. There they found carpentry tools which, examined under a microscope, had imperfections that matched the patterns of marks left on the ladder's boards. They had also climbed into the attic of Hauptmann's home, where it was evident that several boards had been removed. The wood in the attic, the scientist testified, microscopically matched the cellular makeup of boards used to make the ladder. And, for good measure, he demonstrated how the nail holes in one of the boards lined up with nail holes from the attic.

The jury returned a guilty verdict. A verdict, Hauptmann's attorneys railed, delivered by a scientist in a field no one could pronounce, much less had heard of before.

Hauptmann went to the electric chair on April 3, 1936, still proclaiming his innocence. Science said otherwise.

* * *

Throughout the rest of the century, called by some "the century of the detective," the evolutionary tree of forensic science continued to grow and put forth new branches. By the 1980s, dozens of fields were represented that could not even have been imagined in the days of Vidocq, Orfila, Henry, Uhlenhuth, Landsteiner, Waite, Koehler, or even Doyle.

There was Dr. Wayne Lord, an entomologist working as a special agent for the FBI at the agency's Forensic Science Research and Training Center in Quantico, Virginia. Nicknamed "Lord of the Flies," he once pulled blood from the gut of pubic lice taken from a rape victim and analyzed the DNA. The analysis proved that the blood in the lice belonged to the rapist, who had infested the victim with a case of the crabs. The man was convicted.

The FBI center often represented the cutting edge of forensic science. The bureau even had a team exploring the possibility of using geophysical technology originally developed for mineral exploration and subsurface engineering to help locate buried bodies.

But the feds weren't the only ones in the forensic science business. Virtually every police department with more than a dozen officers had someone trained in basic forensic techniques such as fingerprint analysis. Large departments, particularly in the big cities, had their own crime laboratories and employed "criminalists," scientists who deal with physical evidence from a crime scene, to rival the FBI.

Then there were the experts from outside the ranks of law enforcement. As had been the case throughout the history of forensic science, accidents and inspiration led police agencies to look for help beyond their own ranks. Or scientists, hearing of some case that touched on their area of expertise, called out of the blue and offered their assistance.

Usually this help came from academics teaching at colleges and universities or from private industry. Sometimes the scientists worked in a general field and only got involved in police work out of curiosity or as a challenge. Other scientists attached the word *forensic* to their field of study and actively pursued involvement in police matters as a career.

David Hall, a forensic botanist in Florida, made such a name for himself in law enforcement circles that he was often asked to give seminars at the FBI academy. One of his memorable cases involved a man who had taken a girl into a field and raped her on top of a blanket. The girl took the police and Hall back to the scene, where Hall noted some very unusual types of grass where the rapist had placed the blanket. The police later seized a blanket from the suspect. On it, Hall found bits of the unusual grass. That man, too, was convicted.

Another botanist, Jane Bock, at the University of Colorado at Boulder, accidently found herself in the field of forensics in 1982 when a forensic pathologist asked her to study the stomach contents of a murder victim. Protected by indigestible cellulose walls, plant cells are recognizable even after several hours in the digestive system. By identifying a victim's last meal, Bock and her colleagues, endocrinologist David Norris and plant systematist Meredith Lane, were able to establish the time of death—often a vital task in murder cases. In later cases, they were able to prove or disprove witness statements about the last known meals of other victims.

The expertise was out there. The problem for police investigators was knowing what to look for at a crime scene that might relate to one of the more obscure sciences, even if the investigators had no idea what an entomologist or a xylotomist might be able to do. Or, for that matter, where to find one if they did.

Aside from the FBI, there was no central repository for forensic science. Its practioners tended to work independently of other disciplines. For example, it was rare for an entomologist, a botanist, and an anthropologist to be called together to work with a geophysicist on a murder case. No one thought to use a multidisciplinary approach to one of the greatest obstacles in homicide investigations: the location of clandestine graves.

Drive through the mountains; fly over a swamp or a city; float down a river or on a lake; hike across a desert; and there is a good chance you have looked right past the final resting place of a murder victim.

They could be anywhere, killed by anyone. His neighbors thought John Wayne Gacey was just a nice guy who enjoyed dressing up like a clown for children's birthday parties. Until the police started finding bodies in his basement.

Of the more than 15,000 murders in this country every year since the 1970s, only about 66 percent are cleared by the arrest of the killer. At the same time, thousands of people simply "disappear" every year—most of them murdered. That means thousands of killers go unpunished. Part of that can be attributed to the fact that many murder victims end up buried by killers in clandestine graves or abandoned in such lonely, isolated places that their bodies are never found.

The police may believe someone has been murdered. They may even have a suspect. But without a body, charges may never be brought. It's not that it can't be done; it's just much more difficult.

First, there is the usual hurdle of proving that the defendant is guilty of murder "beyond a reasonable doubt." But when there's no body, two more hurdles have been added: proving that the victim is dead; and, assuming a jury can be convinced of that, proving the cause of death was murder.

Prosecutors are reluctant to press a case in which there is a great likelihood they will not prevail. Usually it isn't so much their egos as the fact that if they lose, the suspect cannot be tried again, even if he later confesses or new evidence is brought to light.

The government is likely to go ahead with such cases only when the evidence is so overwhelming that all three hurdles can be overcome. Or, when they feel the investigation has exhausted all other options, and they would rather lose than make no attempt at all. Up until the 1980s, the successful prosecution of "bodyless" homicides could be counted on the toes and fingers of a single corpse. Despite the problems represented by bodyless homicides, and for all the available expertise, very little research had been conducted on how to identify and locate clandestine graves and human remains.

In the February 1979 issue of the *FBI Law Enforcement Bulletin,* Robert Boyd, an instructor at the FBI Academy in Quantico, Virginia, wrote an article "to provide an investigator with useful guidelines and procedures so that the case of a buried body may be pursued confidently and successfully to the identification and arrest of the perpetrator."

In the article, Boyd suggested that police agencies have "expert assistance" available to assist with the excavation and examination of a grave, including a forensic pathologist, a forensic archaeologist, a forensic anthropologist, an entomologist, and a botanist. He noted several means of locating suspected graves, from visual inspection for grave-sized depressions in the ground and changes in plant life to the use of probes to detect gases created by decomposition.

Other research was peripheral to the topic of locating graves. In the mid-1980s, two anthropologists at the University of Tennessee, Dr. William Bass and his student William Rodriguez, undertook a study on the decomposition rates of human cadavers under different environmental circumstances. They buried cadavers that had been donated to the university at various depths and allowed them to decompose naturally, exhuming them at intervals to make their findings.

The impetus for their work was to assist police investigators in establishing the time of death. As they wrote for the *Journal of Forensic Science* in July 1985, "The time interval since death is considered one of the most important questions crucial to the identity of the victim and linking a suspect to the crime."

However, in pursuing their main objective, they noted several aspects associated with decomposition that they suggested might also help in locating graves. One was the presence of carrion insects and their larvae. Another, a surprise, was that a decomposing body gave off more heat than the surrounding soil—a detectable amount of heat if the right technology was available.

A month after their report was published, a Colorado scientist pondered the possibility of using modern technology to find hidden graves. The impetus was a challenge made by his 15-year-old son.

II

NECROSEARCH INTERNATIONAL

BEGINNINGS

Nothing could have been further from the mind of G. Clark Davenport than helping police find the bodies of murder victims. Davenport, a geophysicist, was running a consulting company out of Lakewood, Colorado, with his partner, Linda Hadley.

Geophysicists use a variety of remote sensing devices to "see" beneath the surface of the ground or even water. Davenport and Hadley did geophysical surveys for mining, engineering, and environmental projects. These projects might include foundation studies for dams to determine what sort of rock they were being placed on; or studies on leakage from sewage lagoons; or exploration for coal.

Like most people, Davenport didn't worry too much about crime. He lived in a quiet middle-class neighborhood. Crime was something that happened to other people.

Davenport wasn't naive about the nature of man. After serving in Vietnam as a U.S. Army engineer, he was all too aware of the brutality with which people could treat other people. But here as well as there, he figured it was the other guy who was going to get shot, and didn't give much thought to the problems of law enforcement.

Then one evening, a couple of days before the Labor Day weekend, he was watching the evening news with his youngest son, 15-year-old Sam. Investigators with the sheriff's department in Douglas County, a large rural area south of Denver, were filmed searching for a couple believed to have been murdered over a drug deal and buried in a field. According to the newscaster, the investigators believed that the man and woman had been interred in two 55-

gallon drums. The television camera showed deputies swinging a device over the ground.

Davenport recognized the instrument as a metal detector, not much different than the sort he had used to locate land mines in Vietnam. He snorted, "They'll never find them that way."

The reporter had said that the drums and their grisly contents were buried six to ten feet deep. "A metal detector won't work at that depth," Davenport explained to his son. "I've got something that would work better than that."

Sam rolled his eyes. "Then why don't you do something about it, Dad," the boy said. He was grinning, but the personal challenge was there.

They dropped the subject soon afterward. But that night, Davenport mulled over how the technology he used might help the investigators in Douglas County.

A metal detector like the one being used by the detectives consisted of two coils on the end of a pole. One coil sent an electronic signal into the ground and the other coil received what bounced back. The signal would react to the presence of metal, indicated by a beep or a reading on a meter. A simple, useful tool, but its range wasn't much more than a foot in depth.

Davenport was thinking more along the lines of a magnetometer, which measures changes in the intensity of magnetic fields below the surface of the ground or water.

The Earth is essentially a big magnet with a magnetic field running north and south. Some objects, particularly those made of ferrous metals, also have their own magnetic fields that disrupt the planet's, however slightly. Taking a steel drum from one place and moving it to another would diminish the field at the former and intensify it at the latter.

Also, over time the magnetic fields of particles in the soil will take on the orientation of the Earth's field. Removing and then replacing the soil, as in digging a grave, changes the orientation of the particles.

A magnetometer can detect changes in intensity and in the magnetic orientation of soil. It gives off readings, which the geophysicist plots on paper. The result looks something like a contour map, only the plotted lines denote intensity rather than elevation. Readings different from normal are called anomalies.

Unlike the metal detector, a magnetometer reacts only to ferrous metals—metals that rust, such as iron and steel. However, it is much more sensitive. The size of the object determines the depth at which it can be detected. A large iron ore deposit might be detected at a depth of 300 feet or more.

Davenport knew that a 55-gallon drum could be detected at a depth of seven to eight feet. In fact, magnetometers were one of the techniques he'd used before on environmental projects to locate illegal burial sites of 55-gallon drums containing toxic chemicals.

The next morning, with his son's challenge echoing in his mind, Davenport went to his office and called the Douglas County sheriff. A dispatcher answered the telephone.

"My name is Clark Davenport, and I'd like to speak to the sheriff," he said.

"He's not available," she replied.

"Well, can I leave him a message?" he asked.

"Can I say what this is in reference to?" she asked back.

Davenport thought about it. He didn't want to spend fifteen minutes explaining magnetics to the dispatcher and then have to spend another fifteen minutes explaining it again to the sheriff. Besides, he thought, she'll probably think I'm some sort of kook, or worse, a psychic.

"Just say I have some information about the bodies he's looking for," Davenport said, giving his name, address, and telephone number before hanging up.

Twenty mintues later, several grim-faced detectives entered his office. They wanted to know what he knew about the bodies.

Damn, thought Davenport, *they think I'm involved in the murders.* His face burning with embarassment, he quickly explained why he had called and offered his services.

The next day, Davenport, with Sam in tow, met two Douglas County investigators, Gary Robinson and Kim Castellano, out at the site with his magnetometer. The console of the magnetometer on which the readings would be displayed was about the size of two cereal boxes taped together and was worn strapped to the chest. The other piece of the equipment was an 8-foot pole that had what looked to be a coffee can on top. It was a sensor and the pole was to keep it at a standard height off the ground.

It was obvious that the police were skeptical, but they'd arranged

for a test. They had a backhoe on the scene and used it to bury a 55-gallon drum six feet deep.

"Go ahead," Davenport said. "Run your metal detectors over that." Robinson and Castellano did as instructed and got no readings at all.

In the meantime, Davenport took baseline readings, so he would know what was normal for the area. He explained that he would be looking for anomalies beneath the surface, but there was no telling what they might turn out to be. "There's no instrument in the world that I know of that can find a body," he said, "but I might be able to tell you where to look for one."

Starting some distance away, Davenport began walking toward where the barrel was buried. He stopped every three feet or so, resting the staff on the ground and taking a reading. He called out the readings as Sam took notes and a detective walked alongside.

As they approached the buried barrel, the readings went up. Detective Robinson began peering over Davenport's shoulder at the gauge, as if he thought the geophysicist was making it up. He saw for himself how the numbers peaked as they walked over the barrel, and then began to go down as they moved away.

"Give me that," Robinson said to Davenport, who handed over the chest pack, which the detective quickly strapped to his own torso. "Okay, you follow and tell me what to do," Robinson said.

Everyone was disappointed that day; no oil drums with bodies in them were discovered. But they did find an empty, crushed drum, a car hood buried 5 feet down, and a new respect for the capabilities of Davenport's technology.

By the end of the day, they had walked over every foot of the field and were tired. But there was one more place to look, the detective told Davenport. A warehouse next to the field had been built since the alleged murders, and there was a possibility the victims had been buried beneath it before concrete was poured over the floor.

They tried to run the magnetometer inside the warehouse, but the equipment wouldn't work. As with any technology, magnetometers have their limitations. The instrument may react to the presence of metals inadvertently introduced to the scene, including car keys, belt buckles, steel-toed boots, and even rivets and the zipper on a pair of pants worn by the operator. Care can eliminate some of those problems. However, there are issues that the operator has little or no control over, such as metal fences or power lines, which generate their own magnetic fields. This warehouse had steel trusses in the roof and steel rebar in the concrete, both of which rendered the equipment useless.

Davenport suggested that they were going to need ground-penetrating radar (GPR) to get an idea of what might lie beneath the concrete. GPR sends high-frequency electromagnetic waves beneath the surface, which are reflected back from objects in the ground with different electrical properties. He had first become aware of GPR in Vietnam, where it was used by the U.S. Army to locate tunnels dug by the Viet Cong and North Vietnamese Army. (The open space in a tunnel has substantially different electrical properties than the earth around it.) He had used it a couple of times in his business to look at subsurface conditions for building foundations and mining operations. But he didn't have the equipment or the expertise he felt was needed. He suggested that they contact an engineer he knew at the U.S. Geological Survey who had access to GPR.

The man agreed to meet with them the next day. In the morning, Davenport was back out at the scene, this time with his old friend John Lindemann, a geologist he had known since college at the Colorado School of Mines.

Unfortunately, the GPR search of the warehouse was a disaster, in Davenport's opinion. It began to go awry when the USGS engineer announced that he had "found the barrels." Everybody got excited, including one of the victims' brothers, who had been allowed to attend by the police investigators.

Davenport was uneasy about the engineer's claim. GPR wasn't X-ray vision. It couldn't look beneath the surface and say for sure what was there; it could only reveal the presence of an anomaly, which may or may not be what they were searching for. He thought it was a mistake to make such a positive identification.

In later years, Davenport would call what happened next the phenomenom of "the body ID team"—*ID* standing for "increasing desperation." The closer the investigators felt they were to their goal, the thinner their patience wore. The warehouse was suddenly a scene of pandemonium. Jackhammers were brought in to tear up the floor of the warehouse. The victim's brother jumped into the hole to help dig. But in the end, everyone was disappointed again, especially the victim's brother, who looked as if he had been betrayed. The "barrels" were nothing more than a metal joint and a large boulder beneath the concrete.

It was a lesson Clark Davenport would never forget about not overselling the capabilities of the technology. All it did was hurt the science's credibility. And there was another thing. It was wrong to have let a family member of a victim onto the site. The emotions surrounding the murder of a loved one could only hamper and skew an objective scientific investigation.

Davenport apologized for the lack of positive results. But Robinson and Castellano told him there was nothing to be sorry for; in fact, even negative results were beneficial. They could be reasonably confident that the bodies were not in the field or beneath the warehouse, and could now direct their energies elsewhere. Eliminating possibilities, they said, was as much a part of detective work as digging up new leads.

"Science works the same way," Davenport replied.

He was still thinking of the similarites between science and detective work when he got home that evening. *Might be interesting to look into it a bit further,* he thought, wondering if there was anybody else out there with the same idea. He had heard of remote sensing equipment like GPR being used in archaeology to locate ancient civilizations and burial sites, but never for police work.

Davenport began researching the topic but found very little published material. There was a report about the Army using remote sensing equipment to look for the remains of missing servicemen in Vietnam. And there were studies of infrared equipment being used to detect heat given off by decomposing bodies. But to his knowledge, there was nothing about using radar or magnetometers to locate the clandestine graves of murder victims.

For someone who had never given criminals much thought, he suddenly found himself trying to think like a murderer in order to come up with theories on where bodies would be buried. He was only half joking when he told his wife, Jennifer, that he was thinking of making a career move into "geoforology," a cross between geophysics, forensics, and archaeology. So he was thrilled when word got back to the criminalists at the Colorado Bureau of Investigation (CBI), and he was asked to give a series of talks about the potential of his equipment.

In January 1986, he was giving one of his talks when he again met Kim Castellano of the Douglas County Sheriff's Office. She and her partner still hadn't found the murdered couple, which (she would tell him only much later when she knew him better), in that macabre cop sense of humor, the investigators referred to as the "Janitor in a Drum" case.

The suspects had been running a drug ring from a large piece of property in the mountainous area of the county. They were now in prison on drug charges. But so far Castellano and her partner had been unable to pin murder charges on them, mostly because the couple's bodies couldn't be found to prove a murder had occurred. All they had were witnesses who claimed to have seen the murder, but they were too frightened to testify. "I'd end up in a meat grinder like them," one complained. The couple's remains, according to that witness, had ended up in the river, not buried in barrels.

The case had devolved into chasing one disappointing lead after another, but like any good detective, Castellano refused to give up. She had never planned to be a detective when she was attending Colorado State University in the mid-1970s as a zoology student before dropping out of college. But she had married a police officer and, after three children, decided that life was too tame and she wanted a job in law enforcement. Returning to school for a degree in criminal justice, she signed on with the sheriff's office in 1983.

In 1985, she made detective and was assigned to the crime laboratory. There she often worked in conjunction with neighboring Arapahoe County crime lab technicians Jack Swanburg and Dick Hopkins or called on the assistance of specialists such as Tom Griffin, a forensic chemist with the Colorado Bureau of Investigation.

It was a perfect match, combining her first love, science, with a natural inclination toward solving puzzles. As a mother and a police officer, she found she relied on her intuition, and discovered that the best detectives had similar qualities, though they might refer to why they followed certain leads and discounted others as a "gut feeling" or "a hunch."

An example was the case of Gwen Hendricks, a 37-year-old housewife whose husband had not come home from work one day. His body was found a couple of days later in his blood-splattered truck; he'd been shot numerous times. Most murders are not committed by strangers but by someone close to the victim. Thus, Mrs. Hendricks was immediately considered a suspect, though investigators were split on whether they thought she was innocent or guilty.

Two male investigators were assigned to talk to Mrs. Hendricks, who'd reported her husband missing. But when Castellano heard their report, her intuition or gut feeling told her something was wrong. The Hendrickses had two preteens, a boy and a girl. But according to the investigators, the boy wasn't around. That in itself was not particularly incriminating, but the investigators also had noted that the woman had seemed closed to them. And that made Castellano wonder if Hendricks had a problem with males.

With one of the male investigators in tow, Castellano went back to talk to Mrs. Hendricks. Again, the boy wasn't around. The woman was very solicitous of Castellano, asking her if she wanted anything to eat and jumping up to fix her something before she could answer. She completely ignored the male detective.

Working on her hunch, Castellano became "best friends" with Hendricks to the point that the woman asked for her help balancing her checkbook. In it, the detective saw that Hendricks had recently taken out several insurance policies that paid her if her husband died. More intriguing, she discovered that Hendricks had paid for the plastic flowers used at the funeral and the dress her daughter wore to the funeral . . . before her husband died.

Using a technique police refer to as the "midnight confession," Castellano and a male investigator went over to Hendricks's house at eleven one night and woke up the suspect. The two detectives confronted Hendricks in the family room, where she continued to deny her involvement. After Castellano told her she needed to get dressed, that they were taking her in, Hendricks broke down, sobbing that she could "see blood everywhere."

However, in court, Gwen Hendricks claimed she didn't kill her husband. But the prosecution showed how Hendricks had wanted to use the money from her husband's insurance policies to start a "home for troubled people" near the spot where she'd gunned him down. Apparently, he had made her homicidally angry when he took away her credit cards. The jury found her guilty of first-degree murder and Hendricks was sentenced to life in prison.

It was a case in which a detective's intuition told her to dig deeper.

But Castellano was also a big believer in "more heads are better," and in calling in people with expertise she didn't have, which is why she had welcomed the assistance of Davenport to search for the couple in the barrels.

Davenport had scoffed when he saw the detectives on the television newscast using the metal detectors. But from Castellano's point of view—however ignorant she may have been about the capabilities of the technology—it was a big leap forward from just setting the backhoes loose.

Law enforcement is a close-knit community and, she knew, often reluctant to open its doors to outsiders. But she also knew that the business community usually had access to the latest technology long before police agencies—due in part to the agencies' lack of money and reluctance to try something new and unproven if it meant asking for outside help.

But if it meant bringing a killer to justice and getting closure for the family of a victim, Castellano wasn't about to let ego get in the way. She was fortunate to work for a sheriff who, with his counterpart in Arapahoe County, shared the same philosophy—a philosophy that would soon have an important impact on the evolution of forensic science.

So Castellano found herself attending Davenport's class on ground-penetrating radar at the Colorado Bureau of Investigation. Among those also in attendance was Tom Griffin of the CBI, with whom she'd often talked about the frustration surrounding the "Janitor in a Drum" case. "There has to be a better way of locating clandestine graves," she'd said.

Two months later, Griffin was standing in a bitterly cold wind on an eastern Colorado ranch near the recently unearthed graves of three murdered men, wondering the same thing. Then he recalled something Clark Davenport had said during the class:

"There's no technology in the world that can find a body," the geophysicist had noted. "But I might be able to tell you where to look."

Justice was an important concept to Griffin. As a child growing up in Tuscon, Arizona, where he was born in 1951, and in various other parts of the West including Kansas, Nebraska, and Texas, the television character The Lone Ranger had been his idol. The masked man represented fair play and always arrived on time to aid the weak and oppressed when no one else would. He wanted to be like the Lone Ranger.

It was an ideal that would stay with him long after childhood. His tastes would diversify—from the Lone Ranger to Batman comics to Hardy Boys mysteries—but the theme was the same. Sometimes justice needed a little help.

Science also fascinated Griffin, though he had no clue that his two interests would someday mesh. He was interested in all kinds of science, but after high school he chose chemistry over biology when he found that he was too squeamish to dissect a frog.

While in graduate school at the University of Northern Colorado, located in Greeley, he wasn't quite sure what he was going to do with his degree once he finished, beyond a vague notion of teaching. However, that changed in his second year of graduate school, when he had to choose a topic for a required seminar he was to present.

"How about forensic chemistry?" suggested the professor in charge of the seminar program.

Of course, Griffin thought—chemistry as it applies to solving criminal cases. He had recently rediscovered the adventures of Sherlock Holmes (after reading his first story in the fifth grade) and read everything he could find on the supersleuth. Holmes had made use of forensic chemistry in solving the mysteries presented to him. Forensic science required the sort of objective, detached observation that Holmes was famous for and that Griffin thought he was good at. The young graduate student jumped into the subject and soon found it covered a wider range of topics than he thought. There were chemical analyses for blood and explosives and gunshot residue; tests for drugs and evidence of arson. Through chemistry, substances as commonplace as paint and glass could be traced to their sources.

In 1978, Griffin accepted a position as a criminalist with the police department of Greeley, a mid-sized town on the plains northeast of Denver. Lanky and bearded, he looked more like the college professor he nearly was than a criminalist. The only thing that troubled him was that he wasn't sure he had the stomach for autopsies, which would be necessary in his new job. If dissecting a frog made him queasy, how would he handle death in humans?

As he feared, the first couple of autopsies were a challenge. He struggled, trying not to get sick and still do his job. Eventually, however, repetition made it easier, along with the realization that a body was not the person—not anymore. But what he could learn as a scientist from the body of a murder victim might catch the killer, and that served the cause of justice. The man who couldn't dissect a frog found himself doing such things as climbing onto an autopsy table to straddle a corpse so that he could take photographs that would accurately depict the trajectory of a bullet.

Griffin stayed with the Greeley Police Department through August 1982, when he accepted a position with the Colorado Bureau of Investigation. He enjoyed his time at Greeley, but the CBI had a much larger laboratory, as well as a larger budget for training.

Among the advantages of such work for Griffin was the opportunity to meet others who were combining the worlds of science and law enforcement. One such introduction that would have enormous ramifications on the future was his meeting Jack Swanburg and Dick Hopkins, two older criminalists with the Arapahoe County Sheriff's Office, an unincorporated area south of Denver. They were knowledgeable and professional—and friendly, offering help if he ever needed it.

On a November morning in 1987 he met Swanburg and Hopkins for breakfast at a restaurant in Lakewood, Colorado, a bedroom community washed up against the foothills west of Denver. The meeting was a semiregular sort of thing. They would get together and talk about cases and the latest advances of forensic science.

The three men also shared another interest. All were avid fans of Sherlock Holmes and could talk for hours about his cases. It was fascinating to discuss how Holmes could draw so many conclusions from so little evidence. For instance, in *A Study in Scarlet* the detective deduced the killer's height at more than six feet because a word written in blood on a wall of the apartment was more than six feet off the ground. "And it is our instinct to write above our eyesight," he had told Dr. Watson. He also noted that the killer had an unusually long fingernail on his right hand, because he had written the word using his finger and the nail had scratched the plaster underneath. Holmes's observations were often the sort of things many people might look at but not really see, the three friends agreed.

As they ate, Griffin told the others about the case that was troubling him. It had begun during a bitterly cold week in February 1986.

A frigid wind had swept across the ranch with little to impede its race to the Kansas line 30 miles to the east. The stubble of brown grasses, dormant beneath the oppression of February in east-central Colorado, had shivered in the breeze, as did a dozen officers from several law enforcement agencies who peered into trenches dug by a backhoe that belched black smoke into the gray sky.

Three bodies had already been disinterred by the machinery. All the bodies were fully clothed but skeletonized. There were supposedly as many as six to twelve more buried somewhere on the 2,200-acre spread near the agricultural community of Stratton.

The body count was supplied by Michael McCormick. He had lived on the ranch with his family since his birth in 1956 until foreclosure forced them off in 1981. It was his father, Thomas, Michael told the authorities, who killed the men, mostly drifters and bums he'd hired from Denver's skid row to help work the ranch.

Sometimes his dad had forced him to help put them in the ground. He hadn't told anyone, Michael said, because he was deathly afraid of his old man, who more than once had warned him, "I brought you into the world, and I'll take you out."

Michael McCormick was still afraid of his father, but he had led the police back to the former family ranch—after first taking them to yet another body buried in a sleeping bag 100 miles to the west. It wasn't from a sudden attack of courage or conscience: He was facing murder, kidnapping, and drug charges when he agreed to spill the beans and turned on dear old Dad. The younger McCormick said he had personally witnessed five murders and helped bury as many as nine bodies.

Born and raised near Stratton, which lies 150 miles east of Denver off Interstate 70, Tom McCormick had purchased the land from his father and started a feedlot in 1956, the year his oldest son, Michael, was born. A large man, Tom McCormick had a reputation for running the ranch with an iron hand, which he sometimes used roughly on Michael. He worked hard and expected the same of his two sons. He wasn't much liked in Stratton, and townsfolk wondered about his hiring men off skid row. Some of those men had criminal pasts, while others were simply drifters, always searching for a warm place to sleep and a bottle of booze. Most had lost contact with their families, and few people noticed their comings and goings.

Tom McCormick was said to be hard on the men. He fed them well but had stringent rules: no alcohol; no trips to town; no unauthorized phone calls; and no pay until they left. Some of the men who did leave complained to the Colorado Department of Labor that they'd been cheated of their pay; others said they'd been assaulted or threatened when they tried to go. In 1975, McCormick shot one of his employees in the leg following an argument. At his trial, he claimed the man had a knife, and the jury acquitted him on grounds of self-defense.

McCormick didn't limit his hard ways to bums off the street. He had a reputation for trying to "pull fast ones" on neighbors and local businesses. Once, he blamed cattle rustlers to get his hands on insurance money. The insurance company hired a private investigator to work undercover as a ranch hand for the McCormicks for ten days in late 1980. He reported that the McCormicks were running a number of scams: shorting the count on deliveries of cattle; moving cattle from one pen to another to deceive a loan officer who wanted to inspect their collateral; cheating workers out of wages; and operating vehicles "of questionable ownership."

The investigator described how a ranch cook named Jim, who claimed he hadn't been paid his wages for four months, tried to leave with a truck driver who delivered supplies. Michael McCormick, the investigator said, stopped him from leaving.

Then there were darker rumors about the goings-on at the McCormick ranch. Across cups of coffee in the diners and feed stores of Stratton, people talked in low voices about a tendency for hired hands at the McCormick place to disappear. There was more planted in the ground than wheat at that ranch, according to the town gossips.

Tom McCormick filed for bankruptcy for his feedlot operation in October 1981 and the family had to move off the land, though he still managed to keep a coal mine operation near Gunnison, Colorado. A salesman for the coal company would one day testify that in 1983, Tom McCormick said they would soon have a better truck for hauling coal. Sure enough, Michael McCormick showed up with a real nice one, later identified as a truck owned by a man named Bert Donaho.

Three years later, in early 1986, after signing a plea agreement, Michael McCormick spilled his guts. He claimed that his father and an older man, Donaho, had arrived at Michael's wife's apartment one morning in 1983. They were headed down the stairs to the garage with Michael in the lead when he heard a dull WHUMP! behind him. He turned to see Donaho tumbling toward him, his skull crushed and bloody. His father stood at the top of the stairs with a sledgehammer.

Michael McCormick said he helped bury Donaho and kept the truck. There were more bodies, he told the investigators—many more—out at the old family ranch.

The first murder occurred when he was in junior high, he claimed. A ranch worker who had broken a piece of equipment argued with his father and then tried to leave the ranch. His father, he said, shot the man with a rifle and put the body in the bed of his pickup truck before driving off alone to some remote area of the ranch.

Michael took the police to where Donaho's body had been buried. Then he led them to the ranch where the backhoe operator dug through the heavy clay soil in the general area McCormick indicated. The first body unearthed was that of Jim Plance, the ranch cook the insurance investigator had witnessed trying to leave in 1980. His skull appeared to have been crushed with repeated blows.

It didn't quite mesh with what Michael McCormick told the authorities. He had said that his father had strangled Plance after catching him trying to steal something from a trailer. Also, two shovels were located in the grave, indicating that more than one person had helped with the burying.

A day later, the police found another body when the remains of Jim Sinclair were unearthed. He had disappeared in 1976, when Michael McCormick was 19. An autopsy later revealed he was shot in the back of the head. Michael McCormick said the man was killed while arguing with his father.

Then the third body was discovered two days later. Robert Sowarsh, who disappeared in 1977, had been shot in the face with a handgun and in the back of the head with a shotgun. The use of two weapons again suggested the involvement of more than one killer, but Michael swore his father did all the shooting.

After Sowarsh's body was unearthed, McCormick spent a lot of time scratching his head, trying to recall where other bodies might be buried. It had been a long time, he complained. He also said he suffered from blackouts, which he attributed to having been exposed to so much violence from a young age. The others could be buried anywhere out on that wide, flat expanse of land.

For a few more days, the backhoe roared here and there, digging exploratory trenches. The fields were gone over with a 20-inch plow blade to see if that would turn up any remains. No more were found, and the investigation began to wind down.

Two thousand acres is a lot of ground to cover when searching for unmarked graves. If not a needle in a haystack, the investigators concluded, it was damn close. "It's really difficult to make any progress," Michael Igoe, a CBI investigator, told the press.

"There's no metal detector in the world that's going to find anything three feet deep in this type of soil." Besides, they had four bodies, including Donaho's.

Tom McCormick was charged with the murder of Donaho. Everybody expected that more murder charges for the deaths of the ranch hands would be forthcoming.

Although no metal detector would penetrate far into that or any other kind of soil, CBI agent Griffin thought, there might be a technology that could search beneath the ground, without tearing it, and any evidence, to bits and pieces. Cops had been using such brutal methods to uncover murder victims since the invention of the pick and shovel. But it seemed not only destructive but arbitrary. The backhoe had dug blindly or directed by the vague memory of Michael McCor-mick.

There had to be a better way, Griffin thought. The magnetometer or ground-penetrating radar that Clark Davenport had discussed seemed a good place to start. He was given permission to contact the geophysicist and ask for his help.

Griffin was disappointed to learn that Clark Davenport was leaving for Mexico, an annual trip he and John Lindemann volunteered for, teaching young Mexican geologists. But Davenport asked his partner, Linda Hadley, who said she'd be willing to go to the site and give it a try.

Hadley and a School of Mines intern met Griffin and Wayne Bryant, another CBI agent, at the ranch on a cold and gray Saturday morning. She'd brought an electromagnetic ground conductivity meter, which operates similarly to a metal detector, except that its signal has greater depth penetration. In addition to reacting to the presence of metal, it was normally used to look for metallic ores by measuring conductivity of subsurface materials.

Davenport believed that it might be used for grave location because subsurface conductivity can be related to the amount of moisture in the ground. Once soil has been removed and replaced—as in digging and backfilling a grave—it is impossible to compact it exactly as it was in its natural state. The digger will either overcompact the backfill or undercompact it. That makes the former hole either a moisture shed, meaning moisture flows away, or a moisture sump, which absorbs moisture like a sponge.

It might not be a big difference compared to the surrounding soil. But then, it didn't take much of a difference—5 to 10 percent more or less moisture—for the electromagnetic meter to detect it.

The equipment Hadley brought along was essentially a long pole with antennae on either end and a cable attached that fed back into the meter. She began walking where directed holding the pole crosswise, looking like a tightrope walker trying to cross a void.

Hadley scoured the property for six hours, but the day turned out to be another disappointment.

The equipment had immediately started locating areas of disturbed soil, such as a ranch garbage dump, but their efforts were confused by the trenches and holes dug by the backhoe. There was simply too much disturbance for the equipment to distinguish "noise," in geophysical parlance.

There wasn't much more she could do, Hadley apologized. If they'd come out before the backhoe, then maybe.

Despite Griffin's efforts, the case fell apart. Investigators were troubled that Michael McCormick's description of what happened to the ranch hands didn't match what they had been able to determine from the bodies. They didn't know if it was due to poor memory, or because he was lying about his own involvement.

Other detectives working separately on the Donaho case determined that Michael's story was filled with contradictions. The district attorney's office withdrew the plea agreement it had given him, saying he'd lied. Instead, the district attorney dropped the charges against Tom McCormick and charged Michael with Donaho's murder.

In the summer of 1987, Michael McCormick, still protesting his innocence, was convicted of the first-degree murder of Donaho and sentenced to spend the rest of his life in prison. A post-conviction poll of the jury, however, indicated that they didn't believe that he was the one who wielded the sledgehammer that killed Donaho. They had merely agreed with the prosecutors that Michael was part of the planning and commission of the murder, and therefore guilty as charged.

No one was charged for the murder of the three former ranch hands. Denver newspapers opined that the ranch hands' social status as drifters and bums, and the fact that there were no family members publicly demanding justice, made it easier to sweep the matter beneath the skirts of justice. The McCormick Ranch triple homicide simply faded from the public eye, the men reburied in paupers' graves. But not everyone forgot them.

"There has to be a better way," Tom Griffin said aloud as he had to himself for more than a year. He sometimes talked with Kim Castellano about his frustrations regarding the McCormick Ranch case. Both of them wondered how to get someone like Davenport involved in cases before the backhoes arrived. Now over breakfast, it was Swanburg and Hopkins who shook their heads thinking about the image of the rumbling backhoe tearing through potential evidence like an enormous blind mole. Sherlock Holmes would have been appalled.

At 59 years old, Jack Swanburg was nearing the end of his career. He looked a bit like Santa Claus with his white hair, bright blue eyes, round belly, and fondness for suspenders. Dick Hopkins, a mustachioed 47-year-old, more resembled an English professor than a cop. Together they had been the driving force behind the modernization of the Arapahoe County crime lab, one of the best labs in the country.

Although they had been in the law enforcement business for decades—Swanburg since the 1950s and Hopkins since the early 1960s—they and Griffin were constantly trying to stay up with the latest in crime-solving techniques. It seemed to them that with all the technology and expertise that was out there, using a backhoe to locate graves was comparable to doing brain surgery with a rock.

They knew that no matter how carefully a killer might hide a victim, the body or the container the body had been placed in would change the surroundings. The ground over a grave might sink after rain or snow. Body fluids might attract different sorts of insects or leave traces that cadaver dogs could detect months, even years, later. Disturbed soil might be revealed by the type and age of vegetation that had grown back since, or by remote sensing equipment.

They had all run across, and even used, experts from colleges and universities in Colorado to help with various cases, with good results. They started to list the different sorts of expertise that might be of help in finding bodies.

Griffin told them about the seminar with Davenport. "He seems real knowledgeable and you don't get the feeling he's talking down to you," he said.

Swanburg brought up Boris Kondratieff, an entomologist at Colorado State University in Fort Collins, sixty miles north of Denver. He recalled a case in which a teenage girl disappeared after attending a party; her body was found a month later at a city dump. The police had a suspect, a young man who was seen leaving the party with the girl. But was she killed that night by the young man, or was she murdered some time—maybe weeks—later by someone else?

Swanburg saw that there were insects in the girl's skull, which he took to Kondratieff. By noting the developmental stage of the insects, the young scientist was able to say within a three-day period when the girl had died. He hadn't been told, but the middle day of his estimated range was the day of the party. He testified to that fact and the young man was convicted.

Kondratieff would probably know what sort of insects to look for that might indicate the presence of a decomposing body, Swanburg suggested. He also noted the work of Bass and Rodriguez, which he had read about.

And there were forensic anthropologists Michael Charney up at Colorado State University and Michael Hoffman at Colorado College in Colorado Springs. Once a grave was located, someone would have to identify the remains and get them out of the ground without using a backhoe.

Swanburg knew of a dog handler, Al Nelson, a deputy with Jefferson County, a huge, mostly rural area northwest of Denver. He had a bloodhound trained to sniff out decomposing human bodies.

It was too bad, they agreed, that more police agencies didn't make use of all the expertise. "They probably don't know what's out there," Swanburg said. But what if they could get several of these experts involved in an experiment? See if they could come up with a better way to find graves than tearing back and forth with a backhoe.

The other two men thought it was a great idea. They would invite scientists and law officers to participate. Then they'd publish their findings so that law enforcement agencies could use the information to locate the graves of murder victims.

Swanburg wondered if they might be able to get their hands on human cadavers to bury in some remote spot. But none of them were quite sure what the laws of Colorado were on that, and the public might not take to the idea of their lugging bodies around the countryside.

"How about pigs?" Swanburg said.

The other two looked at him funny. Swanburg went on to explain that he'd read somewhere that pigs were the animal most like humans. They were about the right weight and size; their metabolism and chemical makeup were similar; their fat-to-muscle ratio about the same; and their skin was nearly hairless.

"And nobody will care if we bury a couple of pigs."

It was May 1988 before they had a chance to revisit their idea, again over breakfast. They weren't sure where they were going to get their pigs. Maybe a slaughterhouse or a cooperative pig farmer . . . but they weren't ready yet anyway. They didn't have any place to bury pigs. And, more important, they still needed to contact the scientists and law officers who they wanted to participate in the program.

Tom Griffin had invited Clark Davenport, who brought his friend John Lindemann to the breakfast. Scientists and cops weren't known for harmonious working relationships. Cops were jealous of their turf and wary of even well-intentioned outside help, having had to deal with psychics and charlatans since time immemorial. On the other hand, scientists could be arrogant, or talk above the head of the average detective.

Griffin knew, however, that Davenport had found a way to bridge the chasm between the two. He was good at explaining how his equipment worked without making it sound too technical or exotic. And he seemed genuinely interested in assisting with investigations, rather than trying to lead them.

The three friends told Davenport and Lindemann about their idea for an experiment and asked if they'd like to participate. They both eagerly agreed. The men decided there should be another meeting in a month, this time with the other scientists and law officers.

Someone suggested that they were going to need a name for their experiment. Something catchy. They decided on Project Pigs In the Ground, or Project PIG.

They didn't realize it yet, but the evolutionary tree of forensic science had just grown another branch because justice had not been served in the unsolved murders of Jim Plance, Jim Sinclair, and Robert Sowarsh. Whoever killed them, and any others still buried on a lonely stretch of Colorado prairie, hadn't been held accountable. Maybe they never would be, but some other killers might be made to pay as a result.

It was a serious undertaking. They would be asking a lot of very busy, very knowledgeable people to give their time and expertise.

Still, it would be a hallmark of Project PIG members not to take themselves too seriously. As the men paid their bill and rose to leave the restaurant, Davenport suddenly laughed and said, "I think it's appropriate we started this over a breakfast of HAM and eggs."

The others groaned at the pun. But it wouldn't be the last time he made one at some poor pig's expense.

PROJECT PIG

June 30, 1988

Project PIG officially got underway with its first meeting at the Arapahoe County Sheriff's Department. All told, there were a dozen people, most of them strangers to each other and identified by pink name tags cut in the shape of pigs.

Clark Davenport and John Lindemann couldn't attend, but the three original musketeers—Jack Swanburg, Dick Hopkins, and Tom Griffin—were there. The others represented science and law enforcement.

Among the law officers were Kim Castellano, along with her crime lab assistant Debi Kimball (who had come up with the pig name tags), Jefferson County Deputy Al Nelson, the bloodhound handler, and state trooper Dave Batura, a scuba diver who specialized in retrieving evidence from rivers and lakes.

On the science side were entomologist Boris Kondratieff, archaeologist Jim Grady, geophysicist Linda Hadley, botanist Jane Bock, and Hans Bucher, who ran a thermal imaging company. Falling into neither category was Bill Youngblood. He was a pilot with expertise in aerial photography.

Swanburg, Griffin, and Davenport had spent a lot of time researching the subject of locating clandestine graves, and they were surprised at the lack of material. There was the ongoing work of Bass and Rodriguez, and the article by Boyd, which contained the advice about "recognizing the existence of specialized expert assistance."

Griffin had located a February 1986 article in *Identification News,* the newsletter of the International Association for Identification, an organization of law enforcement and forensic specialists from around the world, that briefly discussed using GPR for locating potential graves. The author, Detective Gary Hoving of the San Luis Obispo Sheriff's Department, noted that the FBI had the equipment and would respond to requests from local agencies. But there wasn't much else he could find in the public domain about the use of remote sensing equipment in law enforcement.

A group of California law officers calling themselves Andermac had published a paper titled "The Detection of Buried Bodies." Those authors, too, noted that they had been unable to find "any written material on the mechanics or the techniques of locating a buried body." The paper was a general overview about a variety of techniques such as site observation, soil compaction, aerial searches, the use of infrared frequencies, probes and gas detection, and metal detectors.

It was the nearest thing to what the Project PIG originators wanted to do. But when they called for more information about Andermac, they were told the group had disbanded. The paper was a one-shot deal. Nowhere could they find any discussion about the idea of bringing scientists and law officers together and pooling their expertise to locate clandestine graves.

Until now. Over several hours, the group was exposed to some of what each member could bring to the table. Hadley and Grady talked about the importance of taking "low-angle sun" photos—when the sun was close to the horizon just after sunrise or before sunset and shadows were longer. As an example of the importance, Grady showed two slides taken of the same site in England, though at different times of the day. In one, when the sun was high in the sky, nothing out of the ordinary could be seen; in the other, low-angle sun photo, it was possible to see the outline of where the walls of an old Roman fort had stood. The walls were gone, but the soil had been compacted over the centuries and was clearly visible given the right circumstances.

Bock talked about her work with Norris and Lane. Bucher discussed the capabilities of the thermal imaging infrared cameras he used for such projects as determining hot spots on electrical transmission lines. Aware of the discovery by Bass and Rodriguez that decomposing bodies give off heat, he noted his equipment could detect differences in soil temperatures as low as one-tenth of a degree.

It was all very interesting, and for many who worked in their own little academic niche or law enforcement specialty, illuminating as far as the potential if they combined their expertise. Then they moved on to the practical aspects of what they were about to undertake. In a nutshell, they would bury pigs and then observe what changes occurred. The individual scientists would each visit the site with a frequency dictated by their field of study. To gain credibility, the group would seek to have their findings published in a respected forensic periodical, such as the *Journal of Forensic Science.*

But maybe the most important accomplishment of the meeting was that it set the tone for how the group members would interact with each other in the years to come. They decided that there would be no titles, no addressing someone as "doctor"; their relationship would be on a first-name basis, with everyone an equal. Everyone would be allowed, and encouraged, to question anyone else. There would be no "I'm the expert in this field and that's why you have to believe me." In order to work with police agencies, they would have to be able to explain what they were doing without putting them off, or their hope to work in the field would be short-lived.

They left the meeting excited, each for their own reasons, and ready to begin. They had no money, but they had a place to bury their "victims." Castellano had worked it out with the Douglas County and Arapahoe sheriffs to allow the group to conduct its experiment on their jointly held and run Highlands Ranch Law Enforcement Training Facility southwest of Denver.

Several days before the meeting, Swanburg, Davenport, Griffin, and Castellano had driven to the training facility to pick burial sites and run background surveys with the electromagnetic and magnetic equipment. As the geophysicist had explained, they first needed to know what was normal to be able to recognize change. Youngblood had also flown over the area taking photographs for later comparisons after the pigs were buried.

They were ready to go. All they needed was a pig.

In August, Davenport, Lindemann, Griffin, and Jim Borowski, another CBI agent, had an article published in *The Leading Edge,* a geophysics magazine, titled "Geophysics: The Leading Edge of Explorations." It documented the beginnings of the group's research, starting with the McCormick ranch case. They hoped the article would put Project PIG on the map as unique in the area of forensic sciences—a multidisciplinary approach.

"Davenport, it is truly criminal what you have done to geophysics," joked Dean Clark, the magazine's editor.

But securing a pig was more difficult than they had imagined. Finally, in September, an Arapahoe County deputy called Jack Swanburg. He had heard about the project and had a contribution to make.

"A bear killed one of my pigs," the deputy said. "I chased him off before he ate much. You want it?"

"You bet," Swanburg replied. The following day, the deputy brought the "murder victim" to the county office complex, where Swanburg slipped the carcass into the morgue. The next day, he and an assistant coroner named Jeff Nielsen loaded the 175-pound pig into the coroner's wagon and drove out to the training facility. There they were met by Hopkins and Castellano.

Swanburg looked around, enjoying the beautiful Indian summer day. The leaves on the scrub oak that spread out over the acres of bluffs and gullies were just starting to turn their fall colors of orange, red, and yellow. He couldn't help but smile and feel they were on the verge of doing something truly important. Looking back, most people can point to events and choices that at the time might not have seemed significant, but many years down the road represent a major intersection in their lives. For Swanburg, who had lived in Colorado since childhood, one of three such events occurred when he was 12 years old and won a camera in a contest.

It was 1941 and soon the country was embroiled in the war, which made it difficult for the budding young photographer to get film. But he managed, and by high school and then college at the University of Denver, he was good enough to earn spending money taking wedding photos.

Swanburg married his high school sweetheart, Connie, shortly after graduating from college. He had plans to attend law school. His father had been a lawyer, even doing a stint as a prosecutor in Chicago during the days of Al Capone, and his stories had whetted his son's appetite for the drama of the courtroom.

Money was tight, however, and Swanburg decided to work for a year before getting back to his studies. He got a job at Heiland Research, a company created to produce seismographic equipment, but which was also the first to develop the synchronized camera flashbulb and shutter. He started on the assembly line, but within a few months was promoted to the sales force, demonstrating the proper use of the equipment to news photographers.

Swanburg was giving a talk on the subject in 1958. In attendance was Captain Jim Schumate, who ran the crime laboratory for the Denver Police Department. Schumate asked the young man if he would help set up a photography lab for his department and teach police investigators how to use the equipment.

The young man had reached another fork in the road. He was soon spending most of his off hours with the Denver police crime lab technicians. They learned how to use the equipment, and he learned crime scene investigation. But if photography put him into contact with the intriguing world of detectives, it was another discovery in 1965 that cemented the relationship.

He was perusing the shelves at the Denver Public Library for something to read when a title caught his eye: *The Hound of the Baskervilles*. Like many others, he'd heard of Doyle's detective, Sherlock Holmes, but Swanburg had never read any of the stories. He checked out the book.

What appealed most to him was the Holmes character's method of reasoning—his analysis of small details that led to a broader knowledge. Holmes might take one, two, or three facts and combine them into a probable theory of what had occurred, although he always remained flexible if more observation and evidence indicated a new direction to follow.

As Holmes told Watson in *The Sign of Four,* "When you have eliminated the impossible, whatever remains, however improbable, must be the truth."

Back in high school, when he was trying to decide which college would serve best as a precursor to law school, Swanburg was advised by his father to "get as broad an education as you can. . . . You never know what will come in handy in a courtroom."

The Holmes character seemed to rely on that principle. For instance, in *The Hound of the Baskervilles,* Dr. James Mortimer was puzzled by Holmes's having been able to definitively state from which newspaper the words in a warning letter had been clipped.

"I presume, doctor, that you can identify the skull of a Negro from that of an esquimaux?" Holmes asked.

"Most certainly," Mortimer replied.

"But how?"

"Because that's my special hobby," the doctor explained. "The differences are obvious. The supraorbital crest, the facial angle, the maxillary curve, the . . ."

Holmes interrupted. "But this is my special hobby, and the differences are equally obvious. There is as much difference to my eyes between the leaded, bourgeois type of a *Times* article and the slovenly print of an evening halfpenny paper as there could be between your Negro and your esquimaux."

Swanburg soon devoured Doyle's other three novels and fifty-six short stories involving his most famous character. By the end, he was considering a career in law enforcement.

In 1970, he left his job with Heiland and took a job with the Arapahoe County Sheriff's Department, accepting a two-thirds pay cut with Connie's blessing "so long as it's less stressful than marketing." It wouldn't be necessarily less stressful, but it was certainly where his heart lay.

Sheriff Roy Vogt had offered the job with the idea of Swanburg working in the crime laboratory. But it was his policy that everyone start first in the jail and work their way up. So for the next three years, Swanburg got a crash course in law enforcement as a jailer, a patrol officer, and a detective before finally moving into the lab in 1973.

One of his first accomplishments was to push Vogt into placing the new 35mm cameras in every patrol car and having Swanburg teach the deputies how to use them at a crime scene. The cameras were lightweight and the film compact and easy to use. Suddenly hundreds of photographs could be taken at crime scenes, to let a jury see later with their own eyes what witnesses in the past could only talk about.

In keeping with his father's advice and the practices of Holmes, Swanburg made it a point to broaden his knowledge. To get over his squeamishness around bodies, he volunteered to work at several autopsies as the "diener", the pathologist's helper who literally must get up to his elbows in gore, pulling apart incisions, lifting out organs. He took a course in locksmithing to learn how to pick locks, which later came in handy to spring the lock of a suitcase, revealing the gun used by a young man to kill his parents.

If dealing with so much death bothered him, Swanburg didn't show it to the outside world. Only Connie really knew how the tragedies of others affected her good and gentle husband—especially the accidental or violent deaths of children. He would come home and hold tightly to his own; then, when they had been put to bed, he would cry over the lost lives of the others.

Life around the Swanburg residence had never been the same after he left Heiland. Connie had gone through her own adjustment period as her husband began bringing his work home with him. Literally. She never knew when opening the refrigerator if she was going to have to confront a finger or hand or some other body part, or shove aside a bottle of blood to reach the milk. As she would tell friends, "You never cook any meat Jack brings home."

As the years went by, Swanburg kept up with the latest forensic advances. He became fascinated with one particular field known as bloodstain pattern analysis, an area pioneered by a private investigator named Herb MacDonell in the 1960s. It involved the examination of a crime scene by looking at the shape, size, and distribution of blood stains. To a trained eye, the stains could reveal the positioning of the victim and suspect at the time of the murder, the sequence of events, and the nature of the wounds. For instance, a fine spray of tiny drops indicated a gunshot wound; large drops would be more in keeping with a knife wound.

It was an interest he shared with Dick Hopkins, a detective and former student in his photography classes who had joined the crime lab in 1977. "Hoppy" got into law enforcement when he got out of the Army in 1964. He began working for the Arapahoe County Sheriff's Department in 1968. Even as a patrol officer, he had earned a reputation as a careful, tenacious investigator who would take every bit of time he needed at a crime scene.

Swanburg introduced Hopkins to Holmes. He thought his friend had a lot in common with the fictional detective in that he could look at a crime scene and see what everyone else had overlooked. A case in point began on the day a man was found lying in a pool of blood on the floor of his kitchen. It appeared he had been executed with a single shot of a .45-caliber handgun to the back of his head. The gun lay several feet behind the body.

Although others were on the case, Swanburg had gone by the scene and concurred that they should be looking for a murderer.

What's more, the killer appeared to have been hurt as well; there was a trail of blood leading from the body out to the parking lot, where apparently, the killer got into a car and left.

Hopkins didn't go to the scene. But he was looking at photographs later, when he turned to Swanburg and said, "Something's wrong."

The blood trail on the sidewalk to the parking lot snaked back and forth. Everyone else thought that indicated that the killer was staggering to his car. But the blood patterns were too regular for Hopkins. And judging by the direction of the splash when the drips hit the sidewalk, they had to have been made by someone walking from the parking lot to the victim's apartment. He said he thought the blood had been planted.

Spurred on by Hopkins's suspicions, detectives discovered that the victim had worked at a hospital where a bag of blood had been reported stolen. When analyzed, the blood at the scene matched the blood of the stolen bag.

The "murder" was a suicide. Hopkins demonstrated how the victim had punched a hole in the bag of blood and then swung it back and forth with his arm extended, moving from the parking lot to his apartment. In his apartment, the man had held the gun to the back of his own head and pulled the trigger; the recoil had sent the gun flying to where it was discovered.

Swanburg thought it was just the sort of detective work Holmes would have admired. As Doyle had quoted his sleuth in *Black Peter*, "One should always look for a possible alternative and provide against it. It is the first rule of criminal investigation."

As he and others laid that first pig in a 20-inch-deep grave and covered it with dirt, Swanburg wondered what Holmes would have thought of their undertaking. He was envisioning a multidisciplinary team of trained observers, taking to the field to locate the remains of murder victims—bringing killers to justice.

"A many-headed Sherlock Holmes," he predicted.

Unlike Bass and Rodriguez, Project PIG intended to leave its "victims" buried. The PIG idea was to study what occurred at a grave site over a long period of time, and ways to detect the graves as they evolved.

But as the idea of offering Project PIG's expertise to law enforcement agencies began to grow among the members, it became imperative to bring a forensic anthropologist on board. They needed someone who could help recover the remains in an organized fashion, identify who their owner might be, and even suggest the manner of death—though the exact cause would be left to a forensic pathologist.

Michael Charney came to mind, but he was in his mid-70s and his health and eyesight were failing. It seemed he might be past the point of scrambling around, looking for grave sites.

Swanburg, Hopkins, and Griffin had paid a visit to forensic anthropologist Michael Hoffman at Colorado College in Colorado Springs. They had all attended lectures of his and knew he had an excellent reputation with police agencies—a hurdle they knew Project PIG would face.

Hoffman had said he was interested and willing to help on occasion. But he didn't have time to commit to a research project. "Why don't you call Diane France at Colorado State University," he said. "She's new and she's good."

Swanburg was aware of France's reputation—she had been appointed director of the CSU Human Identification Lab when Charney retired. He had even met her briefly.

The daughter of a doctor, Diane France had been raised in Walden, Colorado, a small ranching community. The town was set in a nearly treeless expanse of sagebrush and rolling pastures, framed at its outer edges by snow-capped peaks.

For a girl like Diane, it was heaven. A five-minute walk from any point in town and she was in the country. As she walked, her eyes were often on the ground, looking for anything interesting. Her room was full of treasures she picked up: deer antlers, rocks, old bones.

Often, she took the microscope from her father's office on her journeys, stopping to examine the tiniest flora and fauna. Why and how things were put together fascinated her. She was particularly interested in a plastic skeleton that hung in her father's office.

Her parents, noting her predilection toward science, thought she might want to go to college for a career in medicine. However, as a freshman at Colorado State University in 1972, she signed up for a course in forensic anthropology taught by colorful, irascible Michael Charney.

As she soon learned, physical anthropology was the study of the biology of humans and related species. Forensic anthropology is the application of that science to the law.

France would always think of Charney as the ultimate teacher. At any hour—it didn't matter if it was a weekend or a holiday, morning or evening—he would open the campus lab for any students who wanted to study. Then he would wait patiently in his office until they were through in case they had any questions. He taught students to be meticulous. Measurements of bones had to be exact, and just as exactly recorded.

Part of his charm (apart from the enormous walrus mustache he sported) was Charney's ability to weave stories around the bones he exhibited in his classes. The bones themselves told stories, he said, if you knew how to read them. A careful observer could tell whether the person had lived a good life or a poor one, was well fed and healthy or was plagued by disease and malnourished. The bones bore the scars of falls and wounds. From them, a forensic anthropologist could determine sex and, to a reasonable degree, such vital statistics as the height and age of the deceased.

The bones could assist with the identification of their owner by matching them to dental charts or medical records. A skull could provide a structure onto which the anthropologist could add clay to mold into features to spark recognition from some member of the public who might be missing a loved one. Incomplete and lacking flesh, the bones might still leave clues as to how their owner died—even point a phalanx at a killer.

Charney taught that whatever a forensic anthropologist might have to do to bones—disinter them, cut them, remove the flesh by simmering them in hot water—they were to be treated with dignity. "This," he'd say, holding up a specimen, "was once part of a living person, like you and me. He was loved by a mother and father, and loved his children."

Back in Walden, France's parents were surprised when she announced that she was changing her major to anthropology, more so when she said she wanted to be a forensic anthropologist. "You'll never make a living," they both worried aloud. But France didn't care; she was obsessed with bones, arguing with her fellow students about the identity of the tiniest fragments, and usually winning.

France became a graduate student and began working in the university's Human Identification Laboratory, where Charney was the director. The secure laboratory was a place that coroners, police officers, and medical examiners brought or sent human remains for identification. Charney often would then be called upon to testify in court regarding that identity and the circumstances surrounding the death.

It was at the lab that France first experienced what she would call the "goopiness" of her chosen field, and tested her ability to deal with the death of a human being.

One August afternoon in the late 1970s, Charney walked in with a biohazard bag containing what he said was the head of a young woman. She had been murdered and her body covered with brush in the mountains near Estes Park, Colorado. One of her hands was missing, presumably carried off by a coyote, and the body badly decomposed after remaining hidden for what Charney estimated to have been six weeks during the hottest days of the summer.

Charney told France and another graduate student, John Bradshaw, to remove what remained of the flesh from the skull so that he could reconstruct the face in an attempt to help police identify the woman. He then walked out of the room, leaving France and Bradshaw looking back and forth from each other to the bag.

Until then, they'd mostly dealt with dry bones that had little or no flesh remaining on them. This bag, though, smelled bad. And there was a sound coming from the bag, like Rice Krispies in milk.

There were several ways to go about their task. One was to place the head in a dark, dry, warm container box filled with dermestid beetles, which would strip it down to the bone. But the beetles don't like remains that are still too "wet," and the two young students decided that the beetles might not do the job.

They settled on using a large pot and a hot plate and placing the head in very hot water (but not boiling, since that could damage the bone). The idea was that every so often they would remove the head and pick off the flesh, straining the water into a special sink and then repeating the process.

The first shock came when they opened the bag. It was so full of maggots that the larvae were out and crawling up their arms before they could grab the head and close the bag again. The noise from the bag had been the sound of the maggots eating. Repulsed, France brushed them off her arms and fought a desire to run out and, perhaps, change her major.

She stayed and they got the head into the pot, but the ordeal was far from over.

At one point in the rather slow and tedious process, France had to go to class. When she returned to the building where the lab was housed, it was to the scent of something cooking. The air in the hallways smelled like . . . pot roast.

As she drew closer to the laboratory, the aroma began to include the scent of decomposition. Although it wouldn't be discovered until several years later, the fans that were installed to carry fumes from the Human Identification Laboratory weren't working properly. The hood fan in the laboratory did its job, taking fumes to a point halfway out of the building, but the fan designed to finish the job had been reversed—it was blowing the fumes back in.

But even recognizing the smell for what it was didn't prepare France for the scene behind the laboratory door. She slipped in and found Bradshaw furiously mopping at an inch of dirty water on the floor. A lit cigar hung out of his mouth.

The sink, which was full of plaster from another project, had clogged and overflowed. The floor was covered with foul water, necrotic tissue, and dead maggots. The stench was horrible; thus the cigar, Bradshaw said, to cover the smell.

France thought the cigar only made it worse. She was disgusted, but she grabbed a mop and began helping her colleague clean.

Every so often, they took a break and went into the hallway to catch a breath of fresher air. That's how they learned that the guys from the building maintenance crew were running around trying to figure out the source of a foul-smelling liquid that was oozing down the walls of an office one floor below. It just happened to be the office of the dean of the College of Social Sciences.

The maintenance crew thought it must have been a backed-up toilet. France and Bradshaw took a deep breath and headed back into the lab to finish cleaning up their "little secret."

As horrible as the incident was, it was nothing compared to how France felt about the young woman's murder. She found herself wanting to ask questions of the woman as Charney recreated her face with clay. Who are you? Where did you come from? What were your last moments like? Did you suffer?

In the ensuing years, France would silently ask those questions over and over again to one set of remains after another. Sometimes there were answers; often there were not.

In 1979, Diane France went to the University of Colorado in Boulder to pursue her Ph.D. in anthropology with Alice M. Brues, one of the first women to receive a Ph.D. in anthropology, and a noted figure in the field for many years. At the school, France put her ability to deal with death to another test. Her class was dissecting the cadaver of an old woman who had donated her body for science. The students had started with the woman on her stomach so that they could begin the dissection with her back, as was the normal procedure. It was weeks before they rolled her over and uncovered her face.

France stepped back. She'd discovered what others who deal with death know: It's the face that makes a body a person. Most of what she'd dealt with in the past had been decomposed remains or just a skull. This woman looked as though she might wake and open her eyes. France took a deep breath and returned to the business at hand.

Two years later, France was teaching the dissection portion of the class while Brues gave the lectures. In 1983, France received her Ph.D. and was already beginning to attract attention for her work. That included an invitation to join the American Academy of Forensic Sciences, which consisted of the top people in those fields. She returned to CSU as an affiliate assistant professor and was soon offered the unpaid position of director of the Human Identification Laboratory. (Charney had officially retired, though he continued to teach as a professor emeritus.)

There had been many changes in forensic anthropology since France and her classmate macerated that first head. For one thing, all biological material was collected and returned to the coroner, where it was disposed of according to biohazard regulations.

Other changes were much more far-reaching. Technology had made incredible strides. X rays were increasingly being used by anthropologists to compare antemortem and postmortem characteristics of bones. A cross-section of bone could closely give the age of the deceased by comparing the ratio of new to old bone cells.

Photographic superimposition was another technological marvel.

The technique involved using photographs taken while the victim was alive and, through the magic of video and computers, superimposing the images over that of the skull, or another photograph. The object was to see if the general outline of the head, eye sockets, nasal passages, earholes, and teeth lined up. If possible, photos were used from a variety of angles.

Although the layperson might not see much to differentiate one skull from another—other than, say, the size difference between an adult skull and that of a child—to the trained eye they are as different as a birch tree and an oak. All one has to do is look at differences in faces on the street to see this is true. Photographic superimposition was a useful tool. However, it was not ordinarily used as a sole source of positive identification.

There was progress in other areas as well. Forensic science in general and anthropology in particular were gaining more widespread acceptance with law enforcement agencies. Forensic anthropologists like France were slowly changing the way police excavated bodies of buried homicide victims.

Grave sites once excavated with backhoes and shovels were now broached using modified archaeological techniques, like those used to excavate human remains of an ancient civilization. Test holes were dug in suspected graves to reveal the presence of decomposition through odor, or for other evidence such as adipocere—a whitish, soaplike substance that sometimes develops on the body when it decomposes under cool, damp conditions.

Grids, most often comprised of strings tied to stakes, were set up over the suspected grave so that investigators would know where every speck of dirt or piece of evidence—sifted through screens—came from. Instead of bulldozers and shovels, whisk brooms, garden trowels, and bamboo picks were employed so as not to disturb the remains or nick bones. Through this method, the anthropologist could retain contextual, in situ, and locational information, without adding any "artifacts" to the bone, such as scratches that could be misinterpreted.

France was a good scientist, a meticulous one. But all the scientific detachment in the world couldn't shield her from the emotional side of her work. She asked her questions of silent remains, but often she never learned the outcome of the investigations she helped with. Even if she testified in court, she rarely learned much about the victim or the family; sometimes she didn't know the outcome of the trial. The emotional toll of her work reached a critical point in December 1985 when she first, briefly, met Jack Swanburg, following a gas plant explosion in Glenwood Springs.

Swanburg belonged to the Rocky Mountain Division of the International Association for Identification. When the organization formed the Colorado Human Identification team to respond to mass fatalities following the Big Thompson flood of 1976, which claimed more than one hundred lives, he joined that too.

Now in December 1985, he and other members of the team had been called to Glenwood Springs, a town 150 miles west of Denver on the other side of the Continental Divide, in response to a massive explosion at a natural gas plant. Firefighters who responded to the scene had been told to search for twelve victims thought to be in the building. Many of the victims' bodies had been so fragmented by the blast, or so badly burned, that positive identification was thought to be impossible.

The body identification team of photographers, fingerprint experts, and odontologists (specialists who make identification through dental charts) had identified seven of the victims. But what remained of the other victims did not have those kinds of identifying markers anymore; a forensic anthropologist was needed to find different clues to establish their identity.

The coroner had called France. She arrived just as Swanburg and the rest of the body identification team was leaving.

They wished her well, and she found herself alone in the morgue, which was located in the basement of the Glenwood Springs hospital. Even the coroner excused himself and retreated upstairs. France looked around. The morgue was very clean, cool, white. It was as still as only death can be.

Glenwood Springs was a small town. The deaths of a dozen people had to have affected nearly everyone. It was just a couple of days before Christmas, and the remains that lay in body bags in the cooler waiting for her belonged to families who had been looking forward to a joyous holiday. She felt overwhelmed by the fragility of life—the lives of the victims and the lives of those who survived them.

France worried about the emotional health of the firefighters, who had done their best to find what was left of people who were surely at least acquaintances, possibly even friends and family. She also wondered how she was going to deal with such a massive tragedy in her own mind.

She had learned to deal with the physical aspects of violent death. Neither the smells nor the sight nor even the maggots bothered her anymore. The "goopiness" of piercing together shattered, decomposing human bodies was manageable. But no one had ever taught her how to deal with the pyschological aspects.

Standing alone in the morgue, she knew she had to find a way to steel herself and get to work—the families were waiting for their loved ones. She came up with the best she could on short notice.

France visualized dividing her thoughts into two categories: one for emotions, the second for science. Then she pictured a small cardboard box with a lid. Into that box she poured all the emotions. She closed the lid and tied the box shut with a ribbon. Then she placed it on a shelf she built in her mind. *I'll deal with the box later,* she told herself, *when I have time to sit down and examine what I feel about all of this.* The tactic worked, France's scientist side was able to get back to the job.

One by one, she retrieved the body bags from the cooler. The first thing she had to do was conduct an inventory and see what body parts were there to help her determine sex, age, stature, and ancestry. She then looked at medical records for whatever might distinguish one person from another—previously broken bones, for example—and compared what she learned to the list of probable victims and the remains in front of her.

Every half hour, or so it seemed, the coroner called. "I don't want to rush you, but when do you think you'll have the answers?" he asked. The families were getting anxious.

There was no rushing France. These people whose remains she had been entrusted to identify demanded that she be right, that she speak for them. It took her nearly two days, and she was exhausted when she finally walked out of the hospital for the drive home. But she had been able to identify every one of the victims and had made sure the remains went to be buried under the headstones of their rightful owners.

Swanburg knew France had worked alone until she had identified everything and turned the remains over to the coroner for burial by their loved ones. He figured that had taken one tough scientist—the kind Project PIG was looking for. He called France and she accepted the offer.

In the years since the Glenwood Springs Explosion, she had continued to use the boxes in order to deal with the emotional side of her work, but she hadn't followed up and brought them down to examine. They just continued to build up on their shelves. It was one of several reasons why she agreed to join Project PIG. She also liked the idea of working with other scientists toward a common goal and was attracted to the group's intention to apply what they'd learned on real cases.

Swanburg's invitation had one immediate effect. France invited him to attend a class she was teaching with fellow CSU anthropologist Cal Jennings on how to use archaeological techniques to exhume a body for law enforcement officers in Weld County, northeast of Denver. The two-day class included digging up a plastic skeleton buried in the backyard of a county deputy.

The techniques were revolutionary to Swanburg. The accepted method of getting a body out of the ground for most police agencies, including Arapahoe County, was to get a shovel and start digging. If the grave was deep or the exact location unknown, they used a backhoe. Once the body was uncovered, the usual practice was to pick it up, stick it in a bag, and get it back to the coroner's office.

France, however, stressed the importance of carefully excavating the grave. First, she said, establish a grid system of stakes and strings over the suspected grave site so that investigators would know where every bit of dirt, plant material, or evidence removed from a grave came from as it was sifted and catalogued. Use garden trowels, even spoons, rather than shovels to protect the remains, she cautioned, and bamboo picks and whisk brooms rather than metal objects, to dislodge dirt around the remains without nicking the bones and leaving marks that might be misinterpreted later. Leave obvious evidence, as well as the body, in situ (as originally found), so that details such as the position of the body could be photographed before removal.

Swanburg went back home with a whole new appreciation for what was involved if Project PIG wanted to move beyond business as usual. It wasn't long before he got to put France's methods to work. Only a couple of hours after he got back from the class, he received a call. Workers at a rural sand-and-gravel company had discovered a hand sticking up out of the ground on the property.

Swanburg quickly found string, stakes, a garden trowel, and a whisk broom and hurried out to the site. Setting up a grid, he and Anthony Gallardo, a budding criminalist new to the crime lab but interested in this "new" technique, excavated the body of a man. Only after they had completely uncovered the body and removed and bagged the evidence in the grave did he allow the body to be taken away.

In the process, Swanburg found spent bullets and a cartridge case that would later be tied back to the murder weapon and the killer. The criminalist knew that using the old method, the firearms evidence might well have been missed.

Diane France, he thought as he drove home that night, *is going to be a hell of an addition to our group.* He would soon get the opportunity to work with her again.

Swanburg knew that crime solving began and ended with good, hard detective work and a little bit of luck—or divine intervention. One such experience began on a morning that winter when he, Hopkins, and Alan Sprigg, another criminalist with the Arapahoe County crime lab, were called out to a neighborhood where someone had reported seeing a large pool of blood. It had snowed the night before and the bright red stain was easy to see. They collected a blood sample and searched through the mess for other evidence, coming up with three small pieces of what appeared to be skull fragments.

According to what they knew of the apparent crime, an officer had responded to the area the night before when someone reported having heard gunshots. He had found the stain but no body and assumed that perhaps a dog had been struck by a car. Almost in passing, he noticed that someone had been driving down the snowy streets, creating "donuts" by spinning the car in circles.

The criminalists sent one piece of the bone fragments to the coroner, who looked at it and determined that it was nonhuman. The case was closed, but for some reason Swanburg kept the other two pieces in an evidence bag.

Unknown to him, an 18-year-old man named James Bennett had been reported missing by his parents the day the pool of blood was discovered. He was last seen walking home that previous night after work, but had then disappeared off the face of the earth.

Two weeks after responding to the report of a bloodstain, Swanburg and Hopkins were again on the road, this time responding to a request for help from a rural county that didn't have criminalists. A farmer had discovered a body in a well on his property. County deputies had pulled the body out, but the head was so damaged as to make the face of the person unrecognizable.

On the way back to his office, a funny notion popped into Swanburg's mind. He had seen the missing person bulletin about James Bennett and now wondered if the body in the well and the pieces of bone fragments were all connected. What if the fragments really were human? he thought. The timing was about right.

Swanburg went to the autopsy of the body, which was performed by Dr. Ben Galloway, a noted forensic pathologist who freelanced his services, mostly in the large rural counties around Denver. "Can I have the head?" Swanburg asked and explained his theory.

Galloway agreed. He had identified the body through fingerprints; it was definitely James Bennett. The young man had been killed by a single high-caliber bullet that entered his mouth at an upward trajectory and went out the back of his head.

What they didn't have was his killer. Swanburg thought a good place to start would be by proving that the street with the bloody snow was really where Bennett had died.

Swanburg took the head back to his office and set it in hot water to strip the flesh off. What he had left when the flesh was gone was nearly a hundred separate pieces of skull—the effect a large-caliber bullet has at close range.

Painstakingly he pieced the fragments together with hot glue. When he was finished, he had a complete skull, except where the bullet had blown through. He then picked up the two pieces he had kept from the bloody street. They fit into the hole as precisely as those of a jigsaw puzzle.

Now he knew for sure where Bennett died. But he wanted to ask someone with a scientific background for a second opinion that he could use in court to bolster his own testimony if needed. He sent the cranium reconstruction and two fragments to Diane France in Fort Collins.

France matched the arterial grooves—where the arteries run on the inside of the skull—and the thickness of the cranial vault of the pieces to the reconstructed cranium. Everything lined up perfectly, she said. Swanburg was correct; the pieces fit like a puzzle. When she was done, France wrote a report stating that the pieces indeed belonged to the reconstructed cranium, and sent it off to her new colleague.

Swanburg knew he could prove in court that James Bennett had been shot on the street and that his body was then carted many miles away and dumped down the well. The police now knew where to begin looking for his killer, but that didn't mean finding him was easy.

For nearly two years, the police conducted what amounted to psychological warfare. They used a computer to regularly call the telephone numbers of every house in the area with a message asking if anyone had any information that might lead to the killer. A local crimestoppers group also circulated flyers.

At last, a young man called to say that his older brother was the killer. They had been driving down the street that night, spinning donuts, he said, when they had passed another young man walking down the road. Apparently, Bennett thought they had come too close to him and struck the vehicle with his hand when it went by.

The car had stopped and backed up. Words were exchanged. And then, according to the caller, his brother, who was driving, had pulled a .44 magnum handgun and shot the other young man. They had taken the body and dumped it in the well.

The younger brother's conscience, with the constant reminders from the police program, had finally gotten to him. He added that the murder weapon had been buried in the ground beneath where a concrete stairway was about to be poured at a construction site.

The gun was recovered. At a preliminary hearing, the defense attorneys were unable to suppress Swanburg's evidence of the skull, backed as it was by France. Rather than face a potential death-penalty trial with so much evidence against him, the older brother pleaded guilty to second-degree murder and was sentenced to prison for forty-eight years.

Although not officially a Project PIG case, it was an early demonstration of the sort of interdisciplinary and public–private-sector cooperation that would become the hallmark of the group.

December 13, 1988

It was a disaster of the highest order. Everything had been going so well out at the PIG site. But now this . . .

In October, they had buried three more pigs, donated by a veterinary school that used them to practice surgical procedures. And they had fun doing it. Dick Hopkins had marched three jail trustees assigned to help to a spot by the side of the road. "You're going to dig, starting here," he informed the trustees. He kept his face straight as he described what he wanted: three 3-foot-by-6-foot holes, different depths. Grave-sized. The trustees, who had not been told what they were there for except to work, gave each other and Hopkins nervous glances. A sort of "Geez, we know jail overcrowding is a problem, but . . ."

The other Project PIG members present—Griffin, Davenport, Castellano, and Swanburg—laughed at their discomfiture. Hopkins sure had one wicked sense of humor, and sometimes it was hard as hell to tell when he was joking. Although they quickly realized that they were the brunt of some prank, the trustees didn't relax again until the project members pulled the pig carcasses out of the back of a truck.

Davenport and Griffin, who had quickly established themselves as the punsters in the group, claimed the first two pigs had committed "sooey-cide" with the aid of the third, "Dr. Keporkian."

The experiment had then proceeded as planned, with each scientist conducting field studies. Kondratieff set up nets over the four grave sites to trap insects. Davenport took magnetometer readings to see how the readings at the graves changed. Another geophysicist he had invited to join the group, Don Heimmer, also ran ground-penetrating radar surveys. Bock had been out to study plant succession at the sites.

Then this had to happen. Lindemann, who had been working on a geological map of the area, had gone out to the site and discovered that someone—or something—had taken one of the pigs. It had been placed in a ravine and covered with only three inches of dirt, emulating a hurried, shallow burial.

Now, there was no sign of it. On further inspection, it was soon apparent that the thief had disturbed the soil around two of the other pigs, which had been buried deeper.

Lindemann called the others. They were all dumbfounded. And disappointed. They soon realized, however, that they were dealing with the unexpected. Scavengers.

"Maybe a bear or a mountain lion got to it," Hopkins suggested.

Then two more pigs disappeared, one in January and the third in

February. A fourth they had secured by bolting a piece of chain-link fence over the grave. But they worried that the experiment was ruined and they would have to start all over again.

Or was it?

Once the initial disappointment and self-flagellation passed, they began thinking that maybe the theft was a good thing. After all, human remains would be subject to scavenging, too. What could be learned by studying the habits of these animals?

"What we need is a naturalist," said Hopkins. He knew a woman named Vickey Trammell, who taught biology at a local community college and worked as a naturalist at a state park west of Denver. He knew her because they both had sons in a Cub Scout pack that Trammell led.

In March, Hopkins called Trammell, who said she'd love to participate. However, between teaching, motherhood, and playing violin for the symphony, she thought the commitment might turn out to be too much for herself alone. She asked if she could invite a friend and fellow naturalist at the park, Cecilia Travis. "She's also a geologist," she added, "if that helps."

With the addition of France, Trammell, and Travis, a Project PIG tradition was born. If the group didn't know the answer to some question, they would find someone who did and add to their pooled collection of expertise.

Over the next few months, in all kinds of weather, Trammell and Travis traipsed over miles of the rolling, rocky countryside following animal trails, studying tracks, picking up scat, and examining it for bits of pig bone and hair. They looked in thick stands of scrub oak and crawled into coyote dens for signs of the pigs.

There were a lot of similarities between the two women. Physically, they were both small and soft-spoken, middle-aged mothers with older children. At first impression, Trammell seemed more rough-and-tumble—despite her training as a classical violinist—and Travis a bit more "ladylike." But as they soon proved at the Project PIG site, neither was above getting down and dirty.

The one thing they had most in common was a love for the outdoors and a hands-on relationship with nature. It was a trait they picked up in childhood.

Trammell grew up in Canton, Ohio, a steel city. But every summer her mother would pack up the four kids and move them out to a cabin they had on nine acres in the country. It was the 1950s, and she was trying to isolate them from the polio epidemics that swept through the cities during the warm months.

The countryside was a wonderland of deep woods for playing hide-and-seek or "Indian tracker," following the trails of animals. It was a field for studying the ways of insects, and a pond for catching crawdads. When she tired of those games, Trammell would find a secluded spot for a little peace and quiet in which to curl up with a good book. She loved kids' detective stories, especially Nancy Drew and The Hardy Boys, and set up mysteries for her siblings to solve.

What she really wanted to be when she grew up was an FBI agent. But in those days, nobody encouraged a girl to do anything like that. So she did the best she could, including once trying to set a trap to catch hoodlums suspected of stealing hubcaps off cars in the neighborhood. She had stumbled upon a stash of hubcaps that had been secreted in a vacant lot. Her idea was to stake out the lot that night and catch the culprits when they came by to add to their booty. But when her mother found out what she was up to, she dragged Vickey into the house. The next day, the hubcaps were gone. Steaming mad, the girl blamed her mother for spoiling her one and only chance to catch a real live bad guy.

After high school, she went to college to become a science teacher. She didn't lose her love for mysteries, though now her interests shifted to Sherlock Holmes or the characters invented by Agatha Christie. And she found a way to meld her love for a good mystery into her work by taking her young students into the outdoors to play "nature detectives." For instance, showing them how a pile of wood chips around the stump of a recently felled sapling led to the "suspect," swimming in a beaver pond.

Trammell married and had three children, Scott, Jim, and David. The family moved to Denver, where she eventually took a job teaching at a community college.

In 1976, she answered an advertisement for volunteer rangers to lead the public on hikes through the newly created Roxborough State Park, a haven for wildlife including mountain lions and bears. A year later, when the park received a little more of a budget, she was hired to identify plants along the hiking trails, creating signs so that the public would know what they were looking at.

It was at the park in 1984 that Trammell met Cecilia Travis, who had answered another call for volunteer naturalists to serve as tour guides. They became fast friends.

Trammell was used to odd questions from Detective Dick Hopkins. Ever since they met, he had called and posed many along the lines of whether there was such a thing as "carnivorous grasshoppers,"or if temperature had any effect on the life cycle of maggots. She knew it had to do with his work and murder investigations, which piqued her old interest in mysteries, but he was rarely forthcoming with many details, so she remained a frustrated detective.

Then he called with the interesting offer to join Project PIG. More specifically, to discover what had happened to the missing pigs and how that information might fit into the group's research regarding the location of clandestine graves. She knew it would be even better than capturing hubcap thieves.

"We couldn't find any tire tracks or footprints,"he said. "So we thought it might be some sort of animal—maybe a dog."

It was just the sort of mystery she loved. She agreed, telling him she was going to need help from her friend Cecilia Travis.

Travis had grown up in a military family and had traveled quite a bit. However, when her father was overseas during summer months, she, her mother, and sister would stay with her maternal grandparents in Denver. Every Wednesday during those summers, the family would head to the mountains. Once there, they would all spread out to pursue their own interests. Her grandfather, an avid fisherman, would head for the nearest lake or stream; her grandmother would unfold a chair and sit down with something to read where she had the best view of the mountains she loved. Her sister would find some quiet spot to write poetry. And her mother, a self-trained naturalist who seemed to know the name of every flower and the habits of all the local wildlife, would take off for the nearest hill or field.

Cecilia would fish with her grandfather, a former U.S. Army engineer who also knew the names of all the rocks and minerals she would pick up. Or she would follow and learn from her mother. In late afternoon, they would all get back together for dinner. Fish, if her grandfather had any luck; hot dogs otherwise.

Little wonder that Cecilia Travis became a scientist, graduating from Colorado College in Colorado Springs with a bachelor of science degree. She went to the University of Georgia to study geology, graduating magna cum laude, and was then awarded a Fulbright Scholarship to study in New Zealand. But geology was considered a "man's profession."She was usually the only woman in her classes, and was the first woman hired at the major petroleum company where she landed her first job.

Unfortunately, being first didn't mean being equal. She was paid less than male geologists, most of whom did not have her credentials, and given projects no one cared about or understood. She was ahead of her time, but she wasn't a fighter, nor the stuff of which pioneers are made. She was the first to admit that she let the system beat her.

Discouraged by the gender ceiling, she got married and left her chosen field for motherhood. She found that she loved domesticity, raising two daughters and following her husband as he took jobs in South America and then Ottawa, Canada.

In Canada, she reignited her childhood love of being out in nature. During the winter, she took up cross-country skiing and snowshoeing. As she plowed through miles of snow, she noticed animal tracks and began following them to see where they led. Her interest grew, and she bought guidebooks so that she could identify the animals she was following. When winter retreated, she began making plaster casts of tracks she would find where an animal had stepped in mud.

The family eventually moved to Denver. With her children no longer needing her at home, Travis decided it was time to go back to work. She briefly considered geology, but decided that after sixteen years, she still had a bad taste in her mouth and didn't want to fight her way back in. She went back to school and got her certificate for teaching special education classes.

In 1984, she noticed the Roxborough Park advertisement for naturalists. At first, she was too shy to apply; she had no formal training in that science, but her husband told her, "They'd be lucky to have you,"and so she replied—and was surprised when they accepted.

She found a kindred spirit in Vickey Trammell, and they spent long hours discussing their mutual interests. She was much stronger in geology and a bit more proficient in wildlife biology; Trammell was the better botanist. Together they made a good team, and Travis was excited when her friend invited her to participate in a research project that seemed so important. Finding the bodies of murder victims!

Trammell was too busy to start right away, but Travis volunteered to meet Hopkins out at the Project PIG site the next day. Looking at the area, she knew there was a good chance of bears and mountain lions being present—either one powerful enough to dig up and cart away a full-grown pig. Of the two, bears were more likely. They will essentially eat most anything and aren't particularly fussy about the ripeness of the meal. Mountain lions generally prefer fresh meat, though they have been known to scavenge when hungry and the hunting is not so good. But just because those were the two largest meat eaters in the area, it didn't mean they were the only scavengers. There were coyotes, and dogs from nearby ranches. There were also hawks, vultures, crows and magpies, skunks, and badgers. Even rodents were known to gnaw away at bones.

Travis got the lay of the land on the first visit and took a cursory look around the grave sites of the missing pigs. She thought it wouldn't be hard to determine who the pig thief was. There would be hair in feces she should be able to find. Major bones, particularly the skull, probably wouldn't have been devoured entirely.

That got Travis and Trammell to wondering when they met again if they would recognize a pig's skull. From what they had heard, the skull was similar to a bear's. They decided they needed something to compare with whatever they might find.

At their request, Hopkins secured a letter from the Arapahoe County sheriff asking a local grocery store for the donation of a pig's head. Travis went to pick it up and was directed to the butcher department, where she was presented with a great, bloody head in a clear plastic bag.

"It might upset people if I walk through the store with this," she told the clerk, who got her a box to put it in. She nearly made it out of the store without incident, but a curious woman shopper insisted on seeing what was in the box. Impatient to keep going, Cecilia showed the woman, who recoiled and fled.

The woman's reaction was good for a laugh when Travis got the head over to Trammell's house. They put the head in a big pot of water and boiled it to get the flesh off. Soon the whole house smelled like pork roast.

They removed and finished cleaning the skull. After it had cooled, they took measurements and photographs. Then they were ready to return to the field.

For all of their work, however, they ended up with little to show. They found pig hair in coyote feces, but none in the droppings of a mountain lion. There were plenty of bones—the facility had been used to dump the bodies of dead horses by a group that hunted coyotes from horseback—but only a single bone from a pig, a shoulder blade.

At first they were somewhat embarrassed by the lack of results, especially with a big conference coming up in May, at which members of Project PIG would first present their findings. But the other members of the group said they weren't looking at it right.

In a laboratory, the scientist can control the experiment. The theft of the pigs had demonstrated that it was much more difficult to control an experiment outdoors. But, as members on the law enforcement side pointed out, neither could a detective control what he would find at a crime scene. Detectives had to work with what they were given. Project PIG would have to do the same. If it was difficult to find the scavenged remains of the pigs, it might be equally difficult to find the scavenged remains of a human being—a lesson they would soon learn.

On January 23, 1989, with a flip of the switch, 7,000 volts of electricity jumped into the body of Theodore "Ted" Bundy in the execution chamber of a Florida penitentiary. Thus ended the life of one of the world's most notorious serial killers.

A handsome and charming former law school student on the outside, the monster Bundy was executed for the 1978 murder of a 12-year-old girl he had raped, strangled, and left in a pigsty. He had also been convicted and sentenced to death for the earlier murders of two Florida State University students.

Before he died, Bundy confessed to thirty other unsolved murders (police would believe that figure too low and place the number between fifty and a hundred) from Washington to Florida, including two in Colorado. One of those was Julie Cunningham, a beautiful 26-year-old Vail ski shop employee and part-time ski instructor who disappeared on March 15, 1975.

In a four-hour interview just three days before his death, Bundy told Vail police detective Matt Lindvall and members of the Garfield

County district attorney's office that he feigned injury to approach his intended victim. He said he was on crutches and carrying ski boots when he approached Cunningham near a parking garage in Vail. She even carried his boots to his car.

While she was helping him move items in the car, he knocked her unconscious with a crowbar, Bundy said. He handcuffed her and drove her 80 miles west of Vail, to a desolate spot several miles north of the town of Rifle in Garfield County. There he raped and strangled her, then buried her body.

Bundy told the investigators that he had returned and reburied her "a number of times." He described an area at the base of one of the tall buttes that rose from the valley floor. There was a circular drive and large trees. He said he couldn't be more specific than that.

Matt Lindvall believed that he and other investigators assigned to the case had found a place that fit Bundy's description. But it was still a large area to search for a buried body.

As it turned out, Lindvall had often taken evidence in other cases down to the CBI in Denver, where he had met Tom Griffin. One day, he was talking to Griffin when the agent mentioned a new group that was trying to combine a number of scientific fields to locate clandestine graves. Lindvall asked if Project PIG would help him find Cunningham.

It wasn't so much to find justice for Cunningham. Bundy was already dead. But Lindvall had known the young woman, knew her family. The wound of not knowing what had happened to her had never healed. Even with Bundy's confession, they didn't know if he had lied. There could be no real closure until her remains were returned to her family.

Lindvall had some concerns about bringing civilians in on a murder case, but Griffin assured him that the people he was working with were dedicated and professional—good people who would understand and respect the sensitivity of the investigation. Besides, Griffin added to break the ice with humor, if other members of the group agreed to participate, he wouldn't bring many people, "just a skeleton crew."

Lindvall traveled back to Denver to present his case to the Project PIG members. The group brainstormed about how best to approach this, their first case. They asked Lindvall about the area and what had been done to narrow the search site. He described the area investigators had focused on. How deep did Bundy say he buried her? Two to three feet, Lindvall said.

The group decided to accept the case. They didn't ask for any remuneration, just that the investigating agency provide room and board. The next step was to decide whom to send. Davenport would take his equipment; Lindemann, his eyes. Griffin would act as the law enforcement liaison with the investigating agencies. The group decided that they should also send a new member—or members—of the group: Al Nelson with his dogs.

On the morning of April 29, 1989, the Project PIG team headed west and met Detective Lindvall in Vail, and then the Garfield County investigators who went with them to the site. They arrived a little after noon, ready to put their first multidisciplinary, grave-hunting team to work.

Al Nelson got out of his truck and checked the wind. Out of everyone there, he was the most experienced in this business of looking for bodies. Bloodhounds, whose sense of smell is thought to be in the neighborhood of 300,000 to 3 million times that of humans, have been used since the seventh century for man-tracking: first as a means of finding lost people, and then in law enforcement to track suspects and criminals. But only in the 1970s did a few dog handlers begin to train dogs specifically to locate decomposing human remains.

Nelson first became interested in bloodhounds in 1982 after reading an article about them in a police magazine. Then in 1984, he was visiting relatives in Kansas City when he noticed a bloodhound kennel near Leavenworth, the site of a federal penitentiary. The kennel was run by Glenn Rimbey, who, along with Bill Tolhurst in New York and Jerry Yelk in Wisconsin, was considered one of the leading experts on bloodhounds.

At Rimbey's invitation, Nelson visited the kennel. His first look at a bloodhound convinced him that there was something wrong with the dog. It was drinking out of a bucket, but instead of lapping the water like most dogs, it had its face submerged up to its eyes.

Noticing Nelson's expression, Rimbey laughed and explained that the dog was rinsing out its supersensitive nasal cavities, the better to smell.

There were other aspects to the evolution of this particular breed of dog that, while unproven, Rimbey explained, were generally accepted as some of the reasons they were so well suited to their work. The long ears that flapped as the dogs ran with their noses to the ground stirred up dust, and thus the scent. While on track, the dogs also wrinkled the folds of skin above their eyes to store a scent in case they needed a reminder. The skin on the dogs was loose, and an extra fold protected the eyes, the better to push through brambles and thickets with their thick, powerful bodies.

No one was quite sure why a bloodhound is so good at tracking human scent, but it is generally thought that the dogs recognized the chemical odors of dead skin cells. The human body has somewhere about 73 trillion skin cells, which constantly die off and are replaced. Dead skin cells work their way up to the neck and are then shed at a rate of about 50 million per minute. They float to the ground, where moisture in the air causes bacteria to grow, producing the scent the dogs pick up on. At least that's the theory.

As people walk, they lay down a scent trail. It's carried on the breeze, attaches to foliage, dirt, car seats, and weapons. When a person stops, the dead skin cells continue to shed, creating what the handlers call a "pool scent." Since every person is an individual, the scent of her decomposing skin cells is unique—as unique to the dog's nose as a fingerprint to an examiner.

The dogs indicate interest in a scent with varying degrees of intensity. They may "hit," a sort of head jerk to test the air. It doesn't necessarily mean anything more than that something has caught their attention, whether it's the scent they're supposed to be finding or another animal.

But there's no mistaking when they're on the track of their intended target. Their heads are down, noses close to the ground; their tails go up. They work the "scent cone," a triangular-shaped area that starts at the subject and radiates out. Although it is the bloodhound's natural instinct to track, not all are suitable for the job; a dog has to make several verifiable tracks before it is considered a proven manhunter.

In their work, most bloodhounds prefer to follow the scent of a living human being. However, some also show ability—and inclination—to find decomposing human remains. These are the morbidly labeled cadaver dogs (or, as Nelson preferred, "decomp dogs").

Rimbey had some pretty incredible stories about his dogs'capabilities. There was a case he worked in which a farmer's wife had been missing for eleven months. The farmer was the chief suspect, but he maintained that she had left him.

Called in by the local police, Rimbey went to the farm with his dog, who immediately hit on a spot in the middle of a field. It didn't look very promising, but he flagged it and then pulled the dog off to sniff around the rest of the property.

When they returned, the dog hit on the spot again. The investigators dug down three feet and struck an underground stream. Obviously, the body hadn't been buried there.

Rimbey was puzzled. He'd known dogs that didn't feel like working on a certain day. Some just didn't have the knack at all. And cadaver dogs would hit on all sorts of decomposing human "remains," including feces, urine, and old bloodstains. But this dog was one of his best and was adamant about where they had dug the hole.

He looked around and saw a brush pile fifty feet away. The dog hadn't indicated there, but he walked over anyway. Covered with the brush was an old well.

Suddenly he had an idea about what the dog was doing. Sure enough, the body of the farmer's wife was discovered down the 40-foot-deep well. The scent of her decomposition had been carried underground to a spot where the stream pushed within three feet of the surface.

"You don't train these dogs so much as they train you," Rimbey told Nelson after recounting the story.

Nelson bought Amy in 1984 and brought her home, where she immediately became part of his family. So much so that he interpreted her expression when she "hit" on something as, "Look what I found, Dad!" And as Nelson found out, Rimbey was right about who trains who. Something else he learned was that while he might make mistakes in how he used the dog, he never caught her making a mistake on her own.

It was a lesson he learned in 1987 when he was called by the Greeley police to work on the case of a young woman named Mona Hughes, who had been kidnapped out of the drugstore where she worked. Her car had been found a couple of days after her disappearance in a field, but there was no trace of the woman.

After he got Amy, Nelson had trained her and offered her services to his own department. But the sheriff at the time wasn't interested. So he formed a nonprofit agency, Colorado Bloodhound Tracking, in

1985 and worked on his own time for other departments without charging.

Now Nelson responded to the scene with Amy and a new blood-hound pup he'd only just started training, Becky, along for the ride. The first thing he noticed was a field full of men and their dogs; apparently, the police didn't want to rely on one team. The detective who met him motioned to the other dogs and said, "Sorry to have called you out here. These guys haven't had much luck, so you might as well go home."

Nelson shrugged. None of the other dogs were bloodhounds; they were search-and-rescue dogs, used mostly to find avalanche victims. "Well, I'm here; might as well give it a try," he said. He got Amy out of the truck and put her on a shoulder harness and leash. A blood-hound can't be allowed to just run, because once they hit the scent, they're gone.

The detective provided an article of clothing from the missing woman. Nelson could tell he didn't think much of a dog's ability, but Amy immediately picked up a scent trail and took off with her owner trotting along behind.

After about a hundred yards, Amy stopped and began moving in a small circle. The detective showed new interest. "What's she got?"

"Don't know," Nelson replied. "She's telling me, 'Dad, I got something here.' So either something was dropped or the girl stopped here."

The detective looked at him funny, and at the dog with new respect. Before Nelson and Amy arrived, he admitted, searchers had found a personal item from Hughes's purse at that spot.

Nelson nodded. "Good. That confirms she's on track."

They moved on, but pretty soon Amy indicated another pool scent. The detective raised an eyebrow, but this time it was Nelson who asked, "Why don't you tell me?" The detective confessed that it was the place where they'd found a piece of paper from the missing woman's car.

Amy kept hitting on spots where the investigators had picked up items belonging to Hughes. She also found several more items from Hughes's purse that the searchers had missed.

Nelson eventually lost the detective, who had discovered how difficult it was to keep up with a bloodhound on track. It was getting on toward evening when he and Amy worked their way up to a farmhouse. An old woman came out and asked what he was doing.

Nelson explained: they were looking for a missing girl. While he stopped, Amy sat down. And it was then that he made a mistake.

Usually, Amy sat down when she lost the trail, looking back at him as if to say, "Sorry, Dad, lost it. Can you help?" He thought that was what she was saying now. It was dark anyway and, believing that Amy was finished for the day, he took her back to his truck.

Nelson found the detective and told him what had happened. "Okay, well, we appreciate it," the detective said. The bloodhound had done more than the other dogs, but still there was no victim.

A few days later, a Saturday, the detective called Nelson at home. "Can you get up here with your dog? And I mean like now." He explained that a female had called the day before, claiming to have information about the missing girl. "She said, 'I know where she's at. She's in a field.' "

Nelson and Amy met the detective in the field described by the young woman. The dog immediately took off on a track that led right back to the same farmhouse. It was then that Nelson realized that when Amy had sat down that first evening, she was only waiting for him to get going again—not giving up. He knew she was really on when Amy, who detested cats, passed several as she worked her way around the house without reacting, even when a couple of the felines swatted at her.

As Amy sniffed around, a truck pulled up. Inside was the young woman who had called the Greeley police. The dog hit on the truck and then the young woman. The missing woman's scent was in the truck, Nelson told the detective.

It didn't take long, with Amy's nose pointed right at her, for the girl to partially confess. Her boyfriend, Don Long, was involved in the disappearance and he'd used her truck, she admitted.

Nelson would have liked to stay, but the Greeley detective thanked him and said his agency would take it from there. "You tied it in for us," the detective said. "Now go home; we've taken enough of your time, and she's going to lead us to the body."

It turned out that the body wasn't in the field. It was found a couple of days later in a shed twelve miles away. However, her clothes were covered with bits of vegetation as though she had been in a field at one time. When he heard that, Nelson wondered if Amy would have found her that first night if he hadn't misread what she was telling him.

With all the evidence pointing to him, Long pleaded guilty to an earlier murder in Fort Collins and the Greeley murder to avoid the possibility of the death penalty and received two life sentences. Caught by the long nose of the law.

After Amy's work resulted in the apprehension of her third murderer, Nelson's boss decided maybe there was something to bloodhounds, and she and Becky were added to the department's canine unit. A couple of years later, however, a new division commander took over and the bloodhounds were out again.

Nelson was getting a little tired of the doggie roller coaster when Jack Swanburg called. The criminalist said that he and some others were starting a new group that was going to do research into locating clandestine graves. "I heard you have dogs that find bodies and wondered if you'd be interested in joining us?"

Nelson said he'd give it a shot. He was always learning new things about the dogs, especially at seminars with the men he referred to as "the Gods" of bloodhound human-trackers, and this project to bury pigs was even better for working with the dogs than Swanburg knew.

Just about any animal can find another decomposing animal. The trick was to get a decomp dog to focus only on human remains. The funny thing about Swanburg's project was, the only scent that the dogs couldn't differentiate from human was pig.

Amy had never shown much of an inclination for decomposing remains; she wanted live people. Becky, on the other hand, had a real talent for it. And like any "expert," she had her own idiosyncrasies, particularly in how she indicated a hit.

When the dogs were tracking and found the living person they were looking for, they would run up and give them a gentle nudge as if to say, "Tag, you're it."

With decomp dogs, there might not be anyone to nudge, so the idea was to train them to sniff and paw at a site. That's how Nelson tried to train Becky; then as a reward for good work, he'd give her a doggie treat out of his pocket. Becky put two and two together. When she hit and knew it, she would sniff and paw and then head straight for "Dad" and go for the pocket. Rather than try to bend Becky to doing it his way, Nelson learned to accept her method of showing that she had done her job.

Three pigs were missing before Nelson and his dogs had any real involvement at the site. That was when Swanburg called to see if the dogs could join the search already under way with naturalists Vickey Trammell and Cecilia Travis.

Nelson took Becky out to the site. She went wild but couldn't seem to fix on any particular direction. They ran up and down the mesas and gullies that made up the area, without success.

Later, when he had time to think about the lack of success, Nelson decided the dog must have been confused. There was a big difference between tracking a living person and decomposition work. He had thrown Becky a combination of the two out at the PIG site, and maybe she simply didn't know what he wanted her to do. "Track a dead thing, Dad?"

The old joke went that in the beginning of time, when God was handing out attributes he asked the bloodhound if he wanted a nose or a brain. The bloodhound chose the nose. But if the dog was not "smart," it was single-minded; a good dog would stay on a track until stopped by its handler, or it collapsed. It wasn't Becky's fault that her instructions were unclear in regard to the dead, but still mobile pigs.

At the Project PIG meeting in June 1988, he'd been intimidated by all the academics in the room. Everyone seemed to have *ology* attached to what they did for a living. *Man, what am I doing here?* he thought. *I haven't got a clue what some of these people are talking about.* He only began to feel better when he realized that the geophysicist didn't understand what the archaeologist was saying any better than he did.

He quickly realized that even the most distinguished doctor among them was just another member of the team. His own experience in the Greeley case was a good example of how such a team might have worked. His dog had been the initial phase; a botanist could have been called in to tie the vegetation on the Greeley woman's body back to the field where the girlfriend said she had been left. The end result turned out okay with the guilty pleas, but when might such links be crucial to a case?

Nelson began to feel that he belonged with this group. And for fun, he began referring to himself as a "slobber-ologist."

The Julie Cunningham case Detective Lindvall had brought them was pretty straightforward. Somewhere in the acres of high desert country near the circular drive, Ted Bundy one of the most vicious predators in history, said he killed and buried a young woman far from the people who loved her.

This time it was Amy who was along for the ride, and Becky who would be doing the work. It was a cool, cloudy day, which was good—Nelson found that the dogs worked better when the barometric pressure was down.

The wind was gusting up to 30 miles an hour, which might scatter or cut down on the downwind strength of the scent cone but wasn't fatal to a search. The air was dry, which was both good and bad. Good because dry ground cracks, in what is called the desiccation effect, and allows scent to rise from a grave. Bad because moisture seemed to strengthen the scent of decomposition.

The age of these bones didn't bother Nelson. He had a friend whose dog had recently discovered several graves more than 100 years old. He felt that if his friend's dog could do it, then Becky could, too.

The Project PIG members talked about what to do next. Nelson said he would begin working his dogs downwind of the area. The others would spread out looking for things that looked out of place: pieces of clothing or, perhaps, grave-sized depressions in the ground that Davenport could check with his equipment.

Lindemann said he wanted to climb a nearby hill to get a look at the land, to see if there was any area of softer, deeper soil that would lend itself to digging a grave. He didn't say it so as not to discourage the others, but privately he didn't think they were going to have much luck.

Having grown up in Grand Junction, about 60 miles to the west, Lindemann was very familiar with the geology of the place they were searching. It was a land given more to rocks than to living things, except where the Colorado River cut through what was essentially high desert; a wind-and-water-sculpted land of tall, red or gray mesas, so eroded that their sides looked like the folds of an accordion.

Plants were few except for hardy grasses, a few tough, scattered bushes, and spots where gnarled piñon trees could put down their deep roots to underground water sources. Animals were also the sort best suited for desolate climes: jackrabbits, rattlesnakes, magpies, crows, and hawks. And coyotes.

This was where Lindemann had caught the geology bug as a boy in the 1950s. His father had introduced him to Al Look, an amateur paleontologist and rock hound who wrote a well-regarded book called *In My Backyard,* an autographed copy of which he gave the boy. Most Sundays, the boy and his mentor would be scrabbling about in the wilds, remarking on particular rock structures, stuffing rocks in their pockets like shoplifters in a candy store.

After high school, Lindemann had wanted to go to the Colorado School of Mines in Golden, Colorado, one of the top engineering schools in the country. His grades weren't good enough, so he joined the Army.

When he got out in 1959, he applied again and was accepted. He had only been there a few days when he walked into a corner drug-store and was razzed about his Army-style haircut by a loudmouth in the corner booth. He invited the lout outside to settle their differences. Nineteen-year-old Clark Davenport sized up the tall, thin young man who confronted him and, while pretty good-sized himself, decided that prudence was the better part of valor. He apologized and they had been best friends ever since.

Over the years, that friendship included a lot of good-natured debates about the differences between geophysics and geology. Davenport joked that the difference was that "I passed the math." Lindemann shot back by comparing geophysicists to "diviners" who walk across fields with willow sticks to find water.

Beneath the jokes, they had enormous respect for each other. Geophysics relied on equipment to remotely sense what was below the surface. The geologist depended on direct observation, whether it was of massive landforms or tiny rocks or core samples taken from deep inside the earth.

Geology had the drawback of actually having to burrow into the Earth to learn what was below the geologist's feet, which was time-consuming and costly. Geophysics, on the other hand, was highly susceptible to subjective interpretation of the data.

Lindemann had learned to be a little leery of Davenport's "invitations"; there was no telling where they might end up. But what eventually turned out to be Project PIG had sounded fascinating, and he believed that geology could make a contribution.

If nothing else, he could look at a site and distinguish between what was normal from a geological point of view and what was not. For instance, while not a soils geologist, he knew enough about that field to realize when the soil horizon, the distinct layers of soil, had been disturbed by something such as grave digging. Although there are many subcategories, a soil horizon has three basic features: the topsoil, which contains organic matter and is generally dark in color; the leached soil beneath it, through which water from the surface percolates, giving it a lighter or bleached look; and below that, the easily identifiable line that represents the water table and the generally brown or red soil beneath it, where rock is decomposing into soil. Below the soil layers is bedrock.

It was all in knowing what to look for. In the Project PIG situation, police investigators might be taught to recognize that leached soil on the surface could indicate where someone had dug.

At the beginning of the project, Lindemann mapped the geology out at the training facility, a task that had taken two months. Trenching into hills, he defined the soil horizon for the area, supplemented with state soil conservation survey maps developed for agricultural purposes.

One of the main aspects he was interested in at the PIG burial sites was how rapidly the disturbed soil recovered, or changed back into a natural-looking state. He documented this by taking monthly photographs. He noted that sandy soil generally recovered more quickly than clay, unless there were a lot of freezing temperatures and precipitation.

It was interesting work, but not too exciting until Davenport called and asked if he wanted to be part of the team that was going to look for the remains of one of Ted Bundy's victims. Now that sounded like an adventure! Lindemann figured that he might be able to spot things that were out of place—rocks that did not belong in a particular setting or were arranged unnaturally. Or he might note a depression in the soil that wasn't normal for the area.

Out at the "Bundy" site, he climbed the hill and surveyed the area around him through field glasses. He was looking for a place that might have adequate soil for Bundy to have buried a body two to three feet deep.

From Detective Lindvall they knew that Bundy said he had pulled off the highway and driven a short distance to a circular turnaround near some large trees. The only trees in this area were piñon pines.

The site where they were fit those parameters, but supposedly Bundy had said that after he hauled his victim's body out of the car, he hadn't carried her very far. Lindemann surveyed the area for a hundred yards from the circular drive and didn't see any place with enough soil to bury a body more than a foot deep.

The land was a series of sandstone shelves covered with a thin veneer of very sandy soil. There wasn't enough moisture in that arid place to create good, deep soil. The only places deep enough to dig down a couple of feet were dry washes, but the first good thunderstorm would send what he called a "frog strangler" flood down through the washes.

The sand would be carried away, as well as any body beneath it. An exposed body wouldn't last long. For that matter, neither would one buried only a foot deep, which was about as far as a shovel would go without a whole lot of work—more work than someone like Ted Bundy was likely to do.

The problem was that the bodies of most animals are extremely frail when exposed to the environment of the earth's surface. It was the reason 85 percent of the fossil record came from marine fossils, creatures that died and sank into the silt, which covered and protected their remains. On the surface, there were burning summers and freezing winters, which broke down rock, let alone bone. Bacteria and hungry insects made meals of decomposing material. If their experience at Project PIG had taught them anything, it was that scavengers would carry off unprotected remains.

The only evidence that Julie Cunningham had been brought to this lonely place and left would likely be whatever the scavengers didn't want: a belt buckle or piece of jewelry; perhaps a jawbone with some identifiable dental work. Locating any of it, Lindemann knew, would be like finding the proverbial needle in a haystack.

Still, it would be helpful to find anything—a question answered for Julie's family and friends. Not closure, perhaps, but at least some bit of the truth.

It would have been nice to give them something more, but the realization that this was unlikely didn't disappoint Lindemann. As a geologist, he was used to what one of his old professors called "an exercise in controlled failure"—no coal, no oil, no iron ore where he had hoped to find it. It was all part of the science: You went out, applied your knowledge to a problem, and sometimes you were successful, sometimes not.

Lindemann could look at it objectively. The detective could not. As they searched, the geologist heard him pleading to the tall, mute rock formations. "Talk to me, Julie. I know you're out here; talk to me."

The scientist didn't begrudge the detective's response. He knew the other man was emotionally involved, and death was something humans had never taken lightly—particularly when it involved someone they knew. Even Neanderthals had placed flowers and trinkets in the graves of their loved ones.

However, he was concerned about what he perceived as the team's emotional response to Lindvall's need. The more it was apparent that they weren't going to find her, the more they believed that she just had to be there. They got caught up in something that wasn't science and, to him, bordered on mysticism.

Julie Cunningham didn't have to be there. Neither did any other victims. If the fossil record was any indication, Project PIG was going to experience a lot more disappointments than successes if finding a body was the only way they were going to define the latter. They had to look at these things as learning experiences, as research; if they found what they were looking for, that was just icing on the cake.

In the end, they were all disappointed, but felt they had done the best they could. Becky had worked hard, found every deer and rabbit carcass in the area, but indicated interest in only one spot, and that was half-hearted. They dug down a foot but ran into hard ground that didn't appear to have been disturbed.

That night, they all went out to dinner with Lindvall and some of the Garfield County team. It was an eye-opening experience for the two non-law enforcement guys in the group, Davenport and Lindemann.

Bundy was the worst, said one of the prosecutors who had come to help with the search. But there were many more like him: men who traveled around looking like the boy next door, but with rape and murder on their fevered minds. For two scientists with daughters, it was a sobering thought and brought home the importance of what they were doing. Someday it might just be up to them to stop some of these guys.

Another eye-opener came from the investigators who told them that they had withheld some information about the efforts Bundy sometimes made when hiding a body. They wouldn't say what, and the search team now felt as if they had been asked to look while half blind.

It was clear when they left the restaurant that Lindvall was still pretty upset. All they could do was tell him that if something else came up, if he developed any new leads, they would be back in a flash.

Nelson packed up his dog and left. As usual, he preferred to dwell on the things he had learned rather than the success or failure of the search. He had wondered what Becky's reaction would be to a large decomposing carcass such as a deer they had run across. She had checked it out but didn't try to indicate as she would have had it been human, and that was a good thing to know.

The others went to a trailer that had been provided for them. In what would become a Project PIG tradition, they reviewed the day's events, and "debriefed," over a few beers. They theorized that if Julie Cunningham had been buried in that area, her remains had been scattered by scavengers. It was another lesson along what would be a sharp learning curve: Without the "mistake" of the pigs being abducted from the graves at the site, they likely would never have considered that possibility.

Of course, the revelation that information had been withheld left their interpretation open to question. Some, including Griffin, thought that perhaps some day they would return with the new information and have more luck. In the meantime, they learned valuable lessons that would help them make better choices in the future about which cases they took. Their resources were limited; they would need to apply them where they could do the most good. Complete information was critical. They had perhaps rushed in too quickly and got everybody's hopes up, including the family, who had been apprised of the search, when a little more circumspection would have been in order. But Bundy was a high-profile name, worth a lot of publicity if they had succeeded in finding his victim.

They bounced around ideas on how they might do better the next time. One idea was to come up with a questionnaire to get more information from the requesting agency. Another was to simulate the supposed grave and duplicate it at the site so that they would have a better idea of what to look for with the geophysics technology. If the victim had been buried with a suitcase and a rifle, they should dig a grave and bury a suitcase and a rifle.

This idea would have ramifications at the PIG site. Future pigs would be buried rolled up in carpets and shower curtains. Lime would be poured on graves—a practice of some killers to speed decomposition and throw off dogs—to see if Nelson's bloodhounds could still detect the "victim." They had to remember that this was science. They had to work smarter, not harder. But they still managed to have fun; little signs would appear at the grave sites to describe the conditions under which the pigs were buried, such as the tongue-in-cheek "Pig in a Blanket." Still, it was a grim group that packed up the next morning and headed east toward the rising sun, leaving the ghost of Julie Cunningham to the silent cliffs.

LE COCHON CONNECTION

May 19, 1989

A month after the search for Bundy's victim, Tom Griffin stepped up to the podium and adjusted the microphone. He looked out over the crowd in front of him.

More than 140 law enforcement officers, coroners, prosecutors, and criminalists were sitting there waiting for him to begin. Most were from Colorado: police and sheriffs' departments, agents from the CBI, and investigators with the state police. However, there were also representatives from nearly all the surrounding states and as far away as Alaska. They represented agencies as diverse as military criminal investigation units and the FBI, which had sent a half-dozen representatives from its headquarters in Washington, D.C., and from the training academy in Quantico, Virginia.

Hosted by the sheriffs offices of Douglas and Arapahoe Counties, it was the largest audience ever for a Rocky Mountain Division of the International Association for Identification symposium. The RMDIAI was started in 1967 by criminalists in Colorado and Wyoming and sponsored two symposia every year to spread the word on the latest in forensic science. Jack Swanburg, Tom Griffin, and Kim Castellano, all RMDIAI board members, had volunteered Project PIG to be the topic for the spring symposium.

It was maybe jumping the gun a little bit. After all, they had only been conducting the research for nine months, part of that interrupted by the thefts of the pigs. So the presentations made by different members would be more of an introduction to their field of study and its applications to Project PIG and law enforcement than the presentation of any major findings.

To be honest, the symposium was as much advertising as anything else. The "Bundy case" wasn't a success in terms of locating human remains, but it had excited the members about the possibilities of working in the field. The symposium was a way of letting the law enforcement community know they existed, what their capabilities were, and that they were ready to help.

Appropriately enough, the symposium was titled "Le Cochon (The Pig) Connection." A drawing of a pig in Sherlock Holmes attire—deerstalker cap, pipe, and magnifying glass—and holding up a human skull graced the cover of the binder handed to each member of the audience.

Griffin knew that much of the interest was because many in the audience had run up against the problem of bodyless homicides. All he had to do was think of Detective Lindvall in Vail and his quest to find Julie Cunningham to know how deeply these cases could affect even long-time police officers. Lindvall had called Griffin to tell him that he'd sent photos of the search area to Julie's family. It was a stark but beautiful landscape for her grave, and he said he thought it might bring the family peace to see it. They had replied that they appreciated the effort and that the photos brought at least some closure.

There was also the McCormick Ranch case, which still haunted Griffin and many others. In fact, Sharon Heinz, the sheriff of Kit Carson County, where the McCormick ranch was located, was sitting out in the audience. It was with a description of that cold, windy day on the plains of eastern Colorado more than three years earlier that Griffin began his talk. He recalled the image of what the group's members now laughingly referred to as "a forensic backhoe" ripping up the remains of three men whom no one else in the world had cared about. "I thought, 'There has to be a better way.' "

Griffin turned the meeting over to Swanburg, who recalled a breakfast meeting "over *ham* and eggs" where the idea of using pigs to simulate the bodies of human beings buried in clandestine graves was broached. Dick Hopkins, Debi Kimball, and Kim Castellano then each took a turn discussing the length and purpose of the project.

"It's a team effort," Castellano said, explaining how the police and scientist members of the group could complement each other's skills and expertise as they worked toward a common goal.

Only recently, Castellano had been involved in a case that exemplified that symbiotic relationship between sleuths and scientists. In 1987, the partially clothed bodies of known prostitutes began showing up along roadways in the Denver metro area.

A task force was formed of detectives from the counties where the dead prostitutes were found. Castellano was the representative for Douglas County. The difference with her victim was that she wasn't a prostitute. The young woman had been walking down Colfax Avenue in Denver, in an area known for prostitution, however, trying to get home at 2:00 A.M. Her body was dumped along a roadside in Douglas County, south of Denver, partially clothed like the others. Semen was found on her body, but otherwise Castellano had few clues, except the possibility that a large oil stain on the road near the body may have come from the killer's car.

The task force got its first break when a prostitute flagged down a police officer on Colfax Avenue and complained that a man was harassing prostitutes. She pointed him out to the officer, who took down the make of the car and its license number. Then another prostitute told police about a man who had tried to strangle her until she fought him off and got away. She pointed out the man's car, which matched the car from the first prostitute's complaint.

The car's owner, Vincent Groves, who was identified by the second prostitute as her assailant, was arrested for the assault. The task force began looking at him for the murders, especially when they learned more about his background.

Groves had already served time for strangling a girlfriend to death. A bright, articulate, and religious man, Groves had actually driven his truck to the Jefferson County Sheriff's Office with the woman's body in the back. He claimed she had died of a drug overdose, but an autopsy revealed she had been murdered.

When he got out of prison, Groves married a woman who was even more religious than he was. He believed that she was so pure that he shouldn't have sex with her. Instead, he went to prostitutes, whom, the task force believed, he then killed. But how to prove it?

Groves was interviewed by the Denver police and said enough for Castellano to get a warrant to search his car. Nothing much was found, except that the car leaked oil. On a hunch, Castellano had the car measured and learned that if the trunk of the car were lined up with where the victim's body was found, the leak from the engine would be directly above the large stain.

When Groves was shown a large board on which the task force members wrote down what evidence they had, he noticed the oil stain remark by Castellano. "That looks bad; my car leaks like a sieve," he said, though still maintaining his innocence.

It wasn't enough to charge him with murder. However, the many heads of the task force were working together much like contractors building a house. Someone poured the foundation; someone else nailed together the frame; someone else put a roof on it.

Semen had been found on the body of Castellano's victim in Douglas County, as well as on the body of another victim in Jefferson County. If Groves was a "secretor," the semen samples could be matched to his blood type. DNA testing would narrow the possibilities even further. However, there wasn't enough evidence to get a warrant to take a blood sample from Groves.

Then a witness in Adams County, west of Denver, came forward to say she'd seen Groves with the victim from that area before she died. That was enough to get a blood sample, which was then shared with Douglas and Jefferson counties. They soon had a DNA match to the semen found on those two victims. With the ghost of Dr. Karl Landsteiner hovering, Groves pleaded guilty to second-degree murder in both cases. Without the sharing of information and interagency cooperation, followed by the application of forensic serology, Groves might have gone right on killing. Instead, he died in prison a few years later.

The task force reminded Castellano of Project PIG's premise that more heads are better. As a detective, she had always believed that there was no such thing as having too many resources to solve a crime. The new group could be an important tool for law enforcement all over the country, not just for its braintrust, she told the audience, but for its practical applications.

For instance, few police departments could afford to buy, or even rent, something like ground-penetrating radar and then hire someone to run it—and that was if they knew what it was and where to find it. But if they knew about Project PIG, they could get answers to those questions, as well as hands-on assistance in the field.

"One person can't do it all," Castellano said, concluding her presentation. Then she turned the podium over to the first of the day's scientists, James Grady, an archaeologist with special expertise in the use of aerial photography.

"With it you have the ability to record in infinite detail minute changes in soil color or vegetation type," he said, "and document physical evidence of past human behavior."

Hundreds of years after they were gone, ancient agricultural plots and walls could be distinguished using the photographs. "These abilities often permit the archaeologist to make discoveries in places where there is no visible surface evidence of past human activity."

Comparing photographs taken of the Project PIG site by Bill Youngblood before and after the pig burials, Grady pointed out how someone with a trained eye could spot the differences. The characteristics made aerial photography "an equally useful tool to the police investigator."

Hans Bucher, the president of a thermal imaging company in Boulder, was the next speaker. He began by discussing some of the uses of thermal imaging systems, which detect infrared radiation, or heat. Many in the crowd were already aware of some of its uses, such as night vision lenses that allow the wearer to "see" in darkness, haze, fog, rain, and snow. They all knew of the practice of being able to follow a car at night from the air by detecting the car's hot engine.

Bucher said the equipment was capable of detecting much smaller differences, to tenths of degrees. Out at the PIG site he had been detecting temperature variations caused by the decomposition of the pigs and by the disturbance of the soil created while burying the pig.

"During the day the surface at the sites is heated by the sun," Bucher said. "After sunset the soil releases the heat in various amounts depending on how much energy it was able to store." Loose soil released heat differently than tightly compacted soil. "Also the surface emissivity is different from sites with different or no vegetation and where some digging was done recently."

After a lunch break, John Lindemann began his talk by describing the site as "rolling uplands and badlands." "Under dry conditions the recovery of soil disturbance at individual burial sites tends to be slow. Under wet and freezing-thawing conditions the clay soils tend to break down and recover at a more accelerated rate."

He discussed how soil is created and layered. "If you're out there looking and see the third layer on the surface, you know something is wrong."

Lindemann demonstrated how these disruptions to the soil could last decades by showing slides of an old Denver cemetery where the coffins had been disinterred and moved to another site. Usually, the former grave sites where invisible to the casual observer. But with the right light—or, in one slide, a blowing snow that filled in the shallow depressions—the former grave sites could be clearly seen.

It is nearly impossible to dig a grave, put a body in it, and backfill without leaving clear signs, Lindemann said. For one thing, soil taken from a hole expands roughly thirty percent. "With a body now in the hole, that means a lot left over," he said. "Pile it up and you might as well put up a big sign that says 'Grave.' Level it off and it will sag as the body decomposes and the soil compacts."

Clark Davenport followed his friend, stating, "There is no technology that I know of that can 'find a body.' But geophysics may be able to tell you where to look for one."

Crediting the CBI as "pioneering the application of geophysical techniques to crime scene investigations," Davenport said, "A problem that faces many investigators is how to locate a body or weapon in a large area, such as a field. Earth scientists have faced a similar problem for decades—how to locate an oil field or mineral deposit. Geophysical techniques have proven to be very cost-effective in oil and mineral exploration, and based on the experiences of CBI, these same techniques, on a scaled-down basis, have the same potential for success in forensics."

Davenport discussed the "most applicable geophysical techniques" for land crime-scene investigations—ground-penetrating radar, electromagnetics, and the magnetometer—and the capabilities and limits of each. Recalling what they had discussed a month earlier, following their search for Julie Cunningham, he said it was important to determine "what type of information is required prior to applying geophysical techniques." He concluded his part by going over—in lesser detail because he had not yet attempted it himself—the potential for using geophysical techniques for underwater investigations.

Geophysicist Don Heimmer followed Davenport and soon had those in the room chuckling about his slide show. One slide was a "Missing Pig Poster."

"Have you seen these pigs?" was the caption below four "mug shot" photographs of three pigs and a piglike dog, all with small notices of when they were last seen. He followed that with a slide called

"Rooters of the Lost Ark," starring Harrison Boar-d and directed by Steven Squeal-berg. When he got down to serious business, it was to elaborate on the use of ground-penetrating radar.

The last speaker of the day was Al Nelson, who began by talking about the history and capabilities of the bloodhounds. "There are documented cases of dogs finding skeletal remains several hundred years old." He detailed the Greeley case and Amy's role in the capture of Don Long. "Give us a shot," he said in conclusion. "We're happy to help."

The second day of the symposium began with Boris Kondratieff and what he had seen at the PIG site as it related to carrion insects. To make his study, he had dug pits to trap crawling insects and erected mesh tents directly over the burial sites to catch insects that attempted to leave by flying. The most common were species of blowfly. "The particular arthropod fauna attracted to a buried corpse varies with the nature and depth of burial."

Jane Bock followed the entomologist. She said there were two sorts of botanical evidence that could be great aids in locating burial sites.

"The biblical description of '. . . ashes to ashes, dust to dust' describes the first process," she said. "The breakdown of organic remains enhances the organic matter and minerals of the surrounding soil, especially when the remains are located within 18 inches of the soil surface.

"For up to a decade following burial, the vegetation on the site may reflect this nutritional enrichment by appearing more bright green or lush than the surrounding plants."

The second use for vegetation in detecting burial sites, she said, involves the process of plant succession. "If vegetation is removed or seriously disturbed at a site and then left to recover on its own, a pattern of revegetation occurs.

"First, weedy species that flourish on denuded soils appear, to be followed over succeeding seasons by other predictable communities of plants. This sort of evidence can persist for several decades.

"These lines of evidence can be used directly by investigators in the earlier stages of decay and succession, but they may need to seek assistance from local vegetation specialists to seek older burial sites."

Vickey Trammell and Cecilia Travis presented together their study of the pig thefts and their conclusion that the "majority of dining"at Project PIG was done by coyotes and large ranch dogs.

"Understanding which carrion eaters live in an area is important," Travis said. For instance, bears eat carrion in the vicinity where they find it. "Bears will kill and eat humans and aren't too concerned as to whether they are dead or not." Lions, on the other hand, rarely eat carrion unless sick or starving. Lions may cover the carcass with dirt or vegetation if they have to leave.

Some animals may take off with what they can carry, either to feed young or to eat where there is no competition from other scavengers. Knowing which animals are scavenging in a certain area can be determined by watching for the signs they leave of their existence: tracks, scat, and hair. The women cautioned that personal experience had taught them to watch out for beehives and poisonous snakes in caves.

Diane France wrapped up the presentations by discussing the techniques forensic anthropologists use for identification. She had not done much work with the pig graves per se, but had taught members about the proper excavation of grave sites, which she now detailed for the symposium attendees.

After France finished, the visitors were taken to the Project PIG site. There they were shown the graves and different methods to detect them. For instance, Lindemann had scraped off the side of a small hill to demonstrate the different layers of soil and thus, how to identify a disturbed soil horizon.

Although one visitor was overheard grousing that he still didn't see what was so bad about backhoes, all in all, the symposium was a tremendous success. "I'll never be able to look at the ground in the same way," Sheriff Heinz told the press.

Le Cochon Connection concluded with dinner under a large tent erected at the site. The main course? Roast pig. Small wonder that as word of the group began to grow in law enforcement circles, they were affectionately known as "the pig people."

May 1991, Metaponto, Italy

It had been two years since the Le Cochon Connection symposium. Clark Davenport and Tim Deignan, another geophysicist who would later be asked to join the group, were in Italy teaching engineers there how to use ground-penetrating radar to locate underground utilities. On a day off, they decided to take a drive along the seacoast, where the "arch" of the Italian boot would be.

The countryside was a rich, rolling green land of ancient vineyards and farms on one side of the road and the azure Mediterranean Sea on the other. As they passed through an area that had long ago been colonized, first by the Greeks and then the Romans, they happened upon several archaeological excavations.

They pulled into one area where, according to a friendly Italian guard, an American team was excavating the site of a sixth century B.C. Greek colony called Metaponto. Because it was Sunday, the archaeology crew wasn't working, but the guard let the men onto the grounds to look around.

One of the areas under excavation was the necropolis, the Greek word for "city of the dead"—a cemetery. It struck Davenport that what the archaeologists were attempting was related to the work at Project PIG, only the graves were much older. It gave him an idea.

Davenport returned a few days later and met Dr. Joe Carter, a professor of archaeology at the University of Texas at Austin, who was leading the excavation. Carter said the existence of the colony had been known since 1959, when aerial photographs revealed "division lines," or depressions in the ground, where the Greeks had erected stone walls to divide their fields. The walls were gone and the depressions so slight that an observer on foot would never notice them. Even in photographs taken from the air, it took experts who knew what they were looking for to discern where the walls had been.

Because the aerial cameras could not look below the ground, the work in the necropolis was slow, Carter explained. Finding the graves was hit-and-miss, and great care had to be taken not to damage any bones or artifacts by digging too hastily.

Davenport, noting yet another connection between this excavation and Project PIG in the use of aerial photographs, broached his idea with Carter. "Ever thought about using radar?" he asked.

"Sure," Carter said. As a matter of fact, GPR had been used for years in archaeology to detect underground structures and objects—less so on graves, but it had been done. "But," the archaeologist noted, "it costs more than we can afford, and we don't have anybody who knows how to run it."

"What would you say if I could get radar up here—at no cost?" Davenport said.

The professor's answer was predictable: an enthusiastic yes.

As soon as he got another break from the seminar, Davenport borrowed some of the Italian equipment. He drove back to Carter's dig, where GPR soon proved its value, locating the best areas to search, including giving an idea of the depth and size of anomalies that might be—and often were—graves.

Whenever there was free time, Davenport, and sometimes Deignan, went back. One grave in particular impressed Davenport. It contained the complete skeleton of a man the archaeologist labeled "the musician" because the tortoiseshell sound box of a lyre had been buried with him. He was lying on his back, his skull tilted up as if looking at something above his left shoulder. Davenport asked for a photograph of the musician.

As Davenport packed up the equipment to take back to the Italian engineers for the last time, Carter thanked him profusely. Davenport, who had told Carter about Project PIG, held up his hand and said he was the one who was grateful for the opportunity to test the equipment. *Geez,* he thought, *if we can find a body after more than two thousand years, we ought to be able to locate one after considerably fewer.*

Although Project PIG had responded to a dozen cases over the past two years, they had yet to participate in the recovery of any remains. Of course, the graves they were looking for weren't the sort found in a cemetery. They weren't meant to be found at all.

Most of the cases so far, such as the one involving Ted Bundy, didn't stand much of a chance for success from the outset due to the lack of good information, the passage of time, or the simple fact that a body wasn't in the area being searched. Some cases were last-ditch inquiries from agencies that had exhausted all the other possibilities and hoped for a miracle, only to find that scientists don't deal in such things.

Project PIG members were realizing that they were going to have to accept the fact that they were the option of last resort. They weren't going to get the "easy" cases, where the potential for success was high. The locals could solve those on their own. The group had to consider itself as just another tool and, generally, the last one out of the box.

Metaponto was as close as Davenport had come to finding a "hidden" grave, and he returned home still thinking about the excavation. It was certainly a confirmation that geophysics techniques could produce the results they were looking for at Project PIG. They just needed to get the word out that they were capable, and that, he thought, would take a change in the way they were going about the "business" of finding bodies.

Before he left for Italy, Davenport had been pushing for the group to incorporate as a nonprofit organization. In part, that was so the group could accept donations and apply for research grants on a nontaxable status. But he also believed it would add a degree of professionalism that would sit better with law enforcement agencies. The law officers he had talked to both inside and outside the organization were leery of volunteer organizations that wanted to help solve crimes. Amateur detectives, psychics, and wanna-be cops would give the shirts off their backs, but unfortunately they tended to rip the shirts getting them off.

It wasn't as though Project PIG was immediately accepted by law enforcement agencies. It helped that some members were in police occupations and could vouch for the others. But many agencies retained the age-old police skepticism about "amateurs" sniffing around on their turf, some even suggesting that the scientists weren't much different from a high-tech, overeducated version of psychics—at least until they had seen the group work.

There had been some grumbling among some Project PIG members that incorporating would require a break from their original intention to avoid titles (to emphasize that they were all equals). Up to this point the official business of the group had been conducted by a steering committee. Forming even a nonprofit agency would mean corporate officers: a president, treasurer, secretary, and so on.

Others complained that they were moving too far away from research as they took on more field work. It wasn't that they had to avoid helping when asked, these members argued, but the emphasis should be on conducting studies and publishing reports to be used by others.

However, shortly after Davenport returned from Italy, the group swung around to his way of thinking—so long as the "officers' " duties were limited to the official business of the group, such as conducting the meetings. Everyone was still free to voice an opinion or ask questions at the meetings. Team leaders were appointed for the cases the group accepted—usually whoever took the call from the investigating agency, as well as someone whose expertise the others judged might be particularly helpful on a given case.

With the vote to incorporate, all they needed to come up with was a name. The research at the training facility would continue to be known as Project PIG, but the members thought they needed something that sounded a bit more serious.

There had been some good-natured kidding from law enforcement types about the word *pig* having a double meaning as slang for "police officer." To outsiders it was a derogatory holdover from the antiestablishment 1960s. But among themselves, police officers turned a negative into a positive, claiming that it stood for "pride, integrity, and guts." However, the group didn't want anyone getting the wrong impression.

Davenport was home with his son, Jad, mulling over potential names when they got on the subject of the excavation in Italy. "What about something with *Metaponto* in it?" Davenport suggested.

Jad wrinkled his nose. "Nobody would get it," he said. The boy thought for a moment, then asked, "What's Greek for *dead?*"

Davenport recalled the cemetery where he had worked with Carter. "Necro," he said.

"How about combining *necro* and *search?*" Jad said. "That's what you're doing, searching for the dead."

Davenport brought up the name NecroSearch at the next meeting. The group liked it. *International* was added when someone suggested that it only made sense: they were the first group of their kind and had even discussed helping set up other similar organizations in other states and overseas to share information, resources, and even members. Besides, *International* added a little flair.

In June 1991, NecroSearch International was incorporated, with Clark Davenport as its first president. But the decision to incorporate was not the only debate that had gone on within the group. Some of the other discussions were philosophical in nature, such as the argument over whether to concentrate more on research or fieldwork, a point of contention that would later cost them their first member.

Another was, did they work "for" the police and prosecutors? Certainly law enforcement personnel would most likely be the people who brought them on board, but what if what they found disputed the "official" version of the case? Both the law enforcement members of NecroSearch and its scientists agreed that what they were after was the truth, however it turned out. Otherwise, what they were doing wasn't serving science or justice.

Most of the discussions, however, fit more in the category of brainstorming sessions on the practical aspects of their field studies. One of the major concerns quickly became how to get more and better information from the investigating agencies before getting involved themselves.

A comment by FBI instructor Robert Boyd, in his work "Buried, Buried, Buried Body Cases," became a NecroSearch maxim: "The more that is known about the circumstances of the crime and burial, the greater your chances are of locating the site." It was important, they all agreed, that the investigating agencies get as far as possible on their own before NecroSearch stepped in. "My great fear," Davenport worried, "is that some of them will rely on us too much and not do the good, hard detective work first."

To that end, the group developed a questionnaire to send to agencies when they called asking for assistance. Some of the questions gave NecroSearch an idea of how solid the information was that the investigating agency was relying on. For instance: When and where was the victim killed? And was that information based on witness statements, a suspect's confession, or even psychics?

Certain questions were designed to give the group an idea of which of the sciences would be of the greatest use. For instance, answers to, "What was the time interval between death and burial? and, Where was the victim's body during the interval?" might tell the group that an entomologist could be useful in determining the time of death by noting the life-cycle stage of maggots found on the body.

Some questions were to lay such important groundwork as the size of the search area and whether it could be narrowed down still further by the investigating agency before NecroSearch arrived on the scene. How did the victim reach the site to be searched? Did they walk under their own power? Were they carried? Dragged? By vehicle? The answers could make an enormous difference in determining whether the search area involved square miles, acres, or a few square yards.

What about the weather at the time of burial? Was the ground frozen and therefore the digging more difficult? Was it a moonlit night, giving the killer more light to perfect his job?

Other questions were aimed at knowing the capabilities of the suspect. Did the suspect have the strength to carry a body for a distance? Did the suspect know the area well? Might the suspect have access to equipment such as a backhoe and the expertise to use it to help bury a body?

Was the body thought to be intact or dismembered? It might indicate more than one grave site.

What jewelry might have been buried with the body? For both geophysics and identification purposes.

Was the body clothed or nude? Clothing slowed the decomposition rate of a body. And if clothed, birds'nests should be checked for threads, or a metal detector might be used to locate a belt buckle.

Some questions dealt with legalities. Who owned the property to be searched, and had the proper steps been taken to obtain a warrant or permission? It would be disastrous to find a body only to have the evidence thrown out of court because of an illegal search.

The questionnaire asked what maps were available and suggested places for the investigating agency to look for pre- and post-burial aerial photographs. (Even police agencies were often unaware that there were many potential sources for the photographs, including local surveyors' and tax assessors' offices, as well as utility firms and highway departments.)

Agencies were asked to look into what expertise was already available in their area. NecroSearch wasn't trying to monopolize the game and gladly offered to consult with experts outside the organization. If the needed expertise wasn't available locally, and it was necessary for NecroSearch to send a team, they also wanted to know what equipment—from GPR to aircraft to cadaver dogs—was available. Such items could be expensive to rent or transport, and NecroSearch didn't have much of a budget.

Some of the information they asked of the investigating agencies was based on profiles of killers developed by behaviorists, such as those at the FBI Behavioral Sciences Unit. In this they were aided by the addition of private investigator Ed Killam, who had received his master's in anthropology as a student of Diane France and had compiled the latest profiling theories for his thesis.

Such information could be crucial to how they went about their task. For instance, their planning might be dramatically altered according to whether the suspect was thought to be an "organized" killer, who planned out the details of his crime, including where to bury the victim. A "disorganized" killer, on the other hand, murdered on the spur of the moment and simply dumped the body in some isolated spot, or only hurriedly and poorly buried his victim.

As the Surete's first director, Vidocq, established many years before, many criminals, including killers, follow recognizable patterns. Perhaps the killer was a hunter known to frequent a certain mountain, or he was known to give special meaning to or have an affinity for particular kinds of places, such as riverbanks. The more Necro-Search knew about the suspect, the better they might narrow down the areas to be examined.

By studying thousands of cases, the behaviorists had established general guidelines under which killers disposed of their victims. These parameters were both physical and psychological. For example, most killers won't carry a body uphill. Nor will most killers drive more than an hour with a body in the car—both because of the fear of discovery, and ancient, often subconscious taboos about dead bodies.

The guidelines were useful in the planning stages of a Necro-Search case. However, they would learn (sometimes the hard way) that the reason some killers are more difficult to catch is precisely because they "break the rules."

Over the years, the questionnaire would be refined and expanded as NecroSearch learned both from their successes and their mistakes. They would become choosier about which cases they took on, so as to devote their limited resources where they would do the most good. They might ask the investigating agency to go back and try another approach or gather more information before agreeing to help.

Sometimes after a little brainstorming with a NecroSearch member, the investigators would find they needed no further assistance. Other times they realized they had a lot more work to do before a NecroSearch team could be expected to accomplish anything.

Whenever possible, the group asked that the requesting agency send a representative to present new cases and answer any questions at one of the monthly meetings. If this was not possible, the member who had been contacted did his or her best to provide the information and act as a representative of the requesting party.

The group met monthly, originally at a restaurant and then, as they gradually gained acceptance, in space donated at various Denver-area police agencies on a rotating basis. At the meetings, they debriefed about recently completed cases with an eye toward what they might have done better, as well as discussed, debated, and brainstormed ongoing and proffered cases.

As they took on more cases, they also took into consideration the research of others. Diane France knew Drs. Bass and (now) Rodriguez through the American Academy of Forensic Anthropology and began a regular exchange of information. Among the results were discoveries having to do with determining time of death.

For instance, although bodies decomposed at different rates in wet Tennessee and dry Colorado, they still went through the same identifiable stages. Therefore, it was important for investigators to adjust their decomposition rate timetable according to climate to arrive at the proper conclusions. They also learned from each other, as in the example of NecroSearch taking a cue from the Tennessee "Body Farm" (the name given to the research site and later to a book on the work there) as well as the Bundy case, by burying pigs in different materials such as blankets, clothing, and a variety of containers.

Project PIG/NecroSearch operated on a shoestring, its members donating their time and expertise, often participating at considerable expense to themselves. They did not charge the agencies, except to ask that transportation and room-and-board expenses be covered. Yet in those first two years, as word about the group grew, so did the number of applications to join. However, they generally only added members when they had no current expert in a particular area, or when they needed additional support in a field.

Information gathering, credibility issues, memberships, fieldwork: those were the practical aspects that NecroSearch members needed to consider, and they got better at it as time passed. However, the one thing the non-law enforcement members of the group had no experience with was how to deal with the emotional aspects of murder and its impact on others they might have to work with, including families of the victims and even each other.

As Lindemann had realized from the reactions of the detective in the Ted Bundy case, what they were doing wasn't just science in a vacuum of objectivity. The victims had been real people whose tragedies weren't limited to themselves, but extended to those who cared for them or, like the Vail detective and NecroSearch members at the scene, invested a part of themselves in bringing a resolution to a case. Law enforcement members were more experienced, though not immune, to this; the scientists would find it more of a challenge on both a professional and a personal level.

Some agencies just expected too much, especially if money for plane tickets and hotel rooms was involved. In June 1991, the Alaska State Highway Patrol called Tom Griffin. They had a suspect who had confessed to murdering another man but then recanted.

Supposedly, the victim had been buried a year earlier in a shallow grave in a bog area laced with "finger dikes." The suspect had generally described the area before clamming up, but the investigators discovered that there were forty-eight such dikes in that locale and no clear signs of a grave.

The investigators asked if NecroSearch could come to Alaska to help, provided they could get their bosses' okay on expenses. Davenport, Griffin, and Lindemann were all set to go when one of the detectives called back. The higher-ups "want a guarantee" that the body would be found before agreeing to pay to bring in the NecroSearch team, he said, obviously embarrassed.

There was no way they could provide such a guarantee. And to do so would have been unscientific. It could have also set a bad precedent, *especially* if they were successful—every agency after that would expect the same assurances.

Instead, the NecroSearch team brainstormed and gave a number of suggestions to the Alaska detectives, including where to find their own local scientists and a contact for geophysical equipment. Not long afterward, Griffin received a telephone call from the Alaska detectives saying that the suggestions had paid off. The body had been located.

The NecroSearch members felt good about having helped bring a resolution to the Alaska case (though they would still be shaking their heads years later over the request for a "guaranteed" body). Still, it wasn't the same as being in on the actual discovery.

NecroSearch also made itself useful in other ways, particularly in the role of consulting on cases. If nothing else, law enforcement members of the group knew where to go for help if needed on a local case.

In the summer of 1991, Jack Swanburg was called to a remote field where the badly decomposed body of a young woman had been found in a ditch. She was eventually identifed as 18-year-old Heather Ikard, and she had been shot to death. Even more horrifying, she was the mother of a 12-week-old baby, who was missing.

Although not officially a NecroSearch case, Swanburg turned to his colleagues there, starting with Al Nelson and his bloodhound, Becky. A greasy spot had been discovered in the field near Ikard's body, and the investigators feared that the baby had been killed and left there until a scavenger carried it off. But Becky didn't hit on the spot, and so the investigators could work in the hope that the child was still alive.

Swanburg noticed that large sunflower plants had been pulled from the ground and thrown over the body in a hasty attempt to hide it. Using a cellular telephone at the site, he called Jane Bock, who asked him to bring a couple of the uprooted plants, as well as samples of sunflowers still growing at the site. He took the plants to the University of Colorado in Boulder the following day and gave them to Bock and her colleague, David Norris. Also at the site, Swanburg collected maggots from the body and delivered them to Kondratieff at Colorado State University in Fort Collins. The scientists at the two universities soon got back to him. Independently, they reached the same conclusion: the body had been left in the field two weeks earlier.

It wasn't a case in which they had located a grave, but Swanburg's combined use of NecroSearch experts in two distinct fields—the sort that could be found in other states if police officers knew where to look and whom to ask—would play a vital role in convicting Ikard's killer.

Investigators learned that a male friend of Ikard had killed her for her baby, which he then sold to a couple in Kansas. The child was recovered and returned to Ikard's family, and the suspect was charged with her murder. At first he proclaimed his innocence, but he was the last person seen with her two weeks earlier, the time fixed by Bock, Norris, and Kondratieff as the time of death. They were prepared to testify to that fact when the suspect decided they had him and pleaded guilty.

As in the Alaska case, the successful closure of the Ikard murder demonstrated the value of forensic scientists working together and with the police to solve murder cases. But the fact that NecroSearch hadn't found a body themselves was making Swanburg a little anxious.

They had worked on cases from as far away as Texas, Nebraska, Massachusetts, and Alaska. They had consulted with small county sheriffs' offices, big city police departments, and the FBI. Swanburg still believed in what they were doing and that someday there would be a payoff for all the work. He just hoped the others wouldn't lose interest in the meantime.

NecroSearch members were as dedicated to what they were doing as any paid, professional group he had ever worked with. They had learned a lot from Project PIG and its field cases, especially on how to work with each other and police agencies. The camaraderie of the group was extraordinary. In hindsight, Swanburg realized that the scientists wouldn't define success as finding a grave. These were people who for most of their lives had pursued knowledge for its own sake, and a success to them happened any time they learned something new. They often expressed the opinion that one of the best things about NecroSearch was the free education they were getting in fields they might otherwise never have the opportunity to learn about.

There had been an extra bonus in that many of the scientists were closet detectives—had been since their youths spent with Nancy Drew, the Hardy Boys, and Holmes. Then again, he realized scientists were doing detective work, relying as much on observation and deduction as the most intuitive homicide cop.

Swanburg knew that scientists often labored for long periods of time, years even, before (and whether or not) their work paid off. However, it would have been good for them to experience the thrill of solving a crime and bringing some closure to a grieving family. Besides, NecroSearch could use the publicity in the world of law enforcement.

He was wondering when the breakthrough would come when he received a call from a Gunnison County Sheriff's Office investigator named Kathy Young, asking if he knew of a group called "the pig people." When he told her she had found them, she began to tell him a story, one that began nearly twenty years earlier with a meeting of two men in a bar.

III

THE MICHELE WALLACE CASE

THE CRIME

August 29, 1974, Gunnison, Colorado

Chuck Matthews was tossing back a few drinks at the Columbine Bar just off the main street that ran east to west through town. He was a Vietnam veteran and worked hard as a ranch hand on a spread south of Gunnison. He also drank hard and was a well-known figure around Gunnison's bars. On this day, he had just gotten off work and was minding his own business when the fellow at the other end of the bar struck up a conversation.

The man said his name was Roy. It would be one of the few times Roy Melanson told Matthews the truth. There would be many lies and a lot that more that Melanson simply omitted while talking to his new drinking buddy.

One such omission was that Melanson, a 37-year-old drifter, had an arrest record for forgery, impersonating a federal officer, and burglary that dated back to when he was a juvenile in Louisiana and Texas. He had spent a year in juvenile hall.

As an adult, he had been convicted of a variety of lesser crimes from burglary to contributing to the delinquency of a minor, accompanied by short stints in jail. Then in 1964, he was convicted of rape, for which he served a little more than five years, getting out of the Huntsville, Texas penitentiary in 1970. Two years later, he was again accused of two more rapes but took off and was on the run when he arrived in Colorado in June 1974, the same month a 25-year-old photographer named Michele Wallace moved to Gunnison.

Melanson was 6 feet, 1 inch, and weighed 190 pounds. While no longer a kid, he had a certain blue-eyed charm that lingered into adulthood, and he considered himself a real ladies' man. He was also a world-class bullshitter, which was how he landed the job that brought him to the Gunnison area.

The day after arriving in Colorado, he was sitting in another bar, this time in Grand Junction, Colorado, 100 miles northwest of Gunnison, and got to talking to a 40-year-old man named Frank Spadafora. Spadafora told him he owned a sheep ranch in Somerset, a small town west of Crested Butte on the other side of Kebler Pass.

Looking at a map of the area with the town of Gunnison on the bottom, or southern end, the Black Canyon of the Gunnison lies directly to the west and Montrose another 40 miles beyond it. The town of Crested Butte is about 28 miles north of Gunnison. In Crested Butte, the main road forks. One branch runs west over Kebler Pass to Somerset and beyond; the other continues north a few miles to the ski area, Mt. Crested Butte, then turns to gravel as it reaches the town of Gothic and then climbs over Schofield Pass, elevation 10,700 feet.

Spadafora said he had a couple of Basque herders, but he needed someone to shoot coyotes that were preying on his flocks in their summer range near Schofield Park. Melanson convinced the sheep rancher that he was just the man for the killing.

It was a perfect setup for Melanson, who had nothing more than the clothes on his back. Not only did he get free use of a rustic but serviceable cabin in a remote and beautiful part of the country, but Spadafora loaned him a rifle and sleeping bag.

Melanson, however, didn't spend a lot of time working, especially after he discovered the Burton family. Lucille Burton and her five daughters were spending a few weeks of their summer in a Schofield Park cabin while her husband remained in Pueblo. The log cabin had been in the family for several generations and wasn't much more than four walls, a roof, and a floor. But it was soon home, sweet home to Melanson.

He was glib and worldly. He claimed to speak fluent French and soon had the girls and their mother enthralled. It was obvious he enjoyed the company of any young woman, even gallantly offering to take a friend of one of the girls, who had come for a visit, for a horseback ride. Nobody remarked on the fact that after they returned, the girl was quiet and subdued.

But of all the women, Melanson took a particular interest in 14-year-old Sally Burton. He began to spend so much time with her that on August 17, Spadafora fired him and took back the gun and sleeping bag he had loaned.

Melanson shrugged and moved in with his new friends. Such were his charms that a week later, when it was time for the Burton family to return to Pueblo, Melanson talked Sally's mom into leaving the teenager, 23 years his junior, with him.

It wasn't long before Sally saw at least part of what lurked beneath Melanson's charm. He kept her a virtual prisoner in the cabin. If she questioned his authority, he'd lunge at her as though to strike, then laugh as she cringed away. When he wanted sex, he demanded sex. If she protested that she wasn't in the mood, he got angry and insisted. She soon learned that if she didn't go along, he would force her anyway, and so, afraid of his temper, she acquiesced. Adding insult to injury, he gave her a case of body lice.

Sally, however, was lucky. She got to leave. On August 28, Melanson let her catch a bus home to Pueblo. However, he told her he would be joining her soon. The next day, Melanson decided to head for Pueblo, 160 miles to the east. He didn't own a car, so after hitchhiking to Gunnison from Schofield Park, he purchased a bus ticket.

With time to kill before the bus departed, he decided to throw back a few drinks at the Columbine Bar. Maybe find a new sucker for his lies . . . or something even better.

Over a half-dozen beers, Melanson told Matthews that he owned a cabin, horses, and land in Schofield Park. He was having trouble of late with a bear that was harassing his animals, he said. He didn't suppose Matthews knew of anybody who could help him out with the bear.

Well, sure, Matthews said. He had a rifle back at his place. He'd fetch it and a saddle; then they could go get a couple of Melanson's horses and together they'd get rid of that danged old bear. The two men staggered off to Matthews's beat-up car, took off for the ranch where Matthews worked, and picked up the rifle and saddle. They left for the Burton cabin, but by the time they arrived it was too dark to look around for the "bear."

The next morning, Melanson had another story. He'd rented his horses to a guy who obviously hadn't returned them. The other man owed him money, too. The guy lived in a cabin on Kebler Pass.

Would Matthews mind driving him there? They might just spot that pesky bear along the way.

As the crow flies, Schofield Pass is only about ten miles north of Kebler Pass. But 12,809-foot Mount Baldy stands between them, and the only way to get from one to the other was to go back to Crested Butte and then head west up the other fork in the road to Kebler. Melanson knew the drive. To get from the Schofield summer range to Spadafora's place in Somerset, he'd been over Kebler Pass several times.

Matthews agreed to the new plan. So after tossing Melanson's toolbox in the car (in case of engine trouble) and stopping to buy more beer, they were rattling down the road again.

On Kebler Pass, however, Melanson couldn't seem to locate the cabin, his horses, or the guy who owed him money. To make matters worse, Matthews's car kept breaking down. If it wasn't something with the engine, then it was a tire gone flat, and even the spare had a slow leak. Still, Melanson wanted to explore several dirt logging roads that ran south from the main road. He said that if he couldn't find the man who owed him money, he at least wanted to find that bear.

It was worrisome, considering they didn't see a soul on the logging roads, and couldn't expect much help if the car broke down permanently. But Matthews, fortified with beer, gamely tried to help his new friend.

Driving along one such road, about ten miles up the pass from Crested Butte, Melanson suddenly asked him to pull over; he thought he'd seen something. Maybe the bear.

Matthews did as asked, then got out of the car. "Hand me the rifle," Melanson said. Again Matthews complied and even turned his back on his pal and walked over to the edge of the road where Melanson had pointed. It was pretty country with steep north-facing slopes covered by coniferous trees and aspen tumbling down to a flatter area through which a creek ran along the edge of a meadow.

When Matthews turned back around, Melanson had a strange look on his face, as if he had just thought better of something. "Let's go," Melanson said and tossed the rifle back into the car.

The pair made it back to Crested Butte, where they stopped at a gas station to see if they could fix the leak in the tire. It couldn't be fixed, so they pumped it up, bought another six-pack of beer, and headed up the road to the Burton cabin.

About the same time, Michele Wallace was trudging down a gravel road beneath a backpack containing her sleeping bag, camping equipment, and her most prized possession, a camera. Okie, her black, German shepherd dog, paced alongside laden with his own saddlepack.

The 25-year-old woman was returning from a Labor Day weekend of hiking in a mountainous area of south-central Colorado known as Schofield Park. As she walked, she must have had mixed feelings: a little melancholy, perhaps, about her plans to soon leave the mountains she loved, but also excited about the future.

Earlier that summer, she had driven from South Carolina, where she had been photographing a rare bird species on the remote barrier islands, to her hometown of Chicago for her brother George Jr.'s wedding. There she regaled her family with tales of her latest adventure—camping in the marshlands for a week waiting for a nest of eggs to hatch, covering the lower portions of her legs with tin cans as an improvised defense against rattlesnakes.

"She's got more balls than I ever had,"her father, George Sr., remarked to his wife, Maggie, as they shook their heads and laughed over Michele's escapades.

Michele was the bright light of Maggie Wallace's life. She lived through her daughter, listening raptly to the stories, encouraging Michele along whatever roads she chose to take. Michele returned the devotion, talking to her mother at least once a week, and often several times.

The Wallaces had almost grown used to Michele's sometimes harrowing accounts of her life. "Mush," as she was known to her family, had always been independent and inclined to go against the grain.

At 5-feet-6 and 120 pounds, she was much stronger than she appeared, and seemingly fearless. She had once taken a job exercising polo ponies for a Chicago club, dashing full tilt across the fields. Later, she worked on a ranch, helping castrate young bulls at roundup time. Michele took up rock climbing and tried skydiving. She enrolled in martial arts classes. There was nothing a boy could do, her father boasted to friends, that she couldn't.

In her mid-20s, Michele was also a beautiful young woman, with rich chocolate eyes and delicate features. She often wore her long, dark hair in two thick braids.

At her brother's wedding, Michele told her parents that she would be moving on to Colorado to spend the rest of the summer taking photographs of the Rocky Mountains. Then in the fall, she would return to North Carolina for her first professional photography assignment, chronicling the lives of the people who lived deep in the mountains there. It was an isolated, backward world where moonshiners still plied their trade and the locals mistrusted strangers, she said, but she wasn't worried about her own safety. Highways and housing developments were pushing ever closer to their homes, and soon the hill people would be carried away by the tide of civilization. She wanted to make a record "before they're gone." Her idea was good enough to win her a government grant.

So Michele moved to Gunnison, Colorado, a small town with about 3,500 residents, in Gunnison County. It wasn't hard to see why: The town was surrounded by some of the most beautiful and rugged country in all of Colorado. It was set in a wide valley through which the Gunnison River flowed. The valley floor was covered with miles of scrubby, knee-high brush and stunted juniper trees interspersed with the cultivated fields of working ranches. Enormous cottonwood trees lined the banks of the river.

In the mountains, the landscape changed dramatically. Rangeland and cottonwoods gave way to steep, rocky slopes blanketed by forests thick with pine, fir, and groves of quaking aspen. The area was a mecca for fishermen and hunters, who every fall more than doubled Gunnison County's population as they traipsed about the hills dressed in fluorescent orange. It was also a magnet for young people drawn to the area's outdoor recreational activities, including nearby Crested Butte ski area, 28 miles north of Gunnison.

Michele fit right in with the outdoor enthusiasts. She was well liked if somewhat quiet. A few of her acquaintances later said they thought of her as lonely, or lost, as if constantly searching for something. But their perceptions may have been clouded by hindsight because in 1974, Michele Wallace had her whole life to look forward to. Her parents had bought her the red 1973 Mazda station wagon with the South Carolina license plates, and her father paid for the insurance. Otherwise she supported herself that summer by working as a flagger for a highway construction crew.

It was how she met her roommate, Theresa Erikson, another flagger. The two young women and Okie moved into a house that had been converted into apartments across the street from the Gunnison County courthouse.

Michele had acquired the dog, named for the Okefenokee Swamp in southern Georgia, fully grown a year earlier. He was something of an enigma; he could be fiercely protective of his mistress or docile as a lamb. If young men came to visit, Okie usually went berserk. The girls had to chain him in the backyard or lock him in the kitchen, where he would continue to snarl and try to get back to Michele for as long as the visitor remained. When Michele visited her family in Chicago for her brother's wedding, he bristled if her father gave her a hug. However, when Michele and Okie visited the home of Theresa's parents in Montrose, some forty miles west of Gunnison, the dog took to Theresa's father like an old friend.

Near the end of August, Michele called her mother. Theresa was going out of town to a wedding, and Michele had decided to take a backpacking trip. It would be her last chance before she left for North Carolina. Michele informed her mother that she was leaving on the twenty-seventh. She said she might not return until September 2, but not to worry; she was taking Okie with her and would be careful. "I'll call you as soon as I get back," she promised.

Some parents might have worried, but the Wallaces believed that their daughter knew how to take care of herself. Michele was well aware that the mountains could be dangerous, especially for someone alone and beyond help in case of an accident. She minimized the risks by letting people know where she was going, as well as when she expected to get back. She also had top-flight camping equipment and a large dog for protection.

Michele had a number of nearby areas to choose from for her trip. Fate, however, took her to Schofield Park, another ten miles beyond Crested Butte. Arriving in the area, she parked her car near the town of Gothic, actually a biological research station inhabited by only a few people, and walked a mile or so up the road to where a hiking trail began. She spent the next three days hiking and taking photographs: photographs of the mountains; photographs of Okie with his red dog pack; photographs of wildflowers and mountain wildlife.

On the fourth day, August 30, Michele decided she was ready to return to Gunnison and, in a few short weeks, get on with the rest of her life. She packed her gear, settled Okie's pack on him, and strapped into her own for the march back to her car.

It was late afternoon when she reached the trailhead and the road to Gothic. As she left the trail, a beat-up car came wheezing up to her and stopped. Two men were inside. The driver offered her a beer.

Hot and grubby from her days in the mountains, Michele smiled and reached for the offered bottle. Not much of a drinker, she took only a sip before handing it back.

"We're only going up the road a bit and will be back in a few minutes if you want a ride," the driver told her.

"That'd be great," she said and waved as they chugged off.

A few minutes later, the men were back. A tire was going flat, they said, but they would probably make it to Gothic if she still wanted a ride. Michelle and Okie jumped in the back.

They had hardly gone a hundred yards when there was a loud clang. The driver got out and looked under the car. He got back in proclaiming it just wasn't his day; a rock had punched a hole in his oil pan. They all laughed. "How about I give you a ride when we get to Gothic?" Michele offered.

When they reached her car, the driver of the other vehicle got in the backseat with Okie. He looked like a ranch hand, tanned and weathered beyond his years. "I'm Chuck," he said.

"And I'm Roy," the other man added as he climbed in. He was the taller of the two and not bad-looking, even if his dishwater blond hair was thinning as he approached middle age. He smiled and shut the door, and said, "Thanks for the lift."

On the way back to Gunnison, Chuck Matthews made friends with the dog, who licked his face and then drooled on his lap for most of the trip. Roy and the girl were talking up front, but he couldn't hear much of what was said.

It was early evening when they arrived back at the Columbine Bar. Matthews was surprised to hear Melanson ask the girl if she would mind driving him a few blocks farther to find his truck.

That's strange, Matthews thought; *I didn't know he had a truck.*

Why'd we bounce around for the past two days in my old rattletrap?
There was no accounting for some people.

Melanson stepped out to let him past. "I'll be back in a bit," he
said to the confused ranch hand; then he got back in the girl's car.

The pair drove off as Matthews headed into the bar. He hoped
Roy wouldn't be long; he wanted to get back to the ranch and figured his new friend wouldn't mind driving him in his truck.

When Melanson hadn't returned by 9:00 P.M., Matthews called
another friend to come get him. He went home and thought no more
about the girl and her dog. The next day, his friend took him to his
car near Gothic so he could pick up his rifle and saddle. He noticed
that Melanson's toolbox was still in the car, so he left it there in case
Melanson came back for it.

The same morning, Roy Melanson walked into the J. C. Penny's
department store in downtown Gunnison. He bought a cotton dress
shirt and polyester slacks, paying with a counter check on which he
wrote "For new clothes."

Melanson left the store and got into a red Mazda station wagon.
Even though the store was only a block in one direction from the
Gunnison Police Department and a block in another from the
Gunnison County Sheriff's Office, he was apparently unconcerned
about being stopped in the car.

He knew there was no one to report it stolen.

THE INVESTIGATION

Back in Chicago, George and Maggie Wallace thought they had it made. They had been married thirty-four years and were still in love. George's Italian restaurant was a success; the money was rolling in.

Best of all, the kids were doing okay. Their son was married to a nice girl and, finally, out of the house. And Michele, a happy, confident girl, was embarked on what promised to be a wonderful journey through life.

The Wallaces were ecstatic that their daughter, an unfocused student for most of her young adulthood, seemed to have finally found something that she would stay with. She had a real talent for photography, both nature and "art" pieces, like the self-portrait she had taken while still a student at a photography school.

The black-and-white photograph was grainy and highly contrasted. It appeared to have been taken in winter when the leaves had fallen from the thin, dark trees of a city park. In the photograph, the slender silhouette of a young woman, Michele, stood in a clearing turned toward a bright light coming up over a hill in the background. George Wallace thought it was a powerful photograph, almost disturbingly so, though he couldn't say why it made him feel that way.

In the fall of 1974, the Wallaces were looking forward to their golden years together without many concerns. Then Michele didn't call on September 2 as she had promised.

Maggie Wallace called the Gunnison County Sheriff's Office to report her daughter missing. Maybe she just forgot to call or decided to camp an extra day, the dispatcher said.

"Not my daughter," Maggie said. "She always calls when she says she will." She insisted that a search begin immediately. "She was going to be in the Schofield Park area."

The next morning, Gunnison County Undersheriff Steve Fry stopped by the young woman's apartment. She hadn't returned, nor was her roommate, Theresa Erikson, back from the wedding yet.

The first seed of worry sprouted in Fry's mind. Schofield Park was rugged country. She may have had an accident and was waiting for help. He called the Mt. Crested Butte Police Department and asked if someone could drive up to Gothic and look around for her car. They reported back later that day. There was no sign of Michele or her car.

The next day, with Maggie calling for frequent reports, a massive search mission was launched by the Gunnison Sheriff, Claude Porterfield, with the assistance of the Civil Air Patrol, Monarch Search and Rescue Team, Mt. Crested Butte Police Department, Crested Butte Marshal's Office, deputies from neighboring Pitkin County, and numerous civilian volunteers.

Officially, Michele was listed as a missing person, but after several days of air and ground searches, Porterfield and Fry worried that she was more than missing. There was still no trace of her—not even her car, which should have stuck out like a bright, red sore thumb.

Fry returned to Michele's apartment and met with Theresa Erikson, who had returned. He asked her to identify Michele's possessions. "Only the things that she alone used," he said. Erikson handed over a brush and eyeglasses.

Just 24 and working on what would become his first major case, Fry did everything by the book. He carefully packaged, sealed, and identified each piece of evidence and placed them in the basement evidence room of the sheriff's office, not knowing if his diligence would someday pay off.

On September 6, Chuck Matthews was listening to the radio as he sat with the other ranch hands at the kitchen table of his boss, waiting for breakfast. The morning news was led by a story about a missing girl. Matthews nearly choked on his coffee when he heard the description of the girl, her dog, her car, and her last known whereabouts: Schofield Park.

Matthews realized that they were describing the young woman who had given him and "Roy" a ride to Gunnison on August 30.

Why, he thought, *I rode in the backseat of the red Mazda station wagon with that same dog.* He called the sheriff's office and gave the deputy who answered a brief description of meeting a girl who sounded like their missing person. The last time he had seen her was outside the Columbine Bar as she drove off with a guy he had met the day before. "Said his name was Roy."

It didn't sound good to the sheriff's investigators. If the caller was correct, Michele had made it back to Gunnison but disappeared in the company of a man she did not know. In fact, nobody seemed to know who this Roy might be. Or where.

The news got worse the next day when Bob Niccoli, a rancher who lived ten miles south of Crested Butte, called the sheriff's office to report having killed a dog matching the description of the missing girl's German shepherd. The dog was chasing his cattle on September 4, when he shot and then buried the animal.

A deputy and Michele's cousin, Debbie Fountain, who lived in Denver and had come to Gunnison to help with the search, were dispatched to Niccoli's ranch. He took them to the field where he had buried the dog. But they didn't have to dig the animal up; he had kept the dog's collar, on which hung a tag with both the dog's and Michele's names on it.

It was further evidence that something had happened to Michele, that she hadn't simply picked up and moved on. The dog and the young woman were said by the mother and the roommate to be inseparable.

Other people called to say they had seen the dog wandering in the area since August 31. Still more reported seeing girl backpackers, some of whom had dogs with them, in the Schofield Park area. They were all checked but none panned out; there were a lot of female hikers in the mountains.

On September 11, the sheriff's office located Frank Spadafora. At some point, Melanson had told Matthews he had been killing coyotes for a sheep rancher who grazed his stock in Schofield Park. Matthews had passed that on to the deputy. Spadafora was the only one who fit the description, and they had tracked him down.

Yeah, Spadafora said, he had employed a Roy, a Roy Melanson, to be exact. He noted that his former employee didn't own a vehicle or much else for that matter. "I had to give him an old coat," he added, "and bought him a sleepin' bag to use." He had had to fire him, but heard he was living in a Schofield Park cabin "with a bunch of hippies."

Up to now, the searchers and police had hoped that Michele was all right. Injured, maybe, waiting for rescue, but alive somewhere in the mountains around Schofield Park. Now they didn't know what direction she had gone—or been taken. Nor would they for a long time. More than 400 volunteers and law enforcement personnel would search in the months after she first disappeared. In all, 164 hours were flown by air searchers. Another 5,000 man-hours were spent walking a 150- to 200-square-mile area on foot; and an additional 300 square miles were covered by vehicles.

It was the largest search ever in the area in terms of personnel and resources, but it was also a lot of ground to cover. Gunnison County, in south-central Colorado, is 3,266 square miles of mostly uninhabited wilderness. Still, they should have found something if there was something to find, but it was as if the earth had opened up and swallowed the mortal remains of Michele Wallace.

It didn't take the police long to find Roy Melanson, however. What they didn't know at first was that by the time they caught up to him, he had already driven the red station wagon more than a thousand miles.

Melanson arrived in Pueblo on August 31 in the evening and went to a bar where he called the Burton house. He learned that Lucille and her husband were out of town. One of Sally's older sisters, Becky, was left in charge and said she didn't want Melanson to come over. He shrugged and went anyway. After spending the night with Sally, he got another sister to drive him to where he had parked the Mazda. He explained that a friend from Boulder had left it for him to use.

Melanson seemed to be doing much better than when Sally had last seen him a couple of days earlier. He was wearing new clothes and had acquired all sorts of new possessions. He had new camping equipment, including a backpack, sleeping bag, and stove. And he had a nice camera, even allowing Sally to take his photograph as he lay smiling on a couch behind one of her friends.

On September 3, the day Michele's mother reported her missing, Melanson drove the "borrowed" Mazda to G&G Loans, where he pawned the camera and a lens. He signed the pawn ticket using his real name. However, when he checked into a motel with Sally later that afternoon, he signed in under the name Allan King, giving an address of General Delivery, Nile, South Carolina. He didn't provide a license plate number when registering, but the owner of the motel took it down later that evening anyway.

Soon Melanson was on the road again. Leaving Sally behind, he went first to Kansas. Then he was off to Cedar Falls, Iowa, where on September 8, he pawned the sleeping bag and Kelty backpack at Ken's Pawn Shop. From Iowa, he headed south to Elk City, Oklahoma, where he ran into 34-year-old Thurman Gene Wilder.

Melanson was again drinking in a bar when Wilder came in and the two men started talking. Wilder said he was looking for work as a heavy-equipment operator. He had transportation—a white Cadillac he was mighty proud of—but no job opportunities.

"It's your lucky day," Melanson said. It just so happened that he had a friend who owned a big construction firm in Pueblo, Colorado. He was sure he could get Wilder a job driving a bulldozer.

The next day, they headed west, Melanson in the Mazda with South Carolina plates; Wilder in his 1963 Cadillac. They got as far as Amarillo, Texas, where they stopped for a cold beer at The Hard Hat Lounge. Melanson announced that he needed to take the Mazda to a garage for repairs. First, though, he had Wilder assist him with transferring his stuff from the Mazda to the trunk of Wilder's Cadillac. Then, telling his new friend to wait for him in the bar, Melanson left.

A half hour later, Melanson returned, saying he had had to leave the car at the garage. It was going to take a few days for repairs. "We'll have to go to Colorado in your car," he said, "and pick mine up when we come back this way."

On September 12, the day after the Gunnison Sheriff's Department heard from Frank Spadafora, an anonymous caller reported a suspicious white Cadillac with two men in it prowling around a Pueblo high school. "It keeps coming and going," the caller said. "I think they may be selling drugs."

Officer Russ Laino responded and pulled over the Cadillac. Melanson was driving and said he and his friend, Thurman, were just waiting to give one of the students, Sally Burton, a ride home from school. He handed over a Texas driver's license; Wilder handed over his as well.

Laino went back to his car to run the licenses through the police computer to check for any outstanding warrants. "The computer's down," he was told. He read off the license numbers to be checked later and went back to where the two men sat in the Cadillac and handed back their licenses.

It was a half hour later when Laino got a sudden message from dispatch. The computer was back up: The guy from Texas was wanted for aggravated rape. Alarmed about having left the suspect, Roy Melanson, at a high school filled with young women, the officer stepped on it. But the white Cadillac was nowhere to be seen.

A "be on the lookout," or BOLO, was issued, and a couple of hours later, Laino spotted the white Cadillac in front of a motel room. He went to check with the motel manager, who said one of the men had checked in under the last name of Allen. Laino called for backup and Melanson and Wilder were arrested at gunpoint.

Wilder gave the police permission to search his car. There they found a number of things that seemed to belong to someone named Michele Wallace. That included a vehicle registration for a 1973 Mazda, her driver's license, her Amoco Motor Club membership card, and an insurance card in the name of George Wallace. In the car, the police also recovered camping equipment and a dog pack, as well as a Mazda tool kit.

At the jail, Melanson was stripped. In his pants were two pawn tickets: one for a sleeping bag and backpack; the second for a camera. They also recovered an unused bus ticket from Gunnison to Pueblo—and a set of Mazda car keys.

The Pueblo detectives were sharp. One of them recalled that a BOLO had been issued by the Gunnison Sheriff's Department for a red Mazda station wagon owned by a Michele Wallace. They didn't know what they had yet, but they knew that there was no good reason Melanson would have the young woman's personal effects.

They called Gunnison and learned about the search. Undersheriff Fry said they had a warrant out for Melanson's arrest on check fraud charges from another case. "Hold him until I can get down there," he said.

The evidence from Wilder's car and Melanson's pockets was

handed over to Officer J. E. Trujillo. Meanwhile, Wilder told detectives Jimmy Smalley and Bob Silva about meeting Melanson and how they had left a red Mazda station wagon in Amarillo.

Following a telephone call, the Amarillo police soon turned up the car. It had been abandoned one block from The Hard Hat Lounge. Amarillo PD crime lab technician G. W. Dickerson checked out the car for evidence of foul play but found none.

In separate interviews, Melanson and Wilder both mentioned that the former had spent time with the Burton family in Pueblo. Melanson even admitted to having a relationship with Sally, although he denied it was sexual, since that would have landed him in more hot water for having sex with a minor.

Other detectives interviewed Sally Burton, who admitted knowing Melanson, saying she had met him in late July near her family's cabin. She told them about Melanson's arrival in Pueblo and the little red car she and her sisters had traveled in. She even pointed out the room at the Bell Motel where she spent the night of September 3 with Melanson. And yes, she said, they did have sex.

More detectives talked to the motel owner, who remembered Melanson, though under the name Allan King. He still had the license plate number he took off the Mazda. It belonged to the car owned by Michele Wallace.

In the meantime, Melanson was being raked over the coals regarding Michele by Smalley and Silva. At first he said he didn't know her. Then he seemed to remember that she may have been one of a group of "hippies" who had shown up at his cabin in Schofield Park before moving on.

On September 13, Undersheriff Fry drove to Pueblo, where he met with the Pueblo detectives, who brought him up to date on everything they had learned. Fry asked to speak to Wilder and Melanson. He began with Wilder, who told him about meeting Melanson. "What kind of car was Roy Melanson driving?" Fry asked.

"A red Mazda station wagon," Wilder said.

"Did you ever hear Roy say anything about a girl by the name of Michele Wallace?"

"No," Wilder replied, shaking his head. "Never."

Fry finished with Wilder and asked that Melanson be brought in. A few minutes later, he was told that Melanson didn't want to talk to him but did want to talk to the FBI.

FBI Special Agent Lad Scroggins arrived and talked to Melanson for several hours. At first, the ex-con stuck to his story. But with the agent pressing, he suddenly "remembered." Yes, he had met Michele Wallace. He had gone into a bar with her to have a drink. "We left the dog tied outside," he said. Melanson said he made an excuse to borrow her car. Then he left. "And that was the last I seen of her," he said.

Neither Scroggins nor the other detectives were fooled by Melanson's confession. As an ex-con, he knew that taking a stolen car across state lines was a federal offense—the only crime in this case the FBI would have jurisdiction over. They figured he was hoping that the FBI would charge him for the car theft, with a maximum penalty of five years in prison, and in the intervening time period, the Michele Wallace case would be forgotten.

The next day, Fry arrested Melanson for fraud. He was suspected of having broken into a car in the Schofield Park area and then forging his name and cashing checks that belonged to the car's owner. Fry took possession of the evidence related to the Wallace case, including her camera from the Pueblo pawn shop, and put his prisoner in the back of his county car.

The drive back to Gunnison was uneventful. Melanson was sticking to his story: The last time he saw Michele Wallace, she was alive and drinking in a bar.

Melanson was booked into the Gunnison County Jail that night. The next afternoon, Sheriff Porterfield and Fry questioned him about Michele Wallace. Again, he denied having anything to do with her disappearance.

"What are you going to do when she shows up back in Chicago?" he retorted in response to their questions. "I'll be in the clear then."

Melanson asked what was going to happen with the fraud charge. When they replied that it would be up to the courts, he indicated that he was through with the interview but that he would think about it and "decide if I want to say anymore."

He decided against. But the investigators were hearing a lot more about Melanson. There were three rapes in Texas; one of the victims still had not recovered from it psychologically and had been hospitalized. Texas authorities also wanted to talk to him about a murdered woman whose body had been found in a field; they knew he had been in the area at the time, but they had little else to go on.

Louisiana police wanted to question him about a series of strangulation murders in that state.

Fry made arrangements to retrieve Michele's sleeping bag and backpack from Cedar Falls. On September 20, Chuck Matthews was asked to report to the Gunnison jail. They wanted to ask him more questions and see if he could identify Roy Melanson as the "Roy" he had met the day before Michele Wallace disappeared.

There was soon no question about that. Melanson was being led from his cell when Matthews came in. "That's him," Matthews yelled and with his fists clenched, advanced at the other man. He might be a drunk, but he had served his country honorably and wouldn't abide a man who attacked women. "You son of a bitch," he shouted, "you did somethin' to that poor girl!"

"I didn't do nothin'," Melanson snarled back.

The two men moved toward each other. Matthews was smaller, but he was more than willing to mix it up with Melanson. Deputies quickly stepped between them.

Matthews settled down quickly in an interview room and gave a more detailed account of his time with Melanson and Michele Wallace. There was something curious, he added as the interview drew to a close. The morning after Melanson left him at the bar and drove off with the girl, a friend gave him a lift back to his car to retrieve his rifle and saddle. Melanson's toolbox was still in the car, he said, and that's where he left it. But when he returned to the car the following day, the toolbox was gone. "That means he stuck around long enough that morning to come back for his tools."

Matthews said they had been in the Kebler Pass area, about eight miles up. They had taken several side excursions on tracks south of the main road. He recalled one in particular because they drove through two streams to get to the place where Melanson had him stop and hand him the rifle.

With Matthews's positive identification, the Gunnison County Sheriff investigators were certain they had the right man and that Michele Wallace had been murdered. It was unlikely he had taken her very far, which meant her body was somewhere in the mountains. But they couldn't find her, and without a body the prosecutor wasn't going to go after murder charges.

The circumstance became even more aggravating when, a week

after picking up Melanson in Pueblo, Fry had the film in Michele's camera developed. Most of the photographs were from her camping trip. But the last frame on the roll was a photograph of Melanson lying on the couch at the Burton home, a young girl sitting in front of him, a smirk on his face as though daring the investigators to catch him.

As hundreds of searchers combed thousands of square miles in Colorado from the ground and the air, the Wallaces told each other to keep their hopes up. She might have been injured on the trail or slid off a treacherous mountain road in her car. But day followed day with no word, no trace of their daughter.

They struggled to avoid accepting the unacceptable. Not death. Not Michele. She was too tough, too smart, too able to die. But with each day that passed, hope began to slip beneath the surface of their bravado like a drowning man.

The waiting was hard on all of them, but particularly Maggie. She was always on the telephone: calling the sheriff; calling the FBI; calling the governor of Colorado. A brother who was a colonel in the Air Force had jets fly over the area. She called anyone she thought might help, but no one could.

What news there was, was always bad and nothing came along to make it better. A convicted rapist claimed to have left Michele and her dog alive and well in Gunnison when he took off with her car. They knew the story was a lie; Michele rarely drank, and she certainly wouldn't have loaned her car, with her camera in it, to a stranger. But there was no evidence he had killed her—no evidence that she was even dead.

Still, Maggie knew, and she deteriorated day by day. Hollow-eyed and dazed, she cried and wandered around the house like a lost child. She pored over photographs of Michele, caressing the likeness of a face she would never again touch in the flesh. Six weeks after Michele disappeared the Colorado authorities called and asked for Michele's dental records. It meant they had given up hope of finding her alive. Maggie reached the end of the rope she was grasping.

The Wallaces were in bed. Maggie was reading and George was going over the books from his restaurant. "How'd you like some tea?" Maggie asked, getting up.

It was a strange question for the time of night, but George, aware of his wife's fragile state, humored her. "What the hell," he smiled, "if you're up and around, sure."

When she returned with the tea, he took a sip and wrinkled his nose. It tasted terrible. "Where in the hell did you get this tea?" he teased. "You been keeping it in a pot for a week or something?"

Maggie didn't say anything but took the cup from him and left the room. He shrugged and turned out the lights. He was almost asleep when she returned a few minutes later and lay down beside him.

George woke the next morning knowing that something was wrong. You don't sleep next to a person for thirty-four years without becoming attuned to their breathing and heartbeat, the warmth of their body beneath the sheets. But on this morning, though he could feel the weight of Maggie beside him, there was no hint of her gentle breathing or the quiet thumping of her heart through the mattress.

With tears already welling in his eyes, he sat up and looked at his wife. She appeared peaceful, more at rest than anytime since Michele had disappeared—still beautiful. But she was cold when he reached over to touch her, and he knew that she had gone on to join Michele.

Maggie Wallace had taken an overdose of barbiturates with her tea. Waiting had been too great a burden for her to bear, but in dying she placed a heavier burden still on the husband she loved. "If you ever find our daughter, please bury her next to me," she wrote in the note she left for him to find.

George promised he would try. As he stood next to Maggie's grave a few days later, he swore that someday he would face the man he now believed had killed his daughter and his wife. He would look him in the eye and send him back to hell.

But not all of his anger was directed at Melanson. He was disappointed with the Gunnison County Sheriff's Office as well. If they had found Michele's body, he believed his wife would have still been alive. She would have been grief-stricken, yes, but he was convinced that it was the terrible not-knowing that had pushed her into taking her own life. He called the sheriff and said as much.

That bastard, Roy Melanson, was telling the cops to go screw themselves and to get out of his face. If they would let him, George said, he would gladly fly to Gunnison and shoot "the mad dog" in his cell.

Back in Colorado, there was nothing much anyone could say to placate George Wallace. But he was from Chicago and had no concept of the sheer immensity of the land into which Michele had disappeared. Thousands of man-hours had been spent in the search.

They had a suspect, but he wasn't talking. They had a lot of circumstantial evidence, but the district attorney wasn't willing to prosecute.

"There's no way we can file charges without finding her body, or evidence that she met with foul play," said Lynn French, the deputy district attorney prosecuting the fraud charges.

Maybe that fall, during elk or deer season, someone would stumble across her body, the district attorney suggested. When winter came to the high country, dumping hundreds of inches of snow, the search for Michele Wallace froze as well.

Melanson's trial for the fraud charges was set for March 1975. He was alleged to have broken into the car of Alice Moss and then cashed checks he found inside. But everyone knew that fraud charges weren't what was keeping Melanson in the Gunnison County Jail while Texas authorities waited to prosecute him for rape. It was Michele Wallace.

The day of Melanson's trial arrived, but the prosecution's main witness didn't. Although Moss was prepared to testify, the day before she was scheduled to appear at the trial, she received a telephone call at her home in Boulder, a six-hour drive from Gunnison. The woman on the other end of the line said she was the Gunnison County court clerk and that Moss didn't need to show up. A deal had been worked out.

Without the victim, Melanson's female public defender was able to convince the jury to acquit him. Now there was no legal reason for Gunnison authorities to keep him. They shipped Roy Melanson off to Texas to stand trial for rape. He was accused of kidnapping a young woman and forcing her to drive back and forth from Texas to Louisiana, raping her repeatedly over a period of several days. To control her, he had wrapped a pair of nylons around her neck. If she struggled or cried, he would tighten the nylon garrote and caution her to stop, or else. The woman got away from Melanson but had been institutionalized with severe psychological problems ever since.

The jury there found Melanson guilty. Under a "three strikes" habitual offender provision in the Texas legal system, he was automatically sentenced to life in prison. Back in Colorado, those who believed that Melanson had killed Michele were relieved that at least they would know where to find him if her body ever turned up. They were mistaken.

For many residents, Gunnison would never again be as innocent as it had once seemed. The community was reminded again of that five years after Michele Wallace disappeared.

On July 26, 1979, a hiker named Thomas Kolz was walking along a logging track off the main road over Kebler Pass. It was a little-used path, just wide enough for one-way traffic and intersected twice by a shallow stream. The day was hot, and Kolz had stopped to rest when he spotted something dark lying in the middle of where the road forked. It was a mass of hair, parted down the middle into two long, dark braids.

Kolz returned to Gunnison and gave the hair to the sheriff's office, and suddenly, Michele Wallace was back in the news. The hair was sent to the Colorado Bureau of Investigation. There criminalist Nelson Jennett confirmed that the hair was definitely human. But without a specimen known to have come from Michele, he couldn't positively identify it as hers.

Another search was launched, this time concentrated near where Kolz had found the hair. It narrowed the search area considerably, but that hardly made it easy. The tree-covered hillsides were so steep that searchers mostly had to walk along the roads and peer over the edge.

In the end, the searchers again went home empty-handed. No one could say how the hair got to the middle of the logging road. It could have been thrown from a car window, or a scavenger might have carried it there from miles away. The searchers wondered how long the hair had been on the road, and why no one had seen it before.

The hair was returned to Gunnison County, where it was bagged, labeled, and placed in a box to be taken to the evidence room. There it remained for ten years, forgotten until a 33-year-old rookie detective named Kathy Young and a longtime deputy, Scott Jackson, reopened the box—and the case.

Kathy Young had moved to Gunnison a year after Michele Wallace disappeared. She was 19 years old and wanted to spend a summer camping and hiking before returning to California to attend college. The name Michele Wallace had come up wherever people gathered—at softball games and picnics, in bars, and around campfires. Adventurous young women like Kathy were warned about going into the wilderness alone. It didn't necessarily stop them, but it sure was on their minds when they met strangers on the trail.

Prior to coming to Gunnison, Young never imagined working in law enforcement. Her first experience was as the city's animal control officer in 1977. She soon learned that the term meant more than dogcatcher in a rural setting, such as when some pranksters at Western State College left a bawling calf on the third floor of one of the dormitories. She and an officer had to carry the hefty creature down three flights of stairs and then spent several hours trying to locate the unbranded calf's owner.

Another aspect of the job wasn't quite so appealing. Dogs allowed to run loose by their owners sometimes chased cattle. In this part of the country, ranchers were legally within their rights to shoot dogs that endangered their livelihood. Young was taken aback. As a California girl, she wasn't familiar with laws meant to protect livestock in ranch country.

The more Young was around police officers, the more interested she became in becoming one. In 1978, she was accepted as the first female officer on the Gunnison Police Department. It wasn't easy. A typical response from a drunk on the street was, "Screw you, you're not a real cop." She always felt as if she had to go the extra mile.

Young put her law enforcement career on hold after she married and had two sons. In 1985, she joined the sheriff's department, again as the first female deputy on the force. Three years later, she became the county's first female investigator.

A short time later, Detective Young got a call from Roland Turner, the chief of the Mt. Crested Butte Police Department. He had been digging through some old files and thought there was a case she might be interested in: "a girl that disappeared up here in nineteen seventy-four, named Michele Wallace."

Turner said he had been cleared to talk to her by her boss, Sheriff Ric Murdie. "This case has been bothering me for a long time," Turner said. "I'd appreciate it if you'd take a look."

Young asked Murdie for permission to work on the old case. He said to go ahead as long as it didn't interfere with her current workload. He knew that the disappearance of Michele Wallace had been hanging over his community for too long.

Murdie had been born in Gunnison, but his family had moved to Denver when he was a boy. He had joined the Marines out of high school and then returned to Denver and joined the police force. After thirteen years with the Denver Police Department, however, he tired of the big city violence and crime and returned to Gunnison. In 1986, he ran for sheriff and won.

One of the first things he had done was to create the position of investigator, the county version of a police detective, giving it to the man who was Young's predecessor. He had followed that by reviewing the department's unsolved cases. He had seen the Michele Wallace reports. No one in law enforcement liked knowing that a case of that sort was unresolved. A guy getting away with murder was something he took personally.

Experience told him the case was solvable. The district attorney at the time had declined to prosecute without a body, but there was a new man in office, Mike Stern, and maybe he'd be willing to take a chance. Murdie had heard of bodyless homicides being prosecuted successfully—not often, but it had been done. He harbored no illusions about the possibility of finding Michele Wallace's remains after more than fifteen years.

The problem was freeing the time to allow his only investigator to pursue such an old case. Gunnison had grown a lot in the intervening years, and there was plenty for his deputies and investigator to do. When Young requested permission to pursue the case, however, he felt he had to agree.

Young began talking to deputy Scott Jackson. He wasn't around when Michele disappeared, but he had been in on the search after the hair was found on Kebler Pass. "It's still in the evidence room," he said. "You have to see it, Kathy."

When they pulled it out of the box, still sealed in a plastic bag, Young was startled. Jackson hadn't told her that the hair was still in braids. She had pinned a photograph of Michele up on her office wall; she was wearing braids. Now here was a tangible link between the girl in the photograph and the case that she was so completely immersing herself in.

Young, and Jackson when he could spare time from his patrol duties, began to pore over the 15-year-old files. The more she saw, the less she understood why Roy Melanson had not been prosecuted.

There was the interview with Chuck Matthews. The description of the logging road he had taken with Melanson sounded as though it was near the same place where the hair was later found. She wondered if Melanson had planned to shoot Matthews when he got out of the car that day but had decided against it because of the condition of the car. It wouldn't do to break down in another man's car, near where the owner's body lay, she thought. Michele's car, on the other hand, was dependable. . . .

Young was curious about the dog, Okie. He had been shot and buried on the road north of Gunnison, nearly 20 miles from where the hair was discovered west of Crested Butte. Had Michele persuaded her killer to let the dog go? Or had the killer found a way to separate her from her protector and then taken her somewhere else to kill her? Maybe the dog wasn't as protective as he was made out to be. According to Matthews, Okie sat next to him all the way back to Gunnison with no problem, even licked the ranch hand's face.

Other old reports caught her eye. On April 30, 1975, just a few days after Melanson was shipped off to Texas, another Gunnison County inmate, John Paul Steele, told Undersheriff Fry that Melanson admitted killing Michele. "He said he was glad that he wouldn't be around in the spring when y'all would start digging around for her," he said.

Steele had asked if they had found her dog.

"Yes," Fry said without volunteering any other information.

"Was it up north near Crested Butte?"

Fry said it was, but the dog was dead. Steele scowled and said, "He said he didn't kill the dog."

The undersheriff then told Steele that Melanson didn't kill the dog. The inmate's information was accurate and surprisingly detailed, such as when he noted that Melanson had told him that Michele had extensive dental work. "He must have been real close to notice that," he added. Melanson had told him that he dug a grave and poured lime over the body to speed decomposition before burying her. Even more gruesome, he claimed to have used an axe to knock out her teeth, to hinder identification if her body was discovered.

Young found a report that another inmate, Jack Hassig, had told Fry a similar story, including the part about Melanson talking about his alleged victim's dental work. She knew that Michele had indeed had extensive work done, including a gold molar.

"This is solvable," she muttered. She just didn't realize what it would take.

In early 1990, Kathy Young called the Texas Department of Corrections to inquire about Melanson. She was horrified to learn that he had been released from the Huntsville penitentiary in 1988. His "life" sentence had lasted 13 years. Melanson's habitual offender conviction had been overturned. Nobody wanted to release Melanson. He was suspected of beating a young black man to death on his cell block, but prison authorities hadn't been able to prove it. His life sentence was vacated and he was resentenced to time served.

Young could only wonder how many women had suffered as a result. It wasn't long before she found out. The Gunnison investigator contacted the legendary Texas Rangers in an attempt to locate Melanson's sexual assault victims. She wanted to know if there was anything in his attacks on them that might help make a murder case against him in Gunnison.

Young was put in contact with Ranger Haskel Taylor, who had spent a good number of years following the trail of Melanson. He was the one who had pursued him on the rape charges and extradited him from Colorado. However, there wasn't much he could tell her about Melanson's early years. The suspect had graduated from high school, where his grades were satisfactory if not spectacular. Apparently, his parents were dead.

Taylor provided her with Melanson's criminal record. He had never been able to find the earlier rape victims to interview them. The last one was still institutionalized, he said, and wouldn't be of much use to her investigation.

Melanson was a suspect in a number of killings, Taylor added. Besides the beating death of the young inmate, there was a woman who had been found in a field after having been seen with Melanson. The police at the time hadn't had enough evidence for charges to be filed.

"More recently, he's the prime suspect in the disappearance of a Port Arthur woman," Taylor said.

After he got out of prison in 1988, the ranger explained, Melanson had gone to the Gulf Coast town to stay with a relative who lived in a small apartment complex. In July, Melanson was seen offering to help the landlady transport a television set to a repair shop. The next day, the woman's car was found parked in front of a grocery store, the television still in the front seat. However, the woman was never seen again, and it was believed she had been killed and dumped in the vast swamps around Port Arthur.

The police had questioned Melanson, who, as he had in the Wallace case, claimed to have left the woman safe and sound. He had disappeared shortly thereafter but couldn't stay out of trouble with the police.

In 1989, a warrant was issued for his arrest for burglary in Kentucky. He fled but authorities caught up to him, living on a ranch in Montana owned by a woman. She couldn't believe what the police told her; he had convinced her that he was the wealthy owner of a ranch in Texas. Taken back to Kentucky, Melanson, now 53 years old, was convicted for burglary and sentenced as a habitual felony offender.

It was supposed to mean he would serve as much as twenty years in the Kentucky state penitentiary. However, Young was told by prison authorities there that Melanson would be up for parole in another five years or so with good behavior.

For the time being, Young knew where to find Melanson, but she didn't yet have enough for Murdie to take to District Attorney Stern. She was going to have to locate as many of the former witnesses as she could and try to reconstruct the case.

Over the next two years, Young worked on it whenever she could find time outside her regular workload. She was often assisted by Jackson. On March 22, 1990, Young found Jack Hassig, who was living in Montrose, Colorado. He repeated the story Melanson had told him about burying Michele near a stream and pouring a sack of lime into the grave. "He said he cut out her jaws, top and bottom, with an axe or a hatchet so she couldn't be identified."

Others weren't so easy to locate. She spent months trying to find Chuck Matthews until someone recalled that he had a sister in the area. The sister told the detective that Chuck had moved to Truth or Consequences, New Mexico, so she drove there and interviewed the old ranch hand.

He was hazy about some of the chronology and names of places he had gone with Melanson. But he was clear about most things, including the part about his drinking partner driving off with the girl to "find his truck."

As a police officer, Young knew that she couldn't rule out Matthews as a suspect even if everything else pointed to Melanson. But it didn't take long before she thought to herself, *He wasn't involved. . . . He just isn't the kind of guy who attacks women.*

After all these years, Matthews was still angry at Melanson, recalling the confrontation at the sheriff's department—and maybe feeling a little ashamed that he had just stood there, anxious to get into the bar, when "that son of a bitch" drove off with the girl. He said he would be happy to return to Gunnison to testify. "Just tell me when."

Young located Lucille Burton in Denver. She was in frail health but readily recalled the summer she and her daughters met Roy Melanson. There was one other thing she had never told anyone else. The young girl who had accepted Melanson's offer to go horseback riding later told her daughters that he had raped her. She was afraid of him and had said nothing at the time.

Lucille Burton said her daughter, Sally, was living in California, so Young made arrangements to go and interview her. On the way, she stopped in Las Vegas to see Frank Spadafora, who had given up sheep ranching to run a small casino off the strip.

Spadafora stood Young up, so she moved on to Sally Burton. She found a mixed-up young woman who had been through a series of disastrous relationships. She remembered Roy Melanson real well.

Yes, she said, her relationship with Melanson had been sexual—whether she wanted it that way or not. His moods could swing from one extreme to the next in an instant. He never hit her, but he always let her know who was in control and that she had better not cross him. "One time I wanted to leave the cabin, but he said I couldn't," Sally recalled. "He didn't say what he would do if I tried, but I saw his eyes and knew I wasn't goin' nowhere."

Burton recalled the red Mazda station wagon with all the camping equipment in the back and said she would be willing to come back and testify to that if charges were ever filed.

On the way back to Colorado, Young called ahead to set up another appointment with Spadafora, who claimed to have mixed up the previous appointment time. She arrived in Las Vegas only to be stood up again.

When she returned to Gunnison, Young called the Las Vegas Police Department and reached a detective, Parker McManus. She started to explain what she was trying to do when he interrupted her.

"You know Punch McManus?" he asked.

Sure, Young said. Punch was a popular school teacher in Gunnison who had retired just a few years earlier.

"She's my mom," McManus said. "I grew up in Gunnison, and I remember when Michele Wallace disappeared." He said he would personally go "take care of the problem" with Frank Spadafora. The former sheepherder called the next day. He agreed to meet with Sheriff Murdie, who was going to Las Vegas on other business. This time he kept the appointment.

John Paul Steele, the former inmate who had told Fry a similar story to what Hassig had related, also took months to find. Young had finally found a parole officer in the state of Washington who gave her an old telephone number he had for Steele. The number was for a garage where Steele had worked as a mechanic. A woman answered and said Steele still worked there; in fact, she was his wife.

"He's not in any trouble," Young explained. "I just want to talk to him about an old case and a guy named Roy Melanson. Ask him to call collect."

Steele called back that evening. He remembered Melanson and related what he had told Fry many years before.

Young was impressed that the stories both Hassig and Steele told her remained consistent with their nearly 16-year-old statements. Their recollections of what Melanson had told them were almost exact.

As difficult as it was to locate some of the witnesses, there were two with whom she had no luck at all. They were dead. Kolz, the hiker who had found the hair, had died in a crash. Kolz's widow was still in the Montrose area, so Young talked to her about where they had been hiking that day.

Young heard that Thurman Gene Wilder also had died in a crash. The detective took no chances and persuaded a Louisiana State Trooper to go to the cemetery where Wilder was buried to check for his headstone. It was there, as was Wilder's body.

Young felt such measures were important. Without a body, how were they supposed to prove that Michele Wallace was even dead, rather than living anonymously in some other part of the country? The prosecutors would be trying to prove a negative by demonstrating there was no evidence that Michele was alive. No messages to her family or friends. No credit card activity. No bank loans. No applications for a passport or driver's license. No contact with law enforcement for nearly two decades. It was more than suspicious, but was it proof?

Even if the jury concluded that she was dead, how could the prosectution prove beyond that same standard of reasonable doubt that she had been murdered? That she hadn't died in an accident up in the rugged mountains that made up this part of Colorado, her remains lying at the bottom of some cliff she had failed to climb?

The prosecution would get one shot at Melanson. If they missed, they could never try him again for killing Michele. After so long a time, and without Michele's body, it was going to be doubly important to show a jury that they had left no stone unturned. A detective was even sent to Spain to reinterview the Basque sheepherder who had been a potential suspect.

Young would have had a difficult time explaining why she was so driven. Part of it might have been the closeness in age between herself and Michele, and that they had both come to this same beautiful, rugged country as independent young women looking for adventure. One had found a home, a family, and a career; the other had found death.

Part of it, too, may have been that Michele's was such a sad story. Jackson had told her about the suicide of Maggie Wallace and the note asking that her daughter's body be buried next to her. Young assumed that George Wallace was deceased. There had been no contact with him for more than ten years.

In late 1990, she was talking to a member of the Civil Air Patrol who had been in on the original search, when she learned that Michele had a relative living in Arizona. She called the relative and was surprised to learn that George Wallace was still alive. As a matter of fact, Debbie Fountain and her husband had just left to return home to Florida, where George and his second wife were also living.

Young called Debbie Fountain only to hear from the other woman that she wasn't sure that reopening the case was such a good idea where George was concerned. He had remarried, with a wonderful woman named Melba, but had never really gotten over the deaths of his daughter and first wife. George was near 70 and frail, and Fountain insisted that Young funnel any questions or updates on the case through her, "so I can choose times when he's strong enough."

"Just tell him we're working on the case again," Young said.

After conferring with his investigator and Deputy Jackson, Sheriff Murdie had broached the subject of charging Melanson with Michele Wallace's murder to District Attorney Stern. The prosecutor hadn't said no; in fact, he told Young that if she could find the witnesses after all these years, he might try a bodyless homicide. But, he also cautioned, they were a long way from making a case stick.

A major turning point occurred in early 1991 when Young and Jackson decided to reinventory everything in evidence for the Michele Wallace case. The evidence lists were long, but not very detailed. For instance, they noted the presence of a South Carolina driver's license, but the list didn't specifically state it was Michele's. The investigators were wasting a lot of time when questions arose by having to go and search out individual items; they wanted a master list with complete details.

In the evidence room, they opened one old box and began matching items to the list. Young pulled out a bag with a hairbrush in it. There was a case number on it—Michele's case—written by then-Undersheriff Steve Fry, with a date and the address of Michele's apartment. There was no mention of who it belonged to or where it had come from.

Fry had retired from the department but was still in town, running a sporting goods store. Young called him and asked about the brush. He remembered it well. "I asked for things that only she had used," he said.

Now Kathy Young was really excited. Apparently, when the mass of hair was found in 1979 and sent to the CBI, no one had recalled the hairbrush. Young had noticed that it still contained several long, dark strands of hair.

It would be just one more stone in a field of boulders she had overturned, but she now had a way to prove that the two long braids found on Kebler Pass belonged to Michele Wallace.

Sidetracked by more current cases, Young finally sent the hairbrush and the mass of hair back to the CBI on August 1, 1991. This time to their lab in Montrose. Twenty-seven days later, CBI Agent Joe Snyder called. The hair from the brush and the hair found on the pass were a perfect match.

Not long afterward, Young ran into Nelson Jennett, the former CBI agent, in the Montrose County courthouse. "Mr. Jennett," she said, walking up to the tall, dark-haired criminalist, "I don't know if you remember me, but I used to take classes from you." She knew that Jennett was the agent in 1979 who had confirmed that a "mass of hair in the form of two braids approximately twelve inches long" was human.

Jennett smiled down at the short redheaded woman. "Of course, I remember. What are you up to these days?"

Young explained what she had been doing for the past two years. "I wanted to let you know that we're working the case again," she said. Jennett might be asked to testify, and she was letting him know as a professional courtesy. "And I hope to file charges someday . . . soon."

Jennett nodded. "I always wondered what had happened to that case," he said. "How's it going?"

Young briefed him on what she had. And what she didn't: a body.

Jennett paused and thought a moment, then asked, "You ever hear of the 'pig people'?"

When she shook her head, he went on to explain that a criminalist colleague of his who worked for the Arapahoe County Sheriff's Department, Jack Swanburg, had told him about a new group he was working with. "It's a bunch of scientists and cops who've been burying pigs to see if they can figure out how to find clandestine graves. . . . Maybe you ought to give him a call."

Young didn't hold out much hope that this group with the morbid-sounding name would be of much use. She believed that if she was ever to get Roy Melanson in court, it would be because she had finally filled in enough blanks to convince Stern to go forward with the case. She was even prepared to lose. Anything would be better than letting Melanson just walk away.

Still, she was willing to hear what this group might have to offer, so she called Jack Swanburg at his Arapahoe County office. He seemed intrigued and asked her a few questions.

* * *

In October, Kathy Young made the four-hour drive east to Denver and presented her case to NecroSearch International. To be honest, she had contacted NecroSearch to be able to say to a jury or, through his relatives, to George Wallace that she had exhausted every possibility to find Michele's body.

Swanburg had told her, "We're a real casual group. Just a verbal presentation, and they'll ask a lot of questions." So she had brought her main file and photographs of Michele and Melanson.

The first thing that impressed her about the group was their degree of interest—and not just in those details directly related to the search for Michele. They asked about Michele's family, and she told them the story of Maggie Wallace's suicide, which seemed to further motivate the group.

They began discussing the next steps to take. A scout should be sent ahead to look at the terrain, someone suggested. Cecilia Travis asked if there were any aerial photographs available, something Young had not thought of but said she would look into.

It was apparent to Swanburg in that first telephone call that he was talking to a detective who did her homework; she had an answer to everything he asked. Still, a 16-year-old case in which not a few but hundreds of others had searched with no success wasn't too promising. He wasn't sure why he found himself telling Young that he thought NecroSearch might be able to help.

At the meeting, NecroSearch members were just as impressed with Young's detective work in tracking down old witnesses and linking together the pieces of evidence. They were particularly taken with a timeline chart that Young had prepared depicting every single incident in the case from just prior to Michele's disappearance practically up to the present moment.

So many times, the presentations they were given were full of generalities. Or the presenter would finish and then say, "Oh yeah, I forgot to tell you . . ." Young's presentation was packed with details that she laid out in a chronological, easy-to-understand fashion. The group had no problem agreeing with Swanburg: they wanted to help.

A few weeks later, Cecilia Travis was sent to Gunnison to reconnoiter the area and make recommendations on what sort of team might be the most appropriate. She met with Kathy Young, and the two women went to the U.S. Forest Service headquarters for the area to look at aerial photographs. They found some taken in 1979 and then more taken ten years later. The photographs showed that in the 1970s the logging road where the hair had been found was clear enough to drive a Mazda station wagon up, but had since become somewhat overgrown.

Young next led Travis, who had brought her dog, to the logging road, leaving the scientist there to explore. It was hunting season, so she had found bright orange vests for the scientist and her hound.

Travis spent the next three days searching, driving back to Crested Butte at the conclusion of every exhausting day of scrambling up and down the area near the "hair site." Of course, she dreamed of stumbling upon the remains on her own, but her main objective was to be the eyes of the group so that they could plan a search.

She recorded that the slope dropped down to a wide creek bed and a level area of meadow, marsh, and stream. In this bottomland, she noted the prevalence of pocket gophers, which indicated extensive soil development—more so than on the rocky slopes above—and therefore easy digging.

A body could have been buried in the soft soil near the stream, as Melanson had indicated, and then dug up by scavengers, one of which could have carried the hair up to the road. "Just as we follow animal trials when we build roads, animals like to use our roads," Travis wrote in her report to the group. "This might explain why no other sign has been found near the hair."

Travis trenched into prospect pits dug by miners a hundred years earlier to see if there were more recent disturbances. She crawled beneath downed trees and noted that wood rat nests and other animal dens would need to be checked.

"Since the hair was available to scavengers, it seems likely that the grave was dug up and what bones remain are scattered," she wrote. "There is bear sign in the area and plenty of coyote sign." Dogs might be useful, she noted, although the dogs might be thrown off because of the widespread use of the area by human hunters, whose urine and feces give off the scent of decomposing human tissue.

"Geophysics," she noted as a trained geologist, "would be impractical on the wooded, steep slopes of Wasatch sandstone.

"I do not believe that experts in any particular discipline are needed for this search. Just trained observers who will not pass up anything unnatural or manmade."

Travis recommended that a grid system be used to make sure that all areas on the hillside were covered. She also suggested that the searchers examine the aerial photographs to familiarize themselves with the area and plan for the distribution of the searchers.

The report was presented to NecroSearch at the next meeting in November. Because the members agreed with Travis's assessment that the best plan was to conduct a "pedestrian sweep," common to archaeological surveys for evidence of human habitation, Diane France and a new member, archaeologist Steve Ireland, were selected as team leaders.

However, the search was going to have to wait. Winter had already come to the high country, blanketing the slopes of Kebler Pass under many feet of snow.

Early Spring 1992, Montrose, Colorado

Snow deeper than a man was tall may have postponed the search, but it didn't stop Kathy Young from pursuing her suspect. She didn't want to place too much hope in NecroSearch; she needed to go forward as if Michele's remains would never be found. It was under that premise that Sheriff Murdie set up another conference with District Attorney Stern, whose offices were in Montrose, nearly 70 miles west of Gunnison.

The Seventh Judicial District was comprised of six large rural counties, of which Gunnison County was just one. This meant that Stern's resources were stretched thin. Also, the Seventh District wasn't exactly on the cutting edge of homicide trials. In all the years since Michele had disappeared, there had been a handful, all garden variety, quickly solved, and quickly adjudicated.

Stern didn't have the trial experience to handle this one and he knew it. To his credit, he brought his second in command, Wyatt Angelo, an experienced trial attorney, into the conversation.

Still, Stern brought up the usual arguments against prosecuting a bodyless homicide—starting with the need to prove that the victim was not only dead, but that she had been murdered. The first was perhaps easier to get past a jury now that seventeen years had elapsed without any word from Michele. However, the second issue—was she murdered?—was more difficult.

Even assuming that the jury agreed that Michele had been murdered, could they prove beyond a reasonable doubt that it was Melanson? His past criminal record, including his rape convictions, would probably not be allowed to be presented to the jury. So how could they prove that he was the killer, rather than Matthews or some unknown assailant who had accosted Michele after Melanson took her car? And finally, what murder charge should they file?

Young and Murdie wanted first-degree murder. At the time of Michele's disappearance, Colorado's death penalty statutes had been struck down as unconstitutional; it had since been reinstated, but they would only be able to charge Melanson as the law applied in 1974. Still, a conviction for first-degree murder would mean life without parole. No woman would ever have to fear him again.

For first-degree murder, the prosecutors would have to prove deliberation—that Melanson had thought out the act of killing Michele before he committed the crime, even if only for a few moments, the time it takes to deliberate. Or would they have to settle for second-degree murder—that Melanson acted "knowingly," that he knew that what he was doing would likely lead to Michele's death?

Throw all that on top of the fact that the case was nearly two decades old—some of the witnesses were dead; others' memories might be faulty—and they were looking at a difficult conviction at best. At worst, it was a trial they could easily lose.

Wyatt Angelo weighed all this as he listened to Young, Murdie, and Stern. He had been practicing law in Gunnison since 1973 and recalled the disappearance of Michele Wallace. It had been all over the radio and television news, as well as the local newspapers. Other than the media, however, all the information he had up to this point had been through the courthouse rumor mill. It was clear then that Melanson was the main suspect, and Angelo had always wondered what happened to the case. Angelo joined the district attorney's office in May 1987 and was promoted to second in line in January 1988. A year later, he had heard about it when Ric Murdie broached the idea of reviving the Wallace case.

Young had with her a photograph of Michele, taken by some unknown person, smiling as she stood with her dog and an unidentified family at some trailhead in the Rocky Mountains. Her hair was in two long, dark braids, just like the hair found on the logging road. This was the young woman they would present to the jury.

The detective had already done a lot of the homework for the "victimology" Angelo said he would need to try the case. A detailed profile of Michele: her habits, her goals, her relationships with family and friends.

It was apparent to Angelo that he would be able to point out to a jury that Michele had had many reasons to live. She was bright, attractive, engaged with life. She never missed a telephone call to her mother. They might not be allowed to use Mrs. Wallace's suicide in court as evidence of how deep the relationship went, but it was clear that Michele loved and was loved by her family.

She was a budding photographer who would not have blown her first big assignment. Her dearest possession was her camera, and look whose hands it had wound up in, and whose photograph was on the last frame of the roll found in her pawned camera—Roy Melanson. It was a striking piece of circumstantial evidence.

By the time Young had finished answering his questions, Angelo was convinced that, win or lose, they needed to try this case. It was going to be tough; no prosecutor he knew had ever won a bodyless homicide trial. Still, when asked by Stern what he thought, he replied, "I'd go with it tomorrow morning."

On April 13, 1992, Michele Wallace's birthday, Kathy Young finally met Roy Melanson face to face. She wanted to know everything about this man before they met, so she had flown in to Brandenburg, Kentucky, a couple of days earlier to pursue several leads.

One involved two Kentucky inmates who claimed that Melanson had bragged about "disposin' of an unwillin' woman" in the Colorado mountains "where it's hard to find a body." According to one, Melanson added that he "liked it" when women got "feisty" and he had to get rough with them.

The next lead was a little more unusual. Demonstrating that Melanson had lost none of his charm, he had met a widow through her son, a fellow inmate, and after a brief courtship, talked into her into marriage while he was still in prison.

Young had arranged through Detective Tommy Stiles of the

Kentucky State Police to meet another one of the woman's sons—one, Stiles had told her earlier, who wasn't very happy about his mother's marriage.

This son invited Young to their home, where he begged her to speak with his mother. "You tell her about the crimes he's committed," he said. "She won't listen to me. She's head over heels."

Young said she would try. As far as she was concerned, Melanson had victimized enough women, and maybe she could prevent this one from wasting any more of her life on him. Later that day, she met with the new Mrs. Roy Melanson.

She told the woman about the rape cases her husband had already been convicted of, but the woman brushed them off. Roy had told her all about it. "He was wrongfully accused," she said. He had been let go after receiving a life sentence in Texas, he told her, because the authorities there had discovered they had the wrong man.

Young told her it wasn't true. He was let go because his habitual offender conviction was overturned, but nothing the detective said could change the woman's mind.

Young tried a different tack. "You realize that Roy is suspected of beating a man to death in prison?"

The woman smiled as she leaned forward and put her hand on Young's arm. Her husband had told her about that as well. She explained away the alleged beating with a racial slur.

Investigating this case, Young had thought she had encountered just about the worst of human nature. Now, she realized there was always a little room at the bottom of the barrel. But at least she no longer had to feel sorry for the new Mrs. Roy Melanson. She left her and later told the son what had transpired. He shook his head and thanked her for trying.

Then there was nothing left to do but meet with Melanson himself. Young hadn't planned it so that she would see him on Michele's birthday, but it did seem appropriate. She would have been 43 years old today, the detective thought.

Young was nervous. Not so much for her own safety, although because she was meeting him alone there was that factor, but because she didn't want to take any chances on slipping up. Arrested in Montana, Melanson had fought extradition to Kentucky, but Detective John Carr of the Kentucky State Police had at last brought him back in 1991. He was convicted of burglary with the added sentence en-

NecroSearch International was incorporated in June 1991.
(Photo courtesy NecroSearch International)

G. Clark Davenport, geophysicist

Diane France, forensic anthropologist

Jack Swanburg, criminalist

Cecilia Travis, naturalist

Al Bieber, geologist

Dick Hopkins, criminalist
(*Photo courtesy Linda Hopkins*)

Vickey Trammell, naturalist
(*Photo courtesy Jack Swanburg*)

Jim Reed, computer specialist

John Lindemann, geologist
(*Photo courtesy Jack Swanburg*)

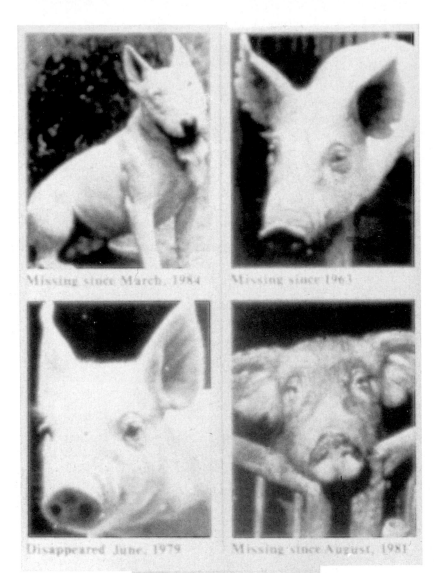

Missing since March, 1984   Missing since 1963

Disappeared June, 1979   Missing since August, 1981

MISSING PIGS
BULLETIN

"Missing pigs" bulletin was part of Project PIG's (Pigs In the Ground) early presentations to law enforcement agencies. *(Photo courtesy NecroSearch International)*

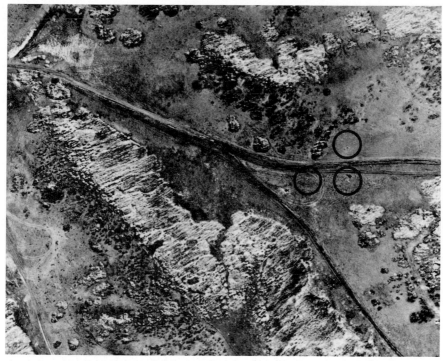

Aerial view of Project PIG site at the Highlands Ranch Law Enforcement Training Facility with grave sites of original three pigs circled.
(Photo courtesy NecroSearch International)

Blanket-wrapped pig carcass waits in an open grave for burial.
(Photo courtesy Tom Griffin)

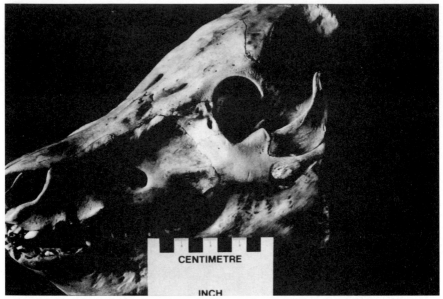

Intact pig's skull used for identification of partial remains. *(Photo courtesy Cecilia Travis)*

NecroSearch members consulted the research on the different decomposition rates of cadavers studied at Dr. William Bass's "Body Farm" at the University of Tennessee at Knoxville. *(Photo courtesy Tom Griffin)*

Geophysicist G. Clark Davenport uses magnetometer to note disturbances in the ground's magnetic field. *(Photo courtesy Cecilia Travis)*

Davenport inspects vegetation over buried pig *(Photo courtesy Tom Griffin)*

Davenport pushing ground-penetrating radar over pig grave site.*(Photo courtesy Tom Griffin)*

An insect capture net is put over buried pig. *(Photo courtesy Cecilia Travis)*

Dogs such as Al Nelson's Becky are trained to find human remains. *(Photo courtesy Cecilia Travis)*

Pig grave site is excavated
with grid system commonly
used by archaeologists.
*(Photo courtesy NecroSearch
International)*

Geologist John Lindemann
studying soil *(Photo courtesy
Cecilia Travis)*

Criminalist Jack Swanburg excavates body of drug dealer using archaeological grid system *(Photo courtesy Jack Swanburg)*

Forensic anthropologist
Diane France descends
abandoned mine shaft
to locate victim's
remains *(Photo courtesy
NecroSearch International)*

Victim Michele Wallace, 25, disappeared while backpacking over Labor Day weekend in 1974. *(Photo courtesy George Wallace)*

Investigators found the last photo of Wallace, her hair in braids, with her dog, Okie, on the roll of film in her camera.*(Photo courtesy Gunnison County, Colorado, Sheriff's Office)*

The search area was marked off with flags and carefully excavated. *(Photo courtesy Cecilia Travis)*

Anthropologist Diane France using a bamboo pick, so the bones would not be marred or nicked. *(Photo courtesy Cecilia Travis)*

Naturalist Cecilia Travis screening dirt and debris from excavation site. *(Photo courtesy Diane France)*

A cleaned grid shows one of Wallace's leg bones in the exact position in which it was found *(Photo courtesy Cecilia Travis)*

Vegetation caught in Wallace's braids, found five years after she disappeared, helped naturalist Vicky Trammell in 1994 to determine that the body was probably nearby and unburied. *(Photo courtesy Cecilia Travis)*

Boot with bones of left foot still inside. *(Photo courtesy Gunnison County, Colorado, Sheriff's Office)*

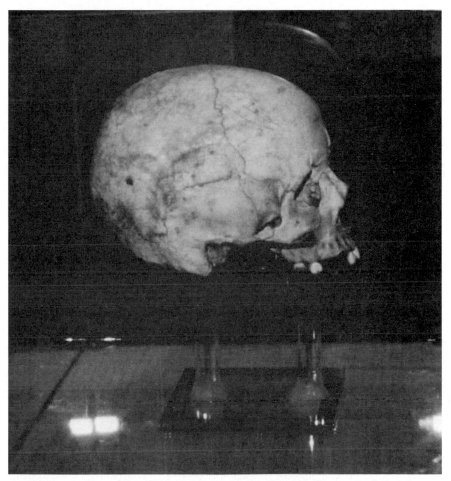

Wallace's skull mounted in a glass case for display during her murderer's trial. *(Photo courtesy Gunnison County, Colorado, Sheriff's Office)*

Investigator Kathy Young.

Sheriff Richard Murdie *(Photo courtesy Richard Murdie)*

Assistant District
Attorney Wyatt
Angelo.

In 1994, Roy
Melanson, 56, was
sentenced to life in
prison for murdering
Michele Wallace
twenty years earlier.
*(Photo courtesy
Gunnison County,
Colorado, Sheriff's
Office)*

Victim Diane Keidel, 34, disappeared in 1966. *(Photo courtesy Phoenix, Arizona, Police Department)*

Gene Keidel, 58, was convicted in 1995 of murdering Diane Keidel
(Photo courtesy Phoenix, Arizona, Police Department)

Geophysicist G. Clark Davenport uses ground-penetrating radar to search for Keidel's body under four inches of concrete. *(Photo courtesy G. Clark Davenport)*

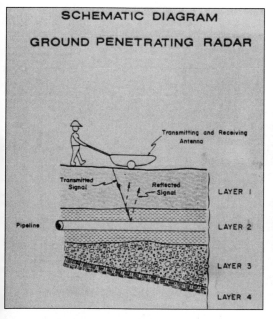

Schematic drawing of how ground-penetrating radar works. *(Photo courtesy G. Clark Davenport)*

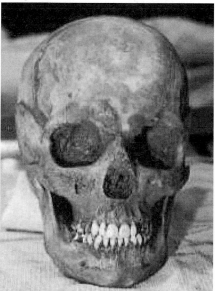

Keidel's skull was found less than an hour into the dig. *(Photo courtesy Phoenix, Arizona, Police Department)*

Corner of the backyard of the former Keidel home prior to excavation. *(Photo courtesy G. Clark Davenport)*

Keidel's remains were found exactly where the ground-penetrating radar had indicated. *(Photo courtesy Phoenix, Arizona, Police Department)*

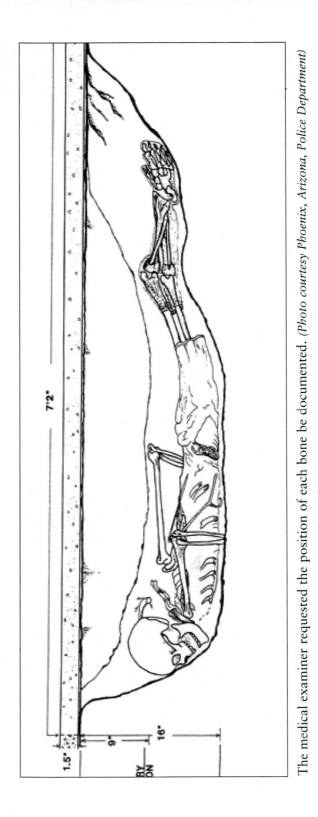

The medical examiner requested the position of each bone be documented. *(Photo courtesy Phoenix, Arizona, Police Department)*

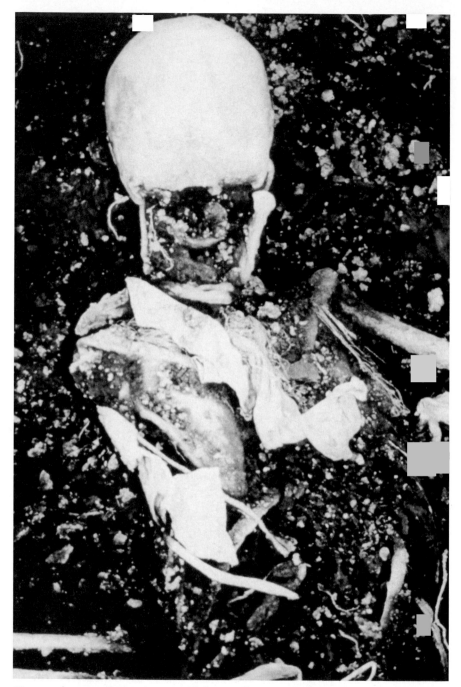

Two nylon stockings were still knotted around the victim's neck. *(Photo courtesy Phoenix, Arizona, Police Department)*

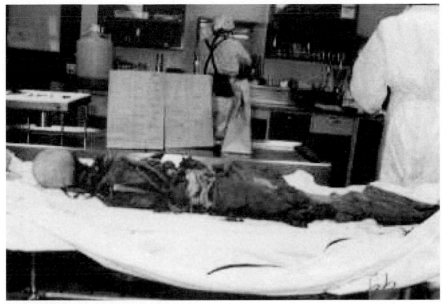

Carefully removed from the grave, the bones were placed on a sterile sheet for transport. *(Photo courtesy Phoenix, Arizona, Police Department)*

The nylon stockings helped establish the date of the crime because panty hose had not been introduced in Arizona until after 1966. *(Photo courtesy Phoenix, Arizona, Police Department)*

Victim Cher Elder, 20, shortly before she disappeared in March 1993. *(Photo courtesy Rhonda Edwards)*

Elder had been buried under a pile of large rocks. *(Photo courtesy Lakewood, Colorado, Police Department)*

NecroSearch excavated the grave site over several days. *(Photo courtesy Lakewood, Colorado, Police Department)*

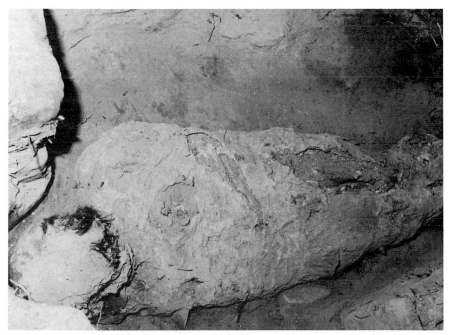

Elder had been shot three times at close range behind her left ear. *(Photo courtesy Lakewood, Colorado, Police Department)*

Detective Scott Richardson *(Photo courtesy Scott and Sabrina Richardson)*

Thomas Luther, 38, was convicted in 1996 of murdering Cher Elder. *(Photo courtesy Lakewood, Colorado, Police Department)*

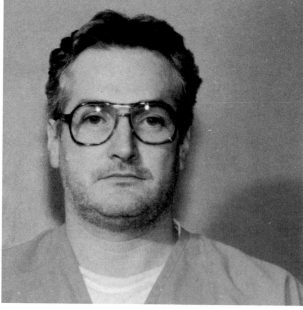

Victim Christine
Elkins, 32,
disappeared in 1990.
*(Photo courtesy
Maryville, Missouri,
Police Department)*

NecroSearch pinpointed the location of Elkins's car in the Missouri River.
(Photo courtesy ATF)

Bureau of Alcohol, Tobacco and Firearms agent Mike Schmidt *(left)* and Detective Randy Strong hold license plate found by divers. *(Photo courtesy ATF)*

Convicted in 1998, Tony Emery was 34 when he murdered Elkins in 1990. *(Photo courtesy Maryville, Missouri, Police Department)*

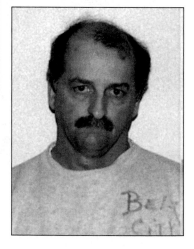

Herbert "Tug" Emery Jr., 50, was convicted in 1998 of killing Elkins with his cousin Tony. *(Photo courtesy Maryville, Missouri, Police Department)*

The car is removed from the river. *(Photo courtesy ATF)*

Elkins's body was found in the car's trunk. *(Photo courtesy ATF)*

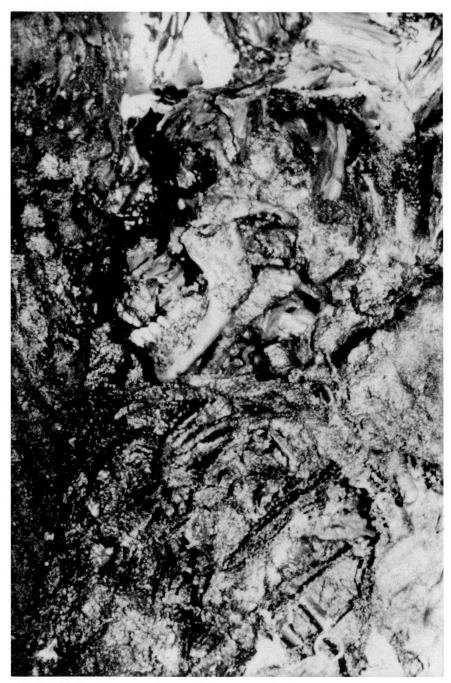
The victim's skull was shattered into several pieces. *(Photo courtesy ATF)*

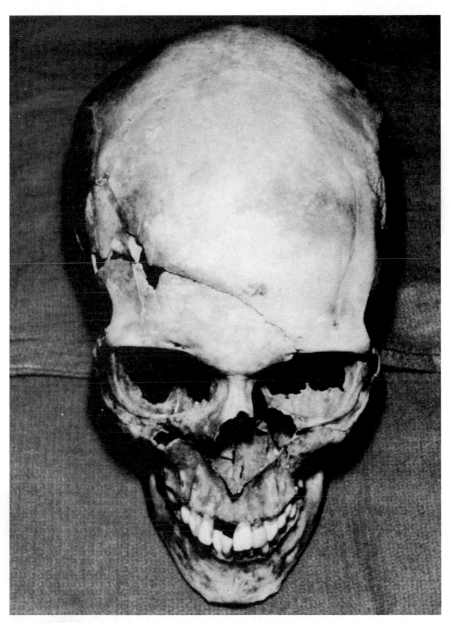
Elkins's reconstructed skull showed she had been hit from behind.
(Photo courtesy ATF)

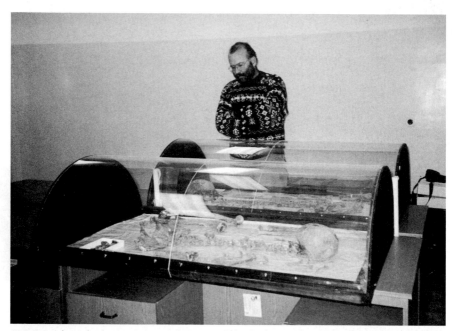

Jim Reed with the remains of Czar Nicholas and Czarina Alexandra. *(Photo courtesy Diane France)*

Diane France was asked to determine if this skeleton had been Princess Anastasia. *((Photo courtesy Jim Reed)*

hancement of being a habitual criminal, and sentenced to twenty years. He would be eligible for parole in the year 2002, and if he got out, it would only mean more pain and suffering for some other woman.

This would probably be the one shot a police officer would get at interviewing Melanson about Michele before he "lawyered up," and Young was worried whether she was the right officer for the job. She believed that Melanson hated women, and if her presence was going to wreck any chance of his talking, she was willing to put her ego aside and let a male officer conduct the interview.

Before coming to Kentucky, she had consulted with FBI experts at the agency's behavioral science unit at Quantico. They agreed that Young knew the most about the case and therefore needed to be the one to conduct the interview. And she would have to do it without a male officer present or Melanson might ignore her.

Detective Stiles, who had taken over the case from Carr, escorted her to the Meade County Courthouse, which adjoined the jail. The conversation would be taped and monitored, and they had arranged certain verbal signals to be used if she felt Melanson was going to attack her. Young soon found herself alone, sitting at a table across from the only door in a small room.

There was a knock on the door. She had been told by Texas Ranger Taylor that Melanson tended to put on weight in prison, but she was surprised when he entered in shackles and handcuffs. He was as big as a bear and had huge hands that seemed disproportionate even for a man as large as he was.

What surprised her more, after he sat down across from her and they started talking, was his demeanor. He was exceptionally polite. "Yes ma'am," he said when they were introduced. "What can I help you with, ma'am?" And it continued through their conversation.

They talked in generalities at first. She explained who she was and what case she was working on. He asked if the old sheriff, Claude Porterfield, was still in office. Melanson considered himself quite an artist, and he had given one of the paintings he'd done in the Gunnison County Jail to the sheriff back in 1974.

Melanson's tone was reassuring. He didn't try to come on to her, or give her the once-over with his eyes she had expected. He was every bit a gentleman.

She felt herself relaxing. Then suddenly, the hair on the back of her neck stood on end and she felt a chill. *Oh my God,* she thought to herself, *this is how he does it!* The nice guy. Polite. Yes, ma'am. No, ma'am. . . . Until his victim relaxed.

Young shook off her antipathy as if waking up from a nap. She knew who he was and what he was, and yet she had felt herself lulled by his pleasant manners. She was glad Stiles was just outside the room. "I'm letting you know that I'm not giving up on this case," she said firmly. "This case will go to a conclusion, and you're the main suspect. There is no one else but you."

For the first time, Melanson dropped the veneer, just slightly. He continued to address her politely, but there was now an edge to his voice when he declared, "You people were wasting your time back then, and you're wasting your time now."

Young got to Melanson again by showing him a photograph of Michele's hair. He stopped what he was saying in mid-sentence and looked stunned. His mouth twitched. Then he quickly changed the subject.

Their conversation only lasted about twenty minutes before Melanson abruptly ended it. If she tried to talk to him again, he said, he would want a lawyer present.

Young had gained nothing that could be used as evidence in court nor any hints about what he had done with Michele's body. But it wasn't a complete waste. She had a keener insight into Melanson's psyche, and she knew that he could be rattled by his victim.

As she turned in for the night, Young murmured, "Happy Birthday, Michele. We're still working on it."

Young flew back to Colorado more determined than ever to take this to trial. Her boss agreed, and on April 22, Roy Melanson was served in his cell with a murder warrant.

A heated discussion followed between Sheriff Murdie and Stern, who had wanted to delay serving the warrant. But the sheriff and Young had agreed: no more stalling.

Stern wasn't the person most upset about the warrant. That fell to Melanson. He soon wrote a letter to Gunnison County District Judge Tom Goldsmith.

Melanson demanded that Kathy Young be removed from the case. She was prejudiced against him, he claimed. She had had him hauled out of prison in shackles and handcuffs and dragged down to the courthouse to grill him. No other prisoner was ever treated so rudely, he claimed.

Besides, contended Melanson, who after spending most of his adult life in prison had become what he considered quite the jailhouse lawyer, the state had no case. "There's no corpus delicti," he pointed out. No body.

Angelo said he was willing to prosecute the case regardless. "We'll do the best we can," he told Young. "If Melanson walks away from Michele's murder, at least we'll know we tried." And Young was willing to try just about anything to succeed, including when she got a call from Swanburg early that summer. If she was still interested, he said, NecroSearch would send a search team in August.

Why not, Young thought to herself. She didn't hold out much hope, but if they wanted to try . . . She was willing to let just about anybody have a go at it.

In July, the town marshal of Crested Butte called to offer some unusual help. There was a "psychic fair" in town with practitioners from all over the United States, he explained, many of whom claimed to have had great success helping with police investigations in the past. "I know it sounds corny, but it might be worth letting them try," the marshal said.

What the hell, Young thought. She didn't place a lot of faith in psychics, but it probably couldn't hurt.

At Crested Butte, Young was introduced to the half-dozen psychics who wanted to participate. They were all women, ranging in age from 30 to late 50s. There was nothing strange about their appearance or actions; they obviously wanted to help and believed in what they did.

There were local psychics in the bunch, so the whole group knew quite a bit about the case from what had been in the media. As a test, Young didn't take them directly to the site where the hair was found. She stopped on the road well short of the area, and they all got out and began to walk up the road.

It was a beautiful day in the mountains, with not a cloud in the sky. Young was leading in a general sort of way; every once in a while, one or another of the psychics would "get vibes" and suddenly plunge a little way off the road before returning with a perplexed look on her face.

They were walking past a large rock formation when from behind

Young came the most blood-curdling scream she had ever heard. Automatically she reached for her sidearm as she spun around. The first thing that had come to her mind was that a bear or mountain lion had jumped one of the women.

However, it was only one of the younger women, who stood in the middle of the trail looking at the rock formation and screaming.

"I sensed that Michele wants her hair back," the woman said.

Young fought to keep her jaw from dropping too far. It became tougher as the others chimed in.

"He's committed several rapes," said one.

"He doesn't like women," said another.

Fortunately, there were no more outbursts, though they did leave a stick to mark a place in the road where they thought NecroSearch, who Young had told them about, should concentrate their efforts. It was some distance from the hair site, but Young promised to tell the group.

Young didn't really think that NecroSearch would be much more successful than the psychics. She had been impressed by their attitude and the questions they had asked. But she was convinced that wherever Melanson left Michele's body, her remains had been claimed by the forest.

Still, she was willing to work with them—even when Swanburg called on July 20 and asked if she would mind sending the mass of hair that had been found on the logging road in 1979. "I have someone in mind who I'd like to take a look at it," he said.

Young checked the hair out of the evidence room and sent it to Swanburg in care of the Arapahoe County Sheriff's Office, where it arrived three days later. When he received the package, Swanburg called Vickey Trammell.

When she first started with Project PIG, Trammell felt out of place. For one thing, she wasn't prepared for the occasionally macabre sense of humor of some members. Davenport in particular intimidated her with his sometimes acerbic wit. Naturally shy and quiet, she wasn't sure if most of the others even knew who she was.

She learned differently, but unfortunately it came as a result of her own personal tragedy. In April, her youngest son, David, and a friend were riding on a motorcycle when a drunk driver ran a stoplight and killed them both. Grief-stricken, she felt lost, asking the sort of questions any parent would about why such a thing happened—the sort of questions that never get answered.

But in that dark hour, she found she had more people who cared about her than she knew. First, Hopkins and Swanburg had stepped in to help the best way they knew how. They oversaw the autopsy and counseled her on legal issues she would face.

Trammell was grateful for the help. But even more, she was surprised and moved when every member of NecroSearch came to David's funeral. It was then she realized that they considered her a part of the whole; they were there to share her grief. She realized she needed to stay involved with those good people, even if she couldn't say exactly why.

When Trammell got to Swanburg's office, he took the hair from the package and laid it on a large sheet of white butcher paper. Without giving her much information, he asked what she could decipher from the evidence in front of her.

Trammell wasn't exactly sure what to look for, but then a picture began to emerge. The first thing she noted was that the hair was surprisingly clean, with no large pieces of soil or leaf litter. By pulling apart one of the braids, she could see where the exposed hair had been bleached but beneath it the hair was a rich, dark brown. The cleanliness and bleaching told her that it was unlikely that Michele Wallace had been buried.

The botanist separated the obvious plant material from the "geology" pile. The plant material consisted mostly of conifer needles, which she took home. She obtained known samples of dried branches for all twelve conifer trees that grew in Colorado. Using her microscope, she compared each needle from the hair and was surprised that she was able to identify each needle. She was also able to identify other biological material as grass and wood particles.

All told she found: twelve full and more than twenty partial needles of subalpine fir, *Abies lasiocarpa;* one needle of Engelmann spruce, *Picea engelmannii;* small pieces of wood from either an aspen or cottonwood tree; and one tiny dried stem with "opposite leaf scars" from a low-growing shrub called Mountain lover, *Pachistima myrsinites.*

It was like assembling the pieces of a puzzle. Trammell found the proportion of subalpine fir to Englemann spruce needles to be particularly telling. The subalpine forest grows in mountains above 9,000 feet in elevation and is generally a mixture of Engelmann spruce and subalpine fir, so finding both was not unusual. However, usually Engelmann spruce dominates, except on very moist north- or northeast-facing slopes. In those wet, cool areas of the subalpine forest, the fir is dominant.

One conclusion led to the next. If the fir species grew above 9,000 feet, then she could assume that the nonconiferous wood pieces belonged to an aspen because cottonwood didn't grow at the higher elevations. Aspen, she knew, grew in areas that had been cleared by fire or by man, such as in road building or logging.

The absence of some species told her as much as the presence of the others. There was no lodgepole pine, which grows up quickly in an area exposed by fire until crowded out after eighty to a hundred years by the fir and spruce.

Also, if the hair had been brought up the mountain by a scavenger, she would have expected to find evidence of ponderosa or piñon pines, which grew at lower elevations. If carried over an exposed, windy ridge (such as between Schofield and Kebler passes), she thought it likely that she would have discovered some limber pine.

Trammell concluded that the hair had spent the time since Michele disappeared in an area that had not been exposed to fire but had been cleared; was above 9,000 feet in elevation, and was a cool, moist, north-facing slope.

If Trammell was right, the searchers could concentrate on the logging road with confidence that they weren't wasting their time. If Trammell was right, the remains would be found close to the surface, covered by vegetation or not at all, and on a moist north slope in the vicinity where the hair was found.

When she shared her findings with Swanburg, he was flabbergasted. He knew Trammell was smart—that she played violin for the symphony, taught anatomy, worked as a naturalist—but he was impressed that she had deduced so much.

Hell, he thought, this was about as close to Sherlock Holmes as you could get.

August 6, 1992, Gunnison, Colorado

NecroSearch International arrived in Gunnison on a Thursday night. The team was led by forensic anthropologist Diane France and archaeologist Steve Ireland. The others consisted of Cecilia Travis and several nonmembers from among France's anthropology graduate students at Colorado State University: Julie Kovats, Todd McCabe, Shannon Morgan, and Russana Youngblood-Evans.

They met Kathy Young at her home on the outskirts of town, where she lived with her sons, Josh and Steve. One of Young's friends, Deputy Maralee Gotsch, and her daughter, Jaime, were also there and ready to go. Maralee worked at the detention center and had often been a sounding board for Young as she discussed the case or vented her frustrations. She probably knew the case as well as anyone except Wyatt Angelo and Scott Jackson by now, and had volunteered to help with the search.

The NecroSearch team made it clear that they were there to assist, not take over Young's investigation. She didn't know it, but that was by design. Law enforcement members of the group had warned their scientist counterparts that nothing would start the group off on the wrong foot like a bunch of eggheads coming in and telling a police officer, who may have worked on a case for years, what to do.

Young reviewed the evidence with them, including handing around the affidavit submitted for Melanson's arrest on the murder charge. They also looked over the aerial photographs to get the lay of the land.

Young then showed them a copy of the letter Melanson had written to the courts pointing out that there was no "corpus delicti." The group took it as a challenge.

The visitors spent the night in a dormitory at Western State College that had been arranged for them by the sheriff's office. Early the next morning, they rendezvoused with Young and the Gotsches and headed north to Crested Butte. There they stopped to pick up lunch at a store. Ireland purchased a supermarket tabloid newspaper and was soon regaling the others with stories from it.

Steve Ireland was one of the newer members of the organization but already well respected by the others. For one thing, he had found more graves than the rest of them put together, albeit in graveyards. As an archaeologist with the U.S. Bureau of Reclamation, he had worked for a number of years finding and relocating historic graves in old cemeteries in Oklahoma, Texas, and New Mexico to make way for new dams and water projects.

This was more difficult than it sounded. Many cemeteries were never maintained or properly documented in the old West. It sometimes took pioneer families years before they were able to buy and place a headstone over a grave, if ever, and sometimes when they did get around to it, the exact location had grown fuzzy with time, and the marker set haphazardly. Or sometimes all the markers had simply been moved, often by volunteers "cleaning up" an old cemetery. Ireland and his group had once found an unmarked grave beneath a stone wall that bordered a family cemetery in south Texas.

Ireland had been reassigned to an administrative post in Denver and rarely got to go out in the field anymore. He was missing his old work when, in 1990, he had noticed an article in a Denver newspaper about Project PIG. He thought that his expertise might be of value and called the Colorado Bureau of Investigation and asked for Tom Griffin, who had been mentioned in the story.

By coincidence, the two men worked near each other. They met over lunch, where Ireland explained his former job. He was familiar with many of the techniques that Project PIG was incorporating in its multidisciplinary approach.

It wasn't long afterward that Griffin nominated Ireland as a member. Michele Wallace was his first field case with the group.

From Crested Butte, the searchers took the Kebler Pass road west. About ten miles out of town, they turned off on a side road. After driving through two shallow streams, they came upon the old logging road where the hair was discovered.

On the way, Young pointed out what she now thought of as "Screaming Rock," and told them the story of the psychics. Over the next couple of days, whenever they passed the point, they would all started screaming, which was how the Gunnison detective learned about the NecroSearch sense of humor.

They arrived at the fork in the logging trail where the hair had been found. After reconnoitering, the decision was made to begin the search up the road from the site. The idea was that loose items generally moved downhill.

It was rough country. On one side of the road the terrain rose as steeply as a pitched roof, while the other side fell away just as quickly. They began by marking off an area to be searched on the downhill side of the road toward the creek. Downhill because the general consensus was that even a large man would have difficulty carrying a body uphill. Young had told them that Melanson was probably too lazy to have gone through much effort.

The group also took into consideration that he had probably killed her the night they were last seen together. There wouldn't have been much light for stumbling about in the woods carrying, or burying, a body. That fit with Trammell's theory from studying the hair, that Michele had not been buried.

It was going to be hard enough moving on the steep hillside in the daylight. The group saw that they wouldn't be able to walk upright and keep their balance on their "pedestrian sweep," which would essentially be moving across the search area shoulder-to-shoulder with their eyes on the ground. So they got down on their hands and knees.

It was hot, dirty work. An afternoon thundershower only added to the miserable conditions, making everything wet, the air muggy, and the ground a slippery, muddy mess. It also brought out mosquitoes "as big as sparrows."

Still, they worked with a purpose and kept their spirits up during breaks. The latter was helped during breaks by Ireland's reading from the tabloid newspaper, as well as the mushroom fights that broke out at intervals.

By the end of the first day, they had covered the slope as far down as where the hair had been found. They had also searched up the other fork where the psychics had left their stick. One never knew. . . .

The sun was setting behind the mountains to the west when the exhausted crew called it quits and headed back to Gunnison. They had found pieces of a leather strap, some bits of logging machinery and tools, and fragments of nonhuman bones. But none of it was tied to Michele Wallace.

In town they cleaned up and then gathered at Young's for dinner and a discussion over what to do next. Although nothing of importance had been found, Young was impressed by the amount of work the NecroSearch members had put into their day. This was no walk up the road with a group of psychics. She was beginning to think that if Michele's body was somewhere near where her hair was found, this group just might locate it.

The pedestrian sweep was a much more intensive event than it had sounded when she originally started talking to the group. They had literally crawled over hundreds of yards with their faces only a couple feet, and sometimes inches, above the ground.

Ireland had explained that the relatively simple technique of the sweep was used all over the world by archaeologists looking for the most minute evidence of human habitation. More than once, something as tiny as a fragment of pottery thousands of years old had led to much more extensive finds.

Scientists, even those in nonarchaeological fields, were trained observers, he said. It was part of their education and personal makeup to notice things out of the ordinary.

Kathy Young felt close to this group of dedicated volunteers. She hadn't really known what to expect. She had talked to Jack Swanburg and knew Cecilia Travis from her earlier visit. But there hadn't been much time at the first meeting with the group to get to know them.

Although they had a lot of pretty impressive credentials, and had carefully explained what they were doing and why, Young never felt talked down to, just included as part of the team.

They were fun to be around too. Professional while working, they were people who knew the value of laughter in what could otherwise be a troubling and somber task.

That night she found herself sharing some of the more personal thoughts she had about Michele. Stuff she hadn't really shared with anyone. Stuff like the kind of person she felt Michele was, and how they had both come to these mountains within a year of each other, but to such different ends.

August 8, 1992

The searchers were back in their cars at sunrise the next morning and soon on the logging road. They revisited a couple of spots they had flagged the day before as deserving a second look, such as probing and cutting exploratory trenches through suspicious-looking mounds.

They also followed a different road to a rockslide that a sheriff's deputy, who had spent some time with Melanson in 1974–75, thought might be the burial site. They found a car jack, some animal scat, and a few porcupine quills. Meeting back at the hair site to regroup, the decision was made to do a sweep across the slope downhill from where they were standing.

It meant another miserable day of crawling through the underbrush, wet and muddy from the passing rain showers. Slapping at mosquitoes, they tried to maintain their handholds to keep from falling into their downhill partner. About 2:00 P.M., they took a break. They had covered the section up to the hair without any luck and were a little discouraged.

The conversation turned to whether Melanson might have carried Michele's body uphill after all. "I think you're giving Melanson too much credit," Young said, shaking her head. He was a lazy son of a bitch, and she felt certain he wouldn't have put much effort into taking Michele anywhere. Of course, if he had forced her to walk . . .

The discussion was interrupted by someone yelling off in the woods. "Yoo-hoo, I found it!" the voice said.

Up on the road, the others stopped talking. They were a little cranky and, for once, not inclined to appreciate a practical joke.

"Found what?" someone yelled back.

"Michele," said the voice they all now recognized as belonging to Cecilia Travis.

"Yeah, right," the others replied, looking at each other and rolling their eyes.

"No, damn it, I found her—a skull with a gold molar," Travis yelled again. Now she sounded ticked off.

Shannon Morgan said Travis must be kidding. "Cecilia doesn't kid," France replied, beginning to stand up from the log on which she had been resting.

All hell broke loose. Scientific detachment went out the window as they rushed toward where Travis continued to insist that she had "found Michele." One of the interns fell flat on her face in the charge. The others reached the edge of the road and plunged over the side. Travis stood on a game trail, pointing at something white lying on the trail, partly obscured by foliage.

Travis explained. When the others went up to take a break, she had remained behind "answering the call of nature." She was walking back to join the others, conscious of what Young had said about Melanson probably throwing Michele's body from the road, when she saw what she thought was an unusually large, white mushroom. She was moving closer to identify the species when a ray of sunshine struck the object, which shot back a glimmer of gold.

Suddenly, Travis said, she realized she was looking at a human skull, minus the lower jaw. A gold filling in an upper molar gleamed, and there was considerable other dental work. She recalled that was one of the physical descriptions they had of Michele. "Yoo-hoo," she had yelled, trying not to sound too excited. "I found it!" Then they had come running pell-mell down the slope.

After the initial jubilation wore off, the scientists felt chagrined. They had stampeded like a . . . like a herd of rhinos, someone said. Their carelessnes could have damaged evidence. They had behaved as if they hadn't expected to find anything. They hadn't even planned what to do if something was found.

It was just so exciting. *Our first success,* the NecroSearch members thought. *Michele,* thought Young. They pulled themselves together and stopped jumping around congratulating each other.

France leaned over to look at the skull more closely. As a scientist she was loath to give absolutes. However, without moving the skull she could see that it was consistent with the gender, race, and age of the object of their search.

For example, on a male, the browridge would have projected forward more and the forehead sloped backward; the bump of bone behind the ear, known as the mastoid process, also would have been larger. On this skull, the markings where the temporal and masseter muscles used for chewing had been attached to the bone were slight, as were the markings left by the muscle at the back of the skull. The larger and stronger the muscle, a male characteristic, the more rugged and raised are the places on the bones where it connects.

What's more, the mid-facial area of the skull was consistent with that of a female of European ancestry. The nasal area was narrow with a sharp lower border, known as the nasal sill.

The skull by itself was not as useful for ascertaining age. Although some of her colleagues were using cranial suture closings (those squiggly lines on the top of the head that grow together over time) for estimating age, France had found the method to be unreliable.

Judging by the development of what teeth were left in the skull, it appeared to be consistent with that of a female of European ancestry in her mid-twenties. Young produced copies of Michele's dental records, which France said seemed to be a match.

It wasn't a positive identification. But barring the unlikely coincidence of another young white woman with extensive dental work having died only 150 yards from where Michele Wallace's hair was found, they all knew whose eye sockets they were peering into.

Travis flagged the skull by placing a thin PVC pin with a brightly colored piece of plastic attached next to it (PVC because metal pins might throw off metal-detecting equipment). She left the skull in situ until they could get photographs and begin the process of collecting evidence.

They needed to plan the next steps. It was getting late in the afternoon and there was a lot to do. But the first thing was to get the heck out of the search area while they regrouped for the next stage.

France led the way out, crawling on her hands and knees, clipping the vegetation in front of her and carefully examining the ground to make sure no evidence would be trampled. Young followed behind her with a roll of crime scene tape for the others to follow single file. This would be their "walk line" to and from the search area.

Back on top, they gathered around France and Ireland, who began to lay out the order of what to do next. Young took off in her four-wheel-drive police vehicle to drive back to Crested Butte. She needed to reach some people but didn't want to call out on her police radio. The media monitored the police bands, and the last thing they needed now was a circus of camera operators and reporters stumbling around the scene. Other people listened to the police radio as well, and she didn't want any gawkers around or any rumors starting. She knew in her heart and mind that she had just been in the presence of Michele Wallace's mortal remains, but official confirmation would have to come later. There would be plenty of time to let the press in on it.

As she drove, Young had to fight to keep her emotions in check. Not always successfully. "Yes," she yelled, punching her fist into the air. "Yes!" She felt like laughing, and so she laughed.

They had done it! That crazy little group of scientists and students had accomplished what hundreds of other searchers had not. And that didn't include all those autumns' worth of hunters who follow game trails looking for quarry.

When she got to Crested Butte, the first person she called was Jack Swanburg, who had been unable to make the trip. "Eureka!" she yelled when she got him on the telephone. "We found her!"

Young said there wasn't time to tell him everything. She had a lot of calls to make and wanted to get back up to the site as soon as possible. Besides, she thought, she should leave some of that up to members of his group. Swanburg told her to get going, he would get the word out to the other members of the group who couldn't go.

The next person Young called was Wyatt Angelo. "I guess we won't be hearing any more about 'no corpus delicti,'" he said after congratulating her. He told her that he would meet her and the others at her home later that night, then go out to the scene the next day.

Young's boss, Sheriff Murdie, was out of town, as was the undersheriff. Regrettably, so was Deputy Scott Jackson, who had been such an integral part of the reopening of the case. She knew he would be disappointed, but at the same time happy.

Still, with the two main bosses out of town, it essentially left Young in charge, and she promptly called dispatch to have a deputy sent to the scene, and arranged for 24-hour security.

Young also called the county coroner, C. J. Miller, to ask at what point he wanted to come to the scene to prepare a death certificate. Miller congratulated the detective; he had been around a long time and knew how important the case was to her. He figured he could show up a little later into the excavation, and they planned for him to come up on Monday.

By the time Kathy Young got back to the site, NecroSearch had established a perimeter around what would be the initial search area: a square 100 feet by 100 feet, with the road as one border. The hair site was at the far west end. The skull lay within the perimeter.

Diane France and Steve Ireland had organized six-person units to begin sweeping through the square, beginning down near where the hair had been found and moving toward the skull site. They were going to have to crawl on their hands and knees, and decided that they had better rope themselves together.

There were two reasons. One was to keep their lines straight as they worked their way across the slope perpendicular to the road. When they arrived at trees or brush too thick to crawl through, they would need to maintain the integrity of their lines so that nothing was overlooked. It would mean untying when they reached obstacles and then retying on the other side, but it was the only way they would move together without any gaps in the sweep.

The other reason was to keep themselves from tumbling down

the hill. Just getting across the hill was going to mean having to grab plants and roots for handholds. Being anchored to someone else would help if they had to release handholds to look under brush.

The searchers turned up a Chap Stick, beer cans, a human femur, and part of a pelvis. All evidence was left as found but marked by pin flags. The cranium and other bones were photographed in place.

The plan was to find where Michele's body had been initially deposited. There were no other bones apparent around the skull, which could either have been brought to that spot by a scavenger or rolled downhill.

Eventually, the searchers reached an area at the base of a tree almost directly above where the skull had been found. There they found the greatest concentration of bones, including ribs and vertebrae.

France figured that they had found where Michele's body had been left. By the end of the day, she, Ireland, and the CSU students were establishing a grid system of one-meter squares, using string and stakes, beginning at the base of the tree. It was getting late and so the decision was made to put off the actual excavation until the next morning, Sunday. Gunnison deputies and Crested Butte police officers arrived to help secure the area; a guard was posted.

The others returned to Young's house, where a small celebration ensued. They were soon joined by Assistant District Attorney Angelo, whose prospects of winning the case had improved considerably.

Chances were that the skull would have been found the next day if Travis hadn't spotted it. It had been the plan of France and Ireland to sweep that section, one more down from the hair site, next. But Travis had saved them a day's hard work, and there was always the chance that it might have been overlooked under different circumstances. A little luck and the trained observer's eye of a scientist had combined for Travis's discovery.

Barring the stampede, NecroSearch had done everything right to increase their chances of success. They had the right people on the scene: an anthropologist, an archaeologist, and a naturalist, as well as the anthropology students. Although they had worked hard, they had also worked smart, dividing up the search into sections and sweeping meticulously through each section.

They had good reason to be proud. But at last, reluctantly, the group said their good-nights and headed off to their dormitory rooms. The real work, they knew, would begin in the morning.

The next day, the search party had grown considerably. The Gunnison undersheriff, Ted Michael Smith, had returned and told Young she could have two detectives from the combined Gunnison Drug Task Force: Len Smith of the Gunnison Police Department and Bill Folowell of the sheriff's office. He also said Maralee Gotsch could skip work at the jail to continue helping along with her daughter. Ted Conner of the Crested Butte Marshal's Office also joined in.

Ernie Nesbit, a surveyor with the county, came to the scene to "shoot" the corners of the perimeter area and the grid area. One of the big goals in any archaeological work is to locate where material has been found precisely enough to maintain the context between the materials found at the site and the site itself. Although what they were doing was a modified archaeological dig, the goal of Necro-Search was to be able to return to the site, fifty years later if necessary, with a jury and still point out exactly where each item was discovered. There is no statute of limitations on murder, and the idea was to be ready whenever called upon.

The survey points would also give them a three-dimensional picture of the excavation. They would know which bones lay on top of others, how far they were found from the site of deposition (where the body was originally placed), or whether a weapon recovered at the scene lay beneath or on top of the victim. Such precision could, if interpreted correctly, identify the sequence of events surrounding the deposition and decomposition of the body.

Everyone had a job to do. Young was appointed to keep the main log where every piece of evidence—its type and location—was recorded. Only one person was assigned to excavate one grid. That person also kept a log of the evidence found in their grid and that information was also transplanted to the general log.

During the excavation of a grid, material was removed ten centimeters at a time using brushes, small trowels, and bamboo picks. After a layer was removed, a photograph was taken whether there was anything to see or not.

The location of all evidence, such as bones or pieces of clothing, was mapped out on graph paper. The evidence was photographed in place before being moved and bagged by Young. All of the other material removed from the grids—leaves, sticks, dirt—was carried uphill in buckets that contained a slip of paper noting which grid it had come from.

On the road, the material was carefully dumped on tarps in separate piles, which were gone through by hand. Then Travis sifted all of this debris through a mesh screen. She found a surprising amount of artifacts, including small pieces of other bones, buttons, parts of a bra, and orange thread later determined to be the sort used for Levi's jeans at the time of Michele's disappearance. There was also one side of the zipper from a pair of Levi's pants, notable because several teeth from the other side were still engaged, as if the zipper had been violently yanked apart.

As she located items, Travis recorded them in yet a third log and then relayed the information to the person at the grid and to Young, so that it was noted in their logs as well. Evidence from the screen was put into separate bags, each marked with the depth and quadrangle of the grid from which it came.

Everyone else helped as they could. A police officer was posted as a sentry on the main road that ran above and parallel to the logging road to keep traffic from stopping. The scientists joked that the tourists might think they were some sort of strange cult—Steve Ireland and his "harem" of women roped together and crawling through the bushes. Other officers pitched in by hauling buckets of the debris up to the road for screening, taking the buckets back down, running errands, directing traffic.

Young's 8-year-old son, Steve, earned the nickname "Rebar" for carrying the steel rods for Nesbit and France as the perimeter and grids were surveyed and marked. He and Josh, 11, also did their share of carrying buckets. Josh even made a few dollars by taking care of Diane France's dog, Moki, and keeping her away from the site.

Every time the searchers turned around, it seemed there was something to be remarked on. Such as when someone knocked over an empty bucket on the road above the grids. It rolled down the hill and, to everyone's suprise, came to rest exactly where Michele's skull had been found (and since removed and bagged as evidence). When it happened again, everyone had a pretty clear idea of how the skull had ended up where it had. It became known as the "bucket test."

The skull had been found late Saturday. The next four days, France and her compatriots carefully removed material from the grid sections until they got down to "sterile" soil, that is, soil that had not been disturbed—probably since it was first laid down.

CBI agent Wayne Bryant, who now worked out of the Montrose office, videotaped the entire process and took photographs. Additional photographs were taken by Travis, an accomplished nature photographer in her own right.

On Monday, Cal Jennings, another anthropologist from CSU and future NecroSearch member, arrived. Jennings brought Global Positioning Satellite System equipment to determine the precise location of the site in relationship to the outside world.

The problem with using regular surveying equipment to get a precise fix on their position on Kebler Pass was a lack of visibility. The vegetation was so dense, it was difficult to see more than a few yards in any direction but up. And that's what GPS does by using satellites to pinpoint the exact location on the planet.

Each day they met at sunrise and didn't get back to Gunnison until well after sunset. It often rained during this period, creating a new problem with erosion now that so much of the top layers of plant life and debris had been removed. It also made getting up and down the hill a slippery, messy adventure. But no one minded too much now that they had found Michele.

The group conducted more shoulder-to-shoulder transects of the hillside, especially down from where the skull was discovered. They found another femur, gnawed on by a carnivore that Travis believed to be a coyote.

As they worked, France could see how Michele had ended up where they found her. Clearly, her body had been thrown from the road and rolled downhill until it came to rest against the base of the tree. The hair had probably slipped off her skull within a few days and was at some point carried by a scavenger up onto the logging road.

Other scavengers also had been at work. The first would have been flies, laying their eggs, which became maggots that eat dead tissue. On a warm late-summer day, that would have begun within a matter of hours, even minutes.

Coyotes, foxes, and bears would have continued the process, removing the parts that were easiest to carry, especially the appendages. That's why the two femurs had been found some distance away.

France could tell that the site of original disposition was up against the tree. At some point, the skull had come loose from the rest of the body—perhaps due to the tugging of an animal—and then rolled down the hill to where it was found.

After 18 years, France didn't expect to find everything. In fact, she was surprised they found as much as they did. Altogether they had a cranium, both femurs, the pelvis, part of the sternum, vertebrae, six ribs, and numerous bone fragments.

Studying these bones, particularly the long bones of the legs, she was able to confirm her earlier judgment from the skull regarding age and gender. There was no evidence on the bones of osteoporosis or arthritis—diseases associated with age—in what joints had been located. Again, the places where the muscles had attached were not as rugged and pronounced as those generally associated with a male.

It still awaited official confirmation, but there was no question in anyone's mind at the site that this was Michele. Nor, with a road so close, would arguments that she had died in some climbing or hiking accident far from help wash if claimed by a defense attorney.

The cause of death could not be determined at the site. The skull had not been crushed. There were no obvious knife or gunshot marks on the rib bones. They had found no weapons. But the searchers were convinced that any jury that saw this place would agree that she had been killed and dumped.

The question then would become: by whom? The evidence pointed only one way: to the charming Roy Melanson. He had Michele's possessions, including her car, her camera, and her driver's license. And, there were his prison friends who told the police what he'd claimed about killing an "unwillin'" woman in Colorado.

A defense lawyer was likely to point out that Melanson's statements didn't match the facts unearthed by NecroSearch. She had not been buried, or even covered with much in the way of brush, nor had she had her teeth axed out. But there were other explanations for why he might have altered the truth. He may have wanted to sound more ruthless to his fellow criminals. Or he was attempting to ferret out jail snitches by feeding them red herrings to pass on to the guards, or creating a ruse to throw searchers off, even discourage them from trying to find a "buried" body.

Whatever his reasons, it made him a liar. And that could work against him in the eyes of the jury because anything else he said was then suspect.

"Filthy and elated, tired and satisfied, we left the site about five P.M., August twelfth, for the last time," Travis noted in her report for the NecroSearch files.

That same day, local and regional newspapers reported that human remains had been found on Kebler Pass. Bones thought to be those of Michele Wallace, according to Kathy Young, who the papers noted had doggedly pursued the case for two years. The detective and the district attorney's office were quick to give credit to NecroSearch.

"We're very, very pleased that they were willing to come up here and work with local authorities," Stern told one newspaper in a story picked up by the Associated Press. Word was spreading about the little group with the unusual specialty of locating bodies. The reports also noted that a convicted rapist, originally suspected of the crime but let go, Roy Melanson, 55, was fighting extradition.

On September 24, Dr. Wilbur Richie, a forensic odontologist in Jefferson County, Colorado, announced that he had examined the skull and dental records and reached an official conclusion. It had belonged to Michele Wallace.

A couple of days later, Richie was among a number of outsiders invited to a NecroSearch meeting. Kathy Young was there with her two sons, her friends the Gotsches, and Sheriff Murdie. Diane France brought her students who had participated.

All of the adults who had been part of the search and excavation crew were given honorary NecroSearch memberships. Josh and Steve Young were presented with their own archaeology trowels.

Sheriff Ric Murdie thanked NecroSearch. "This has been a cloud hanging over our community and my department," he said.

It was the first opportunity the group had to debrief since the Wallace recovery. Congratulations were in order all around, but it didn't stop the group from discussing where mistakes had been made, or areas that needed improvement. In this they were aided by a slide show from Travis and the playing of Bryant's videotape.

Among the recommendations and cautions that came out of this feedback:

- Once a discovery has been made, the crime scene should be treated as though the group might be camped there for an extended period of time. This would include establishing latrines and "clear" pathways in and out of the search area, with safety ropes for steep inclines.
- Searchers should follow animal trails if scavengers were present. After NecroSearch left, a hiker wandering through the area discovered one of Michele's hiking boots on such a trail, somewhat gnawed but otherwise in good shape, with a sock and the bones of her foot still inside.
- Try the "bucket test" on hillsides where evidence might have rolled or been thrown.
- Other members of the group should be taught how to set up excavation grids in the event that the group's anthropologists and archaeologist weren't available. It was noted that every searcher needed to carry flagging tape to reduce the travel in and out of a search area.
- No rhino charges. There should be a preplanned response to discovery. Tape or rope should be used to limit travel through the area before any further entry. Upon discovery, time should be taken out to regroup and plan the next steps.

At the end of the meeting, Kathy Young turned over the bones of Michele Wallace to Diane France. There hadn't been much time during the excavation for the anthropologist to examine them, and she had had to leave the area quickly afterward for a family emergency. But now the anthropologist was going to take them to her laboratory to examine microscopically for evidence of wounds caused by a weapon.

Although no such marks were readily apparent, there was good reason for this examination. In another case, France was asked to help identify a badly decomposed body in which no cause of death had been determined.

Normally, a body decomposes more quickly around orifices such as the eyes, nostrils, ears, mouth, and, if unclothed, the anus. However, she noted that the area of the front of the neck was just as far along in the process as the orifices.

Now wait a minute, she had thought, *what's going on?* It was evident that there had been a great deal of maggot activity on the neck, indicating the skin had been broken. She carefully cleaned the remaining flesh off the bones and, under her microscope, she discovered the tiniest scratch on the vertebra—a scratch consistent with the pattern of a knife wound. It wasn't very obvious, and probably wouldn't have been noticed in a visual inspection by a pathologist. But her work had established that the man in question had his throat cut.

There was the possibility she might find equally telling marks on Michele's remains. Considering what they had been through, the bones were in good shape.

During the excavation process, France had cautioned Young to rotate the bones a couple of times a day to dry them before they were packaged. If the bones had been put in plastic evidence bags without being dried, the moisture would quickly have caused them to get moldy or even decompose and fall apart. She had also warned her not to dry the bones in the sun, for that might cause them to crack. Young had done as she had been told and gone into the evidence room twice a day, where the bones were laid out on paper towels, to turn them over.

France took the bones with the solemnity the occasion demanded. It was a big responsibility to the victim, to Young and her incredible investigation, and to her colleagues at NecroSearch.

THE TRIAL

Over the course of Roy Melanson's trial, the prosecution would call thirty-nine witnesses, including the Pueblo cops and FBI agents originally involved in the investigation. Amarillo Police Department crime lab technician G. W. Dickerson testified that he had checked out the car for evidence of foul play but found none. But what he remembered most was "the car had been wiped totally clean of any fingerprints," even Michele's.

The prosecutors also presented fifty-five exhibits, such as Michele Wallace's driver's license and car registration and an unused bus ticket found on Melanson in 1974. The most stunning exhibits, however, were Michele's remains.

In February 1993, prosecutors Wyatt Angelo and Mike Argall had taken a chance at a hearing to explain to a judge why Melanson should stand trial for the murder of Michele Wallace. Although, thanks to NecroSearch, they had proof that Michele was dead, they still couldn't prove how she died. France's examination of the bones had turned up no new clues. The trial was anything but a shoo-in. Not that it was unexpected, but they weren't going to be allowed to bring in testimony about Melanson's previous rape convictions or current incarceration.

The legal reasoning for such exclusions is that a defendant shouldn't be held accountable for past offenses, and the jury should only consider the present charge. However, the ruling meant the defense attorneys could raise questions about what motive their client would have had to kill Michele. The prosecutors would have to bite their tongues rather than answer: "Because he rapes women and likes it when they get feisty and he has to get rough with them." Meanwhile, any criminal acts or other foibles of the prosecution witnesses would be fair game for the defense attorneys.

The only clue the jury would get that Melanson was something other than a 56-year-old drifter was a weak explanation of how he came to know prosecution witnesses John Paul Steele and Jack Hassig. The prosecutors were going to be allowed to introduce into evidence the fact that Melanson had been in the Gunnison County Jail on forgery charges in 1974–75 but had been acquitted.

On the day of the hearing, Melanson was led into the courtroom in handcuffs and shackles and wearing a jail jumpsuit. He glanced at a stand in the middle of the courtroom, on which something square had been placed beneath a black cloth.

As Argall outlined the government's case, he had moved up to the stand. "Your honor," the prosecutor said, "People's Exhibit . . ." and removed the black cloth.

The cloth, which Argall had purposely made sure was black for mourning, had covered a square glass case. Mounted inside the case on a glass rod was the skull of Michele Wallace. At all previous hearings, Melanson had hardly done more than look bored. This time, he blanched, and his right hand, which had been resting on the table, began to shake as he leaned back in his chair to look at Young, who was sitting to his left at the prosecution table.

Surely his lawyers told him that we'd found her remains, Young had thought as she returned the look, but this seemed to have taken him by surprise. Angelo had told her to watch for Melanson's reaction; maybe it could be used in court. She recalled how he had behaved in Kentucky when shown the photograph of Michele's hair. This had hit him even harder.

As he caught her eye, he had nodded, and ever after Young would wonder if the expression on his face was a smirk, a grimace, or an acknowledgment that she had him beat. *Gotcha,* she had thought, *that will teach you to underestimate the police.*

The trial opened August 23, 1994 without the presence of Roy Melanson, who refused to attend. Instead, he sat in his jail cell listening over an audio system created just for him. The telephone was provided in case he wanted to confer with his attorneys.

Melanson had called the local newspapers to explain his reasons. He was innocent, he contended, but he also wasn't going to participate as long as he was forced to wear a "shock belt," otherwise known as a custody control device. One wrong move to escape or otherwise cause trouble, and a deputy sheriff in the courtroom could press a button and send 50,000 volts of electricity for 8 seconds into the wearer.

Sheriff Murdie had insisted on Melanson wearing the belt for the safety of those attending the trial. Melanson claimed the belt was "degrading. . . . It's intended for nothing but pain and suffering." Melanson had taken his complaints to the judge. In documents filed for him by his lawyers, he contended that the sheriff was "motivated by malice, vindictiveness, intolerance, and prejudice." The authorities, he added, were "seeking to vindicate their otherwise absolute power over me while I am under their control."

The sheriff's office had assured Melanson and the court that he would be given loose-fitting civilian clothes to wear during his trial, which would disguise the bulky contraption from the jury. It wasn't good enough for Melanson. Defense lawyer Harvey Pelefsky told the press that there was another reason Melanson was boycotting his trial: His client was upset that Michele's remains would be presented to the jury.

The prosecution team believed this probably had more to do with Melanson's absence than anything else. Those remains were in the courtroom within three rectangular boxes of various sizes and covered by black cloth, awaiting the right moment for their display.

Angelo opened for the prosecution, outlining the case and the various characters who would be introduced, such as Chuck Matthews, Sally Burton, and Michele's father, George. He talked about how Melanson, Matthews, and Michele Wallace had met, and noted the statements the defendant made to inmates in Gunnison and Kentucky: remarks made about a shallow grave and knocking out the victim's teeth. "He said he had to dispose of an 'unwilling girl' in Colorado."

The prosecutor paused, then, looking into the eyes of the jurors, he concluded his opening: "That sexually unwilling girl was found a year ago this month. She was found on Kebler Pass, where Roy Melanson went with Chuck Matthews to look for a nonexistent cabin. She was murdered on or about August thirtieth, when she fell into the hands of Roy Melanson."

When Angelo finished, attorney Natalie Frei opened for the defense. She was a young, pretty public defender appointed to the case at the taxpayers' expense. She had worried the prosecution team at early hearings with what they felt was her overly solicitous manner around Melanson, placing herself, they felt, at risk of being taken hostage.

Addressing the jury, Frei said the evidence would demonstrate that Melanson was a thief but nothing more. "He stole Michele's car. He stole her camping gear. He stole her camera. That's what the evidence in this case will show. . . . What it doesn't show is that he murdered her."

When Frei took her seat, Judge Richard Brown instructed the prosecution to call its first witness. Angelo rose and announced, "The People call George Wallace.

Young had finally contacted George Wallace after the remains were found. Up to that point, she had been going through relatives. But she felt she had to write to Wallace directly, and told him that, if he wanted, she would be glad to hear from him personally.

She wrote that as a person and a police officer, she wanted to let him know that the door was open. "I'll answer any questions I can," she said. If she didn't hear from him, she would construe that to mean that he was satisfied with the current arrangement.

A month later, she got a phone call from George, and he very much wanted to talk. Soon they were speaking often by telephone. He told her a lot about Michele—the little things that rounded out her personality—and Young found herself wishing they had begun communicating sooner.

George Wallace had remarried, but he had never gotten over the loss of his daughter and his first wife, often breaking into tears as he recalled old memories for Young. Receiving the news from the search had been bittersweet in more ways than one, for it came at the same time he had learned that his second wife, Melba, had cancer. It only deepened his hatred for Roy Melanson—something bad seemed to happen whenever he heard that name.

It had eaten at him that the man who he knew had killed his daughter and caused the death of his first wife went unpunished. It had looked as though he might get away with it forever until Kathy Young had come along, and then this wonderful group of people, NecroSearch, who found his daughter's remains.

Wallace had shown a great deal of interest in the concept behind NecroSearch. He would always be grateful to them and Young, who he regarded as something of a miracle worker. But there was still a trial to get through. Only when it was over, one way or another, would he at last fulfill his promise to Maggie Wallace. He would be able to bury their daughter next to her.

The night before the trial, Young and Angelo met George Wallace at the Gunnison airport. Angelo had work to do, so Young drove George to the motel where he would spend the night. As they parted, the stocky, white-haired old man handed the young detective a large envelope and asked her not to open it until she was alone. It would be too emotional for him, he said.

When she opened the envelope later, Young found a black-and-white photograph inside. It was grainy and highly contrasted, and it appeared to have been taken in winter, when the leaves had fallen from the thin, dark trees of a park. The slender silhouette of a young woman stood in a clearing, turning toward a bright light coming up over a hill in the background.

Young turned the photograph over. On the back, there was a message, as if written by Michele:

> To Kathy Young,
> Though I have been gone for so long, I am glad you remembered me!
> Thank you, "Mush," Michele Wallace.

Below that:

> This was written by my appreciative father for me. My mother will be so happy when I am at her side. May God bless you and your family. My picture is titled, "Coming Home."

The next morning Wallace found out that Melanson wasn't going to attend the trial. He exploded and told Angelo that he wasn't going to show up either.

"I want to see that bastard," he yelled. "That son of a bitch. I want to look him square in the eye." He had waited all these years to face Melanson and accuse him to his face. Now, he would be robbed of even that satisfaction.

The disappearance of his daughter and the death of his first wife had nearly killed him twenty years ago. All the joy had gone out of his life, and he let his restaurant go downhill. He didn't care. His weight had dropped from 240 pounds to 175 pounds, which under other circumstances would have been a good thing. But it wasn't healthy. He was just wasting away.

Wallace had never touched alcohol. He had always believed that drinking was the downfall of many a restaurant/bar owner. Yet, a year after the two women left him alone, he was seriously considering drowning all his sorrows in a bottle.

Then he was saved by love. George had sold the restaurant and was going through the motions for a couple of days more before walking away for good when a middle-aged woman came in for dinner. She was alone, and they got to chatting. She said her name was Melba. She had been recently widowed after thirty years of marriage.

Melba was so easy to talk to. In minutes it seemed as though they were old friends. After a while, she noticed a photograph of Michele he had on the wall behind the cash register.

"That's my daughter," he had said when he noticed her gaze. He told her the tragic story, not caring that he cried in front of this woman he hardly knew. She then asked for the photograph and, from that day on, carried it in her purse as though Michele had been her daughter, too.

Melba and George were both lonely and needed someone. It wasn't long before he proposed and they were married. A few years later, they had moved to St. Petersberg, Florida, where they began a new life and lived happily ever since. She was the most understanding woman he had ever met. She wasn't jealous of the other women who had been part of her new husband's life and for whom he still grieved.

In fact, she worked to keep the memory of Maggie and Michele alive in her home. She was there also to hold him when some new piece of news came out of Colorado regarding his missing daughter. She told him it was okay to cry, that you never lose the feelings you have for someone you loved.

"I am very lucky," George Wallace had told Kathy Young after they began talking. "I found love twice in my life."

They had been married nearly nineteen years. Good years. But that, too, was coming to an end. Melba was very sick with cancer, and he was going to lose her.

Finding Michele after so long had seemed like a miracle. He couldn't say enough good things about NecroSearch. Before they found Michele's remains, he had been warned through his relatives that the prosecutors thought that charging Melanson was risky. Wallace felt that they should try him anyway—better to lose than not make the attempt.

The prosecutors were now a whole lot more optimistic since Michele had been found. Wallace had been a little taken aback by the site of her skull in the glass case. But he had been happy to hear how it shook up Melanson at the pretrial hearing. *Anything to get that bastard,* he thought. It was too bad Melanson couldn't get the death penalty. But thanks to Young and NecroSearch, there was a good chance he would never get out of prison again.

Wallace had looked forward to seeing that knowledge in Melanson's eyes. But now they were telling him that his daughter's killer didn't have to face his accusers. It was as if he was sitting back there in some little room, laughing at them all again. Wallace wasn't even going to be able to stay for the whole trial; there weren't too many more days left for Melba, and he needed to be near her.

Angelo tried to settle his witness down. They were both from the same area of Chicago originally, so the prosecutor talked about the old neighborhood and about Michele's childhood there before bringing up the subject of Wallace's testimony again.

"George," Angelo said at last, "we have the case whether he comes or not."

But Wallace was still too angry. "I want to see that son of a bitch in front of me," he demanded.

Angelo got District Attorney Stern on the telephone. "I'll tell you why you should appear," Stern said to Wallace. "We can put that man away without him being there. And if we do, he'll never hurt another woman like Michele again."

It was that thought that finally swayed George Wallace. Maybe the deaths of Michele and Maggie wouldn't be in vain if a monster like Melanson never saw another day of freedom. He didn't like it, but he said he would take the stand and testify against a man who didn't have the balls to face him in court.

Wallace entered the courtroom and strode up to the area in front of the judge, where he raised his right hand and swore to tell the truth. George Wallace was 54 when Michele disappeared; he was 73 now and angry. He had also been told that he wouldn't be allowed to talk about Maggie's suicide. It might infringe on the bastard's rights.

Tears began to roll down his cheeks when he was asked the name of his first wife. "Maggie Wallace," he said. They continued to fall as the questions dragged up the past, one painful memory at a time.

"How long?" Angelo asked.

"Thirty-four years."

"Children?"

"Two. One boy and one girl." The boy, he said, was named George Junior. The girl was Michele.

In the summer of 1974, he and his wife were living in Chicago, running a successful Italian restaurant, he said. His daughter had moved to Gunnison "to photograph Colorado."

"That summer were you all in good health?"

"Excellent," Wallace answered. "Perfect."

"When Michele was away from home did she maintain contact?"

"Always," her father replied. "At least weekly, in between all her activities."

"Who made the calls?"

"My wife and Michele, mostly. One or the other was always calling."

"If I asked you to describe Michele's personality traits, what would you say?" Angelo asked.

"She was an adventurous girl," Wallace replied, but he was then overwhelmed by the image of his lively daughter. "Sorry . . ." he stammered. Some members of the jury were also dabbing at their eyes.

Wallace talked about his daughter's plans for the future, and about her best friend, Okie. "Would Michele have done anything to protect Okie from harm?" Angelo asked.

"Definitely," Wallace nodded.

"Would she have separated herself from Okie to protect him?"

"Depending on the situation," Wallace agreed. "If it was to protect him from harm, I guess she would have."

George Wallace was told he could step down. "Sorry, I was such a . . ." he began but couldn't finish.

Among the witnesses called by the prosecution was Chuck Matthews. The years and the drinking had been hard on the veteran and former ranch hand; his face was weathered and his eyes bloodshot. He had married and divorced five women. But he gladly answered the call to testify at Melanson's trial, making the long bus ride from, appropriately, Truth or Consequences, New Mexico. He might be a drunk, but he wasn't the kind of man who could abide some guy hurting a woman—he had never so much as slapped one of his ex-wives. And there was another score to settle between him and Melanson.

Matthews realized that when he was driving down all those isolated logging roads at his companion's insistence, he was being set up for murder. In particular, he had recalled the time he handed the rifle to Melanson and then turned his back. "Hell, he probably woulda' shot me," Matthews had told Young, "if he'd a' thought my car would get him to Pueblo."

Neither the prosecution nor Matthews attempted to hide from the jury that he was an alcoholic who had never quite readjusted after the Vietnam War. His memory was a little fuzzy on some of the chronology and place names from his trek with Melanson. But Matthews's candor often provided a little levity to the proceedings, such as when on cross-examination Pelefsky kept hammering at his drinking. "Isn't it true that you were a fixture at every bar in the area?" the defense attorney had asked.

"Well, yeah," Matthews said with a nod and a good-natured smile, "I didn't want to be prejudiced." The defense attorneys were the only ones in the courtroom not to laugh.

Matthews was serious, however, when he discussed his adventure with Roy Melanson. He said he "got along great" with the German shepherd. He was just sorry that he had let the girl drive off alone with his drinking partner.

One of the items Melanson feared was revealed when the first rectangular object, the smallest of the three, was uncovered while the wife of the man Kolz, who had discovered Michele's hair in 1979 and had since died, took the stand. Beneath the cloth was a lovely wooden box with a glass cover, and inside, laid out on light-blue velvet, was the hair.

The prosecution phase of the trial was drawing to a close—just a couple of witnesses left—when Kathy Young took the stand. She was there mostly to tie the rest of it together as the one person who saw the whole picture, but without her, there would have been no case.

Young talked a lot about the evidence, noting such important facts as Melanson feeling comfortable enough to pawn Michele's equipment using his own name, and driving more than a thousand miles in her car bearing South Carolina plates. Using a large map, Young traced Melanson's travels from Gunnison to Pueblo to Kansas to Iowa to Oklahoma to Texas and back to Colorado.

Part of her investigation had been to run down other leads and look at other suspects, including Chuck Matthews, she said. But all other leads had not panned out, or they came back to point at the man who was noticeably absent from his seat at the defense table.

Young described how she and Scott Jackson had found the brush with the hair on it and thought to send it to the CBI, along with the mass of hair the jury could see in front of it. "It came back a match for Michele Wallace," she said.

The hair had led her to NecroSearch, she said, then described her part in the finding and recovery of Michele Wallace's remains. Most of that, however, she left for Cecilia Travis and, particularly, Diane France.

It felt good to be finally telling a jury, the representatives of her community, what had happened all those years ago. She knew from her investigation that a lot of people had never forgotten the name of Michele Wallace or how her disappearance had taken some measure of innocence from their beautiful part of the country.

Cecilia Travis was called to the stand. The petite naturalist matter-of-factly talked about the purpose of NecroSearch and how she came to be crawling around in the vegetation on Kebler Pass.

Then, she described spotting the "mushroom" that had turned out to be the skull of Michele Wallace. As she spoke, Angelo walked over to the second of the rectangular boxes and removed the black cloth. Inside its glass case was the object of Travis's testimony, the reminder of Michele that had so greatly disturbed Roy Melanson.

The jury stared at the case and its contents in fascination. There before them was the reality of Michele's fate. Not some theory proposed by attorneys, but white bone and a gold filling. The skull of Michele Wallace.

Finally, the stage was set for Diane France. By the time she showed up at the Gunnison County Courthouse for Roy Melanson's trial, it seemed to France that every time she turned around, there was a new case involving the murder of a 20-something-year-old woman. At least with Michele Wallace, there was some consolation in being able to give some closure to the family, as well as to a dedicated cop like Kathy Young.

Perhaps, France hoped, she would find some peace in that, too. She had a few butterflies as she entered the courtroom to take the stand. For all of her work at the Human Identification lab, this was the first time she had been asked to testify at a trial.

She had met with the prosecution team the night before and felt confident that she was prepared to answer any questions that might come up. Angelo had told her only to speak to what she knew. She knew that no one else in that courtroom was better able to talk about forensic anthropology and the recovery of Michele Wallace's remains than she was.

It helped that it was not up to her to decide if Roy Melanson was guilty. She had no firsthand knowledge that he had killed Michele. All she had to speak to was what she had learned at the site where the young woman's bones were found.

Some of the law enforcement members of NecroSearch had often talked to other members of the group about the best way to testify. Mostly, they said, listen to the question carefully, and then address the answer to the jury. Surveys showed that jurors tended to believe witnesses who maintained eye contact with them and didn't try to avoid the question or give too much information.

As discussed the night before, Angelo led her through a series of questions about how NecroSearch went about setting up the search scene, how Michele's skull was discovered, and the procedures that followed.

Finally, the last black cloth was removed from the third rectangular object. It was a wooden box about 5 feet long, the insides of which were lined with light-blue velvet. Beneath the glass cover, every bone that had been found except the skull had been sewn into its anatomically correct position. Other items, such as the pieces of bra and the boot with the foot bones had also been included. The jury now had the hair, skull, and recovered bones of Michele Wallace in full view.

None of the witnesses at this trial was able to say how Michele had died; too much time had passed. But France could describe the circumstances surrounding the deposition of Michele's body based on what was found at the scene. In her expert opinion, she said, the original site of deposition was the base of the tree, 25 feet below the road.

At different points in her testimony, Angelo handed her photographs from the scene to describe before passing them on to the jury. She hadn't seen these particular photographs, so she did her best on short notice to describe what the jury would see.

"This is the overall scene," she said of one. "This is a bra clasp . . . this shows bits of a bra . . . that's the zipper to a pair of jeans . . . that's a femur . . . this is her vertebra."

Angelo handed her one photograph that showed her bending over from behind, but for the life of her, she didn't know what it was trying to depict. "And what do we see here, Dr. France?" Angelo asked.

France hesitated, then told the truth. "There's nothing in here but my rear end." This time even the defense lawyers joined the rest of the courtroom in laughter.

Once again, Young found herself impressed by the small anthropologist who had been so tireless at the excavation site. She appeared confident and looked at the jury as she explained the process that NecroSearch had used to recover the bones they could now see. She neither spoke down to the jurors nor used terms they weren't likely to understand, unless she followed their use with a simple explanation.

For her part, France noticed that the jury seemed to be paying close attention. Her testimony lasted less than an hour and when it was over, she felt enormous relief. And, she thought as she left the courtroom, it felt good to have spoken for Michele Wallace.

Before the prosecution ended its case, and against the protests of the defense attorneys, the jury was taken to the site where Michele Wallace's remains were found. The prosecutors had persuaded the judge that it was important for the jurors to see for themselves the site that Young, Travis, and France had described.

On the logging road above the site, with the court reporter perched on a little stool in the middle of the road with her equipment, the judge gave the jury a brief description of what was found. Young then led a tour—the jurors had been told to dress for hiking this day—where she pointed at various spots. "This is where the cranium was discovered. . . . This is the base of the tree where most of the bones were discovered."

After their return to the courtroom, the defense's case was short. The attorneys presented only four witnesses, recalling former sheriff Claude Porterfield and former undersheriff Fry. Both were questioned about the quality of the search at the time of Michele's disappearance, and whether leads regarding other suspects had been followed.

Throughout the prosecution witnesses' testimony, the telephone on the defense table had remained silent. Then one day, it rang loudly. The sudden intrusion jarred everybody nearly out of their seats, and Pelefsky quickly grabbed it and spoke quietly into the mouthpiece.

It turned out that Melanson had seen Sally Burton and her sisters in the parking lot from his jail cell. Recognizing Sally after all those years, he now wanted to talk to her. That wasn't going to happen, but she was called to testify.

The telephone remained quiet while she described her relationship with Melanson. He never raped her, she said, but she also knew that she had no choice but to comply with his demands for sex. She recalled how quickly he could move, and the implied threats when she gave any indication of trying to leave the cabin. She still remembered the little red car he used to drive her and her sisters around Pueblo.

In the end, it was a toss-up whether Burton's testimony had been more beneficial to the defense or the prosecution. Although he had never attacked her, this was a man who had kept a 14-year-old girl a virtual prisoner in a cabin for a week.

At last the moment had come for closing arguments. Angelo began by noting to the jury that in their instructions from the court they had been told to "feel free to apply their life experiences" while deliberating. "This is not a laboratory." Reasonable doubt was not the absence of doubt, but "doubt based upon reason and common sense."

The evidence in the case, Angelo concluded, pointed squarely at Roy Melanson as the man who killed Michele Wallace, "and that he planned to do so. . . . I trust that you will return with a verdict of first-degree murder for the death of Michele Wallace."

Pelefsky began his closing arguments by referring to the movie *Twelve Angry Men*. By "all appearances . . . it appeared that the defendant was guilty," the attorney said. But one man, played by Henry Fonda, had insisted that his fellow jurors look more closely at the government's case, and in the end, the defendant was acquitted. He suggested that the jury sift through the evidence "much as NecroSearch sifted through the dirt, and let's look and see if there was reasonable doubt."

The case was a puzzle, and if the pieces fit together, "then convict him; convict him of first-degree murder if that's the picture you get. But if it's an obscure picture, an incomplete picture . . . then there is reasonable doubt and you must acquit."

"Roy Melanson was a drifter," Pelefsky conceded. "A petty thief. A con artist who used people and lived from day to day. . . . He moved around and got people to do things for him. . . . It was how Roy Melanson lived. Whether you approve or don't, he used his charm to use people. . . . But being a con artist, being a petty thief, being someone who uses people does not a murderer make."

In his rebuttal, Angelo noted, "Mr. Pelefsky suggested that motive is important. I'll give two. If the crime was theft, you don't leave someone to point the finger at you. If the crime was rape, same thing."

Angelo urged the jury to take special notice of People's Exhibit 47, the zipper found by NecroSearch. The zipper clasp was at the top, but the other side was gone. "What's chilling is if you look down the front of the zipper where the other side should be . . . there's a broken tooth ripped from the other side of her Levi's. . . . That's your motive."

Angelo concluded by turning around Pelefsky's remarks about justice and Roy Melanson. "My request to you is that you give Michele Wallace her justice. It is nineteen years, almost to the day, that she died. She is entitled to some."

The jury thought so, too. On September 1, 1993, after just 5 ½ hours of deliberation, but nearly two decades in coming, they returned with a verdict of murder in the first degree.

Following the trial, the jurors met with Deputy District Attorney Kyle Ipson and investigator Kathy Young. They were all impressed by the sheer amount of circumstantial evidence, and each seemed to have picked up on different aspects of the trial. Some were convinced that Melanson's use of his own name to pawn Michele's equipment proved he knew she was dead. They all believed Steele's account of his long-ago conversation with Melanson.

One woman said that not only did she believe every word Matthews said; she "wanted to take him home and feed him." Another juror asked if they had staged the emotions of George Wallace. When they denied it, he shook his head and said, "I thought it was too emotional not to believe."

The jurors agreed that Angelo had done a magnificent job of tying together a complex case. The defense, however, particularly in its closing, acted as if they didn't believe in their client's innocence and were "grasping at straws."

The jurors all seemed to have some one small thing they had picked out. For some, it was the way Melanson had driven around in Michele's car so brazenly, knowing there was no one to report it stolen. One man thought it was incriminating to have found Okie's leash in the car when Melanson had claimed he last saw the dog tied up outside the bar where he left Michele. A woman thought Michele would have had the insurance card on her person unless it had been taken.

However, they all reported having been most affected by the site. For some, it was the remoteness; for others, how it matched Matthews's description of his travels with Melanson: the steep slope, the thick vegetation . . .

It all fit so well with the testimony of Diane France, who had related her findings in such amazing but understandable detail to what they saw at the site. Would they have convicted Melanson without Michele's remains? Ipson and Young didn't ask. But, the jurors said, there was no ignoring the bones of Michele Wallace. "It made her real," said one juror.

That afternoon, Melanson was brought into the courtroom he had sought to avoid. Judge Brown sentenced him to life in prison, to run consecutive to his Kentucky sentence. In pronouncing judgment, Brown read from the U.S. Constitution and the Declaration of Independence, as Melanson stood sullen and brooding, noting that the defendant had deprived Michele Wallace of her "life, liberty and pursuit of happiness."

"Quite frankly, you are nothing more than a big mouth and a big braggart with an empty mind and no conscience," the judge said. "People have a right to be free, Mr. Melanson. People have a right to be free from people like you. You're a waste of humanity."

Melanson showed no reaction. He just sat and stared straight ahead as if bored.

It was a bright, warm end-of-the-summer day when Angelo, Argall, Murdie, and Young at last left the courtroom. There wasn't a cloud in the sky outside, but just as they stepped out the door, there was an enormous clap of thunder.

"I guess someone else approves," Kathy Young said, and they all laughed.

On April 13, 1994, what would have been her 45th birthday, the ashes of Michele Wallace were buried in her mother's grave. Even that simple act had to follow a twisted road to its end.

Melanson had appealed his conviction, so the evidence had to be preserved in case he won another trial. It took a series of special motions to have Michele's remains released, and then only after they had been photographed and catalogued and the defense attorneys had signed off.

Gunnison coroner Miller took the remains and cremated them according to George Wallace's wishes. That accomplished, he called Wallace to ask where to send the ashes. Tragically, the old man had just minutes before returned home from the hospital and the bedside of his wife, Melba. She had died that afternoon.

Michele's remains arrived the same day that Wallace picked up Melba's ashes. It was almost more than one man could bear, and still he had another dilemma to face.

When he was married to Maggie, George had reserved a place for the two of them, side by side in Chicago's Woodlawn Cemetery. He had never dreamed he would have to bury two wives and a daughter before he, too, passed on.

Now, if he buried Melba next to Maggie, there wouldn't be any more space available in the original plot, and Maggie had asked to have her daughter buried next to her. Nor did he want to be separated in death, as he was in life, from the three women he loved. Heartsick and unsure of what to do, George wrestled with the problem until he discovered that Illinois law allowed one body and the cremated remains of a second person to be buried in the same grave.

Michele and her mother were at last reunited, one on top of the other. George Wallace kept Melba's ashes to be buried someday with his own, next to the grave of his beloved first wife and only daughter.

Sitting next to him at the services that day was the detective who had made it all possible when she reopened the case nearly five years earlier. There were a lot of Michele's high school friends, as well as family, surrounding Kathy Young. It felt good that after twenty years it had still mattered that Michele be laid to rest, and Young was proud to have had a hand in that.

As professionally as she had conducted her investigation, it was the personal involvement of Young that had commanded the respect of the members of NecroSearch. So much so that after the trial, Diane France had called and asked her if she would be interested in becoming a member.

"If so, I'd love to present your application to the group," the anthropologist said. "We were all so impressed by what you did."

It didn't take anything more to persuade Young. A killer had been convicted and would spend the rest of his life behind bars. Without NecroSearch, without Michele's remains, the case might have been lost.

But there was more to it than that. Young only had to be present at this ceremony, sitting next to an old man in his grief, to know that there was something else the group had accomplished that was as important as catching a killer.

The people who had loved Michele, and the detective who wouldn't let her be forgotten, could find some peace, could let her go. Michele was turning toward the light; Michele was going home.

IV

THE
DIANE KEIDEL CASE

May 1994, Denver, Colorado

Clark Davenport was getting discouraged, but not because he wasn't trying or important work wasn't being accomplished. The research was also ongoing out at the PIG site, where the NecroSearch members regularly seemed to come up with something new and unexpected.

For instance, Al Nelson was finding that Becky was growing less interested in the scavenged sites, and on certain days might not even hit on them. But she would consistently hit on bushes that grew nearby. Nelson theorized that whatever chemical or chemicals a dog identifies as the scent of decomposition were carried by water to the roots of the vegetation and up into the leaves, where the dog could smell it. He ran his idea past Jane Bock, the botanist.

"It makes a lot of sense," Bock said. "You're turning into a pretty observant scientist."

Nelson took the botanist's comments as high praise. That was one thing about these scientists at NecroSearch; they always listened to his theories as if he were one of them. It felt good to have someone as knowledgeable as Jane Bock validate his conclusion. Not bad for a slobberologist, he thought.

Such a discovery might not seem like much, but it could be important in a search. In the past, if his dog hit on a bush, he might have attributed it to someone taking a "potty break." Now he realized that it might indicate the proximity of a grave. A geophysicist could then determine the direction of the groundwater flow to the vegetation, which could be backtracked in looking for the source of the scent.

The bloodhounds never ceased to amaze Nelson, though Amy and Becky were as different in their preferences as any two humans. Amy had never shown much interest in becoming a "decomp" dog; she wanted the people she was tracking alive and kicking. Becky had a real flair for bodies. They had tried wrapping the pigs tightly in plastic sheets, or burying them deeper, or covering them in lime, and still she found them. He had yet to see an instance, no matter what was used to disguise the scent, that fooled her.

Even Davenport noted that there were a lot of similarities between his instruments and the dogs. "After all, they're both remote sensing devices," he had said, each with strengths and weaknesses.

Other work at Project PIG concerned the more usual scientific endeavors. Much of it involved the mundane collecting of data—changes in vegetation, the numbers and behavior of insects, geological observations of changes in the soil—but there were new experiments with technology as well.

Davenport was conducting two experiments out at the site. One was a "self-potential survey," which operated on the concept that any time liquids pass through porous materials they generate an electrical current. By sticking nonpolarizing electrodes at different spots in the ground and attaching them to a high-impedance voltmeter (all of the equipment available at the nearest Radio Shack), the current generated by the movement of the fluids could be detected and measured in millivolts.

He had used the technique in geothermal and mineral exploration and thought it might work to detect an electrical current at a grave—both from the release of liquids during the decaying process and later, as moisture flowed into or out of the disturbed soil. The survey showed some promise in that the researchers could see changes in the potential, that is, the way currents flowed in the ground. But the measurements were so ambiguous and the effort so labor-intensive that it didn't seem worth pursuing.

The second experiment involved attempting to identify a grave by measuring the gases given off by decomposition—particularly methane. Davenport had used "soil gas surveys" in his business to locate leaking tanks at filling stations.

At the PIG site he sank hollow probes into the ground and then withdrew any gases in the probes using a vacuum pump. The gases were removed from the pump with a syringe, the contents of which were then inserted into a portable gas chromatograph, which identi-fied what gases were present. He got positive results, but the probes had to come within three feet of a grave to detect the decomposition gases, which meant that this technique also was too labor-intensive to use over a large area. However, it might be possibile to sink the probes into a suspected grave for confirmation of decomposition below the surface prior to excavation.

It was interesting work. But the most intriguing research into finding clandestine graves was still in the field, working on real cases. NecroSearch had been involved in fifty-three cases in eighteen states. Usually, nothing they did or said helped, except perhaps to remove some lonely spot from the list of possibilities for a frustrated investi-gator. But there had been some exciting successes.

Finding Michele Wallace's remains had certainly boosted morale at NecroSearch's monthly meetings. Not that it was bad before, but now there was proof that "we can do this."

The case generated a lot of publicity as the media picked up on this group with the unique avocation who had located the most im-portant piece of the puzzle in a two-decade-old murder mystery. "For me, it is fascinating work because we can always learn some-thing new," Diane France had told one newspaper three months after Michele's remains were discovered. "And it's rewarding work be-cause we can find information that may bring someone to trial and bring peace to the families of the victims. That is a powerful feeling."

The group rejoiced that partially through their work a killer was brought to trial, but that was tempered by the knowledge that their "success" involved finding murder victims. "There's a real mix of emotions when you find remains," France told the reporter. "For all of us, there is a real sense of elation and of sadness."

There was also an increase in the number of calls from police agencies. A measure of their growing reputation was that many of the inquiries came from out of state and included such sophisticated agencies as the FBI and the U.S. Secret Service. No bodies were found in those cases, but the group was able to eliminate some areas from consideration and helped the agencies evaluate the credibility of wit-nesses.

The Drug Enforcement Administration called NecroSearch's Clark Davenport and asked for the group to submit a bid for the cost of trying to locate a grave in Guadalajara, Mexico. The victim was undercover agent Enrique Camarena, who was thought to have been murdered by Mexican drug dealers.

NecroSearch submitted a bid based on sending two members, along with ground-penetrating radar. A few weeks later, Davenport received a call "congratulating" NecroSearch on having the successful bid. But the agency wanted a new cost estimate, based on sending one person and reducing the cost of the radar equipment.

Davenport had worked in Mexico on and off for fifteen years. He was fluent in Spanish and familiar with Mexican customs. He thought the idea of sending one person to snoop around in an area where drug dealers buried DEA agents wasn't a healthy choice. NecroSearch politely declined to get involved in the case.

The group was also adding to their expertise by taking on new members. These included geologist and compuer whiz Jim Reed, thermographer Gil Miceli, and a young anthropology student named Tom Adair.

Thirty-eight-year-old Reed's claim to fame as a geologist was that he had found the world's largest deposit of talc, a mineral used in manufacturing many common items, including anything made of plastic. However, when the mining industry took a nosedive in the early 1980s, he got into computers. In 1987, a former geologist-turned-Denver police officer, Bill Nagle, contacted Reed. Nagle had an idea for creating "contour maps," like those commonly used by hikers, except that these would illustrate crime distribution in a city or even a neighborhood. On a standard contour map, the lines represent elevation, but on this map they would indicate concentrations of different types of crimes. The idea was to help police departments decide how best to allocate resources, especially personnel.

In August 1991, the crime-distribution software developed by Reed was written up in a magazine called *Government Technology*. Among those who read the article was NecroSearch's Clark Davenport. He contacted Reed about an idea of developing a similar program only, at Reed's suggestion, they would enter all the data they had—such as criminal behavior statistics, geophysics, botany, the dogs, geology—to come up with an exploration target. Each target site would be different, as would the relative strength of the various disciplines at the site. For instance, GPR doesn't work if the groundwater is salty, so Reed also developed a system of "weighting factors" based on the confidence level of a particular discipline at each site.

When first contacted by Davenport, Reed thought that the geophysicist sounded like some sort of weirdo. But the more Davenport explained how NecroSearch worked, the more intrigued Reed became. He missed going into the field and that adrenaline rush that came with the discovery of something hidden, whether it was a mineral deposit or, in this case, dead bodies. He thought it would be the civic-minded thing to do, too.

In 1984, Gil Miceli was a retired air traffic controller when he and his wife, Monica, started a company called Hot/Shot Infrared Inspections, Inc., which used Forward Looking Infrared, or FLIR, cameras, which detect tiny differences in temperatures between objects, such as between an insulated and an uninsulated wall. The FLIR camera assigns a gray shade to a specific temperature, with very white being zero and very black being 225, and each gray shade equal to one-tenth of a degree. The differences are projected on a monitor, appearing as a black-and-white television picture, only the image is not what the eye would see but temperatures recorded by the camera. A FLIR "photograph" of a person, for instance, may look like the outline of a human being, but in reality it's showing heat given off by blood circulation.

Most of Miceli's work was in the field of predictive maintenance for utility companies—searching for powerline shorts or overloads—or for the owners of commercial buildings concerned about heat loss. The camera could be mounted on a truck or the bottom of an aircraft, usually a helicopter. Like Reed, Miceli wanted to put his expertise to work for his community, and for years he had been using FLIR cameras to help with search-and-rescue missions, looking for lost hikers and children in Colorado's rugged mountains.

In 1993, Miceli got a call from Detective Scott Richardson of the Lakewood, Colorado, police, who was investigating the disappearance of a 20-year-old woman named Cher Elder. The detective asked Miceli to attend a meeting, where he was introduced to Necro-Search's Steve Ireland and Clark Davenport, who were assisting with the case. The meeting led to an invitation to join the group. Miceli acknowledged that there was something of the "thrill of the chase" and catching the "bad guy" in it for him. But the real issue for him was the idea of bringing what peace he could to the families of murder victims.

* * *

In September 1993, after a human skull was found next to a remote mountain road near Colorado Springs, a NecroSearch team had located the rest of the remains of 13-year-old Heather Dawn Church, who had disappeared without a trace in 1991. Earlier in 1994, a team of Diane France, Steve Ireland, and Kathy Young had found the hidden grave of an as-yet-unidentified young woman on a barren, windswept plateau in a Colorado wilderness area after yet another skull was stumbled upon by a hiker.

The calls kept coming. Even the FBI routinely made inquiries or referred cases to the group, a relationship that began with Clark Davenport, who in October 1991 had been invited to speak at a seminar in White Plains, New York, titled "Detection and Location of Human Remains," by FBI Special Agent John Dew. The agent had forwarded a letter to NecroSearch from a woman working on her master's thesis, and Davenport had called him back. They got to talking and the next thing Davenport knew, he was on the list as a guest speaker.

The seminar was very NecroSearch-like in that the speakers represented several fields also found within the Colorado group. Besides Davenport, there were Andy Rebmann, a Connecticut State Trooper and renowned bloodhound handler; forensic anthropologist Spencer Turkle; Detective Kenny Pierce, a profiler with the New York City police; and James Mellett, a geology professor at New York University.

Davenport was particularly interested in what Mellett had to say about his work with ground-penetrating radar. The NecroSearch president claimed to be the first "forensic geophysicist" due to his work with the police in 1985. But in 1988, Mellett had actually pinpointed the grave of a murder victim using GPR.

It hadn't taken Mellet's success to convince Davenport that the technology would work. He had been running magnetics and electromagnetics out at the PIG site every few months, and GPR not quite as often, and the changes were clearly discernible. Once the ground was disturbed, according to the data, it remained disturbed—whether it was a change in the magnetic field, an alteration in the moisture content of the ground picked up by electromagnetics, or, in the case of GPR, soil horizons that were out of whack.

Still, Davenport couldn't help but be a little envious of Mellet. It had helped some when, just before he was to speak at the seminar, he received an overnight delivery parcel. He pulled out a small box, opened it, and smiled. It contained business cards. Very unique business cards—the sort one wasn't likely to forget, he thought.

NecroSearch International, Inc.
G. Clark Davenport
President

The writing and the logo were rust red against a white background. The logo was what made Davenport smile when he recalled where it came from. It was a drawing of a skeleton, arms down by its sides, the "grinning" skull tilted slightly back and up to the left as if looking at something over its shoulder—the "musician" from the Metaponto necropolis in southern Italy. There was a note with the box. "Happy Birthday, Dad!" it read. "I know you can use these now. Love, Jad."

Davenport shook his head. His boys certainly had their impact on his involvement with what he called "geoforensics." First, Sam had prodded him into offering his expertise to the detectives searching for the bodies in the barrels in 1985. Then, six years later, Jad had come up with the name NecroSearch, and now the logo. His whole family, especially his wife, had been so supportive and proud of what he was trying to accomplish. And now, a reminder that he had found a body—a very old body.

Davenport's knowledge—he discussed magnetics and electromagnetics as well as the use of aerial photography—and his sense of humor were a big hit at the seminar. He had ended his lecture with the usual caution about the limitations of technology and the necessity of good detective work preceding its use.

As an illustration, he showed a set of slides taken from his days in Vietnam. They were of his minesweeping team working its way toward him. Even with the metal detector, he noted, the team missed a mine that later blew the track off an armored personnel carrier. Concluding, he asked if there were any questions.

One FBI agent raised his hand. "You must have been a second lieutenant," the man said.

Davenport wrinkled his brow, puzzled. *This guy has to be one heck of a detective to figure that out,* he thought before replying, "Yes, but how did you know?"

"Because only a second lieutenant would have been stupid enough to take pictures standing in *front* of a minesweeping team," the man replied, to general laughter.

Davenport laughed right along with everyone else. It was a good way to wrap up with a pitch that NecroSearch was there to help. The FBI agents present had been impressed with his gadgets and the possibilities the technology represented. The agency had its own team experimenting with geophysics equipment, especially GPR, but their focus was on research, not fieldwork. The NecroSearch investigators, as Davenport explained, were ready to jump in and get their hands dirty.

The next time Dew put on another seminar, he asked Davenport to speak. Beginning in 1993, he became one of a group who were invited to lecture on "The Detection and Recovery of Human Remains" annually at the FBI forensic training facility in Quantico, Virginia. The group included FBI entomologist Wayne Lord; dog handler Andy Rebmann; botanist David Hall; Scott Hill, commander of the Buffalo, New York, police dive team; health and safety specialist Dr. Robert Gaetjens; Dr. Edward MacDonough, medical examiner for the state of Conneticut; forensic anthropologist Robert Sundick; and forensic anthropologist Bill Rodriguez, now with the Armed Forces Institute of Pathology.

Still, Davenport was filled with self-doubt about what he was accomplishing at NecroSearch. Questions ate at him. *Am I using the proper techonology for the circumstances? Have I passed over something and missed it?* He had fielded a lot of calls from a variety of agencies—from the FBI to police investigators in Australia to the Royal Canadian Mounted Police—with questions about the use of geophysical equipment in locating clandestine graves. He was also a guest instructor every year for a course sponsored by the U.S. National Park Service on "remote sensing for archaeology." Yet, he had still not found a single grave outside of Metaponto.

In May 1994, as he had just returned from an FBI seminar, he picked up a message to call a Detective Ed Reynolds in Phoenix, Arizona. The detective said he had been referred by an FBI agent who had taken Davenport's class. He wanted to know if he had something that would "look under concrete."

THE CRIME

In June 1993 Detective Ed Reynolds of the Phoenix, Arizona, Police Department opened an envelope handed to him by his lieutenant that was addressed to Charlie Masino, a detective in the missing persons unit. Masino had passed the letter on to Reynolds because its author, Lori Keidel Romaneck, was purporting to have witnessed a murder, and Reynolds was a homicide detective—not the usual homicide cop, but half of a two-man unit that specialized in "cold cases," homicides for which the case agent has retired without its being solved.

So far, the unit had yet to crack a case after one year of operation. But Reynolds wasn't giving up. It wasn't in him; the lessons he had learned early in life made him particularly well suited for the frustrating task of pursuing cases others had given up as lost causes. Born and raised in Lansing, a suburb of Chicago, as a youth he was skinny as a rail and clumsy. His lack of physical dexterity didn't hinder his love for sports, or his attempts to participate in them all. Even as the worst player on the football team, he wouldn't quit. It only made him try harder.

After he graduated from high school, Reynolds's parents moved to Phoenix and he soon followed. After taking the written test for the police department in 1979, he was told that he might not hear from them for nine months. However, he did so well on the test, he was called six weeks later and offered a spot in the next police academy class.

The 12-week police academy was essentially run like a military boot camp with college classwork thrown in. He was a big guy at 6-feet-4, but he was now overweight and out of shape. Most of the other cadets were college boys, and he didn't know how he was going to keep up with them academically—if he didn't die of a heart attack running the obstacle course first.

Almost daily, he considered dropping out of the academy. However, another cadet, Mark Stribling, whom he had met on the first day, wouldn't let him give up. Between Stribling's pep talks and his own persistence, he managed to keep at it day after weary day.

When he graduated on July 13, 1979, his grades were near the top of the class. He had gained a badge and lost 50 pounds, all because he wouldn't quit—something wouldn't let him.

A year or so later, Reynolds got that feeling of a higher purpose again as a patrol officer. He was down in the holding cell at the county jail when another officer's prisoner attempted to commit suicide by hanging himself. Reynolds quickly grabbed a knife and cut the man down; he then revived the prisoner using CPR. For his efforts, Reynolds was awarded the Medal of Lifesaving.

Early on, Reynolds set his sights on becoming a homicide detective, but he knew he had a lot to learn first. He began working undercover in 1982, helping Detective Chuck Gregory with fugitive apprehensions. Gregory had a real knack for finding bad guys, but like anyone else in that line of police work, that was only half the problem. The other half was getting the fugitives to come out of the house or apartment without having to go in after them—which was dangerous for the officers and suspects, not to mention any innocent bystanders. If the bad guys left the houses on their own volition, they weren't thinking that a cop might be waiting to pounce, nor did they usually bother to carry a gun. However, playing it safe often meant wasting hour upon hour waiting for their subjects to show themselves.

It looked as though that was going to be the case with a guy they believed was holed up in a hotel room. They had found his truck parked in front but didn't know what he looked like. Reynolds had an idea. He got in the undercover car and drove around the block. When he had made a full circle, he gunned the engine and raced toward the suspect's truck, stopping only a few inches away with the tires squealing. He then parked next to the truck. From his hiding place, Gregory noticed that the drapes moved slightly in the room where they believed the suspect was hiding, as if someone was peering out.

Getting his wallet, Reynolds made a show of taking out money. He walked into the hotel and to the suspect's room, where he knocked on the door. A man answered, looking through the crack in the door. Waving five 20-dollar bills, Reynolds told the man that he had accidently hit the truck parked out front and torn up its bumper. "But I got a criminal record and don't want the police involved," pleaded Reynolds, who looked the part with his long hair and full beard. The man was still suspicious, but Reynolds saw him eying the cash. Finally, the man decided that $100 ought to cover the damage.

Not so fast, Reynolds said; he wanted to see some identification in case the man's insurance company came after him. The man pulled out his wallet and showed his identification. He was the suspect they were looking for. With one hand holding out the bills, Reynolds placed his other on the man's shoulder as Gregory appeared and told the fugitive he was under arrest.

"I knew you were a cop," the man muttered to Reynolds.

"Then why'd you go along with it?" Reynolds asked.

"You were waving all that money around, and I couldn't resist," was the reply.

Gregory went on to become one of the top homicide detectives in Phoenix. It was a position Reynolds aspired to when he became a detective in 1989. However, as with most police departments, detectives in Phoenix were expected to put in their time working other units—vice, burglary, auto theft—before being considered for homicide detail.

It took Reynolds until 1992 to be assigned to homicide. He figured he had reached the pinnacle of his profession, but he didn't know he was going to take a different road than most.

In 1993 his lieutenant, Sherry Kiyler, proposed creating a cold case unit within the homicide division. The man who had once wondered if he had what it took to get through the police academy was the first detective assigned to it.

To avoid burnout, Reynolds worked more than one case at a time. He was working the 1988 murder of wealthy Phoenix socialite Jeanne Tovrea and the 1970 murder of a Navajo child when on June 9, 1993, a 32-year-old woman named Lori Keidel Romaneck wrote a letter to the Phoenix Police Department's missing persons bureau. The letter began with a warning from Lori that she greatly feared retaliation by her father if he were told of her accusations. But, she said, "I need to convey to authorities what I witnessed as a child."

* * *

A few days after being handed the letter, Ed Reynolds met with Lori Keidel Romaneck in his office. She was very emotional, often bursting into tears. And yet, he thought, if this was true, the case might be solvable.

Before the meeting, he had gone to Detective Masino, who gave him a missing-persons file labeled "Diane Keidel." She had been reported missing by a neighbor, not her husband. But that wasn't all. The file contained reports of a suspicious house fire five months after Mrs. Keidel disappeared that had claimed the lives of two of the Keidel children, the sisters of the woman who now sat in his office.

Lori was an attractive young woman, though he noticed she wore her hair and clothing in such a way as to hide scars on the side of her face and neck. Scars, she told him, she got in the fire that killed her sisters. But it was the scars he couldn't see, Reynolds soon realized, that ran the deepest.

By all appearances, in September 1966, the Keidels seemed the picture-perfect American family. Gene Keidel was a contractor. Diane stayed at home with their four children: Susan, 12; Greg, 9; Kelly, 7; and 5-year-old Lori. They lived in a brick ranch-style home on West Citrus Way, in a quiet neighborhood of neatly trimmed lawns and palm trees. There was even a new pool in the backyard to get out of the late-summer heat.

When Diane wasn't around, Susan looked after the others, especially little Lori. It was Susan who led the search when Lori's pet turtle, Touché, disappeared one day from its cage in the backyard. The girls looked and looked until Susan noticed a hole that plunged into the dirt beneath the sandbox. She had learned somewhere that turtles will burrow beneath objects to hibernate, and that is what she quickly decided had become of the missing terrapin. She went into the kitchen, and when she returned, she gave her heartbroken baby sister bread crumbs to spread in front of the hole's entrance, "in case he's hungry when he wakes up."

It was reassuring to believe that Touché would someday return, and good to have an older sister to dry her tears and bring a smile back to Lori's face. Especially because, by 1966, it was clear that the portrait of the perfect family was a fraud.

As her ten-year marriage fell apart, Diane Keidel, a petite 34-year-old brunette, carried on a series of affairs with other men. These in-

cluded men from the job site where Gene worked. He learned he was
the cuckold when he overheard his fellow workers laughing about it.
Salt was rubbed into the wounds when his wife became pregnant and
had an abortion—after he had had a vasectomy.

The couple separated, and Gene moved in with his father. He was
seeing another woman but remained jealous of his wife and her
lovers. He was also angry that Diane had the house and wanted the
kids. She filed for divorce, and on September 16 went to talk to her
lawyer about what was shaping up into an ugly custody battle.

That evening, she met with Gene and they took the kids out for
something to eat while the two adults talked in a bar next door.
Sometime later, after midnight but before dawn on September 17,
1966, Diane and Gene Keidel were at it again in the home on West
Citrus Way. Yelling. Name-calling. He pushed her.

Unknown to both, they were being watched by Lori, who had
been awakened by the commotion. She peeked in to see what her
parents were doing in the dining room, near the sliding glass door
that led to the backyard. She noticed that her mother was wearing a
dark-blue dress that she thought of as the "coat dress" because of its
tailoring and half-inch-wide metal buttons down the front.

Lori's father was screaming bad words. Then he hit her mother,
who fell back against the glass door before collapsing to the floor,
where she lay still.

Frightened, Lori returned to her bed. There in the dark, she lay
listening to the sound of someone digging in the backyard.

The next day, her father told her and her siblings that their
mother had left them for another man. A short time later, he realized
he had a problem—a witness. One afternoon, with his friends gathered near the pool, Gene Keidel saw Lori tossing bread crumbs onto
the dirt near the back-left corner of the house. When he asked what
she was doing, she replied that she was spreading the crumbs "in
case Mommy's hungry when she wakes up." Just as her sister had
taught her to do for the turtle.

In front of his friends, Gene Keidel had laughed off her comments. When he had her alone, he told her in no uncertain terms that
she was to stop talking about "Mommy waking up." A few days
later, Keidel covered his entire backyard with six inches of concrete.

Apparently, that wasn't enough. On January 9, 1967, the house at
West Citrus Way caught fire. Lori recalled how she and her sisters

were trapped in a bedroom. They could hear the sirens approaching, but the flames were everywhere. Susan lay on top of her to protect her.

As Lori talked, Reynolds took into account that she was describing what she had supposedly witnessed as a 5-year-old. Yet her story was amazingly detailed, including such fine points as the dark-blue dress that her mother had been wearing, "her coat dress."

Lori thought she remembered later seeing her mother lying in the dirt outside while her father fumbled in the dark with tools. But there was no doubt in her mind that she had heard someone digging in the backyard. The sound of scraping and scooping hadn't left her head for twenty-five years.

Lori had never told anyone her story before. Now, as the words tumbled out in a rush to Detective Reynolds, so did her tears for Susan. "She tried to comfort me. She said, 'I love you and I will never leave you.' " Her brother escaped out his bedroom window, but her sisters died.

Lori said she was hospitalized for four months with burns over 50 percent of her body. The pain was so unbearable that whenever the medical personnel woke her, she begged to be allowed to go back into blissful, drug-induced sleep. But even when that pain was masked, another was growing—that of a little girl who had lost her mother and her two older sisters in less than a year.

The pain of her loss could not overcome her fear. For the next twenty-five years, Lori lived in terror of her father, she said. He rebuilt the home and brought her and her brother back there to live. The abuse she continued to suffer at her father's hands was emotional and physical, she told Reynolds. He would beat her for the smallest infractions, including once with a boat oar and another time with a board. She had no doubt that it was her father who set the fire.

Gene Keidel taught his daughter to distrust police officers. This wasn't as difficult as it might otherwise have been. As far as a little girl, then a teen, and finally an adult was concerned, the police had failed to protect her or her family. Why should she trust them?

Instead, she had tried to stay out of her father's way. If he didn't notice her, she would not be beaten; she would not be killed.

"He used to tell me that he brought me into the world, and he could take me out," she said.

Lori grew up and got married, only to be divorced seven years later. She hadn't even told her husband the story about her mother's death. But, she emphasized to Reynolds, what she was telling him now was not some repressed memory that had only recently floated to the surface of her consciousness. She had never forgotten what happened, but the fear of her father was so great that she had remained mute.

It had taken every bit of courage she could muster, and an epiphany of sorts, to come forward. A devoted horsewoman, she had recently witnessed the birth of a foal to one of her mares and was struck by the immediate, intense bond between the mother and her offspring. She was suddenly reminded of what few memories she had of her own mother's love, and it was then she knew that she needed to say something. Even now she wasn't out for revenge, she told the detective. It was just that she had been living with the heartache and fear for too long and needed to tell someone—and if possible, to find her mother's body and bury her as she deserved.

It was sure one unbelievable story, Reynolds thought, but at the same time she was a believable young woman. It was obvious that she thought that what she was saying was the truth. Whether or not her memories were accurate, he was sure she wasn't consciously lying.

THE INVESTIGATION

Reynolds knew he wasn't going to be allowed to just start digging up the backyard of the house on West Citrus Way based on a hunch, even if the owners gave him permission. It would cost too much money, especially if he was wrong, and any defense attorney worth his salt would attack anything that looked like a fishing expedition. But where to start?

He thought it was a stroke of luck that a short time after taking on the Keidel case, he was told about an upcoming seminar at Hocking College in nearby Scottsdale, to be presented by Dave Rivers of the Miami/Dade County Sheriff's Office's cold case squad. Rivers's unit was one of the first of its kind in the country, and Reynolds thought for sure he would be able to glean a few ideas there.

The seminar was attended by a dozen homicide detectives from the western region. It began with Rivers recounting cases his squad had seen to a successful conclusion. The talk was motivational to Reynolds, but he was a little disappointed that there wasn't more discussion covering the nuts and bolts of how the Miami/Dade unit went about their work.

What had really attracted Reynolds to the seminar was that each participant was expected to make a presentation on a cold case they were working. The group would then brainstorm for ideas, followed by dissection of their suspect by an FBI profiler.

Although he was no closer to solving the Tovrea or the Navajo girl cases, Reynolds chose to present the Keidel case. There wasn't much contained in the original investigation reports into the disappearance of Diane Keidel. Lori was never interviewed, nor was her brother, Greg, or sister Kelly. Susan was talked to briefly, but the only real item of interest there was that she had last seen her mother with her father about 1:00 A.M. the night of her disappearance. That conflicted with her father's statement to the police.

When Gene Keidel was questioned, he initially told detectives that he had spent the afternoon of September 16, a Saturday, with his wife and their children at the house on West Citrus Way. That evening, the couple took their children to a fast-food restaurant. While the kids were eating, they went to a nearby bar to drink and talk.

Afterward, according to Gene Keidel, the children were taken home; then Diane dropped him off at his father's so that she could use his car to run errands. It was the last time, he said, that he ever saw her. Not that he didn't try.

Suspecting that Diane was really going to meet another man, Gene Keidel said he left his father's house later that night on foot to check up on her. On the way to his former home, he called and spoke to his eldest daughter, Susan, who told him her mother was not home. According to his story, he continued walking until he reached the home about midnight. His car was gone and the children were home alone.

"I fell asleep on the couch waiting for her to come home," he said. The next morning, he said, his car was in the driveway, but there was no sign of his wife.

The police were suspicious, yet there was no proof that Keidel was lying. Diane Keidel was officially listed as a missing person. Her children, with whom she had been very close, were told by their father that she had abandoned them.

Reynolds related to the group how Lori Keidel had come to him twenty-five years later and told him what she believed about where her mother was buried, and her suspicions about the deaths of her sisters. He hoped that some detective in the room would have an idea on how to break the case.

Again he was disappointed. Everyone agreed that Gene Keidel had killed and buried his wife. An FBI profiler said that if Keidel was a killer, the murders of his wife and two daughters wouldn't be the only black marks in his past. "He's probably committed numerous crimes for which he's never been caught." No one, however, had a clue on "how to see through concrete."

Reynolds returned from the seminar with mixed emotions. On one hand, Rivers's unit demonstrated that cold cases could be approached methodically and solved by something other than a phone call out of the blue or a lucky break. A plan. But he found himself right where he had started on the Keidel case. If it was going to be solved, he would have to find a way on his own.

There were two possible avenues of investigation: the disappearance of Diane Keidel, and the fire that claimed the lives of Susan and Kelly Keidel. He decided to work both and see which one shook out first.

About the same time that Lori contacted him, she had located the firefighter who had pulled her from the burning house in 1967. Now she put him in contact with Reynolds.

Ray Mullins had been a rookie when he broke a window and entered the home, searching for the children said to be in there. He had seen a lot of tragedy in his years with the fire department, but that fire had stuck with him worse than most, he told Reynolds.

The fire broke out shortly after midnight. Firefighters had arrived on the scene within minutes; several, including Mullins, had risked their lives, and a couple were injured trying to get to the trapped children. The two older girls were pronounced dead at the scene. Lori was still alive but badly burned.

Even as rescuers were treating Lori, other fire and police investigators questioned Gene Keidel, whom they located standing in the crowd that had gathered. Two of his children lay dead in the grass, and yet he was unemotional, as if he were just another bystander. It had taken one of the neighbors to point him out as the father of the children.

Keidel said he was gone when the fire started, having left the children alone while he went to the laundromat. He theorized that Susan may have left a pot on the stove and forgotten to turn the burner off when she went to bed. The fire department arson investigator who went through the house the next day found that the stove was indeed turned on and there was a melted aluminum pot on it. The investigator was in a hurry; he had been given strict orders to reach a quick conclusion. The stove and melted pot seemed to back the father's statement. He officially labeled the cause accidental.

Mullins didn't believe it was accidental. One way to prove it, he told Reynolds, would be to find the autopsy reports of the two dead children. The sequence of events—from when Keidel said he left the house to when the call came into the fire station to when the children were brought from the home—had occurred over a matter of minutes. If that was true, the carbon monoxide levels in the children's bloodstreams could not have been very high—unless accelerants were used.

Unfortunately, because the fire was ruled accidental, the department had destroyed its records after seven years. The only records that remained of the fire investigation—and they were sparse reports—had been placed in the police department file for Diane Keidel.

At Mullins's suggestion, Reynolds tried to find the autopsy reports from the medical examiner's office, but was told that after twenty-five years, there was no way they still existed. With another angle to pursue, he took no for an answer.

Lori had told Reynolds that she believed that her father had buried her mother in the backyard. With the current owner's permission, they had gone over to the property and she had pointed to a spot near the back-left corner of the house. But was she right? She admitted that she had not actually seen her father dig a grave or put her mother's body in it.

However, it didn't take Reynolds long to learn that the story about a woman being buried in the backyard on West Citrus Way was also part of the neighborhood lore. He decided that the "right wind," his plan, would be to track the rumor down and find out where it had originated. Maybe he could find someone else to corroborate Lori's memories.

One of the things he had learned since picking up the Tovrea case was that in certain ways, the passage of time could actually help in a murder case that could not be solved soon after it occurred. For one thing, technologies that didn't exist even a few years earlier—such as DNA testing and computerized fingerprint matching—were now available. He also had learned that loyalties and fears often changed over the years. A witness who twenty years ago wouldn't talk to police or had lied, might now be willing to tell the truth.

The detective located Gene Keidel's second wife, Chloe. Gene had been an abusive, alcoholic husband, she said, and it had been good riddance when they divorced. She had her own suspicions about what had become of his first wife. In fact, she recalled several incidents during their marriage that led her to believe that her former husband had killed his first wife and buried her the backyard.

Keidel had used insurance money from the deaths of his two children and from his homeowner's policy to rebuild the home. But bad business decisions forced him to sell the house in 1971. According to Chloe, not long after the sale, they had gone back to the house to pick up a rollaway bed they'd loaned the new owner. However, when they got out of the car, they could hear the sound of a jackhammer coming from the back.

Gene, she said, had run through the house as if he still owned it. In the backyard, he found the new owner trying to break through the concrete because he wanted to install a Jacuzzi. Her husband quickly told the man that he shouldn't dig in that spot because of electrical wires and the plumbing. He suggested another spot and even volunteered to help, which he later did.

Chloe told the detective about an earlier incident in which she had wanted to plant roses in an area near the pool, to hide the pump from view. Her husband had come unglued. He threatened to kill her, and it was then she realized that the neighborhood rumors might be true; maybe Diane was buried beneath the concrete.

"I never told anybody," she said to Reynolds, "because I did not want to believe she was really dead and that my husband had killed her."

Reynolds knew that he had to take what Chloe told him with a grain of salt. It was obvious she held no affection for her former husband and was frightened of him. But the area of the backyard where Chloe indicated the Jacuzzi and rose incidents occurred was where Lori had pointed. The trail was getting warmer, but he still needed to find out where the rumor had started.

Eventually, he traced it to Gene Keidel's boss at the time of Diane's disappearance. It was a long time ago, the former boss said, but he recalled that Keidel had taken a day off from work and borrowed company equipment to pour concrete over his entire backyard. The boss said he had joked with Keidel in front of the other workers. "What'd you do, Gene, kill your wife and bury her in the backyard?" They had all laughed—even Gene. Everybody knew Diane had been messing around behind Gene's back and then left him with the kids. But murder? However, after the house burned down and the kids died, the joke became a rumor and the rumor took on a life of its own.

There was no direct corroboration of Lori's story, though certainly the timing of the concrete work was more than just a little suspicious. Reynolds knew he still didn't have enough to go ripping up the backyard on West Citrus Way. Neither was the case strong enough to try prosecuting Keidel for a bodyless homicide.

He wasn't about to give up, though. There was something particularly evil about this case, more than the others he was investigating. He believed Tovrea's death was a contract murder—cold-blooded to be sure, but at least it was done by a stranger. The Navajo girl's death was terrible, but from what he was beginning to learn from family members of the suspect, the suspect hadn't meant to kill the girl.

For Keidel to kill his wife and bury her in the backyard, then set a fire to kill his own children to cover up the first crime . . . How could any man live with that? Unless the killer was a man evil enough to watch passively as the burned bodies of his children were laid on the grass outside his home.

But suspicions and hunches weren't worth squat in court, especially when he didn't have Diane Keidel's body to prove she was even dead. What he really needed was Superman's X-ray vision so he could see through 6 inches of concrete.

There was no doubt in his mind that Diane Keidel was dead, but he couldn't assume a jury would see it that way. For one thing, there were reports that she had been seen since her disappearance. Her son, Greg, while a student at the University of Arizona, reported having been approached by a mysterious woman who he believed was his mother. Someone else claimed to have seen her on the television game show *Let's Make a Deal*.

Reynolds had to run down each and every lead. He asked Lori, who was in contact with her mother's family back in the Midwest, to ask if any of them had any reason to believe Diane was alive. But there was nothing, including when Diane's mother had died and her daughter might have been expected to show up.

He talked to Diane's former friends. They said she had been to see her divorce lawyer before going to meet with her estranged husband. Diane had said the breakup was "getting messy," especially over custody of the kids.

Ray Mullins located the arson investigator who had ruled the fire an accident. He and Reynolds went to talk to him together. The man, now retired, said the case had haunted him his entire career.

There had been indications that the fire was set deliberately, he said. The firefighters at the scene claimed the fire was burning from the floor up, unusual if it had started 4 feet up on the wall behind the stove. Also, they had reported that the fire had spread very quickly, which suggested that a flammable liquid, or accelerant, had been present. The arson investigator had noted that the point of origin and "hot spot" of the fire was approximately 10 feet from the stove.

It didn't fit with Gene Keidel's story. But the stove was on and the aluminum pot was melted. Told to finish his report quickly, he had ruled it accidental—and had to live with it ever since.

Reynolds tried to get the Phoenix Fire Department to reopen its case. He hoped they would assign it to Ray Wilson, whom he considered the best of their arson investigators. But the higher-ups gave it to a guy who was about to be medically retired from the department and wasn't particularly interested. He moved about as quickly as Lori's missing turtle.

The detective took it upon himself to go back to the medical examiner's office to see if the autopsy records could be found. Instead of just talking to some clerk, he asked to speak to the woman in charge of the records. He told her the whole story, and by the time he was finished, she was in tears.

"You know, there is a box down there that I've never looked inside of," she said. "Let's go look."

The detective followed her to the old-records room, where they found the box. The very top file turned out to be the medical examiner's report on the deaths of Susan and Kelly Keidel. Sure enough, the carbon monoxide in their blood was very high—too high given the timeframe, unless accelerants had been used.

Throughout his investigation, Ed Reynolds kept Lori Keidel Romaneck informed of what he was doing. They talked nearly every day. She would begin the conversation: "Hello, how are you? Have you found my mother?" But her remarks were not meant to needle the detective or express dissatisfaction with the speed of his investigation. They were a measure of the faith she had placed on the big man's shoulders to carry her burden.

Lori couldn't recall every detail of the last time she had seen her mother. Reynolds didn't want her taking any special measures to improve her memory. Early on, he had cautioned her not to undergo hypnosis. He had made the mistake once of taking a witness with a patchy memory to a hypnotist to see if that might improve the witness's recall. Back then, he was unaware of court cases in which defense attorneys had shown that hypnotists could, consciously or unconsciously, suggest, or plant, memories of events that had never occurred but which on waking, would be remembered as if they had. He nearly lost the use of that witness on those grounds.

It was going to be tough enough to make a case against Gene Keidel, if a case could be made, based on what a 5-year-old child had witnessed twenty-five years before. Arguing with a defense attorney over whether those memories were real or planted wasn't going to help.

Without any such outside help, Lori was able to contribute to the investigation. In one instance, Reynolds had heard the rumor that Diane Keidel had been buried beneath the swimming pool in the backyard. The rumor seemed to gain substance when he talked to a man who had helped install the pool. The man's job was to prepare the foundation for the bottom of the pool by placing rebar in the hole over which concrete would be poured. The man recalled a curious incident at the Keidel house. The day after he had placed the rebar, he returned to finish the job and discovered that someone had moved some of the rebar, dug a hole, and then filled it back in. He remembered because he had had to replace the rebar. The man said he didn't think anything of it at the time. But now that the detective mentioned it, there was something suspicious about the occurrence.

Thinking he may have hit on something, Reynolds asked Lori if she knew when the pool was built. Lori produced an old family movie that showed Diane Keidel swimming in what was then a new pool. If someone or something was buried beneath the pool now, it wasn't her mother.

Reynolds was running out of leads to chase. He needed a body, or at least a way of looking under concrete without removing it. But no one seemed to know how to go about doing that. He asked the U.S. Army Corps of Engineers. He thought they might have some sort of equipment they used to look for land mines or buried explosives, but that was a dead end. He checked with the Bureau of Reclamation, whose engineers, he had been told, used X rays to check concrete dams for weaknesses and fractures, but again, they said they had nothing to help him.

In the spring of 1994, he attended a one-day seminar on the "Medical/Legal Investigation of Death" at Arizona State University with more than 150 other homicide detectives from all over the Southwest. The conference ended with an open forum in which any of the participants could ask questions of their fellow officers.

Reynolds stood up and talked a little bit about the Keidel case. "Does anybody have any knowledge of a device that can look under concrete?" he asked. Surely with so many homicide detectives, someone had to have heard of something, he thought.

One detective said he had heard of some device involving explosions set off at two different points, and a sonar reading made of the ground in between. He didn't know what the device was called or where he had heard of it. Reynolds couldn't imagine being allowed to blow up the backyard of a home in a Phoenix neighborhood, anyway.

Another detective suggested drilling holes in the concrete and then seeing if a cadaver dog might be able to detect the scent of decomposition. Reynolds thought that might work, but again it might look like a fishing expedition if he started drilling holes here and there. Also, what if he missed the grave by a couple of feet and the dog didn't catch a scent? It wouldn't mean Diane wasn't there.

Reynolds had hoped there was something more definitive and even less intrusive. The owner of the home, a real estate investor, had been cooperative so far. He was anxious to disprove the rumor that there was a dead woman buried in the yard, so that he could sell the house. Everytime he had a tenant or potential buyer, it seemed, a neighbor would drop by and bring up the old story. But he might not take kindly to having a bunch of holes drilled if nothing were to be found.

Reynolds couldn't quit, but he wasn't sure where else to turn until he thought of an old friend with the FBI.

In May, he called Steve Chenoweth, the FBI's agent-in-charge of the Phoenix office. They had known each other for years, ever since they worked together on a gang task force. He told his friend about his frustrations. "They're not going to let me dig up the concrete without something more," he said. Did Chenoweth have any ideas—maybe some newfangled device the FBI had stashed away?

"Normally, I would have told you no," Chenoweth replied. But he'd just returned from a seminar in Quantico, where one of the lecturers was a scientist named Clark Davenport. "He uses something called ground-penetrating radar that I think can look under concrete."

As a matter of fact, the FBI had one of the machines, too, Chenoweth said. But the bureau was so busy with its own cases, it wasn't lending it out.

Davenport, on the other hand, belonged to a group called Necro-Search International, which apparently was formed to help police agencies locate the remains of murder victims.

"Why don't you call Davenport and tell him what you got?" Chenoweth suggested

September 12, 1994, Phoenix, Arizona

"How confident are you the body's there?" Clark Davenport asked the big detective in the lobby of the hotel. He was looking for the sort of response that he felt couldn't be gauged from the NecroSearch questionnaires, but only face to face.

Just the day before, a Saturday, he had asked a detective in nearby Scottsdale the same question and knew right away that locating anything was going to be a long shot. The detectives at the scene were all ready to go; they wanted to see this marvelous new technology at work. But the answer to his question was nebulous at best—a big *maybe*.

The Scottsdale case, which had been presented to NecroSearch in July, involved a 7-year-old boy who had been reported missing twenty years earlier. His twin brother had recently come forward to tell the police that he had seen his father beat his brother to death. He claimed that he remembered his father installing a wading pool in the backyard a few days after the murder.

It wasn't just the way the detective answered his question that had dampened Davenport's enthusiasm. Before leaving Colorado, he had asked the Scottsdale detectives to get aerial photographs of the alleged crime scene from the tax assessor's office. They didn't know such things existed and then delayed getting them until just before his arrival. He took a quick look, and it was just what he feared. The detectives could give him a timeline of what the suspect had been doing around the time of the boy's disappearance, but no one had run a timeline for the alleged crime scene. The photographs showed that the wading pool had been installed a year before the boy disappeared.

Davenport sighed over another lesson learned the hard way. Next time, he thought, *insist* that he get the required materials in hand before leaving Denver. There wasn't much point, but he still passed the GPR over the drained pool in the Scottsdale backyard. For good measure, and because he might have gotten lucky, he went over the entire backyard. There was nothing that couldn't be explained—just pipes and wires.

As he went to sleep that night, Davenport wondered if he would ever experience the kind of satisfaction some of his NecroSearch colleagues had been experiencing. Early the next morning, there was no reason to believe his luck had changed. He was tired from the previous day's search and ruing that he hadn't insisted that the Phoenix detective send him aerial photographs beforehand, too. When he asked the detective if he was confident a body had been buried at the site, he felt his spirits rise with the answer.

"Absolutely," Ed Reynolds responded.

Davenport looked in the other man's eyes. They were about the same height, though Reynolds was younger and heavier. But it was the eyes said this detective knew what he was talking about.

On the ride over to the site, Reynolds told him a little about what he had learned since receiving Lori's letter. Davenport asked for the aerial photographs and was relieved when Reynolds produced them— and even more relieved to see that the victim had indeed disappeared before the concrete was poured over the backyard.

Interpreting aerial photographs was something else he had grown accustomed to in Vietnam. He had looked at them before every mission to understand the maps, and quickly learned to identify man-made additions to the natural landscape, such as trails, as well as potential ambush sites. He had used those skills in his work as a geophysicist and brushed up on them some more out at the PIG site, learning what to look for that might indicate a grave, such as missing vegetation and disturbed soil.

He should have known that this detective would have his act together. After that initial call back in May, they had talked several more times, and each time Reynolds had impressed him. Except for the photographs, he had known the answer to every question Davenport had.

Reynolds wasn't even going to need any other sort of Necro-Search assistance. He had explained that he was already trained in clandestine grave excavation. And, he said, the Maricopa County medical examiner had recently hired a forensic anthropologist to help with any possible identification issues. All he needed was a way to look under concrete without having to tear it up first.

While Davenport was sizing him up, Reynolds was doing the same thing to him. He thought the scientist looked like a real "techno-nerd," but he had already run into the famous Davenport humor on the telephone and liked the man.

When they first talked, the detective expected to hear that Chenoweth was mistaken. After all, if the U.S. Army Corps of Engineers couldn't help, how could this group, NecroSearch? The name sounded a bit on the morbid side, and the first thing he had thought when he heard it was *necrophilia;* after all, he dealt with all sorts of strange people. But he didn't care how strange these people were if they could help.

Davenport was very positive about the possibilities. Six inches of concrete wouldn't be a problem for GPR, he had said. At the same time, the detective appreciated that the scientist didn't claim to work miracles.

"I can't really *look* under concrete," Davenport had explained. "It won't even be able to tell me if an anomaly is caused by an object, unless it's made of metal. . . . It *can* tell me if soil has been removed and put back in."

Whatever its limitations, the technology sounded better than anything else Reynolds had heard about. He was no stranger to the forensic sciences, including those that went beyond the scope of normal police work, such as fingerprints or firearms testing. He was aware of the work of forensic entomologists and botanists. Along with several other homicide detectives, he had taken a course in forensic anthropology at the University of Arizona to learn proper grave excavation.

However, forensic geophysics had been new to him, at least until Davenport explained what it could and could not do. Still, he hadn't held out much hope that he would see it at work. Ground-penetrating radar: even the name sounded expensive, and probably more than his superiors would okay for a 28-year-old case. He didn't try to conceal his surprise when Davenport said he would be happy to help at no charge other than travel expenses plus room and board. Even the transportation costs could be split with the police department in Scottsdale, the scientist said, though that had taken a couple months to work out.

Davenport had seemed more concerned about whether Reynolds had done his homework than how he would get compensated. In those early conversations, the scientist had asked a lot of questions, and it had become quickly evident that the detective was being tested to make sure this was not some stab in the dark.

He was really impressed when Davenport asked him to get aerial photographs from the city offices. No one at the police academy, nor any detective since, had told him that such things even existed. He was already sure that the pool was installed before Diane disappeared and the concrete poured afterward; the photographs confirmed it beyond any doubt.

Before Davenport's arrival, Reynolds contacted the current owner of the home on West Citrus Way and asked for permission to bring the scientist and his equipment onto the property. The owner was more than happy to allow the search.

At the home, Davenport got right to work. He said the first thing he needed to do was calibrate the instrument. To Reynolds's consternation, he chose the spot near the back-right corner of the house that Lori had pointed out as the place she believed was her mother's grave. The detective didn't know quite what to do.

As interested as he was in the concept behind NecroSearch, it did not make its members law enforcement professionals, even with Chenoweth's recommendation. Maybe to keep himself from getting too excited, he half thought of Davenport as a sort of high-tech psychic. Most so-called psychics were simply good at turning around information they had gathered by less dubious means and changing it just enough for it to sound as though it had come to them out of the blue.

Now, if he suggested that Davenport calibrate his instrument somewhere else, it might clue him in, just as it would a perceptive psychic. So he stayed quiet and waited to see what would happen.

Davenport worked for a few minutes, then stopped and scratched his head. "God, I hate when that happens," he said.

Reynolds's heart jumped into his throat. He tried to sound as uninterested as possible when he asked what was wrong.

"Well, if I didn't know better, we got a pretty good anomaly right here," Davenport replied.

It was all Reynolds could do not to say something. But he managed and instead just followed along, helping when needed, as Davenport ran his machinery over the entire backyard and across the floors of an addition to the house that had been built after the fire.

At one point, Lori came out to the house, accompanied by Mullins. They were introduced to Davenport, who paused to explain how GPR worked. They didn't stay long; Lori had just wanted to thank him for helping. "It means an awful lot," she said.

Davenport smiled, but in all honesty he was more comfortable when she left. He could still recall the disappointment and betrayal on the face of the brother when the "two barrels" beneath the floor of the warehouse in 1985 turned out to be a metal joint and a boulder. He wasn't overselling the technology, nor did he expect the detectives to start excavating immediately while he was there. But Lori's presence clouded the issue for him. He was a scientist working on a problem, not a cause.

Moving quickly, Davenport was finished by mid-afternoon. After that, he drew the detective a sketch map of the backyard showing where he had encountered four anomalies. Using the GPR readouts, he pointed out how the sites on the map corresponded to the instrument's charts. In that way, he was able to demonstrate that three of the four anomalies had logical explanations—sewer pipes and electrical lines, equipment for the pool.

There was one anomaly, though, that he had no explanation for: the anomaly he had discovered when he was trying to calibrate the instrument. By the readout, he said, it appeared to be 2 feet wide by 6 feet long, with a depth of about 2½ feet.

"I can't tell you that's a grave," Davenport said, "but if I were going to dig, that's where I'd start." With that, he packed his instrument and was ready to be taken to the airport.

Reynolds drove and thanked him for his time. He didn't tell him that he had picked the spot where a little girl had once spread bread crumbs, hoping her mother would wake up.

On the way back from the airport, Reynolds's mind was already preoccupied with the next step: getting his bosses to okay tearing up a certain spot in the former Keidel backyard. Thanks to Davenport, he thought he had the ammunition he needed.

The next morning, armed with the scientist's charts and map, he went to ask his supervisor, Lt. Sherry Kiyler, for permission to start excavating. Just as Davenport had explained it to him, he now explained to Kiyler how the equipment worked and what the disturbance of the lines—the soil horizons—on the GPR readout meant. There was no guarantee that it was a grave, but this was as close as he was going to get. If he was turned down, he didn't know what else he could do. Kiyler told him to go ahead.

Right away, Reynolds arranged for a city street crew to show up at the house to remove the concrete over the anomaly Davenport had marked "Number 1." The crew arrived with their jackhammer and gave him strange looks when he said he wanted them to work carefully and stop as soon as they cracked the concrete. Above all, he said, don't run the jackhammer into the ground. And they were going to have to pull each broken piece out by hand—no heavy equipment. It would take twice as long, but that was how he wanted it done.

Reynolds had his reasons for being so particular. He had contacted anthropology professor Chuck Merbs at Arizona State University and explained what was going on. Merbs told him that one of the important things to consider was the timeframe between the burial and when the concrete was poured.

If it had been a year in between, Merbs said, the body would have decomposed and the dirt sunk into the space created. The killer would have noticed and then probably backfilled the depression to bring it level with the surface before pouring the concrete.

However, if Reynolds was correct about the concrete having been laid down shortly after the burial, Merbs said, there should be a hollow space beneath the slab. That being the case, the detective needed to be extra careful when removing the concrete so as not to disturb the outline of the grave, which would tell him exactly where to dig. Also, there was a danger that any remains might be exposed or covered by very little dirt; with nothing to block its plunge, a jackhammer could rip into the evidence.

It took the crew a couple of hours to remove an 8-by-9-foot section of concrete. There in the dirt, Reynolds could clearly see a depression 3 to 9 inches in depth, 2 feet wide, and 6 feet long. It looked like a grave.

At last it was time to put his anthropology classwork to work. Reynolds already had his excavation crew assembled. Detectives Dennis Olson and Randy Chapman would excavate while Frank Dimodica and Joyce Snodgrass sifted. Reynolds would monitor the whole process. Despite Davenport's charts and now the depression, he was still nervous. If they didn't find anything, he would be the goat, and like the little boy who cried wolf, no one would believe him the next time. The owner had given permission to do this, so long as the city paid to restore everything. The bean counters weren't going to like it if nothing was found.

The team began by dividing the site into grids. Then they excavated the grids using teaspoons and brushes. Every ounce of dirt that came out of the hole went into a bucket, where it was labeled as to which grid it had come from.

The next step was to sift the material through a screen. However, they ran into a problem. The lab exercises for the excavation classes they had taken were done in the desert, where the soil was sandy and easily sifted. The soil in the former Keidel backyard was dense clay and wouldn't pass through the screen. They came up with the idea of using a garden hose and pouring water on the material in the screen. That way, the soil passed through and other items were left behind. Soon Demodica and Snodgrass were soaked to the bone.

A little more than an hour into the dig, Detective Chapman struck something hard. "That was a skull," he told the others, "I can tell by the sound." Carefully, using brushes, the dirt was cleared away. Six inches below the surface from where they had started was the white top of a skull.

As he looked at what he was sure was Diane Keidel's mortal remains, Reynolds felt a rush of exhilaration. After working thousands of hours on this and the other cold cases, he now knew it had not been a waste. But he kept his emotions in check; this wasn't the time to make a mistake and miss something.

The detectives quickly got back to work and, if anything, were even more careful. Every bit of potential evidence found in the grids was saved and catalogued with the exact measurements of where it had come from and at what depth it had been located. At every step, the detectives took dozens of photographs.

Detective Mark Stribling, who had kept his friend Reynolds in the academy, showed up to help. He was assigned to sifting with Snodgrass and was soon just as wet. The work was hard and dirty, but not without its moments of levity. At one point, Stribling was hosing down a new batch when he spotted a piece of crumpled paper. Excited to have perhaps discovered some crucial piece of evidence, he carefully opened the note on which was written, "Sift faster! Diane." The others broke out laughing at the joke, and after a moment of confusion, Stribling laughed, too.

By late afternoon, the detectives stood around a hole in the ground, looking at a complete skeleton lying on its back. Whatever clothing had been present was now mostly gone except for those items composed of manmade materials, such as the elastic in the underwear, bra, and garter belts. A hanger and an old pre-1966 penny were found in the grave. But what demanded everyone's attention were two nylon stockings, knotted and wrapped around the skeleton's neck.

That evening, the press got wind of the story while the detectives were still in the backyard with the exposed skeleton. Soon helicopters were hovering overhead and a crowd had gathered in the street outside the home. The "woman buried in the backyard" had been a neighborhood rumor for a long time, and now it looked as though it was more truth than rumor.

Reynolds became concerned that Gene Keidel would get wind of the investigation. He decided he needed to have his suspect picked up, but they had to be careful. The FBI profiler at the cold case squad's seminar back in 1993 had warned him that Keidel might be dangerous to himself or others if he thought he was going to be arrested. The detective had other reasons to believe it was a possibility.

A few days before Davenport arrived in Phoenix, Lori told Reynolds that her brother, Greg, had confronted his father about the detective's investigation. Gene Keidel's response was an angry one.

"That cop needs to stop this, or I'll drop him if he comes to my house," he had shouted.

Whenever possible, Reynolds had asked Bob Ragsdale, the chief hostage negotiator for the Phoenix SWAT team, to pick up his fugitives. He and Ragsdale now agreed that the best tactic would be to trick Keidel into leaving his home. They didn't know whether he had access to guns, and they didn't want him to hole up in his house.

Ragsdale came up with an idea that rivaled anything Reynolds and Gregory had used in their days of chasing fugitives. Outside Keidel's home that afternoon, Ragsdale and his team made a big show of arresting a man and placing him in the back of a police cruiser. One of the team members then went up to Keidel's house and knocked on the door. When he opened it, the SWAT team officer explained that they had caught a man (actually a plainclothes member of the team) prowling around his house. They wanted him to walk over to the cruiser to see if he could identify the man.

Gene Keidel left his house but quickly found that he was the one the police wanted handcuffed in the back of the cruiser. Ragsdale reported back to Reynolds that his suspect looked dumbfounded when he was arrested—the look of a man who thought he had gotten away with murder twenty-eight years ago.

The next morning, Maricopa County medical examiner, Dr. Philip Keen, arrived at the scene to discuss how to remove the remains. When he saw the nylons, he cautioned the detectives that it was very important to find a tiny neck bone called the hyoid.

"Document exactly where in the grave you find it," he said. If the person in the grave was indeed strangled with the nylon garrote, the hyoid would probably be fractured, helping him establish the cause of death.

Now that word of the excavation was out, everybody wanted to see the grave, including the police chief. But Reynolds wasn't breaking the rules for anyone; only necessary personnel were allowed into the backyard. Instead, a platform was built in the yard next door for viewing the last steps in the recovery of the skeleton.

Not all of the visitors were officials. Reynolds had called Lori Keidel Romaneck the night before and told her the news. She came out to the house in the morning and wanted to see the reality of the nightmare that had haunted her for so many years. The detective wouldn't let her, though. He didn't want her to see her mother in the grave dug by her father.

After she left, the bones were carefully removed from the grave and placed on a sterile sheet. It was then folded and placed in a black body bag and taken to Keen's office by a mortuary vehicle.

After the major bones were removed, the excavation team continued to work until every last bit of evidence was removed and they got down to sterile soil. In the bucket of soil taken from directly beneath where the neck had been, they found the hyoid bone. It was fractured. That afternoon, the Diane Keidel case was changed from a missing person to a homicide.

With all the comings and goings, it was some time before Reynolds could catch his breath and take stock of how he was feeling about the sudden success. For years, he had believed that there must have been a reason, perhaps some divine force, behind his being a cop. Some explanation why he had refused to give up at the academy, or why he made detective when it seemed there were more-qualified applicants. Now he understood that this was why—and not just for Lori or Diane Keidel. But for Jeanne Tovrea and the little Navajo girl and all those who would come after. He knew this could not be the end, but a catalyst to get even better—and never to quit on a case.

It was a moving experience, and he was exhausted. But he still had another call to make, this one to the wise-cracking scientist who had made it possible.

That evening, Clark Davenport was at home watching television while his wife talked to one of the kids on the telephone. He heard her interrupt her conversation to take an incoming call. "I'll have him call you in a few minutes," she told whoever it was. When she finished her call, she told him that the caller had identified himself as a sergeant with the Phoenix Police Department. He wanted Davenport to call as soon as possible.

Davenport called and got through to the sergeant. "Detective Reynolds would like to speak to you," the man said, pausing before adding, "but he can't because he's crying. However, he wants you to know that he found Diane Keidel right where you said to look."

The geophysicist tried to imagine the big detective in tears and couldn't, not that he would blame him if he was. In their phone conversations and their short time together, he had recognized that there was something special about Reynolds, something he hadn't noticed even in some of the better detectives he had met in recent years.

Davenport had heard the stories from his fellow NecroSearch members about their admiration for the tenacity and dedication of Gunnison's Kathy Young. He had been equally impressed by Reynolds. The detective was as professional as they came, and as talented. Maybe it was knowing how deeply the man cared about the victim that made him special. *Or victims,* he thought, remembering Lori.

Stunned, Davenport thanked the sergeant and hung up. All this time, he had believed in the technology. But now all he could think was, *It worked; it really worked!* Unaware that a detective in Phoenix was making the same pledge, Davenport told himself that this success was just a wake-up call to do even better the next time. Grieving people like Lori, detectives like Ed Reynolds, victims like Diane Keidel were counting on him and his colleagues.

It was a sobering thought, so when he picked up the telephone and called Jack Swanburg, there was no shout of "Eureka!" "I just got a call from Phoenix," he said quietly, "and we were a success." We, he thought, because no matter who went out into the field, that person represented the collective brain trust at NecroSearch International.

THE TRIAL

March 1995, Phoenix, Arizona

The trial of Lyle "Gene" Keidel pitted two of the top trial lawyers in Arizona against each other. Deputy District Attorney John Ditsworth on one side; defense attorney Tom Henze on the other.

Henze had a reputation for winning lengthy and complex trials. He didn't come cheap. But Keidel's girlfriend convinced her mother to remortgage her home to pay what would amount to $65,000 for his defense.

Henze let the state know long before the trial began that they were going to be in for a fight, first by trying to convince Maricopa County Judge J. Kenneth Mangum that the case should be dismissed because too many years had gone by. The passage of time "did not merely dim witnesses' memories," he contended, "those memories were dissipated, altered, and in many cases were obliterated."

Ditsworth countered that just because Keidel had gotten away with murder for nearly thirty years, it didn't mean he should be forgiven and excused. The jury should decide the credibility of the witnesses. The state won the argument and Mangum decided the case would proceed.

Henze won the next round when he argued to the judge that the jury should not hear about the house fire that had killed Susan and Kelly Keidel. The tragedy would unfairly sway the emotions of the jury, who would be led by the prosecution to believe that Gene Keidel was responsible for the deaths of two of his children, he said.

Ditsworth and Henze also fought over whether Romaneck should be allowed to testify about her father beating her. Lori had told

Reynolds that she kept her secret about the last time she saw her mother because she was "paralyzed" with fear. She had said that as she was growing up, he repeatedly told her, "I brought you into the world, and I can take you out."

In particular, Ditsworth wanted her to be able to testify about the times her father beat her with a boat oar and a board. Such allegations, he argued, were admissible as evidence of "prior bad acts" committed by Keidel against his daughter, which had frightened her into silence.

Again Henze countered that such evidence, especially with no corroborating witnesses, could prevent the jury from deciding his client's fate solely on the evidence regarding the case for which he was being tried. The judge ruled in favor of the defense.

With those issues out of the way, the opposing sides were at last ready for trial. Thanks to NecroSearch, the biggest obstacle for the prosecution wasn't the lack of a body. However, as Henze was sure to note at trial, the identity of that body was still in question.

It wasn't from a lack of effort. Reynolds had begun by trying to date the age of the grave. He had saved pieces of a tree root that had grown through the chest of the skeleton, which he took to a dendrochronologist, a specialist in using the rings of trees to determine age. The scientist said that the roots were about 15 years old. Certainly, not as old as Reynolds had hoped, but pushing the age of the grave back to when Keidel still owned the house.

In trying to decide where to turn next, Reynolds and Ditsworth thought about the evidence they had, particularly the garter belt and nylon stockings. They wondered if those items might hold a clue. They located an expert in clothing history, particularly women's undergarments. He was able to tell them that panty hose, which had pretty much done in the everyday wear of nylon stockings and garters, were not introduced to Arizona until after 1966. It wasn't conclusive evidence, but the detective and prosecutor knew that some puzzles are completed by the assembly of many small pieces.

The evidence, along with common sense, said the bones were Diane's, but the threshold for juries is "beyond a reasonable doubt." The prosecution was going to need as many pieces of the puzzle as possible, some more of which were provided by Lori's memories.

During the excavation, the detectives found five "gobs" of rust about a half inch in diameter. Reynolds took these to criminalist Lee Garrett, who removed the rust one flake at a time to reveal that the "gobs" were actually metal buttons.

Garrett showed him how the buttons had been manufactured in two pieces, then snapped together with the material between. None of the material from around the buttons had survived. But by prying apart the buttons, Garrett found a few cotton threads inside. The threads were dark blue, and Reynolds knew they had found evidence of the "coat dress" Lori remembered her mother wearing. But would a jury be convinced?

Reynolds hoped that modern science would be able to remove any lingering doubts. A cross-section of bone was removed from one of the femurs. The femur was one of the thickest bones in the body, and the most likely to have preserved a large enough chunk of marrow for DNA testing.

DNA is the large molecule in human cells that contains the genetic information that makes each person unique. It contains four chemicals, called nucleotides, that fit together like teeth in a zipper. They are arranged in pairs, and it is the sequence of these pairs that makes one person different from another. Except for identical twins, no two people have the same sequence.

Laboratories can compare sequences: The more that match between two samples, the fewer the number of people that are likely to have the same sequences in any given population. Family members have more similarities than would unrelated people. Thus, the laboratories can compare the DNA of one person to establish, or discount, that person's relationship to another. In this instance, it was hoped that DNA from the skeleton could be shown to be from a person related to Lori.

The study of these genetic fingerprints is a prime example of how the passage of time could actually aid criminal investigations. When Diane Keidel disappeared, DNA testing didn't exist. It wasn't until 1987, even as the idea for Project PIG was coming together, that serial rapist Tommy Lee Andrews became the first American convicted by DNA evidence.

However, in the Keidel case, time had also worked against Detective Reynolds. The marrow inside the femur had decomposed due to bacteria and the moist conditions of the soil. It couldn't be tested.

* * *

The trial began March 1. The atmosphere in and around the courthouse took on the aura of a heavyweight title bout, complete with the accompanying media circus. The national press was in town, intrigued by a nearly thirty-year-old murder case and the skeleton found in a backyard.

In his opening argument, Ditsworth admitted that much of the state's case would rely on the memories of Lori Keidel Romaneck. But those memories were "vivid," he said, and, also important, not the product of hypnosis.

"She never told, but she never forgot what happened that night. But it took until nineteen ninety-three for her to gather the courage" and write a letter to the police.

It was that letter that eventually led police to excavate the skeleton of Diane Keidel in her family's former backyard, he said. They would hear how that came about through the testimony of a geophysicist from a group called NecroSearch. Among the findings of that excavation: "Two nylon stockings—tied and knotted around the throat—that caused death by strangulation."

The murder, the prosecutor said, was motivated by Gene Keidel's jealousy and anger over his wife's infidelities. After the jurors examined the evidence, he said, he was confident they would return a verdict of guilty—guilty of first-degree murder.

When Ditsworth took his seat, Henze began his opening claiming that by September 1966, "Gene Keidel didn't have an emotional attachment to Diane." She had destroyed their marriage with her extramarital affairs and abortions, he said. The impending divorce, Henze contended, was "amicable." Gene Keidel had a girlfriend and was just as happy to be going his separate way. However, he noted ominously, Diane had four lovers, and one of them may have been jealous enough to kill her in a fit of rage.

Henze urged the jurors not to place too much importance on the remains found in the West Citrus backyard. He was leaving his options open until he heard the evidence and saw how the jury reacted to the witnesses. Then he could argue that the bones either weren't Diane's or that they were hers and someone else had killed her. For now, he left them with the question, "Can you know in nineteen ninety-five what happened in nineteen sixty-six?"

When he finished, the prosecution began its case. Keen testified that the placement of the stockings indicated the victim had been strangled; however, he had to concede that the hyoid bone could have been fractured postmortem. Garrett testified about the buttons and the blue cotton threads he had found inside, though the jury would be left to wonder about the significance of that until Lori's testimony.

Keidel's second wife, Chloe, testified about his panic when he heard the sound of a jackhammer coming from their former backyard, and his efforts to dissuade the new owner from installing a Jacuzzi where he planned. She also recalled his anger when she wanted to plant roses near the pool.

When it was time to attempt to positively identify the bones as belonging to Diane Keidel, the prosecution still had no absolute proof. The first attempt to get DNA from the leg bone of the skeleton had failed. Shortly before the trial, pulp from inside of one of the skull's molars was removed to see if it might contain enough material for DNA testing. But the results weren't going to be back in time. (After the trial, it was discovered that bacteria had rendered that test useless as well.) So the prosecution turned to forensic anthropologist Laura Fulginiti, who had recently been hired by the Maricopa County medical examiner.

Fulginiti testified that the skeleton found in the West Citrus Way backyard was that of a white woman in her mid-30s to mid-40s who stood about 5-feet-1—a description that matched Diane Keidel. The young anthropologist took it a step further with photographic superimposition, the process of overlaying a photograph of the victim when she was alive on that of the skull to see where the general outline of the head and eye sockets, nasal passages, ear holes, and teeth lined up.

Privately, Fulginiti told Reynolds that because of the photo superimposition she was "ninety-nine percent" convinced that the skull belonged to Diane Keidel. However, legally, she could only testify to an 80-percent certainty.

The use of photo superimposition was not accepted equally by all forensic anthropologists. Even under the best circumstances—a good selection of clear photographs and an undamaged skull—some argued there was a 10-percent margin for error. Many leading forensic anthropologists, such as NecroSearch's Diane France, believed the technique was best used to eliminate a person from consideration, rather than as positive identification. But it was another piece of the puzzle.

Reynolds took the stand to discuss his investigation. He was confident and glad to be finally able to talk about his efforts. He had tried to avoid the media crush—not an easy task with their constant calls for interviews—so as not to jeopardize the case.

At the same time, he was working nonstop. Trial all day, the working until eight or nine at night to get ready for the next day's witnesses and to go over strategy. After that there were the weekends; the Keidel murder wasn't the only case he'd managed to move from cold case to the front burner.

The Navajo girl's murder investigation was getting warm and the Tovrea case was red hot. In the meantime, the national and local press were all eager to interview the detective who had apparently solved a 30-year-old murder case. There was no way he could do his work and keep up with the media's demands, so he avoided them when possible.

When he did agree to an interview or quick statement, there was one point he stressed over and over again, and that was to praise NecroSearch. He truly believed that the case might never have gone to trial except for the assistance of Clark Davenport. Without a potential grave site pinpointed by the ground-penetrating radar, his bosses probably wouldn't have let him excavate. Without a body, it was doubtful whether murder charges would have been brought. This trial was probably going to be their only shot at Gene Keidel.

Shortly after Keidel's arrest in September 1994, Maricopa County Attorney Richard Romley praised the efforts of the police, saying it sent a message to Arizona criminals. "You may think you can get away with it at the time, but you won't."

Romley was not so kind to the Phoenix Fire Department, which he said had failed to properly investigate the January 1967 fire that killed two of the Keidel children. He went so far as to state publicly that an accelerant had been responsible for the quick spread of the fire. He called on the fire department to reopen the investigation.

Joe Bushong, the chief of the fire department's investigations division, agreed that the investigation needed to be reviewed. "The problem is, there is no physical evidence other than what the firefighters can remember and what was documented," he told the *Phoenix Gazette*. He turned the investigation over to Ray Wilson.

Together with Reynolds, Wilson found the woman who had been Gene Keidel's girlfriend at the time of Diane's disappearance. She said she had been there in 1966 when the investigator talked to her boyfriend. "He was lying through his teeth about what we did that day," she said. But the investigator hadn't asked her any questions, and she hadn't volunteered any information.

With the concurrence of medical examiner Keen, Wilson reclassified the report on the fire from "accidental" to "homicide by arson." Not that anything would ever come of it; a second trial would cost too much if they lost this one.

When Clark Davenport entered the courtroom and took his seat in the witness stand, he glanced to where the defendant sat. Keidel didn't look like a man who could have killed his wife and, possibly, two of his children. Then again, this was nearly thirty years later—and just what did a killer look like?

Earlier that morning, John Ditsworth had taken him into the courtroom to let him know where everyone would be sitting. The prosecutor said it was up to him whether to stay in the courtroom before his testimony or to wait in a sequestered room. Davenport decided to wait in the room. He didn't know much more than the basics of the case and preferred it that way; he didn't want to come off as biased.

It wasn't as if he was devoid of any feelings. He had been struck by the irony of Diane Keidel's disappearance in the fall of 1966; about the same time he was crawling through rice paddies and jungles trying to stay alive. Her death struck him as incredibly sad.

Still, he couldn't let his feelings influence his testimony. He was a scientist who had used the tools of his chosen field in an attempt to solve a problem. His pursuit was of the truth, not a criminal. If the truth sent a killer to prison and gave a young woman some sense of closure, those were just the beneficial byproducts.

Gene Keidel looked right through Davenport, as if what he had to say wasn't going to matter much. It didn't bother Davenport. Like Diane France in the Wallace case, he didn't feel it was his role to give an opinion on the defendant's guilt or innocence. It was his role to explain that finding the skeleton had involved a lot more than grabbing a shovel and digging. Tom Henze had intimated in his opening, and was sure to repeat in the main portion of the defense case, that there had been a "rush to justice" in charging his client with murder.

Davenport knew that it was important for him to convince the jurors that he was a professional, not an amateur or psychic, and that the search for Diane Keidel's body had been carried out as meticulously and scientifically as possible. On a larger scale, how he presented NecroSearch's involvement would reflect on Reynolds's entire investigation—no stone unturned, and every T crossed and I dotted. No rush to judgment, but only the fine, if sometimes slow, grinding of the wheels of justice.

Although this was his first time testifying in a court of law, he was not intimidated. By now, after all the seminars he had given to the FBI and other police agencies, he was used to explaining to lay people about geophysical technology and how it could be used to detect possible burial sites. He kept his eyes on the prosecutor when he was asked a question, then he turned to the jurors to answer. He explained what he had done in the former Keidel backyard as he would have lectured a group of college students about finding buried toxic waste. The technology he used couldn't find bodies, he said. "But it can tell me where to look."

As professional as he wanted to appear, Davenport couldn't resist letting his particular brand of humor slip into the proceedings. One of the diagrams he had supplied incorrectly labeled the compass directions. It didn't really matter to the case, but it had embarrassed the exacting nature of Davenport.

It was also something that needed to be cleared up for the jurors before Henze made a big deal of it. Ditsworth attempted to explain the error by pointing out that Davenport was used to getting his bearings in Colorado by the chain of the Rocky Mountains that ran north to south through the state.

"How do you usually know which way is west?" the prosecutor asked, expecting the scientist to say something to the effect that the mountains were due west of his home in Denver.

"That's the direction all the Californians come from," Davenport said with a smile.

Ditsworth looked stunned, but the jurors laughed. Later, outside the courtroom, the prosecutor shook his head and said, "Don't ever sandbag me again." But he was smiling and added that it was probably good for the jury to hear from a scientist who had a sense of humor.

Also waiting for him after his testimony was Lori Keidel Romaneck. She hugged him and said thanks. The first time he met her, he had been uncomfortable with having her at the scene. He hadn't wanted to raise her hopes and then see them dashed. Now that the search was a success, he felt proud of his part in bringing her some peace of mind.

Davenport went home without waiting for the end of the trial. On the flight back, he did a lot of thinking. It had always bothered him that the image many Americans had of Vietnam veterans was of homeless men in fatigues standing on street corners, or going over the edge and shooting people.

The truth was that the vast majority had come back to live normal, productive lives. They were guys who carried the mail, or built homes, or delivered babies. They were doctors, and lawyers, and cops—and guys who helped cops find bodies. Considering what he had been asked to do with his knowledge in Vietnam, he was happy that now he could use it to alleviate the pain and suffering of others.

Back in the Maricopa County Courthouse, Lori Keidel Romaneck took the witness stand wearing a dark-blue dress. Around her neck hung a heart-shaped locket.

For most of her life, she had tried to avoid the notice of her father—if he couldn't see her, he couldn't hurt her. She had been told that the mother she loved had simply walked away one night. Not a birthday card. Not a telephone call at Christmas. Just left her with the man who had tormented her throughout her childhood and, she believed, set the fire that killed her siblings. It was hard to say which had been crueler: the violence or his suggestion that her mother was willing to abandon her so easily.

Now, she was sworn in to "tell the truth, the whole truth," but not really. She wasn't to say a word about the fire that killed her sisters. She wasn't to tell the whole truth about her father's violence toward her. The truth was being edited.

She had often expressed, including to the press, that she feared her father's "violent retaliation." She did not attend any of the pretrial hearings, relying instead on victims' advocates to keep her apprised of decisions. Now, she kept her eyes on Ditsworth as he began to question her.

Lori described what she remembered of that night when she was 5 years old. The fight between her father and mother was brief, she said, her voice already cracking from the strain. He struck her, "and she curled up in a ball—just laying there." The courtroom was absolutely silent as she recalled the sound of someone digging in the backyard.

She told them about the disappearance of Touché, the turtle, and how that led her to spread bread crumbs for her mother "in case she woke up."

At the prosecution table, Reynolds felt proud of her. They had talked nearly every day since that first meeting. He had always found that what you saw was what you got with Lori. There was no game-playing, no vengeful recriminations against her father. The only coaching he and Ditsworth had done was to say, "Just tell the truth." He firmly believed that was what she was doing now, and he had never been in a courtroom so quiet.

"Why did you write the letter?" Ditsworth asked.

"It was part of my fears," Lori responded, a tissue in one hand to dab at the tears in her eyes. "I decided I would rather be dead than keep this secret."

"Was there any other reason?" Ditsworth probed gently.

It took Lori almost half a minute to compose herself enough to nod her head and answer. "Yes sir . . . I wanted to bury my mother."

When Ditsworth finished, it was the defense's turn to cross-examine Lori, but Henze announced that he had no questions. He wasn't even going to try to challenge the young woman's memory.

Neither did Henze try to claim during the defense portion of the trial that the skeleton in the backyard was anyone's but Diane Keidel's. Davenport and Fuljenetti were obviously knowledgeable in their fields. He had not tried to put on any expert witnesses to counter them.

In fact, the defense put on only few witnesses. Greg Keidel got on the stand and said he didn't believe his father would have killed his mother. But there were no former boyfriends or neighbors called to testify that someone else may have killed Diane. That was left to Gene Keidel himself.

In an unusual move, because it opens the defendant up to cross-examination, the 58-year-old Gene Keidel took the stand in his own defense. Soft-spoken, wearing a blue blazer, he calmly denied fighting with his wife the night before she disappeared. He said he had no idea why his daughter said the things she did.

But he changed his story from what he had originally told police. In 1966, he said that he had arrived at the house shortly after midnight, but his wife was gone, and he never saw her again. Now, he testified that he didn't even arrive at the house until some time after 4:00 A.M.

Questioned by Henze, Keidel portrayed himself as a man greatly wronged by his wife, who had carried on several affairs. Whatever feelings he might still have had left for his wife were erased nearly two years before she disappeared, when she had an abortion, he said.

"After you had a vasectomy?" Henze asked.

"Yes," Keidel replied, not showing much emotion one way or the other.

On cross-examination, Ditsworth attempted to use those same responses to show that the defendant had a motive to kill his wife. He asked Keidel if it was true that he had learned his wife was having sex with other men from the job when he overheard the others laughing about it.

"I do remember a situation like that," Keidel admitted matter-of-factly.

"And that didn't bother you?" Ditsworth asked incredulously.

"I was upset," Keidel shrugged, but his mouth twisted into a tiny smile when he added, "At that point, I figured there was nothing much I could do about it."

Shortly after beginning their deliberations, the jurors in the Keidel case took a poll to see where everyone stood. They were evenly split on whether to convict.

They all agreed that the skeleton in the grave was Diane Keidel's. The garter belts and stockings were convincing evidence as to the date of the grave, and the photographic superimposition sealed it for them. It was too great a stretch to believe that a different woman had been murdered and buried in that backyard. So the question was, who killed and buried her?

Those against were troubled about sending a man to prison for the rest of his life on the basis of what a 32-year-old woman thought she witnessed more than twenty-eight years earlier. It was obvious that Gene and Diane Keidel fought a lot. But even if Lori did see a confrontation, some argued, who knew if it had occurred the night before her father told his children that their mother had run off with another man?

Maybe Lori had combined different memories, they suggested. Diane was seeing a lot of men. Wasn't it possible that one of them killed her?

But, others argued, when would some other lover have had the opportunity to kill and bury Diane Keidel? Gene Keidel said he spent the night at the house, and then he moved in after she disappeared.

Even the jurors who weren't sure of Keidel's guilt had to admit that Lori's memories seemed amazingly detailed and accurate. The "gobs of rust" buttons had yielded blue cotton fibers, just like the dress she recalled. And she had pointed to the exact spot where she believed that her mother was buried. It had to be more than a coincidence that it would be the same place designated by that scientist, Clark Davenport, as the best place to dig.

Soon most of the jurors were inclined to find Keidel guilty. The last couple of holdouts were swayed by Keidel's changing accounts of what time he went to the house. It seemed to the jurors that he was trying to tailor his story to fit the evidence.

All told, it took less than a day of deliberation before the jurors returned with a guilty verdict. Lori emerged from the courtroom to face the media. After years of living in fear, she had finally told the truth and someone had listened. "I was not out to incarcerate my father," she said to the horde of reporters with their cameras and microphones. "I was merely out to bury my mother with respect."

After the Keidel trial, John Ditsworth and Ed Reynolds met with the jurors. They were highly complimentary of the way Ditsworth had laid out the evidence and led them one step at a time through each tiny bit of interconnecting evidence. They were also emotional and wanted to know more about things they suspected had been withheld from them at trial. For instance, why weren't Susan and Kelly Keidel called to the stand? When they heard the story of the fire, it helped cement the belief that they had done the right thing in convicting Gene Keidel.

The jurors didn't mention Davenport specifically. But Reynolds knew from their comments that much of what left an impression on the jurors during the trial—the remains, the nylons around the neck, the rusted buttons—probably wouldn't have been possible without the scientist. Reynolds called Davenport and thanked him again.

It was another call, though, that provided the inspiration for what would become something of a motto for NecroSearch. A few days after Keidel's conviction, a reporter with the *Wall Street Journal* called Davenport. The reporter asked if he felt happy about what he had helped accomplish.

Davenport paused. He wasn't sure how to describe what he felt. Pride, sure. A sense of having contributed to the community. Satisfaction that he had helped Lori find some closure. But happiness? No. If anything, the opposite: a sadness for all the lost and wasted lives, even that of Gene Keidel.

For the first but not the last time, Davenport shook his head and said, "There's no statute of limitations for murder, but there is also no statute of limitations for grief."

V

THE
CHER ELDER CASE

Empire, Colorado

By January 1995, Scott Richardson, a Harley-riding, cowboy-boot-wearing detective for the Lakewood police department, had logged over a thousand hours of paid time and maybe twice that on his own looking for Cher Elder, who had been reported missing on March 31, 1993. Richardson had been trying to pin her death on Tom Luther, a man he had pegged as her killer a month after she disappeared. Luther was the last one seen with Cher, at a casino in the mountain town of Central City, a former mining community. Luther denied it when confronted by Richardson, but the evidence continued to point to him.

Luther had been convicted ten years earlier of a brutal rape in which the woman was nearly beaten to death. At the time of the rape, he was also a suspect in two homicides near the ski town of Breckenridge, Colorado, but investigators there had been unable to pin them on him. He had been out of jail only a couple of months when Cher Elder disappeared.

Since then, Detective Richardson had talked to more than a thousand people, including crime lab technicians, Cher's family members and friends, and a wide assortment of drug dealers, liars, thieves, and convicts, as well as friends, associates, family members, enemies, and victims of Thomas Edward Luther. Among them was Deb Snider, a psychiatric nurse who had fallen in love with Luther while writing to him in the penitentiary. She was an odd character, torn between her love for Luther and her knowledge, Richardson believed, of what he really was—a sociopathic killer.

In August 1993, Deb Snider had finally confessed that Luther told her about Cher being killed and dumped by the side of the road by others, he said, because she was a police informant. The day after Richardson's first confrontation with Luther in April 1993, Snider said, her boyfriend had gone out to find and bury Cher. Luther told her that the grave was off Interstate 70 east of Denver, near a stone marker where people pulled over to walk their dogs.

Snider also told the detective about arriving at Luther's apartment after a vacation in March 1993 and finding him in bed, with battered hands. That would have been Monday; Cher had last been seen by her friend in Central City about 1:30 A.M. Sunday, getting into a car with Luther. Snider's revelation was just the start.

In May 1993, Snider had suddenly called Richardson and urged him to have Luther followed. She said she thought Luther was going to check on the grave because Richardson, with the help of other police agencies, had used a variety of tricks to make him nervous, and now he was worried that the cops were getting close. The surveillance team had lost Luther, but spotted him the next day in the town of Empire, west, not east, of Denver off Interstate 70. That's when Detective Richardson called on NecroSearch.

Before Cher Elder disappeared, another Lakewood officer had returned from one of the group's seminars talking about their work burying pigs and studying what happened afterward. Richardson had filed it away under useless information. When Snider told him that Cher was buried, he knew he had to find someone with experience in locating clandestine graves. That's when he remembered "the pig people."

Richardson found the literature the other officer had brought back and contacted Jack Swanburg, who invited him to present his case to the group. The detective showed up at the meeting with his sergeant, Don Girson, and laid out what he had so far. Cher Elder had last been seen in Central City in the early morning hours of March 28 with a man named Thomas Luther. The suspect was a convicted rapist and thought to have been involved in the murder of two other women more than ten years earlier. The best information was that he had buried Cher. Where, Richardson had no idea.

The NecroSearch members were impressed by the young detective. They were still on a high from the Melanson case. Michele Wallace's remains had been located the previous September; the trial of Roy Melanson was coming up in August. They figured that now that they had one under their belt, the next success wouldn't be far behind. (It would be several more weeks before Phoenix detective Ed Reynolds opened a letter from Lori Keidel Romaneck, beginning a year-long investigation that led to NecroSearch and Clark Davenport.)

Diane France listened to the young detective and was immediately reminded of Kathy Young during her presentation to the group. Not so much in personalities: both were obviously smart, to the point, and exuded confidence; but Young was a little more reserved and patient, while Richardson was intense, with a bit of a swagger to him. However, when it came to their respective cases, the two detectives could have been twins. It was evident that Richardson was just as emotionally involved with Cher's case as Young had been with Michele. Maybe even a little more, because Cher had not been missing for very long and there was a sense of immediacy. He had apparently had a good deal more contact with the missing girl's family, whom he described to the group as "devastated."

Richardson and Young were also the type of detectives who did their homework before coming to ask NecroSearch for help, unlike some, who came to them unprepared and wanting miracles. Neither had asked anyone to do their investigations for them; they were just using every resource at their disposal, and NecroSearch was only one more tool in the shed.

"She was totally innocent," Richardson told the members. "She's not your typical runaway. But I think she got into a bad situation and now she's dead."

NecroSearch quickly agreed to help. Diane France and Steve Ireland said they would head up the team, with Ireland acting as the contact person if Richardson came up with any leads for them to check out. Richardson finally had one when Luther was seen in Empire, getting into the car of one of his criminal associates, a teenager named J. D. Eerebout. "I need some help in a little town called Empire," he told Ireland when he got the archaeologist on the telephone.

Empire was one of those tiny Colorado mining towns that were built on the hopes and fortunes of gold-seekers in the late 1800s and had somehow managed to cling to existence in the high country when the gold played out. Their diggings—some hardly more than pits, others deep shafts blasted and picked far into the mountains' entrails—littered the area.

Fortunately for Empire, a nearby molybdenum mine—a mineral used to strengthen and add flexibility to steel—continued as a source of jobs for residents. Otherwise the town, about forty-five miles west of Denver, relied for revenue on tourists in the spring and summer, hunters during the fall, and skiers in the winter.

The town, population about 400, consisted of a single avenue of businesses lined up along the highway, and maybe a hundred homes, many of them built in the old Victorian gingerbread style. It was a blink-and-you-miss-it sort of place, battered by harsh winters where snow piled up higher than a man could reach standing on his toes.

Empire was situated near the mouth of a narrow valley at an altitude of 8,600 feet, bordered on the downhill side by snow-fed Clear Creek, a noisy, vigorous stream that makes up in energy what it lacks in depth. Bald-headed mountains from which some of the snow never melts, even in summer, rise on either side of the town and the highway that passes through it paralleling the stream. The sides of the mountains are as steep as a staircase, the pine-covered slopes interspersed with numerous landslides of granite rock that range in size from a man's fist to a small car.

After leaving the town, the highway runs for several miles before suddenly veering and climbing to the right, leaving the valley and the stream behind. Up it winds, through a series of switchbacks until reaching Berthoud Pass, elevation 11,300 feet; then it drops down the other side to the Winter Park ski area a few miles farther on.

Tom Luther and J. D. Eerebout were hardly out of Empire before Richardson contacted Ireland, who called and got the first Necro-Search member to Empire. Within an hour, Al Nelson had shown up with Becky. He got her scented off the rock that Luther had been hiding behind and they began to backtrack. It was more difficult to keep the dog on trail because they naturally prefer to work toward where the person went than where they came from. Becky worked her way partway through town and to the outskirts, to a sewage treatment plant. In the mud at the edge of one of the holding ponds, she came upon a footprint, and there she stopped. A little way out in the pond was a hole in the dried crust on top of the water where it looked like something might have been thrown.

Becky couldn't be brought back on track, even though Luther obviously had to have come from some direction to reach the treatment plant. Nelson didn't know if it was because of all the decaying human remains in the form of the sewage, or because she was trying to tell him that the pond was where the body had been tossed.

Obviously, someone was going to have to take a look in the holding ponds. Nelson was glad that wasn't his area of expertise.

Scott Richardson didn't get to Empire himself until the next morning. The previous evening, he had Luther, who was trying to leave the state, stopped at the Colorado–Nebraska border and brought back to Fort Collins. At a local hospital, the ex-con was served with a warrant forcing him to give hair and blood samples.

Luther became enraged when he saw Richardson approaching in the hospital, where samples of his pubic hair were about to be taken. He began ripping out his pubic hair by the handful and yelling, "Where do you live, Richardson? Where do you live?"

After the samples were taken, they had to let Luther go, and he had promptly left the state. Richardson was concerned about how difficult it might be to find him again, but there was nothing he could do about it. Before he could worry about finding Luther again, he had to find Cher Elder.

Until Luther led them to Empire, Richardson had proceeded as if he might never find Cher's body. He ran credit card checks to see if they had been used; he asked the U.S. Border Patrol to watch out for anyone using a passport under the name Cher Elder. But there was nothing to indicate that Cher was alive.

There was also nothing to indicate she was dead. He ran down dozens of leads about bodies being reported in other parts of the country. He answered dozens more telephone calls from other police officers working missing-persons cases in their districts. Nothing came of any of it.

The Jefferson County District Attorney's Office, which would be handling the court case if one could be established, was reluctant to pursue charges unless Cher's remains could be found. Not that they were ruling it out, said Deputy District Attorney Dennis Hall, who would be prosecuting the case. But at this juncture, they had a weak circumstantial case without conclusive proof that Cher had been murdered.

In the meantime, Cher's family suffered. Her disappearance was almost harder than the probability that she was dead, something Richardson had warned them in early April to begin coming to terms with. It was the not knowing that tormented them.

Earl Elder walked around like a beaten man, his mood swinging wildly from crying jags to rage, and visions of revenge against the suspect Richardson had told the family about.

Cher's mother, Rhonda, and her husband, Van, lived in Grand Junction in western Colorado. Rhonda was haunted by nightmares that always seemed to wake her at about 3:00 A.M. One was particularly troubling. In it, she dreamed of being driven up a mountain road at night; then there would be a loud noise and immense pressure behind her left ear, before she felt herself shrinking into nothingness. Awakened, she often would call Richardson's office number. She knew he wouldn't be there at that hour, but she would want to hear his voice or leave a message begging him to find her only child.

Richardson had promised Cher's family that he wouldn't give up trying. And finally, he had a place to look that seemed promising. In fact, when he arrived in Empire and got out to look around, he thought, *She's here. I can feel it. But where?*

He walked over to the downhill side of the highway. Any one of the rockslides that ran like granite fingers down the hillsides could have covered a grave.

The terrain was so steep that a body thrown from the road would travel twenty yards before it stopped. It would be no problem to send a few rocks tumbling over the body, and then the grave would look like any one of a thousand other piles of rocks in the immediate vicinity. The search that day revealed nothing.

Richardson drove back to Empire again the next day. The Cher Elder case had been a real eye-opener for Richardson about the number of unsolved murder cases there were every year in the United States. He had heard that 65 percent of all homicides went unsolved.

Only a few days earlier, he had been handed a report that the jawbone of a woman had been found near Leadville, which was of interest because Leadville had been one of Luther's haunts before he moved to Summit County in 1981. The jawbone did not match Cher's dental records, and to whom it had once belonged remained a mystery. What about that woman's family, he thought. Where were they? What did they think happened to their daughter or wife or mother?

Thank God this ought to be over pretty quick now, he thought to himself.

Al Nelson was called in again. This time he brought Amy to follow Luther's live scent from the restaurant. She quickly followed it back into town and down by the sewage treatment plant and eventually the rock on the other end of town.

Returning to the restaurant, he got Amy to backtrack up the road and off onto a forest trail. She went for a hundred yards or so before stopping next to the highway. On the other side of the road, there was a turnout from the highway, but beyond that the mountainside rose steeply.

Years later, Nelson would rue that he didn't take the dog across the highway. Whether it would have made a difference, he couldn't say for sure. At the time, according to the profilers, killers—particularly those who act alone—were too lazy to haul a body uphill. A victim might be forced to walk uphill to their execution, but considering Cher had disappeared at night, it would have been extremely difficult to make her walk up the steep slopes on the other side of the road in the dark.

A newer member of NecroSearch, another dog handler named Jerry Nichols brought his dog, Yogi, to Empire to see if he could add anything to what Nelson's dog had already done. Yogi was a small, rather common-looking bloodhound, but he was fresh from his latest triumph.

Earlier in May, 5-year-old Alie Berrelez was abducted from her grandfather's yard. A massive manhunt yielded nothing until Yogi was called in. The dog led Nichols for nearly 10 miles from the apartment where the girl lived to the mouth of a canyon, where searchers found Alie's body, stuffed in a duffel bag and thrown down a ravine by her killer. It was evident that the killer had transported her to that point in a car, yet Yogi, with one of the most sensitive noses in the animal kingdom, had followed a trail that was several days old.

Now, it was hoped that Yogi might help in Empire, but he merely confirmed the trail from the rock to the highway beyond the Marietta restaurant already found by Nelson's dogs.

The searchers surmised that the dogs had stopped because that was the place where Luther got out of the car when J. D. Eerebout brought him up the day before he was spotted. If so, and Luther had gone to the grave, it meant Cher's body might be somewhere between that spot and the rock on the other end of town.

So the dog and human searchers concentrated their efforts on the downhill side of the highway. Searchers walked along the creek at the bottom of the valley, looking for clothing that might have been discarded. Still others combed the hillside between the highway and the creek, watching for any unusual disturbance of the ground that might indicate a grave.

Eventually, the sludge ponds were emptied and searched with the aid of a backhoe. A holding tank was explored by divers. As the days passed, followed by weeks, with nothing to show, the hope that Richardson experienced in those first days after Luther was spotted in Empire began to wane.

Where are you, Cher? he would ask, looking over the rugged terrain. *I know you're up here somewhere.* But the mountains were mute and at last Richardson reluctantly had to leave Empire and wait for another opportunity.

That opportunity came in September 1993, when J. D.'s older brother, Byron Eerebout, was arrested for attempted murder after shooting up the house of a man who owed him money for drugs. The young man faced up to twenty-four years in prison, and several times since his arrest he had hinted that he knew what Luther had done with Cher Elder. But every time he and Richardson got close to working something out, a lawyer jumped in the middle, convincing Eerebout he could get an even sweeter deal. Eventually, Eerebout decided to take his chances at trial rather than "snitch" on Tom Luther. In July 1994, he lost, and in September was sentenced to the maximum. Even with good time, he was looking at ten years in prison. Then another tumbler clicked into place.

Just days before Eerebout's sentencing, Tom Luther was arrested for raping a woman in West Virginia. As with the rape victim in Summit County, Luther had picked up a hitchhiker—32-year-old Bobby Jo Jones—and drove around with her for some time before announcing he was going to rape her. He beat Bobby Jo so severely that he broke her nose and badly separated her shoulder, before strangling her to the point she blacked out. Later, she escaped by jumping out of his moving car when he said he was going to take her back to his cabin in the woods. She told police that she was afraid he was going to kill her and dump her body in those woods.

Luther was subsequently tape-recorded by the West Virginia State Police admitting what he had done to her. While the police listened in, he told Bobby Jo, "I'm a real fucking idiot when it comes to that."

Deb Snider, who had followed Luther to West Virginia to pursue their on-again, off-again relationship, told police that Luther also confessed the rape to her. After trying so hard to avoid it in the Elder case, Snider now found herself in the position of being called as a witness against him.

Scott Richardson felt bad that another woman had suffered because Luther was still on the loose. He knew she probably wasn't the only one. After a notice was sent to police agencies in states around West Virginia inquiring about unsolved cases involving murdered or missing women, he had heard from the Pennsylvania State Police. They had a couple of such cases. One victim was found in December 1993, raped, beaten, and strangled in a remote wooded area near Newport. The second, a fashion model on her way to a job in New York, had stopped in Newport in April 1994 when she disappeared. Her clothes were found in a motel room she had rented, and her car was only 5 miles from where the other woman's body had been discovered.

Richardson confirmed that Tom Luther was known to have been in the area at that time. In fact, Luther was working at a construction site outside Newport where the first young woman, whom police still had not been able to identify, was seen hitchhiking in the days before her body was found. Another incriminating fact was that blood found on that victim's sweater—the only article of clothing with the body—wasn't hers, but did match Luther's blood type (though not conclusively enough to charge him with the murder).

The detective had no doubt that Luther was responsible. It was too much of a coincidence that the attacks on women in Summit County in the winter of 1982 and the attacks on women in the Newport, Pennsylvania, area in 1993–94 both stopped when Luther was arrested for sexual assault on the two victims.

Counting Cher Elder, that was five murders Richardson believed Luther had committed. And that didn't include a story he had been told about a blond hitchhiker who had arrived with Luther in his hometown in Maine after leaving Colorado in 1993. She had disappeared one day, according to witnesses there, and Luther left the state for West Virginia the next morning.

At least women were safe for the time being, Richardson thought. Luther's rape trial was coming up in a couple of weeks. The case sounded pretty solid, but it was the sort that could fall apart. The woman admitted going with Luther voluntarily, apparently to find drugs. It didn't mean she deserved to be beaten, strangled, and sexually assaulted, but you never knew how a jury would see it. Or the victim might refuse to testify.

Even if Luther was convicted, he would still get out again someday. Sooner if he could win on appeal, or possibly in as little as ten years if not. Even if he served every year for a rape conviction, Richardson thought, it still wasn't enough for what he had done to Cher and her family.

In the fall he had talked again to Dennis Hall about the possibility of prosecuting a bodyless homicide. Hall, a boyish-looking yet tough prosecutor known for piecing together the most complex cases, had researched the possibility already. The news wasn't good. He had found one case where the prosecutors had been successful "and dozens more where they weren't." The danger, of course, was that if they prosecuted Luther for Cher's death without her body and he was acquitted, they wouldn't be able to try him again if her body was found later.

Richardson called her family and told them about the option and its pitfalls. One drawback from the family's point of view was if they went to trial, the official motivation behind the search for her body would end; her grave might never be discovered. "Don't do it unless there's no other way," Earl Elder said, and his former wife, Rhonda, had agreed.

Richardson and Hall decided to wait at least until after the hunting season and the snows had melted. As the Gunnison County sheriff had once hoped after Michele Wallace disappeared, hunters don't keep to the regular paths and are often the ones who stumble upon clandestine graves.

And there was always the hope that Eerebout would talk.

When the deal with Byron Eerebout fell through, Richardson thought he would try another avenue. He began looking for a former convict named Dennis "Southy" Healey, a methamphetamine addict and small-time burglar with a heavy Boston accent. The younger man had spent a lot of time with his friend Luther in the days before and after Cher Elder disappeared. The detective had heard, from sources including Byron Eerebout, that Healey was somehow involved in the case.

On January 9, 1995, Richardson finally got a break when Healey was arrested on a felony menacing charge for waving a gun at a couple he thought had ripped him off in a drug deal. The detective had Healey pulled from his cell in the early morning hours, when he would be tired and strung out. At first, Healey played around, giving hints that he knew something and then claiming ignorance. He wanted a deal. Richardson discovered that he had a soft spot for his sisters, and appealed to the young man by bringing up what Cher's family was going through.

It worked even better than Richardson had hoped. A couple of days later, Healey contacted the detective and said he had been doing some thinking. "Especially what you said about the family wanting Cher's body for burial. . . . I don't care about the deal no more. I don't care if my information gets me outta anything.

"I'll give you Cher."

According to Healey, Cher was buried outside "a tiny town in the mountains." Richardson immediately pictured Empire, but he kept a straight face as Healey told him a story about driving through this town with Luther and Byron Eerebout when Luther pointed up the hill and indicated that was where he had buried a girl. The grave was shallow, Luther had said, because the ground had been frozen, and he had had to pile rocks on top of it.

Healey conceded he had rarely been sober during that time period. However, he thought he might be able to lead them to the area.

Richardson and his partner, Stan Connally, picked up Dennis Healey the next morning on the pretext that he had to appear in court. The detectives could scarcely contain themselves as Healey guided them to Interstate 70 and west into the mountains. But they didn't say anything. For this to stand up in court, Healey was going to have to get them there on his own. It was all they could do not to grin when Healey directed them to take the exit off the interstate to Empire.

Richardson had told Healey that he would not be prosecuted so long as he had no direct hand in Cher's murder or burial. Now, as they arrived in Empire, Richardson decided to test him. "We think we're going to find physical evidence at the grave," he said.

If Healey had something incriminating to worry about, now was the time he would back down. But the young man just shrugged. "I don't give a fuck," he said. "There's nothin' around her grave that's gonna connect me."

They had passed through Empire when Healey spotted the Marietta Restaurant on the left-hand side of the road. A mile farther up the road, he nodded at a horseshoe-shaped turnoff on the right side of the highway. "This is it. Slow down; slow down. It's right here on the right; slow down.

"That's right where it is. That's right where Luther showed us."

The turnoff was a 50-foot loop on and off the highway. A man-made rock formation with a wooden pole stuck in the center stood inside the loop. *The stone marker that Luther told Deb Snider about,* Richardson thought, *only west on Interstate 70, not east.*

Out of the car, Healey pointed up the hill from the turnoff. "That is where Luther was pointing when he said he had taken care of business."

Richardson looked in the direction Healey was pointing. The hillside was steep, which went against all the conventions about killers taking the bodies of their victims downhill. *No wonder we missed her,* he thought.

He climbed about 50 yards up the hill and discovered the old, partially collapsed mine entrance. A perfect hiding place. Healey said that Luther claimed to have buried Cher, but he might not have been telling the truth—even to his pals.

Down below, Healey was lighting up a cigarette; a pack was the one thing he had asked of the detective for his information. Richardson gave the mine one more glance and walked back down the hill to the car, where he got on the radio to Al Nelson and NecroSearch.

"If he brings that dog up here right now," Healey said, "he'll find it."

NecroSearch had participated in sixty-seven cases by September 1994, when Clark Davenport went to Phoenix and located the grave containing the skeleton of the woman believed to be Diane Keidel.

He was now waiting to testify at the upcoming trial of Gene Keidel in March.

Back in Colorado, however, nothing had come of the searches for Cher Elder.

Forward Looking Infrared built into a high-altitude FBI jet had even been used. When the crew from the jet landed in Denver to be briefed about the case, they were met by Clark Davenport and Sgt. Girson of the Lakewood Police Department. It was apparent that the crew were puzzled, and a little miffed, about what they were doing with their expensive high-tech equipment helping a local law enforcement agency. And what was this group with the strange name, NecroSearch? This wasn't a federal crime.

Then Davenport mentioned that NecroSearch had been experimenting with FLIR, trying to locate the bodies of buried pigs. "Wait a second," the pilot said, "are you the Pig People?"

After Davenport confirmed that they were sometimes known by that nickname, the crew's demeanor did an about-face. They'd been told in the past to render whatever assistance the Pig People might want. Suddenly, they couldn't do enough. Davenport felt as if he had been welcomed into an exclusive club.

From such altitudes that a person on the ground would hardly even note the presence of the jet, the FLIR crew circled above Empire. Inside the plane, Davenport guided the searchers on the ground, who looked like small ghosts of men on the monitor he was looking at, toward "hot" areas that appeared as white blotches.

In keeping with the theory that most bodies are located downhill, that was where the FLIR crew and Davenport concentrated. By doing so, they had searched to within a hundred yards of the entrance area of the mine, but not close enough.

While he continued to check out leads that Cher Elder had been seen in another part of the country or was buried south or east of Denver, Richardson never quit believing that she was waiting for him somewhere in the rugged valley north of the town. She had to be the reason Luther had come to this town when the psychological game they had played got to be too much.

During the ground sweeps of the area, local townspeople or tourists would stop and ask what all the fuss was about. They were told that it was practice for search-and-rescue missions. Despite the wild-goose chases, the NecroSearch team respected the cop who seemed to eat, drink, and sleep his case. They were all aware of the thousands of hours he had put into it, and how much he wanted to give Cher, whose picture hung on his office wall next to those of his wife and kids, back to her family. If anything, the NecroSearch members worried about his health as the passing days took their toll on him. Not that it saved him from their sense of humor.

Steve Ireland in particular had begun to razz Richardson good-naturedly about their needing to write a travel brochure because, "we've seen so much of the countryside." Each time he got into the detective's unmarked car, he would inquire if this was "another Richardson pleasure cruise." Then he would settle back in his seat, as if to take a nap beneath the ball cap he always wore, while the detective directed a few choice words in his direction.

But when Richardson called, they always came. This time Al Nelson arrived first with Becky.

It was a sad time for Nelson; Amy had passed away just a few days earlier. She had never cared much for finding bodies, but she had helped put twelve murderers in prison, and there were still several more awaiting trial. And that didn't count the rapists and burglars she had tracked, nor the lost children and hikers she had found. Now it was up to Becky to carry on her legacy.

Becky immediately "hit" at the edge of the turnoff and again at the mine entrance. Then, when Nelson pulled Becky away from the mine to explore the surrounding area, she began hitting all over the mountainside. It was clear that at least some of what she was finding were old campsites. The area was popular with hikers and hunters. Becky couldn't tell him if what she was smelling at the mine entrance was a decomposing body or decomposing human waste.

After Becky hit on the entrance to the mine, Richardson crawled partway into the opening with a flashlight. The mine pitched away from the entrance at a 30-degree angle. It seemed to end in a thick, oily pool of water, next to which he could just make out a spade with a broken handle. Recalling a story from Deb Snider about Luther having broken one of her shovels the day he purportedly buried a box of assault rifles, the detective thought, *This is it. This is where he put her.*

The mine was unstable; rocks fell from the ceiling without any provocation, so Richardson decided to take Healey back to jail. It would give him a chance to ask a few more questions, and he wanted to get NecroSearch and the mine rescue team from neighboring Gilpin County involved.

When he delivered the young man to the jail, Healey suddenly reached out and grabbed Richardson's arm. "Tell Cher's family that I'm sorry I didn't say something sooner." Leaving the jail, Richardson had to smile. Who would have thought that a scraggly-haired meth addict would be the only one of these guys with a conscience?

On the way back to Empire, Richardson picked up Steve Ireland. When they arrived, the Gilpin County mine rescue team was already at the site. They said the water was going to have to be pumped from the mine and the ceiling reinforced to make it safe to search. Ireland and Richardson agreed that it would be better to start the next day.

The two men got back to the site early in the morning. Al Nelson returned with Becky, and NecroSearch members Dick Hopkins, Cal Jennings, and Jim Reed also responded. The detective was sure that this would be the day he found Cher. However, while the others worked, there was not much for him to do, so he decided to take a walk around the area.

Following a light trail through the woods and snow, he came to a bowl-shaped clearing among the tall pines. On one side was a shelf of gray granite that hid the clearing from the highway 50 yards below. The wind whispered through the trees and he could plainly hear Clear Creek tumbling down the valley floor on the other side of the road.

It was a peaceful spot, almost like a chapel beneath the boughs of the trees. But what caught his attention was a pile of large rocks, perhaps 2 feet tall and the length . . . of a body.

It's a grave, he said to himself.

Richardson quickly returned to the mine and summoned the NecroSearch team members, who were waiting for the rescue team to finish pumping water from the mine. They went with him to the clearing and agreed with him that the pile of rocks was not naturally occurring, but that didn't necessarily make it a grave. Hunters or hikers might have stacked the rocks to clear a camping spot, make a windbreak, or create a cairn to mark a trail, someone suggested. Was

Luther the sort of killer who would have gone through the considerable effort to place the rocks, and would he pile them where they were so clearly visible?

Nelson took Becky over to the pile of rocks. He had responded when called but was leery of bringing her in for a search in February, the coldest month of the year. In warm months, cracks in the ground caused by desiccation helped by letting scent seep to the surface. But they could also fill with water and freeze in the winter, trapping the scent beneath the surface. The pile of rocks lay in the bottom of the bowl, where water would tend to collect. He was afraid of missing something.

Becky paused when she reached the rocks and sniffed, as if interested. She turned her head back to him and gave him a look, but he wasn't sure what it meant—the look wasn't her usual signal for a hit.

Yet Hopkins noticed it. "What was that about, Al?" he asked.

Nelson shrugged. "She smelled something." But the dog gave no further response and moved on, so who knew what she'd noticed?

The searchers removed the rocks until they had a bare piece of ground. Using a hand auger, Ireland drilled a hole the diameter of a tennis ball into the frozen soil. He bored in 18 inches and still there was no sign of human remains. He shook his head. "The ground is really compacted," he said, looking at the core of soil removed by the auger. "It doesn't look like it's been disturbed."

The team gathered their things and wandered back to the mine entrance. Nelson told Richardson he would like to come back in the fall when the ground warmed up. As he turned to follow them, the detective cast one more look back at the clearing. Something in him didn't want to leave. He remembered Healey mentioning that Luther covered the grave with rocks. But reluctantly, his boots scuffing through the snow, he returned to the mine.

In the end, the mine yielded only the broken spade, which didn't match the one lost by Deb Snider. The searchers learned nothing more, other than the fact that a mountain lion had been using the spot as a den. The rescue team and NecroSearch members quietly packed up their equipment and headed back down the hillside.

On his own, Richardson took the trail back to the clearing and stood for a moment looking at the cleared space where the rocks had been. Then he walked down around the rock shelf, got in his car, and left, with the scene burning in his mind.

* * *

On February 23, 1995, Richardson was again thinking of the pile of rocks as he drove up the winding mountain highway toward Empire. The last of the tumblers appeared to be falling neatly into place.

Back in West Virginia, Luther had been convicted of first-degree sexual assault and sentenced to fifteen to thirty-five years in prison. He wasn't going anywhere for a while, but that didn't bring any peace to Cher's family, nor had he paid for what he had done to her. Hopefully, he would soon.

Shortly afterward, the Jefferson County District Attorney's Office reached a deal with Byron Eerebout. His three eight-year sentences would run concurrently, instead of consecutively. He would be transferred to a halfway house out of state to finish serving his time. In exchange, he was going to have to testify against Tom Luther and take Richardson to Cher Elder's body. "Does a pile of rocks mean anything to you, Richardson?" he had said, looking sideways at the detective during a meeting to work out the details of the deal. Richardson just didn't know how much it meant.

Sitting in the backseat of the car with his lawyer, Eerebout directed Richardson and Connally to the town of Empire, through it, and to the little horseshoe-shaped turnoff up the road from the Marietta Restaurant. It was the same spot Healey had brought them to a month earlier. They pulled in, followed by another car carrying crime scene technicians. Eerebout pointed to the path that led up past the gray rock shelf. The grave was up there, he said.

The ground outside the car was covered with a fresh layer of snow, but the sky overhead was clear and blue as a robin's egg. A lot of traffic was passing by, most of the cars topped with skis and heading for Winter Park Ski resort. The detectives waited until there was a break in the traffic before jumping out of the car and pulling on overalls that covered their suits. They didn't want to attract attention; in particular, they didn't want any media nosing around.

Richardson hauled Eerebout out of the car and up the hill into the trees. When they had been joined by the others, Eerebout set off up the trail, taking the fork that led to the clearing. He stopped, as if trying to get his bearings. He moved a little way off the trail toward the rock shelf. "I was standing over here lookin' over the rocks and watching him. It was two in the morning. . . . Yeah, this is it," he said. He pointed to the middle of the clearing, where a large number of rocks lay scattered about and covered by snow.

"He came up here to put rat poison on the body so the dogs and the wild animals wouldn't dig it up. He said it wasn't too far down; it wasn't deep enough, and he wanted to come up here to dig it deeper. . . . But then he said to stay out of his fuckin' business."

Eerebout's slight confusion was probably the result of expecting to see a pile of rocks, Richardson thought. The detective quickly escorted the prisoner back down the hill. He and Connally then drove him and the lawyer back to Denver while the crime scene technicians remained in the clearing.

On the way down, Richardson asked the police dispatcher to place a call to Steve Ireland. He had warned Ireland the night before that something was likely to happen, and now that it had, he wanted Ireland and Diane France up at the site as soon as possible. NecroSearch had passed on what lay beneath the rocks the first time; he doubted they would again.

Diane France got down on her hands and knees to sniff at the hole she and Steve Ireland had drilled into the slight depression on the wooded slope outside Empire, Colorado. Cher Elder had been missing, and presumed dead and buried, for two years. The presumption now was that they had found her, though that remained to be proved through scientific analysis. Assumptions had already proved costly in this case.

The spot where France knelt had been dismissed after a cursory examination a month earlier. Good old-fashioned detective work, not NecroSearch expertise, had brought them back to this snowy, chapellike clearing in the pines.

If anything, the Elder case was proving to be one of those where the group learned more from their mistakes than from whatever they accomplished—but that just made France and Ireland more determined to do everything right this time.

Late the night before, Ireland had called France to say that Richardson wanted them to stand by; something might break in the morning. "He wants to know if we're game," Ireland chuckled.

As committed to finding Cher Elder as Richardson was, Ireland was just as committed to NecroSearch. From all of his years working for the government, he got a lot of annual leave time every year, most of which he now used up on NecroSearch investigations. An avid reader of mystery books since boyhood, he enjoyed the chance to play detective and get away from his desk job and back out in the field to use his archaeology training.

The conviction of Melanson was bittersweet. Ireland had found it sort of anticlimactic after the exhilarating moment when they had found Michele Wallace. Then again, he reminded himself, they were scientists in pursuit of the truth, not necessarily of bad guys. Once the case was turned over to the justice system, it was someone else's problem. Most of what interested NecroSearch members was on the ground or under it, not on the floor of a courtroom.

Ireland had often teamed up with Diane France, and they got along like old friends. She was so easygoing, and yet her experience and credentials were incredible.

In 1991, France had been elected to a six-year term on the board of directors of the American Board of Forensic Anthropology. A few years later, she had accepted another prestigious invitation to the federal Disaster Mortuary Team, or DMORT, which was charged with responding to mass fatalities, such as airline crashes, to help recover and identify the remains of the victims and prepare them for return to their families. She was also a frequent lecturer at the American Forces Institute of Pathology. Yet, despite her bona fides, Ireland had never heard her grow impatient with or belittle members of the group who asked questions.

"I just can't tomorrow," France replied when he told her about Richardson's latest request. She was busy trying to catch up with her "real work"—as director of the Human Identification Laboratory at CSU, and as the owner of a private business that made anatomical facsimiles.

"Yeah, I know. It's tough for me, too," Ireland said. "But he says this time it's for real and that we really need to do this."

France sighed. The boxes with their ribbons that she had shelved in her mind continued to pile up. A series of brutal rapes and murders of 20-something-year-old women, beginning with the woman found in Estes Park and continuing through Michele Wallace and culminating with Cher Elder, was eating at her. The hardest to deal with were the remains that were never identified but remained in her laboratory mute to her questions. *Who are you? Where did you come from? Did you suffer?*

Lately, she had been plagued by a recurring nightmare. In her sleep, a man stalked her through a house. She never saw a face, but she knew that he wanted to kill her. She would flee to the basement, but he would find her. She would run up the stairs, but he would follow. Then, just as he was about to show himself, she would wake in fear.

Finally, under Ireland's teasing, she said she would go. But she might have to leave early, so she said she would meet them in Empire.

The next morning, Detective Richardson arrived at Ireland's house. The archaeologist got in the front seat, stretched out, and pulled his cap over his eyes. "Another Richardson pleasure cruise?" he yawned.

Richardson smiled. "This time we got a body. I guarantee it. It's at the same spot we looked before."

Ireland looked up skeptically from under his cap. But for once, he said nothing in response. There was something about the detective's voice this time that made him wonder. Scott could be a real bulldog, and once he set his teeth, you had to wait until he decided it was time to let go.

They arrived at the site to find that the technicians had already photographed the scene and established a perimeter. France put the auger into the same hole Ireland had begun in January. After a couple turns, she got down to sniff.

"I can't say for sure, but I think something is decomposing under here," France said aloud.

Scott Richardson was lying on a rock behind the NecroSearch investigators with his arms crossed and his eyes open to the overcast sky above. He was still as a statue and didn't move when France spoke.

France and Ireland glanced at each other, shrugged, and went back to drilling the hole a little deeper. A few inches farther down, they struck adipocere—the whitish, soaplike substance that sometimes develops when a human body decomposes under cool, damp conditions.

"It's likely that it's human," France said, looking again at the balding 35-year-old detective with the dark eyes and Fu Manchu mustache. She couldn't have said how, but France was reasonably sure she could tell the difference in odors between human adipocere and animal adipocere.

Again Richardson didn't respond. Then quietly, without taking his eyes off the sky above, he asked in a deep Texas drawl, "What's next?"

Noting that it was already late afternoon and most of the narrow mountain valley was already in shadow and getting colder by the minute, France replied, "Well, it's up to you. But we should probably come back tomorrow. We're going to need to set up a grid and start excavating."

Richardson jumped off the rock and walked over to stare down at the hole they had drilled. For two years he had been working toward this moment—two years of missing his young sons growing up; Two years of putting his wife and himself through hell. All to put a predator back in his cage and give Cher back to her family.

Without looking back up at the scientists, he announced, "I'm staying here tonight."

France nodded. She knew what it was to be haunted by the ghosts of young women, of boxing her emotions and putting them on a shelf because there was a job to do.

Richardson and Connally spent the night in their car. They couldn't take the chance that some curious local would come on the site now and call the media. Richardson wasn't worried about the local mountain lion; cougars won't eat decayed flesh. But there were also bears in the area that might be attracted to the escaping scent of decomposition, and they might try to unearth the body.

"What if it ain't Cher?" Connally asked as they tried to get comfortable in the cramped vehicle.

They couldn't be sure. Luther might have moved the body since Eerebout followed him up here, leaving enough decaying material to give off an odor and produce adipocere. Or it could be somone else in the grave, a red herring Luther had heard about through his criminal sources and used to confuse investigators.

There had been so many lies, they couldn't rule anything out. They had two witnesses—Dennis Healey and Byron Eerebout—and one of them was lying. Healey said he had been to the turnoff with Eerebout and Luther in the daytime. But according to Eerebout's story, he and his brother, J. D., had followed Luther into the mountains at 2:00 A.M. after the older convict told them he was going to put rat poison on the body. He made no mention of Healey being present.

"I don't want to think about it," Richardson said, and each detective turned to his own thoughts. Neither slept much, and they both greeted the dawn stiff and cold. They were soon joined by the police and NecroSearch teams, who brought coffee and breakfast.

Under the direction of France and Ireland, the tedious process of exhumation began. They had realized the night before that digging was going to be difficult because the first 6 to 12 inches of soil was frozen, which probably explained why the cadaver dog hadn't detected anything.

It was snowing as they began, and shields were erected to keep it out of the site. A special electric heating system run off generators was brought in to warm the ground. But the air was still freezing cold as they worked.

First, the grave site was sectioned off into grids, delineated by pieces of string tied to stakes. Everything that came out of the excavation went into buckets marked for the appropriate grid space. The contents were then sifted through a screen and examined.

The dirt and debris were removed centimeter by centimeter, as slowly and carefully as if they were unearthing the tomb of some queen of ancient Egypt. By the end of the first day, they had exposed one of the walls of the original grave. France was so precise, using toothbrushes to clear away dirt, that they could see the tool marks left by the grave digger's shovel.

The sun was going down behind the nearby hills when they called it a day. Richardson and Connally spent another uncomfortable night in their car below the grave site.

By late the next afternoon, the searchers knew that at last most of a human body remained in the grave under the light-tan soil. About 4:00 P.M., France bent over and tugged at a small root in the bottom of the pit. It came up along with a small lock of dark-brown hair.

The searchers were silent. Richardson said quietly, "It's Cher." Everyone cheered. Hands patted him on the back. Voices said, "Congratulations, you got her." They all knew what this case meant to him, and its enormous personal toll. But Richardson just wanted to get away from the celebration.

Numb, he walked off. On the other side of the clearing, he sat down on a rock outcropping that offered a view of the mountain that rose above the grave site and the chapellike clearing that held the remains of Cher Elder. Clear Creek sang in the valley below, sounding different now as it appeared and disappeared beneath an icy sheath.

It's so beautiful, he thought again. *Peaceful. A shame we have to take her away . . . except that Thomas Luther put her here.* Anger filled his mind. Luther's presence could stain even the most heavenly place; he sullied everything he touched. Richardson hated him for it.

The detective sat for a long time trying to sort out his feelings. His mind exulted one minute, only to be overwhelmed by sadness the next. He was surprised to discover that even he had held out the tiniest hope that Cher was alive somewhere. *She's dead,* he told himself. *She's dead.* It sounded so final, so unfair.

He stood up as the last light from the west bathed the snows on the mountain above briefly in pink before leaving the world in gray twilight. A chill wind swept down from the slopes with the setting of the sun, and Richardson shivered. But not from the cold.

I found her, he thought. *Soon I'll have to tell her family.*

The sleepless night in the car, the cold, and the emotional toll of the discovery had done in both Richardson and Connally. They were nearly asleep on their feet when the crew called it a day. Although they argued to remain behind, their sergeant ordered them both to go home and rest.

When he got home, Richardson was pumped up. He could hardly stop pacing. Finally, he was going to nail Tom Luther's hide to the wall for what he had done to Cher Elder.

His wife, Sabrina, was relieved for her husband's sake. He had put himself under a lot of stress, juggling the investigation, keeping it fresh, while giving Cher's family a shoulder to cry on. He had lost a lot of weight and wasn't sleeping well—waking up in the middle of the night to write a note to himself, then lying awake with his mind going over what he should do next. Scott was always tired. He had no energy for the boys. About the only time he seemed like his old self was when riding with Sabrina on his Harley. Those rides were few and far between.

But she was also relieved because now she hoped they could go on with their lives. Tom Luther was like a ghost in the house, always there. Scott couldn't seem to think of anything else. If they went to a gathering of friends, the Luther case became a topic of conversation; nothing else mattered.

* * *

The excavation team returned to the site early the next morning only to face a new problem. An avalanche had swept across the highway farther up the pass, burying two people and slowing traffic down to a crawl past the turnoff. When the occasional curious skier poked his head out the window to ask what they were up to, the detectives pointed up the road and yelled, "Avalanche."

Near-panic gripped the searchers when a television news helicopter began circling overheard. It was there to record the effects of the avalanche, but had a bird's-eye view of the partially exposed grave site through the trees. Everyone breathed a sigh of relief when the road was reopened and the skiers and the helicopter went away.

Throughout the excavation Diane France and Steve Ireland had maintained a tight control over who was allowed through the perimeter to where the work was being done. As word spread that the long search was at last a success, a lot of people from law enforcement and the district attorney's office came to the site. None of them were allowed past the perimeter unless they had been assigned a specific duty, and that included Scott Richardson.

The investigators were after the maximum amount of evidence possible. Metal detectors were used to sweep the area for shell casings—an important task to establish whether Cher had been killed at the site or elsewhere.

NecroSearch botanist Vickey Trammell was called to the gravesite to take a look at the roots in the grave. Guided up the hill, she found it emotionally difficult to approach the grave.

Back before Michele Wallace's remains were found, Trammell had been having doubts about her ability to handle the psychological aspects of working with NecroSearch. Then, as case after case of missing women and missing children made their way into NecroSearch files, the majority never being resolved, she realized how naive she was about the amount of evil in the world. It frightened her, and she wondered if she had the heart to deal with so much tragedy on top of her own after her son, David, was killed by the drunk driver.

Then when Michele Wallace's remains were found and Roy Melanson convicted, she had heard about how grateful George Wallace had been. She had seen firsthand how the Cher Elder case had affected Scott Richardson over the past two years. She knew from him how devastated Cher's family was and how they were counting on him to find her. She admired his tenacity and how deeply he cared about someone he had never even met.

At least she had known what happened to David. He had not just disappeared one day. She couldn't imagine the pain of wondering, sometimes for years, sometimes forever, what had become of a child or spouse or parent. When Richardson found Cher, she had realized that NecroSearch was something she needed as much as her colleagues needed her. It somehow made her son's death easier to bear knowing that she might be able to help lessen the pain for others.

Trammell's work had been essential in determining the time of death in several NecroSearch cases. Now she was trying to use her knowledge of plants to determine the age of this grave.

Like many of the other NecroSearch members, she was feeling somewhat embarrassed about NecroSearch's role in the Elder case. *We were willing and well intentioned,* she thought, *but we certainly made mistakes.*

The first, and possibly the worst, had been to forget the scientific principle of accepting nothing as fact unless it had been proved. They had taken as gospel the profilers' generalization that a killer acting alone wouldn't carry a body uphill. All of their searches, the FLIR flyby, even the dogs, had been directed at the land on the downhill side of the highway.

Then, against Al Nelson's better judgment, they had used a dog in the dead of winter when the ground was frozen. Steve Ireland had missed finding the grave by only a couple of inches with that first hole they drilled. They had also talked themselves out of the possibility that Luther was determined enough to dig a grave nearly four feet deep *and* cover it with bowling-ball-sized rocks. Which had all added up to NecroSearch initially ruling out the spot where Trammell now knelt to clip root samples.

We just plain missed it, she thought. For all of NecroSearch's expertise and high-tech gear, it had taken a bulldog of a cop to teach them a lesson about staying open-minded about possibilities.

It was clear now, however, that the excavation team was missing nothing. The dirt had been removed millimeter by millimeter. The sides of the grave were exposed so precisely, Trammell could see the shovel's impressions and where the roots, which had been collected from the dirt in the grave for her examination, had been cut off by the killer's digging.

New roots were coming through the walls of the grave, some of them growing into the mummy-shaped object in the bottom of the grave. Trammell felt depressed looking at the sad scene. The dirt-encrusted object had once been a beautiful young woman—a young woman she and the others almost felt they knew from Richardson's descriptions.

Trammell knelt by the side of the grave. She could smell death. She bent over and clipped several of the roots that came through the walls, and those that pierced the body. When she finished, she took her clippings and walked away, never looking back.

It wasn't until 6:00 that evening that the excavation ground to a halt. Cher Elder's remains lay exposed except for the crusty soil that encased her. Ireland thought that she looked like a sand sculpture of a woman that had been rained on.

For the most delicate work near the body, France supplemented her toothbrushes with thin bamboo sticks. Bamboo, she had explained to Richardson, wouldn't scar bone as would a metal pick.

The man who buried Cher had not made the grave long enough, and she lay awkwardly on her back with her head bent forward by the end wall of the grave. Her left arm lay across her stomach; her right, underneath her. All that remained was to dig beneath Cher to loosen her gently from the ground on which she had rested for two years. France decided to wait until the morning light so that the body could be removed without missing or damaging any evidence. In particular, she wanted to make sure that the position of the head remained the same. If Cher had been strangled, there might be key evidence on her neck that needed to be preserved.

Before they left that last night, France and Richardson stood alone next to the grave, preparing to cover the remains with a tarp. They were so different and yet so much alike.

Richardson had been amazed by the strength and determination of the petite anthropologist. Long after husky police officers needed a break from the work, France would still be at it, crawling around in the cold. Even Steve Ireland suffered, though he lasted longer than all but this female colleague.

In Scott Richardson, France found a kindred spirit. He cared about this girl in a way that went beyond the scope of his duties. He felt about Cher the same way France felt with the victims—particularly the women—who ended up in her lab. None of them had deserved what happened to them.

She was not surprised when Richardson announced that he and Connally would spend the night on the ground in sleeping bags next to the body. He said it was to protect the remains from scavengers, but she knew, even before, much later, she heard the truth from him, that he didn't want Cher to spend another night alone in a grave dug by Luther.

They lay the tarp gently over the remains and folded the edges under as best they could. Stepping back, France looked up at Richardson; his eyes were dark and he looked sad and tired. She reached out to touch him on the arm. He smiled wistfully and said, "It's like we're tucking her in for the night."

France nodded. "I understand why you took this so personally," she said. Turning toward the grave, she added, "Good night, Cher. We'll be back for you tomorrow."

Cher Elder may have been the only one who slept peacefully that night. In her sleep, the man again chased Diane France. He wanted to kill her and nowhere she ran was she safe.

Scott Richardson dreamed of death and heaven. In the morning, he was awakened by something wet that dripped onto his neck. He opened his eyes, puzzled that all he could see was white. He wondered if he was still dreaming.

It took a moment to realize that it had snowed again, so gently that it didn't wake him when several inches piled up over the small space he had left open in his bag for his face. He sat up to a world pure and innocent; even the horror of the grave was disguised beneath the white blanket.

That night they gently placed the remains in a body bag and transported them to the Jefferson County coroner's office. There the remaining dirt was carefully removed and the skull x-rayed. Comparing the X ray to dental records, the coroner was able to make a positive identification: The body belonged to Cher Elder.

In January 1996, the trial of Tom Luther for the murder of Cher Elder lasted six days. Arrayed against him were prosecution witnesses that included Dennis Healey, the Eerebout brothers, and Deb Snider.

The presence of NecroSearch was felt in a variety of ways. Aerial photographs of the grave site were provided by one of the newest, and definitely the youngest, member of the group, 24-year-old Brannan Gamber. The photos weren't taken in the usual manner, however. Gamber used unmanned, radio-controlled aircraft.

The founder of MicroFlight Technologies, Gamber had always thought his aircraft might have law enforcement uses, such as photographing accident and crime scenes. But he was shocked after being introduced to Jack Swanburg and Dick Hopkins by their idea of using low-level aerial photography to search for clandestine graves. Even the skeleton on their business cards seemed rather morbid. He met them out at the Project PIG site, where he launched his airplane and took photographs of the area. Even though he knew the resolution on his low-altitude photographs would be good, he was surprised how good. It was easy to pick out the nearly two dozen pig grave sites, even the older ones.

The NecroSearch membership were impressed and quickly invited Gamber to join them. The "toy" aircraft had several advantages over normal-sized airplanes. The unmanned planes flew slower and lower than their large counterparts, and the photographs were much clearer, particularly for small objects. Gamber's aircraft could also fly low over populated areas, where regular airplanes and helicopters would have to fly impractically high for detailed photographs due to FAA regulations. Also, important from the always budget-strapped NecroSearch perspective, they were much cheaper to use.

The Cher Elder case was the first for Gamber. Shot from just above the treetops, the photographs showed even the rocks as they had been left. His photographs made it easy for the jurors to visualize where the grave was in relationship to the turnoff from the highway, as well as the rock shelf where Byron Eerebout claimed to have spied on Luther. The photographs were then related to another NecroSearch addition: the model of the hillside based on the work of Cal Jennings, Steve Ireland, and Jim Reed. Reed testified during the trial about how accurately the model had been prepared. When Byron Erebout spoke about sneaking up the hill to watch Luther, the jury could see from the model how he did it.

Al Nelson would also be called in to testify about the searches conducted by his dogs in 1993. The purpose was to back up the human witnesses who had already testified about seeing Tom Luther walk through town. A little levity was also introduced when prosecutor Minor, who kept getting more and more specific about how the dogs operated, asked what Nelson did when Amy found Luther's trail.

"I held on," Nelson deadpanned. Judge, jurors, lawyers, spectators, and even Luther laughed out loud.

NecroSearch's work didn't always get credit during the trial, though Richardson praised them in the press whenever he got the opportunity. For instance, the care used to remove Cher Elder's body resulted in bullet fragments being discovered in her skull. A ballistics expert testified that those fragments had been fired from a gun of the same make as one traced to Luther.

Some of what NecroSearch had done simply prevented the defense from countering the prosecution's theory. One such example was Trammell's work with the root cuttings was able to prove that the grave had been dug when the prosecution said it had been (ruling out the possibility that someone else had killed and buried Cher at a later date).

Luther was eventually convicted of second-degree murder and sentenced to forty-eight years, to run after his West Virginia sentence. (He would also later be convicted for the 1993 attempted murder of a Denver woman, Heather Smith, and sentenced to an additional fifty years.) Most of the jurors in the Elder case wanted to convict him of first-degree murder, which would have exposed him to the potential of the death penalty, but a single holdout juror forced the others to settle for the lesser verdict.

After the trial, the eleven jurors who voted initially for first-degree murder were questioned about the witnesses. They believed Healey when, under accusations by the defense attorney, he said, "I'm a thief and a conniver . . . but I ain't a killer," and pointed the finger at Luther, who had confessed to him. Taken on his own, they might have dismissed Byron Eerebout as a pathological liar. He was a smirking criminal without a lot going on upstairs. But even his critics conceded, Eerebout had acquitted himself well. "[Defense attorney] Enwall just kept pushing and pushing," one juror noted, "but Byron just sat there and said, 'I didn't kill Cher Elder. Tom Luther killed Cher Elder.' I believed him."

Of all the prosecution witnesses—at least those who weren't there in an official capacity—Debrah Snider was the most convincing and did the most to sew up the loose ends and tie it all together. It helped that she was obviously, however strangely, still in love with Luther. So much that it had looked like it physically hurt her to tell the truth. She hadn't tried to elaborate on what she knew—she never said that Luther confessed to her—and yet she had damned him just the same.

Detective Scott Richardson, however, was the key. The jurors all agreed he could be trusted, and had kept his cool while the defense hammered at him. No one bought the argument that he had focused on Luther to the exclusion of other possibilities; he had checked them out and still arrived back at Luther. They had also seen how emotionally involved he was in the case, how he had cared about Cher's family.

Richardson had recounted how Cher Elder's body was found, and the steps taken to carefully exhume her remains.

"Did you maintain security up there when people weren't working on the grave?" Prosecutor Hall had asked.

"Slept by it," Richardson replied. His sleeping by Cher's grave had left a lasting impression with the jurors of his dedication and humanity.

All in all, the prosecution had provided the little pieces of the puzzle, much of it provided by NecroSearch. All the small details, such as the bullet fragments matching the type of gun, the model of the hillside, and the aerial photographs so that the jurors could visualize the actions of the various characters. It was obvious how painstaking the prosecution's experts had been—and the jurors didn't know the half of it, because the defense had not tried to challenge the Necro-Search investigators.

The reaction of NecroSearch members to the verdict in the Luther case was mixed, reflective of their varied personalities and backgrounds. Too many of them had worked this case over three years not to have become emotionally involved. They believed in Richardson; they believed in what their own research had shown; and therefore they believed in Luther's guilt.

Some felt it was enough that he was in prison and wouldn't be able to kill. Others were angered that he didn't receive the death penalty. Jim Reed tore the telephone off the wall and flung it across the room.

Diane France, who had continued to be bothered by nightmares and the still-mounting boxes of emotional baggage she had to deal with, felt that if the jurors had been told about Luther's past crimes against women, they would have voted for first-degree murder and the death penalty. She herself was torn on how she felt about that ultimate punishment: on one hand, it was the only way to make sure Luther could not kill again, in or out of prison; on the other hand, innocent people had been sent to their executions in the past—not that she believed Luther was innocent by any means. What scared her was that Luther seemed like such a normal person. She wondered how many men she might have met—some stranger, perhaps, who drew her into a conversation at a convention or in a university hallway—could have turned out to be a Thomas Luther.

Steve Ireland was pleased that Luther was found guilty, but wished the death penalty were the end result. Because of his close association with Richardson, he felt he almost knew Cher Elder. Still, the most important thing to him, and what he felt was most important to the other members of NecroSearch, was that they had helped bring some closure for Cher's family.

And some closure for Richardson. They had all been moved by his quest to catch Cher's killer and bring him to justice. He had praised their efforts, but they all knew that the real reason Luther was behind bars was because of him. It had been a marathon of a case, and he had run every mile of it.

For just the second time in their history, the members invited one of the detectives from a NecroSearch case to become a member. In doing so, they presented Richardson with a ball cap with the NecroSearch logo, on which they had embroidered the nickname he had earned: "Bulldog."

VI

THE
CHRISTINE ELKINS
CASE

May 1997, Lakewood, Colorado

Mike Maloney of the U.S. Naval Criminal Investigations Service in Camp Lejeune, North Carolina apologized to Clark Davenport for the lack of introductions. "But I got your name from the folks at the FBI training center in Quantico."

Maloney said he was calling on behalf of an agent with the Bureau of Alcohol, Tobacco and Firearms in Kansas City, Missouri, who had asked if the Navy could lend him a magnetometer. The agent, Mike Schmitz, thought he might have a body in a car somewhere in the Missouri River and that a magnetometer might help him find it.

It's possible, Davenport thought to himself. He doubted the agent would know how to go about it, but it did sound like a job for . . .

"He called the Navy, who called me, and I called the FBI, who asked me if I had ever heard of the 'Pig People,' " Maloney continued. "They said I should check with NecroSearch in Colorado and gave me your number.

"I don't know if this is the sort of thing you people do, but I think Schmitz would like to talk to you."

The Pig People, Davenport thought; funny how the name stuck. Actually, activity out at the Project PIG site had slowed down considerably. People tended to work quietly on their own individual projects at the facility. For instance, Al Nelson still used the site to train his dogs, and have them train him, or they were out of the research aspect altogether.

In fact, the reduction in pure research was getting to be something of a point of contention among the membership. Some thought the group was straying too far from the originial concept of compiling information to pass on to law enforcement. The rift had even lost them a member, Tom Adair, who had switched his major in college to entomology so as to have an area of expertise needed by the group.

However, Clark Davenport and most of the others were much more interested in hands-on work with the police. They felt they had already done plenty of research in their respective fields. Going out and applying their knowledge as NecroSearch was a way to help on a personal basis, though each was affected by the cases in different ways.

For instance, there was the Lois Kleber case. She had disappeared from her home in Arvada, Colorado, in July 1992. The case had been assigned to Detective Scott Buckley, who had worked for the next four years to pin her disappearance and murder on her husband, Jim.

Diagnosed with terminal cancer, Jim Kleber had eventually confessed and told Buckley, who had called in NecroSearch for help, that he would lead them to the grave. He had taken them to a remote area in the mountains but had been unable to find the exact location. Buckley had asked Diane France to talk to Kleber to see if she could get any useful information out of him. What struck her about their conversation was that Kleber did not care about anything. He referred to his ex-wife as "it." Never she or Lois. He came to epitomize all the killers of the women whose bodies came through her laboratory or whom she learned about working with NecroSearch. But quitting was not an option to France. More firmly than ever before, Kleber had convinced her that as a forensic anthropologist, it was her role to speak out for the victims.

Though not everyone was as dramatically affected by their work with NecroSearch, the idea of being the advocates for the victims and their families was a common one for the group's members. It had helped that in the Kleber case, they were able to find the final resting place of Lois Kleber months after her husband and killer died.

The group had survived the research–fieldwork debate and the departure of Tom Adair, and had even grown with new members such as Chuck Fisher, a police psychologist and profiler, and the latest addition, geophysicist Al Bieber. And their reputation continued to grow.

When Davenport received the call from Mike Maloney, it had been nearly five years since Cecilia Travis spotted Michele Wallace's skull in the woods on Kebler Pass; three years since Davenport got the call from Ed Reynolds in Phoenix; two years since Cher Elder was found in Empire; one year since the search for Lois Kleber on Grouse Mountain.

There had been other successes as well, though the group tried to refrain from calling only those cases in which a body was found "successes"; to them a success was something learned.

They had been instrumental in the conviction of Jill Coit, the so-called Black Widow Killer, who, with her boyfriend Michael Backus, had murdered her husband in 1993. However, that success had nothing to do with finding a body. Rather, Arapahoe coroner Michael Doberson and Swanburg had been able to match marks found on the body of the murder victim with those of a stun gun found in Coit's car, by using the gun on an anesthetized pig. It was the only hard evidence tying Coit to the murder of Gerry Boggs.

In September 1995, Diane France and Steve Ireland had crawled down a collapsing mine tunnel and retrieved the bones of Ike Hampton, who had been murdered in 1977. By examining the remains, France was able to determine that what a police informant had said about the nature of the murder was in fact true, and two men, Randy Bird and Mark Prieur, eventually pleaded guilty to the murder when confronted with the facts.

A year later, the team of France, archaeologist Cal Jennings, Ireland, and Swanburg excavated the body of George Legeza, who had been the unlucky odd man out in a love triangle with Jim and Bonnie Taylor. The dogs of Nelson and Nichols had located the body in a shed in Loveland, Colorado. The police detectives in the case, John Spreitzer and Bob Coleman, had been told by one of the guilty parties that the body was there; but in case the "confession" was lost in the legal maneuverings, they had wanted NecroSearch to find it on their own, after being taken to the general area.

There had even been occasions for humor, such as the time a "human hand" had been found in the mountains, identified as such by the local coroner, and a press conference scheduled to announce what the authorities thought were the remains of a young girl reported missing. NecroSearch identified the hand as having belonged to a bear, whose hands are similar to those of humans. There was the time Dick Hopkins had borrowed Clark Davenport's equipment to help a police department locate buried explosives. He had searched the whole field with no luck until someone suggested that he check the ground beneath where he had parked his car, and sure enough, he found the explosives.

The calls kept coming, though the skeptics weren't always convinced. In August 1996, Janet March, a 33-year-old artist, had disappeared from her home in Nashville, Tennessee. Her husband, Perry, didn't report her missing for two weeks. He told the police she had left a note saying she needed a "vacation" from him and their two young children, but that he thought she would return. He admitted that they were having marital difficulties but, in the face of finger-pointing by the police, denied having anything to do with her disappearance.

In February 1997, NecroSearch was asked by the Nashville Police Department to send a team to search several sites where they thought Janet March might have been buried. The NecroSearch team, including Davenport, spent a weekend searching six sites. They didn't find a grave, but certainly seemed to worry March, who referred to them in the press as "high-tech witch doctors." The Nashville police investigators thanked the team for helping "rule out" the sites, though the police were cautioned not to remove them absolutely from the list. The team then left, assuring the Nashville police that they would be happy to return if other potential sites were identified, and were quietly amused by the "witch doctor" label.

Despite the recommendations they got from law enforcement agencies all over the country, including the FBI and DEA, there were still police agencies out there that regarded them in much the same way that Perry March had. There wasn't much they could do about it, Davenport reasoned, except approach their work as professionally and competently as possible.

"I don't know if this is the sort of thing you people do," Mike Maloney had said somewhat hesitantly. Davenport hurriedly assured the Navy investigator that the ATF case sounded exactly like the sort of investigation NecroSearch would be interested in.

"He's sort of in a hurry," Maloney replied, giving Davenport a telephone number for Mike Schmitz.

Aren't they all, the scientist thought, hanging up. Still, he couldn't help but reflect on how far the "PIG People" had come in a bit more than eight years: From studying the graves of buried pigs—and with a reputation only slightly above that of psychics—to getting referrals from the FBI, the DEA, and the U.S. military. Not bad for a volunteer collection of eggheads and cops, he thought.

Davenport waited a day for Maloney to call Schmitz to fill him in on NecroSearch, and then called himself. He got an answering machine. "Hey, this is Clark Davenport with NecroSearch," he said after the beep and left his number.

When Schmitz called back a few hours later, Davenport noted right away what he generally thought of as "first-time caller" reticence. Agencies that asked for NecroSearch's help usually did so as a last resort, and not always with a lot of enthusiasm. Good cops are naturally circumspect when it comes to revealing much about their cases, especially murder cases, and really good cops are often emotionally involved and simply not comfortable talking about the intimate details with a stranger—particularly with some civilian like Davenport. With each new agency there tended to be a feeling-out period.

Davenport pegged Schmitz as a really good cop after the agent revealed that his case was nearly 7 years old and that he had been working on it the entire time. That showed a lot of tenacity, which more than made up for the agent's being a little standoffish in Davenport's mind.

Schmitz didn't say much, just that he thought he had a good place to look in the Missouri River for a car with a female murder victim stuffed in the trunk.

That was okay with Davenport. He didn't need to know the whole story. It wasn't from a lack of compassion. His quote to the reporter, "There's no statute of limitations on murder, and there's no statute of limitations on grief," was a NecroSearch slogan, and he wouldn't have been with the group if he didn't care deeply about the cause of justice.

Most NecroSearch members seemed to have some sort of self-defense mechanism to protect themselves from the emotional fallout of dealing with murder victims and their families. Diane France had her boxes. Clark Davenport focused on the technical aspects of each situation.

Who this woman was, or who was suspected of killing her, wasn't relevant to what he could bring to the case. However, there was a car that had been in a major river for a long time with a body in the trunk. Finding it was a challenge he relished.

THE SETUP

Methamphetamine had been around since World War I, when both sides used the powerful stimulant to keep their soldiers awake and alert. Adolf Hitler was said to use it on a daily basis. Since the 1960s, "meth," also nicknamed in various permutations as speed and crank, had gained a sort of hint-and-wink acceptance in American society, from the housewife trying to lose a few pounds, to the businessman who wanted to get a jump on the competition, to long-haul truckers needing a boost to stay awake. But they were all dabblers compared to the real speed freak.

By the 1980s, meth was supplanting cocaine and heroin as the hard drug most popular with that segment of society that sociologists refer to as the lower socioeconomic white class. In less sophisticated circles, it was simply known as the "white trash" drug of choice. The reasons for the drug's popularity were in part economic, in part social. Although meth can be as expensive as cocaine, the high lasts for hours as opposed to minutes. Injected, snorted, or ingested, the chemicals release adrenaline into the bloodstream, which in turn pumps up the production of dopamine, the naturally occurring chemical in the brain that triggers feelings of pleasure, at once creating a sense of euphoria and strength. One hit of methamphetamine and the user instantly rockets (at least in his or her own mind) from the bottom of society to the top, self-confident and invincible for as long as the high lasts.

But meth has several unfortunate side effects. Acne and muscle tics are the least of them. The drug also causes heart irregularities, even failure, as well as liver and kidney damage. It suppresses the appetite, leading to extreme weight loss among frequent users, who must take increasing amounts to feel as good.

The mind is also under attack. Heavy users frequently exhibit paranoia, delusions, and hallucinations. Up for days without food or sleep, they are unpredictable and often violent.

Longtime users look faded, stretched, their skin sallow, their hair and eyes like they have been hooked up to an electrical charge. It's as though for every hour spent on top of the world, the drug exacts a toll, adding a line to the face and a vacancy to the eyes; stealing a day, a month, a year from a life.

Before she got hooked on meth, Christine Elkins was a pretty, petite young woman with a quick smile, trying to get by as a single mother in Maryville, Missouri. However, the drug took its toll on her physically and psychologically. She injected it between her toes and under her fingernails to disguise the needle tracks. Although she managed to hold on to a job working as a waitress in a restaurant-lounge, most of her money went to that next high. She hardly had enough left over to keep her maroon Oldsmobile Cutlass Supreme running, and she had become a thin, burned-out shell of her former self.

Still, she was not a total loss. By 1989, she was raising one son, Steven, age 7; another son, Jeremy, 15, was living with his father. Years before, her former husband had run off to Las Vegas, leaving her with the children. But even when methamphetamine took control of her life, she still wrote to her mother in Oregon on a weekly basis and called often. While some, including her former in-laws, who lived outside Maryville, didn't think much of her as a parent, Steven always had clean clothes and a roof over his head, and never went hungry so that she could feed her habit.

Christine Elkins just seemed trapped in what was, in many ways, a miserable life. Meth made it all right. On it, she wasn't a failure; she wasn't a bad mother. At least not for the three or four hours the high lasted.

Her boyfriend, Clark, regularly beat the hell out of her in front of her son. When she complained and said she would report his drug dealing to the police, Clark and his friend and supplier, Tony Emery, threatened to kill her. Everybody was afraid of Emery.

Once, when Emery's pal Ron Coy was supposed to go on trial for shooting a man with a handgun, the prosecutor arrived back home one night to find that someone had pumped a couple of shotgun rounds into his house. Emery was the chief suspect, but nothing could be proved. A mistrial was declared. Then the charges were dropped when the witnesses expressed extreme reluctance to testify.

Another time, Emery had a job working for a county road and bridge crew; the only problem was, he wouldn't actually do any work. The crew foreman had gone to the Nodaway County commissioners to complain and a commissioner told him to fire Emery. That commissioner's home was set on fire a short time later.

The tales of Emery's misdeeds went on and on. A competitor of the Emery family's trash-hauling business lost his truck in a mysterious explosion. Everyone knew who had rigged the dynamite, which had been stolen from the county road crew's supplies, but no one was going to say it for the record.

After the local newspaper dared print an unflattering article about the Emery hauling business, someone climbed on a bulldozer parked across the street the next night and drove it through the front wall of the building housing the newspaper's offices. But again no one was willing to talk about who might have been responsible.

Emery was suspected of numerous burglaries, auto thefts, and assaults. Stripped vehicles and cracked safes ended up underwater in abandoned rock quarries that pocketed the region. Everyone knew who put them there, but there were no witnesses who would testify and no proof.

Elkins sold drugs for Emery in order to support her own habit. She had done it for years, but she made a mistake in 1989 and sold to a Nodaway County Sheriff's Department informant and then twice, over a period of a few days, to a Missouri State Highway Patrol informant. The third time, she was arrested and charged.

The police sat her down and explained her options. She could help them catch Emery, or she would be looking at a lot of time in prison. Even if she helped, she would have to go to trial, but they would see that the prosecutor asked for leniency—maybe even no jail time, so she wouldn't have to leave her boy alone.

The squeeze was on, and Christine chose to cooperate. The police arranged for her to call Emery to arrange a drug buy.

When Emery arrived to meet Christine, he spotted the surveillance cars and took off. Armed with a warrant, the police arrested him at home. They quickly located the $900 in marked currency the informants had paid to Christine; now it had been traced to Emery. The police also found a cache of weapons, including an assault rifle and a dozen hunting rifles and shotguns—all illegal for a convicted felon.

Hoping to up the ante on Emery, the highway patrol called Special Agent Mark James with the U.S. Bureau of Alcohol, Tobacco and Firearms in Kansas City on the gun charges. James was a former Missouri State Patrol officer who had worked narcotics for a number of years before going over to the ATF. He wasn't big, but he was as tough and solid as mahogany.

At the time, James was training a new agent, Mike Schmitz, who had joined the ATF in 1989. Schmitz, a former University of Kansas assistant football coach, was a big, rugged sort. The attributes that had made him a good coach—show up ready to play and never quit—also made him an agent with a lot of promise. He would need it all over the next seven years.

Emery knew Elkins had set him up and was the key prosecution witness against him on the drug charges, yet he continued to sell meth to her. It was, perhaps, a measure of his arrogance. But he also thought he would be able, one way or another, to persuade Christine not to testify at his trial, slated for August 10, 1990.

In June 1990, the highway patrol and James decided to see if they could use Christine to set Emery up again, to give him a little more rope to hang himself. They wired her several more times and sent her to buy meth.

What the listeners got was small talk. In fact, parts of the recordings seemed to indicate that Christine was letting Emery know, possibly through hand signals, that she was wearing a wire. They suspected that she was playing both ends against the middle.

Emery thought the same. He began to complain to his friends and family that "that fucking bitch Christine" was blackmailing him. He had given her dope and helped her out with cash, including $2,000 in attorney fees for her own drug case. His trial date was getting close, and he was tired of investing with no sign of any return. He decided to poison her.

In late June, he contacted his cousin, Herbert "Tug" Emery in Greeley, Colorado, and asked him to acquire pure methamphetamine from their drug connection, John Watts, a 50-year-old biker. Most meth was diluted and cut with harmless additives before the user ever got it. The stuff Tony Emery wanted was from the bottom of the barrel and extremely strong, and he figured if Christine injected her usual amount, it would kill her but still look like an accidental overdose.

Tug was no Tony. He was a short, paunchy, weasely-looking 42-year-old who drove a long-haul truck and used meth to stay awake on the road. But he would do anything for his cousin, with whom he had been raised in Maryville like a brother. He agreed to get the stuff from Watts, who went by the nickname J. W., which his friends pronounced "Jay-dub."

The day after Tug Emery brought the stuff to Maryville, Ron Coy invited Christine Elkins over to his house, where he gave her the meth. She wanted to shoot it up right away. But worried that she would overdose in his kitchen, leaving him with a lot of explaining to do, Coy shook his head. "No, not here," he said, escorting her to the door.

A few days later, he was surprised to see her again. "You fucker," she screamed, "you tried to kill me." Coy pleaded ignorance when Christine complained that she had injected the "gift" and it made her violently ill. Apparently, Christine Elkins wasn't going to be easy to kill.

Emery was getting increasingly nervous. He pulled Christine aside one night at the lounge where she worked, and though witnesses couldn't hear what was said, it obviously upset her. She later told a coworker that she was terrified of Emery. "He says he's gonna kill me if I testify," she said. She was stuck between the drug dealer and the police.

On July 26, Agent James and Missouri State Highway Patrol trooper Al Riney wired Christine and instructed her to meet with Emery. They took a surveillance position across from his home. Ten minutes later, Emery walked out of the house and up to their car, looking in. He then stood behind their car until they drove off.

A little later, James and Riney met with Christine. She was hysterical and tried to hit Riney. "You fuckers almost got me killed," she cried. Emery had taken her to a house, where he had placed his hands under her clothing to locate the microphone he believed was on her body. He narrowly missed finding it hidden in her panties.

One afternoon soon afterward, Emery and his girlfriend, Mia

Clayton, were sitting in his car when Christine pulled up alongside. Emery and Christine talked a moment about their upcoming trials, and he gave her a gram of methamphetamine.

When Elkins drove off, Emery muttered, "She's blackmailing me."

"What do you mean?" Clayton asked.

"She wants dope and money for her fuckin' attorney to not testify against me," he replied. "But I'm tired of it. Something's gonna be done about her."

Clayton knew how violent Emery could be; he had beaten her up several times. She figured he meant he was going to kill the other young woman, but she didn't dare ask.

This time, Emery wanted it done right. He had another plan and asked his cousin, Tug Emery, to drive down from Colorado again.

On August 2, Christine called Mark James at his office in Kansas City. "Tony says he's gonna give me three, maybe four thousand dollars and some dope, and fix my car, so that I can get out of town. He wants me to leave before the trial," she said.

"It's a setup, Christine," James warned. "Don't go. I've been down this road before. Let me get up there and get you wired up, so we'll know if something's going wrong."

Christine promised to wait and hung up. She knew how thin the ice was; she even asked her former father-in-law to take care of Steven "if anything ever happens to me." But two days after talking to James, she apparently decided to take a chance and trust that Emery only wanted her out of town.

Late in the afternoon of August 4, Elkins arranged for her former sister-in-law, Tonya Green, to take her to retrieve her car from a repair shop owned by one of Emery's friends. Christine told the other young woman that "someone was going to help" her get out of town before her trial.

Then, a little before 10:00 P.M., Christine dropped Steven off at the home of a neighbor, Jerry Moser. Before she left, she asked to use Moser's telephone. From the gist of the conversation, Moser believed she was talking to Tony Emery—something about meeting him near the town park.

When she got off the telephone, Christine told Moser, "I'll only be

gone ten minutes. If I'm not, you can look for me at the morgue."
She hugged Steven; then she turned and hurried into the night.

When Christine Elkins hadn't returned by the next morning,
Moser and the boy drove past Elkins's duplex and noticed that the
front porch light was still on and her wash was still on the clothes-
line. Steven told Moser that they should look for his mommy at
"Tony's." But Moser wasn't interested in riling Emery and instead
took Steven to his paternal grandparents to wait.

Steven's mother never came back for him. Nor did she turn up at
the morgue. Her family—her mother and father in Oregon and two
sisters, one of them who also lived in Maryville—waited in vain for
her to contact them.

Eventually, Christine's landlady let herself into the apartment at
the request of the police and found coffee still in the coffee pot and
Elkins's belongings undisturbed. But as much as the ATF and local
police feared she was dead, there was no hard evidence to support
that she had done anything other than accept Tony Emery's offer to
get her out of town. At least nothing a defense lawyer wouldn't make
mincemeat out of in court. She was a drug addict; God only knew
what she might have done.

Christine's court date for the drug charges came and went. She
didn't show, and a warrant was issued for her arrest, as much as anything to put her on the national crime computers in case she was
picked up in another jurisdiction.

Emery's court date arrived. The prosecutors asked for and were
granted a continuance so that they could try to locate their key witness. Emery walked away from the courthouse laughing. After all,
no witness, no case.

Christine Elkins might have disappeared into the ranks of all the
thousands of others who vanish every year and are never found. But
that fall, the Maryville police caught a break when they got a call
from the Greeley, Colorado, police department.

"You got a missing woman?" Greeley detective Kent Donahue
asked. He explained that they had a defendant in a drug case who
was looking to make a deal by trading information about a homicide
in Missouri.

The Greeley police and DEA agents had arrested John Watts in a large methamphetamine bust. According to the detective, Watts was supplying meth to a guy named Herb "Tug" Emery. "Jay-dub" claimed that he had heard Tug Emery and another friend, Bobby Miller, talking about a murder they had been involved in with Tug's cousin, Tony Emery. The victim was a woman.

Word spread quickly to the ATF office in Kansas City, where Mark James and Mike Schmitz wondered what had happened to Christine Elkins. The guy in Colorado had to be talking about her. Still, it took several months to work out a deal with Watts.

On December 18, James, and Detective Dave Lin of the Maryville Police Department were in Greeley to meet with Watts. Keith Wood, the director of the Maryville Department of Public Safety, made Christine's disappearance the priority case for the department. But the decision had been made to try to get Tony Emery and his cousin, Tug, on federal charges. The federal government doesn't have a straight murder charge. However, the idea was to go after the Emerys by charging them with conspiracy to distribute methamphetamine and, in relation to that conspiracy, the murder of Christine Elkins. A conviction would result in life without parole, or even the death penalty.

There were a couple of reasons for going with the feds. One was Tony's notoriety, which might make it difficult to find a Maryville jury that wouldn't be terrified to participate. A federal trial, though, would be held in Kansas City. The second reason was resources and power: it was simply easier for the feds to deal with out-of-state witnesses, particularly those needing deals in Colorado, and to get subpoenaes for such things as telephone records and bank statements.

Watts now told the investigators that Tony Emery had said that past summer that "a girl" was going to testify against him in a drug case and that he was getting nervous. Later, according to Watts, Tug Emery informed him that he was going back to Missouri to "get rid of her."

"I told them they better think real serious about what they were going to do," Watts said. Tug Emery and Bobby Miller had gone to Maryville in early August anyway. After Watts returned home in mid-August from the annual motorcycle rally in Sturgis, South Dakota, Tony Emery told him over the telephone that the situation with the girl had been "handled."

Tug Emery was even more forthcoming. He told Watts that he, his cousin, and Bobby Miller had killed the girl. They had lured her to a house where, Tug Emery said, he hit her with a blackjack. She had fought, and he had to hit her again with a steel pipe.

"Miller freaked out and took off," Watts told the investigators. Miller left in a rental truck in which they had planned to put a barrel containing Elkins's body and concrete, to take back to Colorado. Later, Miller still received an ounce of meth from Tony Emery for his participation, and to keep his mouth shut.

With Miller and the truck gone, said Watts, Tony Emery had come up with another plan. "They put her body in a car and drove it off a cliff into a rock quarry."

It was exciting news to the investigators. They now had a place to start looking for Elkins's body. But they knew they were a long way from proving a murder case. They only had Watts's word about what had happened, and he wasn't the most credible witness in the world.

James and Lin, working with Detective Donahue of the Greeley police, put a wire on the biker. Then they sent him to meet with Tug Emery at a restaurant with a story about needing to eliminate the witness in his own drug case, a man named Norm Downing. He was also supposed to try to set up a drug deal with the two Emerys.

"You know that fucking Norm Downing?" Watts asked Tug Emery as they sat in his car outside the restaurant. "The one that set us up."

"Yeah," Emery replied.

"He's around, I heard," Watts continued. "I'm going to do that fucker."

"What's he look like?" Emery asked.

"A little short guy," Watts replied. "I can get you a picture. . . . But I don't know quite what to do with the fucking body."

"You have to find somewhere to put the body . . ." Emery said.

"But where?" Watts asked, trying to lead Emery. "There ain't no rock quarries back here, is there?"

"I'm tryin' to think," Emery said. "A mine shaft is what you need. . . . But you've got to be able to, you know, if he's driving something, you've got to be able to get rid of it, too. You can't just leave that sitting around."

To the delight of the listening investigators, Emery quickly referred to Christine's disappearance, saying, "That whole car and everything's gone back there, and I mean everything."

Watts then asked if Emery had gone by the rock quarry on a recent return trip to Missouri. "To see if she was floating?"

Emery shook his head. "She ain't floating." He advised Watts that after Norm Downing was killed, "all you got to do is wrap him up in the rug. . . . That works real good. We just roll the motherfuckers up and put them over your shoulder. . . . You can't even tell what's in there."

"Was there a lot of blood?" Watts asked, referring to the Elkins murder.

"Yeah," Emery replied. "Just a little bit."

"I ain't gonna beat him," Watts said. "You know, he might turn around and whip my ass. That chick damn near whipped your ass, huh?"

"Nah," Emery said. "She didn't fucking whip it, but she was hard to get down."

"She wouldn't go, huh?" Watts asked.

"She went," was Emery's reply.

"Yeah, but it took some . . . that blackjack ain't enough, huh?"

"No, you got to have a steel pipe," Emery said. "Get one of them big flashlights."

"You smashed her," Watts said. "Man, that would be the shits. I bet she was screaming and hollering, huh?"

"Uh-huh," Emery agreed.

The conversation turned to Bobby Miller and whether their friend might have said anything about the murder to his girlfriend. Emery said he didn't think so. "I told him I'd kill him."

"I don't know why you ever took Miller with you back there. You know that's something you always got to worry about," Watts said.

"I'm not worried about it," Emery replied. "He's done been told and not just by me, either."

"Just think," Watts continued, "he got an ounce—"

"He got more than that," Emery interrupted. "He's got that fucking forty-five pistol."

"But he didn't do nothin'," Watts said. "That's why I never could figure out why he had a fuckin' U-Haul truck."

"He freaked out," Emery said. "He fuckin' got lost."

"Then you decided to use the rock quarry, right?" Watts asked, aware the investigators were probably waiting on the edge of their seats.

But Tug Emery was suddenly distracted about a recent spate of drug-dealing ripoffs and double crosses that had set him back financially. Watts tried to steer him around again to the subject of murder.

"So, ah, if I do Norm, ah, will you help me get rid of him?" Watts asked.

"Yep," Emery replied.

"Does it have to be a lot of water?" Watts asked.

"Nah," the other man responded. Besides, he didn't know of any rock quarries in Colorado with water in them. "Too bad you didn't know where a mine shaft was or knew somebody that worked on a farm that has one of them big hay grinders," Emery mused. "There ain't nothin' left when they do that. I mean fucking nothin'."

"No," Watts said. He kept trying to turn the conversation back to the killing in Missouri. "That was perfect back there where you had the water deep enough you could sink the fucking car. . . . Did it go out very far?"

"Fucking right, it did," Emery replied, pointing to another building to indicate a distance of some 25 yards.

"That far?" Watts whistled. "Man, you must have had that fucking pedal down . . . looked like a fucking rocket."

"Put a stick in there," Emery said. "Hell, it was a fucking quarry. I don't know how fucking deep it is."

"It's a long ways to the water probably," Watts said, hoping to get more description to help the investigators pinpoint which rock quarry.

"Yeah, it is," Emery agreed. "There's a cliff there, hell, a hundred feet down. . . . They'll never be able to find that motherfucker."

If the job was done right, Emery went on, people would just think that Watts's problem witness had simply left the country. Just like they did that girl who tried to mess with his cousin.

The two men agreed to set up a major drug buy with Tony Emery for some time between Christmas and the new year. "Be careful," Tug Emery said as he got out of Watts's car.

"Yeah, I'll be good," Watts replied. "If you can't be good, be careful."

*   *   *

On December 28, 1990, Tony Emery and Ron Coy flew into Denver's Stapleton International Airport, where they were picked up in a blizzard by Tug Emery. He drove them to a motel north of the city to meet with James Watts, who waited with 3 pounds of methamphetamine worth $30,000, provided by agents of the DEA.

At first, Tony Emery and Coy wanted to stay in the car and have Watts come outside to complete the transaction. They sent Tug Emery in to speak to Watts, who, knowing that a hidden video camera was capturing all that went on in his room, said he had to wait for a telephone call from his drug supplier.

Tug Emery went outside and returned with his cousin and Coy. After introductions and complaints about the flight, Watts asked Tony Emery about the status of his drug case.

"It comes up the twenty-third of January," Tony Emery said and smiled. "And they're going to have to drop it because that's the last time they can postpone it."

"That's good," said Watts, who used it as a segue into his own case and the witness supposedly lined up against him. "Yeah, I gotta get rid of that fucking Norm."

"That's against the law, ain't it?" Tug Emery joked.

"Huh?" said Watts, not the brightest bulb in the room, before he caught on. "Well, everything we do right now is against the law, you fucker."

Coy feigned horror. "It is?" he said, his beady eyes as big as he could make them. "Oh, I need to go home."

That got them all laughing. Then they settled down to business, with Watts complaining about all the people who owed him money for drugs—as much as $25,000, he said.

"Goddam," Tony Emery exclaimed. "We're gonna have to come out here and help you do some collecting."

"Yeah, you can," Watts agreed. "Sons of bitches all hiding, you know." He made another attempt to try to get Tony Emery to incriminate himself in Christine's murder. "Like Norm—you know how I can do him? He's the only son of a bitch that can testify against me."

Now Emery took a professional interest. He asked if Watts knew where the feds were keeping Downing, or whether there would be an opportunity to get to him when he was brought up to testify. Before Watts could say anything, Tug Emery, another dim bulb, interjected that Watts shouldn't try to kill Downing while he was surrounded by police escorts.

"Well, hell no, Tug," Watts said, rolling his eyes. "I ain't gonna just jump out there in the fucking courtroom and do him, you goofy fucker."

Coy thought that was funny. "They could get you for contempt of court," he said, and the men laughed. But Tony Emery was wrapped up in the serious business of getting to the witness against Watts. "Where's he live now?" he asked.

"Lubbock," Watts replied, referring to a rough-and-tumble Texas city.

"Fuck, people disappear every day in Lubbock," Tony Emery snorted. "And they never fucking even bother to look for 'em."

"People disappear every day in Lubbock," Coy repeated like a parrot, "and nobody fuckin' bothers to look for 'em."

It was yet another opening for Watts. He talked about how Downing had set him up. "He came over one day, and I sold him an ounce and then he came back and, uh, bought two more ounces the same day."

"Shoulda' known something's up, that motherfucker," Tug Emery said, shaking his head.

"That's the way that fuckin' bitch did me," Tony Emery added.

Encouraged, Watts went on. "Some way, some day, I don't care, even if I have to go . . ."

"Yeah, but if you can stop it in its tracks . . . and stay out of the son of a bitch," Tony Emery advised. "The way I see it, a motherfucker like that ain't worth twenty years."

The men turned their attention back to the methamphetamine deal. Tug Emery offered to step outside with Coy while Watts and his cousin wrapped up the deal; he knew his cousin didn't like having a lot of witnesses around when he was doing business. Tony said he could stay so long as it was okay with Watts, who nodded.

"Do you wanna see if I'm wearing a wire?" Tug Emery laughed, not knowing that he was being filmed. The comment, though, reminded his cousin about Christine Elkins.

"Hey, that fucking bitch," Tony said. "I shook her down. She had a skirt, and I pulled it right up over her fucking shirt."

"She wasn't wired?" Watts asked.

"Not on that deal," Tony Emery said.

Tony Emery and Coy left the room with the drugs to wait for his cousin in the car until Watts's drug connection came by to pick up the money. "Miller still got that forty-five Tony gave him?" Watts asked Tug while they waited in the room. The agents listening in noted that it must be the gun Tug had referred to before—the one Miller received from his cousin for helping with the murder.

"As far as I know," Emery said. He was pretty sure his cousin would help Watts take care of Downing, "and it won't cost you a thing."

Tug Emery was just plain proud of his Missouri cousin. "He's the closest thing I got," he said. "And I'll tell you what, they never catch him. You can tell that by looking at him."

There was a knock on the door. It was Watts's "drug connection," actually an undercover DEA agent.

When their business was concluded, Tug Emery thanked the agent and opened the motel room door to leave. Waiting for him were more agents, who entered with their guns drawn.

"Freeze! Police! Don't move! Keep your hands up!" The officers' shouts froze everyone. "Get down! Get down! Get that door. You, too, get down! Get the door closed!"

"Got any chew?"

The DEA agent looked at his prisoner. It was January 8, 1991. They were on an elevator at the federal building. Agent Jay Erickson pulled out his bag of chewing tobacco and handed the wad to Tug Emery, who gnawed off a huge mouthful.

"Geez, think you got enough?" Erickson said, looking ruefully at what was left.

"Don't worry," Emery said between chews. "You'll be gettin' your money's worth in a minute."

Both of the Emerys and Coy had been charged with selling methamphetamine in the drug bust, a felony that could land them in prison for twenty years. Tony Emery and Ron Coy hadn't budged under questioning. But Tug Emery, who the investigators felt all along would be the one to crack, now wanted to make a deal.

"You guys got a map of Missouri?" Emery asked.

"We've got a map of the Maryville area," Erickson replied as they stepped off the elevator.

Emery shook his head. "Ain't gonna be big enough," he mumbled through his full mouth."

"Is it near Maryville?" Erickson asked.

"It . . . ain't near Maryville," Emery said, "and you won't find it without me."

Believing he had the investigators where he wanted them, Emery swaggered into the room where ATF agent James and Detective Lin, an assistant U.S. Attorney, and Emery's lawyer waited. Emery noticed a map on the table and walked over to it and read the legend in the bottom right hand corner.

"This ain't gonna do it," Emery said, pushing the Maryville map away with disdain.

"KEEP YOUR MOUTH SHUT AND SIT DOWN!" Emery's lawyer shouted at him. A former assistant U.S. Attorney, the lawyer had only just been told that the meeting involved more than drugs, that this was a homicide investigation. Nothing had been worked out yet, and his client was already blurting out information.

The investigators were startled. Not so much by the attorney's shout but by the implication that, unless he was blowing a smoke-screen, Tug Emery had just told them they had been looking for Christine Elkins's body in all the wrong places.

Ever since Emery's recorded conversation with Watts on December 18, they had been searching rock quarries. But they had apparently stayed too close to home, all within a 10- to 20-mile radius of Maryville, the area covered by the map he had just shoved away.

Conventional wisdom, including that developed by the FBI's Behavioral Sciences Unit, held that a killer wouldn't drive very far with a body in the car. They had firmly believed that Tony Emery wouldn't have dared take Christine any farther than he had to and risk accidental discovery.

Now, the search area had just been more than quadrupled in size, but only if Tug Emery was telling the truth. James thought he was; the reaction to the map had been too spontaneous, his disdain unrehearsed. However, Emery's lawyer kept a muzzle on his client for the rest of the meeting and did the talking himself. In exchange for any possible information, Emery wanted a free ride: the drug charges dropped and no charges for Elkins's murder.

It was too steep a price for the U.S. Attorney. Emery was, after all, an accomplice to murder, he said. They had to be conscious of how a deal would look to a jury. A man might say anything, even implicate his own flesh and blood, for the deal Emery was demanding, and a defense lawyer would be sure to point that out.

So there would be no deal. Instead, in March the Emery cousins and Ron Coy pleaded guilty to the drug charges. Tug Emery and Coy received sentences of a little more than seven years; Tony Emery got nearly ten years.

It was something, but it wasn't nearly enough for the murder of Christine Elkins.

THE SEARCH

The day was sunny, the sky blue, but the temperature hovered around 20 degrees as the men stood on the ice covering the deep waters of the rock quarry. Around them, the farmlands of northwest Missouri lay shrouded in snow, the trees bare.

Somehow, the bleakness of the landscape was also an apt description of how this case was going to Mike Schmitz. For what seemed like the hundredth time, he and Mark James had driven up to Maryville to meet with Dave Lin to check out yet another rock quarry.

This one had seemed a good prospect. Some of Tony Emery's acquaintances said this was one of his favorite swimming holes, and a place he dumped evidence of his crimes. Although a "fish finder" they'd brought along and dropped through a hole in the ice located the remains of an old boat, there was no car, no body.

Schmitz knew, looking at his mentor and friend James, that there would also be no quitting. James was the one who had worked the most with Christine Elkins, and he was not about to let this go. Tony Emery had gotten away with just about anything he wanted to do for a long time. But not this crime, he would tell his protégé Schmitz, not this time.

James didn't come right out and say it, but Schmitz knew him well enough to understand that he felt guilty over what had happened to Christine. It had been her choice to sell and use drugs, and then to believe Tony Emery's promise to help her get out of town. But she was a pawn in the struggle to bring Emery down; she had worked for James, and he had not been able to protect her.

Schmitz knew that they would spend as long as it took, turn over every stone, peer beneath every surface, to find Christine and make Tony Emery pay for killing her. But on days like this one, with their feet and faces numb from the cold, it seemed they were getting nowhere.

The investigators hadn't limited themselves to looking in rock quarries. They subpoenaed the telephone and credit card records of Bobby Miller and Tug Emery, which showed that the men had traveled to Missouri and back at the time Elkins disappeared. In fact, judging by the records, they had traveled to the "show me" state together but returned to the Rockies separately.

The timing and placing of some of the calls was intriguing and perplexing. Sometimes they were able to fill in pieces of the puzzle by talking to Watts. For instance, at 11:16 P.M. on the night Elkins disappeared, a two-minute calling card call charged to the home telephone of Bobby Miller was placed from Burlington, Missouri, to James Watts in Fort Collins. Watts told the investigators that Miller called that night when he wasn't at home and left a message asking for Tony Emery's home telephone number. A half hour later, Miller had called Watts again and spoken for four minutes, which also jibed with the records.

Watts told the investigators that during that telephone conversation, Miller was "freaked" and claimed that the Emery cousins had killed a girl. "He said he got scared and took off," Jay-dub recalled. "He wanted Tony's number so he could call and say he was driving back to Colorado."

The investigators knew that Miller called Tony Emery's house a couple of times right after talking to Watts, but apparently there was no answer. At 3:23 and 3:45 the morning of August 5, Miller used his card again to call Tony Emery from St. Joseph, Missouri. Again, only a machine answered. Tony Emery was apparently out all night.

Most of the progress the investigators made could be attributed to good old-fashioned legwork. The investigators tried to talk to every known associate of Christine Elkins and Tony Emery, except Ron Coy. They left him alone in prison, figuring he would remain loyal to his friend unless they could come up with something linking him to the murder—something they didn't yet have.

But others talked. One of Tony's meth buyers, Terry Swalley, confided that Emery had told him several times between December 1989 and August 4, 1990 that he was going to kill Christine. One of the small-time dealers Tony forced into his operation, Randy Crail, said Emery often complained about Christine "setting him up" and said that she would be "taken care of."

Kenny Poppa, another of Tony's drug pals, also told them about Emery threatening to kill Christine. "He said, 'No witness, no case.' But he hadn't decided whether to do it or pay her to take off," Poppa recalled.

Emery also said, according to Poppa, that he was talking about getting his problem taken care of by another of the family's model citizens, an uncle who was serving a life sentence for murder in the Iowa State Penitentiary. The uncle had a friend who was getting out soon, " 'and he'll do it for the right amount,' " Poppa said, recounting Tony Emery's boast.

The investigators also talked to Christine's friends, who painted a picture of a desperate young woman trying to get out of trouble. Trouble with Emery. Trouble with the law. Moser, who had been left with Elkins's son the night she disappeared, said Steven told him that his mother was going to get some money, "and that he was going to Las Vegas to see his father." Christine's friend and coworker at the lounge, another once-beautiful young woman beginning to show the ravages of a meth habit, recounted the night Tony Emery had shown up at their work and threatened Christine.

"She was terrified," the woman said. "She thought Tony Emery was going to kill her."

During the winter of 1991–92, the investigators began to present their evidence to a federal grand jury in Kansas City, Missouri. They originally thought they had a very solid drug conspiracy/murder mapped out by James on his computer, complete with phone and bank records. The rug was yanked out from under them when they learned that back in early 1991, the then-U.S. Attorney in Colorado had agreed there would be no conspiracy charges. James was livid. He had told the prosecutor that they wanted to keep that option open to get leverage for the murder case. But he had bargained it away, and now there was nothing James could do about it.

They came up with another idea. The ATF agents hoped they could persuade assistant U.S. Attorney Michael Green to ask the jurors to indict Tug Emery on an obscure federal murder charge based on a suspect's killing a witness to prevent the witness from communicating with a law enforcement officer regarding a federal crime. Their point was that Elkins had been working with James when she disappeared and was allegedly murdered.

The investigators had what amounted to a taped confession made by Tug Emery to Watts in Colorado. The telephone and credit card records placed Tug in Maryville at the time Elkins disappeared. If nothing else, they felt, the added pressure of a murder rap might get him to rethink spending the rest of his life in prison—maybe even the death penalty—and roll over on his cousin.

The real prey was Tony Emery. If Tug and Bobby Miller and maybe Ron Coy were involved, they would go after them, too—even harder if they wouldn't cooperate. But what had happened to Christine happened at Tony Emery's bidding. He was the one they dreamed of bringing down.

The jurors met with Schmitz, James, and Green every other month. They would listen to the presentations of witnesses—including the agents themselves—and ask questions. They seemed to understand the case, but they could make no move unless asked by the prosecutor to issue an indictment.

Green wouldn't go for it. He needed more, he told the investigators. And what he needed more than anything was Christine Elkins's body. Common sense might tell a trial jury that she was dead, he argued, but where was the proof beyond a reasonable doubt?

So it was back to the rock quarries and running down leads. As they developed new information, they took it to the grand jury, hoping that the next piece would tip the scales and an indictment would be forthcoming. They would have to keep on hoping, and working, for many years.

In 1992, ATF Agent Mark James transferred to the Omaha office, and Maryville Detective Lin accepted a position with the ATF office in Kansas City. The two men stayed involved in the investigation, but the grunt work fell to Schmitz and to Lin's replacement, Detective Randy Strong of the Maryville police.

Police work ran in Strong's blood. His grandfather was a police officer; one uncle was a Missouri state trooper and the other a sheriff. But when he got out of high school, he went to college at Northwest Missouri State in Maryville to be an art teacher.

Gradually, he tired of school. Married with kids, he also needed a job. It just so happened that the Maryville Police Department was advertising for new officers. Strong had always admired his relatives in law enforcement, and decided it was a job he could do. He became a patrol officer in 1979 and in 1992 became a detective. Actually, he was the only detective for the Maryville PD.

Strong met Tony Emery and Ron Coy early on as a patrol officer. As he put it, they were "the first badasses" he ran across, and they remained the worst. In fact, he thought Emery was worse than the late Ken Rex McElroy, a more notorious Missouri thug.

McElroy had lived in Skidmore, a little less than 18 miles from Maryville. He'd once committed a burglary with a then-16-year-old Tony Emery, but that was the least of his criminal activities. He was said to have raped and assaulted and robbed the citizens of Skidmore with impunity because he had the locals too cowed to go to the law.

One day during the summer of 1981, citizens of Skidmore had enough. As McElroy climbed in his truck in the middle of town, he found himself surrounded by his neighbors. When the crowd backed away from the truck again, McElroy had been shot dead.

Randy Strong was teaching a class on robbery precautions for bank employees in Maryville when he got a call to assist sheriff's deputies in Skidmore. When he arrived, the deputies were just removing McElroy from his truck. Except for the law officers, the streets of Skidmore were empty. Strong thought it looked like a ghost town.

Though the local law enforcement and eventually even the FBI tried to find out who killed McElroy, no one in town would talk about it. No one was ever arrested for the murder, and not a whole lot of people shed any tears over that, either.

Still, Strong didn't think McElroy, bad as he was, could have held a candle to Emery for meaness, nor was he anywhere near as brazen. McElroy bullied those he thought were weaker than himself, but he stayed away from the law. Emery, on the other hand, seemed to think of the police as a personal challenge. Strong never knew him to back down from anyone. Not the county prosecutor, nor the commissioner, nor the police.

The young detective didn't really know Christine Elkins, but he had seen her around town and noticed the company she kept. He was working at the police department one night in October 1989, when she came in with a black eye and a split lip. It was obvious she was high on methamphetamine as she complained that her boyfriend had beaten her up and that Tony Emery had threatened to take it farther. She eventually refused to cooperate on the assault allegation, so the case had been dropped. Then she disappeared.

At first, Strong was eager to get involved in the Elkins case. But after months and then years passed, he felt emotionally and physically drained by it. As his friendship with Mike Schmitz grew, he knew his colleague felt the same. Days, nights, weeks were spent away from their families. Even when they went home, they were consumed by the case. What hadn't they thought of? What bit of pressure applied here or there might start the crack that would break the whole thing open?

The investigation was an exemplary instance of interagency cooperation among the ATF, the Maryville police, the state highway patrol, and the Nodaway County Sheriff's Office. Those assigned to the case met frequently to report on any progress and go over the to-do lists. The team consisted of Schmitz; Strong, Lt. Ron Christian, and patrolman Bob Seiple of the Maryville PD; Deputy Harley "Stretch" Linnegar of the sheriff's office; and Dennis Randle, a diver with the Missouri State Water Patrol who was in on every quarry search.

The team looked in all the quarries that were easily accessible, and then those more difficult to reach, until they were trekking across farm fields to reach the most remote. They knew the late summer of 1990 had been a wet one, and the fields had to have been muddy. They looked at those fields now and thought that even someone as arrogant as Tony Emery wouldn't have tried to cross them and chance getting stuck. Then again, they recalled Tug Emery's insistence that their maps weren't big enough, which had shot full of holes the conventional wisdom about the distance a killer would travel with a body. So they had crossed the fields to have a look, carrying boats and other equipment by hand.

They had even lugged some pretty sophisticated technology, including the "fish finder," a simple sonar used by fishermen to locate schools of fish, which also could be used to map the bottom of a quarry; and once the Navy had loaned them a magnetometer. They even had some luck and located three cars. Each time one was located, there would be a rush of excitement—followed by disappointment. The cars had all been reported stolen, but none was a maroon Olds Cutlass Supreme.

Mark James, a computer whiz, fed everything anyone gathered into a database. With a flick of the switch, he could immediately bring up a chart that would show what they could prove, what evidence they did (or didn't) have, and all the witnesses and exhibits they would need in court, and at what point in the trial. Strong and Schmitz interviewed dozens of known associates of Tony Emery, many of them petrified and absolutely certain they would be the next to die, in prisons as far away as Iowa, or secretly in Kansas City hotels.

In the meantime, Schmitz and Assistant U.S. Attorney Green had a series of knockdown drag-outs, complete with door slamming and name calling. The agent understood the prosecutor's point that if they messed up, they wouldn't get another chance. But Schmitz, and through him, James, wanted to try. Anything was better than knowing Tony Emery was out there laughing at them.

For instance, the agent wanted to have some of the witnesses subpoenaed before the grand jury and compelled to talk. They might not cooperate, or tell the truth, but it would be one more way to add a little pressure to the situation and see what crack developed. But Green would balk. It was still going to come down to one thing, he said, proving that Elkins was dead. "Bring me a body," he would always say, "and we'll go after all of them."

Schmitz would throw up his hands. There must have been precedent for prosecuting a bodyless homicide, he reasoned. Surely the FBI had pursued some mob-related case in which the victim had disappeared. But while there had been rare instances of such crimes being successfully prosecuted in state courts, he was told, there had been none in federal courts.

Schmitz burned up the telephone and computer lines with James. They hashed and rehashed what they had and what still could be done. It was frustrating as hell. Both ATF agents were black-and-white kind of guys; there was right and there was wrong, and Tony Emery was as wrong as it got.

For Schmitz, it wasn't just about Christine Elkins. He wanted Emery for Mark James, the man who had taken him under his wing, trained him, and now suffered because he had not been able to protect a young mother of two boys. Without James, Schmitz might have let the case go. It really wasn't "his" case. It had been passed on to him. He had other cases to work on, and it wasn't as if the world stood still so that he could track down the killer of a methamphetamine addict. But in the end, Schmitz had to admit, he stayed in it for himself as well. This case was all about the kind of man he believed himself to be. Giving up went against the grain of the football player and coach in him. It wasn't even about winning and losing—it was about showing up, ready to play. They had managed to work their way downfield against Tony Emery. They could see the end zone. They just couldn't seem to get the ball across the goal line.

One of the most heated debates between the agent and the prosecutor involved whether to grant full immunity to Bobby Miller in exchange for his testimony. The night the Emerys and Coy were arrested at the Denver motel, James, Lin, and Detective Kent Donahue of the Greeley Police Department had also paid a visit to Bobby Miller. First, they sent Watts in wired, to see if he could get Miller to say something incriminating. Instead, Miller demanded that he leave. Two minutes later, the officers went to the door and were let in. James told Miller to take a seat. "You got one foot in the gas chamber and one foot out," he snarled. He was bluffing; they had nothing on Miller except what Watts said he had overheard. "Unless you're honest about what happened with that girl in Missouri last summer."

Miller stayed cool. "I don't know what you're talkin' about," he retorted.

James grabbed a .45-caliber semiautomatic lying near Miller. It had to be the gun given to Miller by Tony Emery.

"He give this to you so you'd keep your mouth shut about what happened back in Missouri?" James asked.

"I paid for it," Miller scowled, then lawyered up on them.

Later, word came down that he wanted full immunity to testify. Anything less and he wasn't talking to anyone. Schmitz wanted to give it to him. It wasn't because he liked Miller. In fact, he was just another scumbag meth dealer who had at least known a murder was being planned and did nothing to stop it. However, the way the agent saw it, Miller was the least culpable, and they were going to need him to get to Tug Emery so that they could climb the ladder to Tony.

It wasn't until the spring of 1996, nearly six years after Christine Elkins disappeared, that Green finally warmed up to the idea of giving Miller full immunity. The Justice Department wasn't happy about it. The higher-ups didn't like the idea but at last they relented.

Miller could have his immunity so long as he told the truth and hadn't killed Christine or helped dispose of the body.

Even then, it required U.S. Attorney General Janet Reno to sign off on the deal before it could be offered to Miller. Then he almost scuttled it because it seemed too good to be true. He refused to believe that all he had to do was tell the truth and he could walk away a free man. He demanded a lawyer. When the feds explained the offer to Miller's attorney, he didn't hesitate and told Miller, "You got a good deal, and you better take it."

Miller was brought to Kansas City where, safe from prosecution, he spilled his guts. Tug Emery had asked him to accompany him to Missouri in August 1990, he said. But, he claimed, he didn't know why and didn't find that out until the morning of August 4.

They had driven straight through, arriving in Maryville before dawn that day. They drove to Tony's, where they grabbed a few hours' sleep. After he got up, Miller said, he was standing in the kitchen making a sandwich when he overheard the two cousins talking about killing the girl. That's when he put in his two cents.

"I'd heard on the Discovery Channel or something that concrete dissolves bones and flesh—the lime that's in it," Miller said. It had been his bright idea for them to get a 55-gallon barrel, dump the girl's body in it after she was killed, and then pour in concrete. He had also suggested they rent a truck, which he would drive back to Colorado, then he and Tug would dispose of the barrel.

Tony Emery liked the idea. He gave Miller and Tug cash—so the rental couldn't be traced back to him—to rent the truck in St. Joseph, and to purchase the necessary bags of concrete. He promised to give Miller an ounce of meth and sold him the .45 at a steal for his troubles.

The plan was for Tony Emery to lure Elkins to a rental home he owned near the city park, a few blocks from his own home. The men discussed whether to shoot her there, but Tony Emery decided the noise might attract attention. Instead, he said, they would beat her to death.

Sometime after 9:00 P.M., Miller said, he drove the truck and followed the Emerys to the house. He was directed to park in the rear next to a shed. The house was dark and the yard lit only dimly by a streetlight. Tony Emery went into the house through a rear entrance.

Tug Emery helped Miller string a hose from the house to the truck to add water for the concrete. Tug Emery then left Miller alone and followed his cousin into the house. Miller said he couldn't be sure, but he thought he could just make out the dark silhouette of a man sitting in a truck parked down the street.

A short time later, maybe 10:00, another vehicle pulled up alongside the car Tony Emery had driven. It was an older model GMC two-door. The driver got out and walked to the rear entrance of the house.

"I couldn't see her real well," Miller told the investigators. "But I could tell she was a woman."

The woman went in, and a moment later, Miller was jolted out of his wits by her screams. "Stop! Stop! Stop hitting me!" he said she had cried. "Why are you doing this? Stop!" The screaming seemed to go on for a long time, "at least a minute," until at last there was silence.

Tug Emery came out of the house and told Miller that his cousin had changed his mind. He wanted Miller to drive back to Tony's house and wait. Unnerved by the woman's screams, Miller had been happy to comply. He set out for Emery's house; however, he took a wrong turn and began heading toward downtown Maryville. Then he saw a police officer, who seemed to take a "professional interest" in him.

"I thought maybe we were already found out," Miller said. He decided to hell with Tony Emery; he was getting out of town. It wasn't that easy. He got lost some more and went in another wrong direction. He stopped to call Tony Emery to tell him he was leaving town and to alert him to the police officer he had seen. But he didn't have Emery's number and called Watts in Colorado. Watts wasn't home for the first call, but he reached him on the second and got the number.

The agents listened with straight faces, though their minds were racing. They hadn't told Miller that they had his telephone records. So far, his recollection matched what they knew to be true.

Miller said he unloaded the bags of cement and the barrel at his home and then dropped off the rental truck in Greeley, Colorado, on August 6. Later that day, Tug Emery showed up at his house. To show there were no hard feelings, Emery gave Miller the personal effects he had left at Tony's, including the .45, as well as the promised methamphetamine.

"He said Tony had nothing to worry about anymore," Miller added.

The next day, the investigators took Miller to Maryville, where he amazed them with his recall, pointing out places he had made calls or roads he had gone down. They knew from his telephone records that he had been to these places, but considering he was lost, they hadn't expected Miller to be so accurate. He even took them past Tony's house and the house where Christine had been murdered. It went a long way toward establishing his credibility.

There was something Schmitz didn't understand. Why had Miller been willing to take such a chance for someone he didn't know? An ounce of meth was worth maybe $1,500. So little to participate in a murder? "What were you thinking?" Schmitz asked.

Miller shrugged and shook his head. "You know, I later started wondering, *Man, I must be the stupidest guy on Earth."*

Bobby Miller and James Watts testified before the grand jury in Kansas City. It was the third grand jury, each serving an eighteen-month term, to hear the evidence; every time a new jury was sworn in, Schmitz had backtracked to bring them up to speed.

After those two witnesses, the grand jury was getting itchy to issue an indictment. Green explained the difficulties he would encounter in a murder trial when he didn't have absolute proof that the victim was dead, or had been murdered. Even with a body, it would be a complex case. It was also a matter of timing, he said. He and the agents and police officers had to work on other cases. He urged patience.

Mike Schmitz thought the prosecutor had handled the question pretty well. He had come to a grudging respect for the assistant attorney general's meticulous ways. Green was slow to move for an indictment, but Schmitz figured that if they ever did make it to court, he would be tough to beat.

Still, the agent wasn't sure how much longer he could keep it up personally. At first, when they had learned about the rock quarries, there had been something to really go after—even when the search had expanded to quarries in Iowa, Nebraska, and Kansas. They had tried everything. They had brought in cadaver dogs, flown over the quarries taking photographs, and sent in scuba divers. But to no avail.

It wasn't that they had no luck—a safe, with money still in it, was recovered, as were several cars, including a stolen vehicle out of Oklahoma. It was just never the right car, never the right kind of luck.

There would be word that some prison inmate had a lead, and Schmitz or Strong, and often both, would have to go speak to him. Inevitably it was just some jerk looking for a free trip out of jail with no real information. But they couldn't be ignored for fear they would miss the guy who could crack the case.

As the investigation dragged on year after year, Schmitz began to routinely feel tired and depressed. It surprised him. He had always considered himself a pretty tough guy, able to handle adversity well. But he was beginning to doubt himself, and wondered if they were ever going to get this one over with. He felt like a circus dog, always jumping through hoops.

Even his colleagues urged him to give it up. Some things just weren't meant to be, they would say. "Let it die, Schmitty." But he couldn't.

The worst part was that it was affecting his family life. He would catch himself yelling at his wife or the kids about something trivial. Once he cooled off, he knew that it wasn't them he was angry with. "I'm just spinning my wheels on this damn case," he would confess to his wife. "It's the body; we can't find the damn body." There were many nights when he couldn't sleep, so he would get up and work. He would organize and reorganize his graphs and timelines to see if there was anything he had missed.

The team even tried to talk to Elkins's younger son, Steven, to see if there was some childhood memory that might help. But the boy's grandparents wouldn't let them. He had been told that his mother had simply left him; they didn't feel it would do him any good to hear she had been murdered. The investigators had spoken briefly to Jeremy, her older son. He had grown into a fine young man, who was going to college, but he was angry with the police for what he considered foot dragging in going after the man who had killed his mother.

There were times when Schmitz agreed with him, not that the ball was in his court. What more could he do?

Late that summer, Schmitz had finally had it. He handed his report over to Green. "We've got as much as we're going to get," he said as he turned to leave. "Shit or get off the pot."

On September 19, 1996, Green condensed the ATF case report and laid its essence out for his superiors, asking to go ahead with the indictment of Herbert "Tug" Emery for the murder of Christine Elkins. If they got him, they might get his cousin. "The defendant told Watts that they put her body in her vehicle and drove it off a rock quarry."

However, Green noted, there were two problems for the prosecution. One was jurisdiction: He was going to have to be able to prove that Elkins was killed to keep her from communicating with a federal law enforcement officer. "There obviously is abundant evidence that Tony Emery wanted to kill her to keep her from testifying against him in the state drug case," Green explained. "This fact alone does not give us jurisdiction. However, it is also a fact that on July twenty-third, nineteen-ninety, Elkins became a federal informant when she provided information to Special Agent James.

"It will be a close question. However, the fact that Tony Emery had reason to suspect Elkins was working as an informant on July twenty-sixth, nineteen-ninety, after spotting Trooper Riney and Special Agent James, should support the inference that he killed her on August fourth to prevent her from giving additional information to law enforcement agents. . . . Obviously, the defendant [Herbert Emery] could be held to share Tony Emery's intent or 'state of mind' since he aided and abetted Tony Emery in killing Elkins to silence her."

A bigger problem, Green cautioned, was factual. "Ironically, it may be easier to 'prove' that the defendant and Tony Emery killed Elkins than the fact that she is dead," he noted. "There is no body, no trace evidence, and no vehicle. Obviously, the fact that Elkins has never been seen nor heard from since August fourth, nineteen-ninety would support the inference that she is dead. However, there is no physical proof. Agents have spent more than four years combing rock quarries in a three-state area searching for her body and vehicle."

There were statements from some witnesses, he conceded, that Elkins had talked about leaving for "an Indian reservation in Nebraska or Wyoming." A drug dealer named Dean Smith had testified to the grand jury that Tug Emery once told him that Elkins had gone to the Bahamas. "Obviously, any defense attorney's first line of defense will be that the government has not even proved a murder was committed," Green said.

The reason for indicting only Tug Emery at this point was simple, Green explained. Their best case was against him, not Tony, because of the tape-recorded conversation Tug had with James Watts on December 18, 1990. "The defendant, by appearing alone in an indictment which potentially may seek the death penalty, will have incentive to cooperate.

"If this were to occur, I would recommend making a deal with the defendant even though he participated in the killing. There is no doubt that Tony Emery is the motivating force behind Elkins's murder."

As they waited for the Justice Department to go ahead and seek the indictment, Strong and Schmitz decided to make another attempt to talk to Elkins's younger son, Steven. His grandparents, Bob and Emma, were country people, strait-laced and conservative. They still didn't think much of Christine's mothering skills and were reluctant to let the investigators dredge her memory up again. But at last they gave their permission and brought Steven to the Maryville police station.

Steven was a good-looking boy, polite and quiet. He was aware that something was going on—something bad from the looks on his grandparents' faces—but he was determined to take it like a man.

It fell to Strong to break the news. The boy stayed silent the whole time the detective spoke, but it was obvious it had hit him hard. On the one hand, he had heard that his mother hadn't abandoned him; on the other, she had been murdered.

"We've been working on this for a long time," Strong said. "We're not going to stop until we're done and the people responsible are caught. That's why we're here, to see if there's anything you remember that might help us."

There was nothing Steven could remember. It had been so long, and he had been so little. He thanked them for telling him and left with his grandmother's arm around his shoulder, obviously struggling not to cry.

On November 20, 1996, Tug Emery was indicted by the federal grand jury in Kansas City, Missouri, for the murder of Christine Elkins. "Today's development should be a clear signal to anyone involved in the killing of Christine Elkins that the passage of time neither forgives them for, nor does it allow us to forget, the taking of her life," said Stephen Hill, the U.S. Attorney for the Western District, in a press release issued by the U.S. Department of Justice.

Two hours after the indictment was handed down, Schmitz, James, and Strong were sitting in an interview room at the federal penitentiary outside Denver, Colorado. The door opened and Tug Emery stepped in blinking. He was one bewildered convict. Released to a halfway house the day before to serve the remaining six months of his drug sentence, he had just started a new job when the U.S. Marshalls scooped him up and brought him back to prison. They wouldn't tell him why.

When he was told to take a seat in front of the two agents and police detective, he still didn't know. They shoved the murder indictment across the table for him to read. It noted the possible penalties: life without parole or, with formal approval of the U.S. Attorney General, the death penalty.

"We know the story and think you know it, too," Mark James said. "And you're in a world of hurt."

Tug Emery just sat there stunned; when he started to open his mouth, James held up his hand. "We don't want you to tell us anything right now," he said. "We want you to get an attorney."

"We think you tried to do the right thing six years ago," Schmitz added. "It just got messed up."

At this, Tug Emery started to nod. Then James pulled a photograph out of a file. It was Christine Elkins with her two boys. "We know about the trip to Maryville. We know about Tony," James continued as Tug swallowed hard, looking at the photograph.

"Damn right I know," Emery finally blurted out. "And I ain't takin' a fall on this thing. Unh-uh."

It was music to the investigators' ears. Blood might be thicker than water, but it wasn't thicker than the prison walls Tug Emery would be looking at for the rest of his life. He wanted to make a deal.

Schmitz emerged from the meeting with mixed emotions. They had taken another step forward. Hill had cautioned him after the go-ahead was given to ask the grand jury to indict Tug: "Don't get your hopes up about Tony. We don't have as much on him. We need Tug to give him up—and you need to find Christine."

November 1996, Maryville, Missouri

Back in Missouri and Kansas, not everyone was as thrilled as Agent Schmitz and Detective Strong when news of Tug Emery's indictment hit the newspapers and television news reports. Tony Emery, who was serving his time at the federal penitentiary in Leavenworth, Kansas, heard about it in a telephone call from his mother.

"You been getting your newspapers?" she asked.

"Yeah, why? I got one today," he replied.

"You know what's going on?"

"No."

"Nationwide news," she said cryptically. "Tuggy."

"Oh, no," groaned Tony Emery.

"Oh, no," his mother spat disgustedly. "That's right, 'Oh, no.' First-degree murder charges." She calmed herself and spoke more cautiously in case someone besides her son was listening. "Something to do with a person being missed . . . and drug trafficking."

"Oh, yeah?" said Tony, sounding sick.

"It just blew our mind. It just blew our mind," his mother said, repeating herself. "Great big headlines, St. Joe paper, all the local TV stations are carrying it. Uh, *Maryville* in great, bold letters."

There was silence. Then as if by agreement, they dropped the subject for a moment to discuss other family problems. But it wasn't long before they returned to the most pressing issue. "Well, anyway, it don't sound like it's gonna be a very happy Thanksgiving, do it?" she said.

"No," Tony answered. "Where they got, uh, Tug at?"

"Kersey, Colorado," his mother answered. "They're transferring him to Kansas City for arraignment, but I don't know when. But I assume they would have to put him over at Leavenworth, wouldn't they?"

"Is it state or federal?" he asked of the charges.

"It's federal," she replied. "I think. I don't know. . . . We were so shook up about it."

Tony wanted to know if anybody planned to get in to see his cousin.

"I don't know," his mother replied.

"Well, somebody needs to," he said.

"I don't know if they can or not."

"Yes, they can. Somebody needs to go talk to him. A lawyer or something needs to talk to him," Tony said pointedly. "You know what I mean?"

His mother answered that she didn't know if someone would get the chance before he was brought to Kansas City. It had all happened so fast.

Tony Emery was regaining his composure and thinking ahead. "Well, I think it's a big bluff," he concluded.

"I hope so," his mother said. "I surely hope so. But that's a heck of a thing to do to a person. . . . It's like he's already been tried and convicted."

"Well, see, that's what they're tryin' to do," Tony said. "But somebody needs to tell him to stand his ground, you know what I mean?"

Of course, someone was listening in: Schmitz and Strong. The ATF agent and police detective had spent a lot of time in the basements of prisons, reviewing hundreds of hours of telephone calls by the Emerys and their associates, recorded at the investigators' request by the prison staff.

In one, shortly after his indictment, they caught Tug admitting to his stepmother that what she read in the newspaper was true. Tug would try to talk in code, but when she couldn't understand him, he got frustrated and just talked. "I told you and Dad there was a reason I couldn't come back to Missouri," he complained. He also said he wasn't about to take the fall by himself. "There's a couple of others will take it, too."

It was a pretty incriminating telephone call. The listeners couldn't help but shake their heads. Tug just wouldn't learn. If he had kept his mouth shut around Watts during the tape-recorded conversation they had had in the car in front of the restaurant, the investigators still wouldn't have had a clue about what happened to Christine

Elkins. But lucky for them, Tug was apparently incapable of keeping his mouth shut.

The investigators figured that if they released a little about Tug's indictment to the media, there would be a pretty quick reaction by Tony Emery and his family. The proof that the Emerys were very worried about what Tug Emery might say was gratifying.

Still, the investigators were a long way from making a case against the man they really wanted. The U.S. attorney had made it clear: no body, no case against Tony. And Tug hadn't given up his cousin yet, either.

It took until June 1997 to work out a deal with Tug Emery. His attorney had come in, looked at the evidence the government had put together, and gone back to Tug and told him to take whatever deal he could get.

This time it was Schmitz, Strong, and Green who were waiting when Tug and his attorney were led into the room. The convict had gained a lot of fat in prison, and had aged as well—his hair was even thinner, and his skin seemed nearly as gray as his sideburns. He was dressed in a prison jumpsuit and wearing a belly chain to which his handcuffs and a chain leading to his shackles were attached. The chains and shackles probably weren't necessary—Schmitz alone was twice Emery's size and in a lot better shape. But it was certainly a good reminder to Tug that he had better cooperate or he wouldn't be going anywhere ever again, except back to prison.

Tug recounted how he, Tony, and Bobby Miller had devised the plan involving the rental truck, barrel, and concrete. They even went over to the house earlier in the day to rehearse the murder. When Christine drove up that night, Tony instructed Tug to hide behind the door, facing the stairs that led to the basement. Tony then stepped out front to greet the young woman. The lights were out, and Christine hesitated at the door. Tony suddenly pushed her in and to-ward Tug, who struck her in the head with a blackjack. "She fell down the stairs," he shrugged.

Schmitz scooted his chair up until he was practically knee to knee with Emery. It was a start, but they needed details. He told Emery to go back and start over. "It was a hot night; you're doing crank; are you scared?" he asked.

Tug Emery swallowed hard and reached for a glass of water, having to hunch over to drink because his hands were still secured to the belly chain. "Yeah, scared and nervous," he said.

"You never killed anyone before?"

"No," the convict said, shaking his head. "Never." Emery was trembling now.

"What did she do when you hit her?"

"She screamed and kind of ducked. She grabbed my hand and said, 'Why are you doing this to me?' "

Tug Emery hesitated. He looked like a haunted man; his voice cracked as he continued. "I remember looking her in the eye and asking myself, 'Why *am* I doing this?' "

However, the woman then lost her grip on his arm and tumbled down the stairs, he said. She was still alive because he could see her at the bottom of the stairs in a patch of light from the streetlamp outside the kitchen window, then she crawled off into the darkness.

Emery was having a difficult time catching his breath as he relived the events of that night. Tears spilled from his eyes as he talked about how Tony told him to go get Miller and then come back to finish the woman off before putting her in the barrel. Tony then left, saying he was going to get rid of the woman's car.

Tug said he looked down into the basement but couldn't see the woman anymore. He was scared to go down there, he admitted, and didn't have a flashlight. He went outside, where he found a badly frightened Bobby Miller, whom he asked to go back in with him to murder the woman.

"No," Miller had responded. "I ain't no killer."

"I ain't either," Tug claimed he replied. "Let's get out of here." He took Tony's truck, and Miller drove the U-Haul rental back to his cousin's home. There, Tug said, he got in the Thunderbird he had driven from Colorado and attempted to follow Miller out of town. But Miller took a wrong turn, and they got separated. The next time they saw each other was the following day in Colorado.

The story didn't match Miller's in some of the details. For one thing, the telephone records indicated that Tug was behind Miller on the way back to Colorado, which didn't make sense if Miller took the wrong turn and wandered around lost for a period of time. Besides, it was Tug who had lived in Maryville; why would he follow Miller out of town?

The investigators looked at the story as a whole, and most of what Tug said fit with Miller's account. One of the men, probably Tug, was lying about some of the details—or maybe his memory was affected by the fact that he was on methamphetamine and "scared shitless" on the night of Christine's murder. Either way, there weren't enough differences to worry about. Sometimes it didn't hurt for juries to hear from witnesses whose stories conflicted a little; it made the witnesses sound less rehearsed.

During the interview, Tug Emery said Ron Coy wasn't around much the day of the murder, but he remembered seeing his truck drive past the house where Christine was murdered. He also thought he recalled seeing a truck parked down the street with a dark figure behind the wheel when he followed Miller.

Tug said Tony later told him that after Tug and Miller left, he had gone back down into the basement with Coy to finish Christine. They found her bleeding and covered with pink paint, from when she had climbed on paint cans in an effort to get out the basement window and had spilled some. According to Tug, Tony struck her on the right front part of her head, crushing her skull. Tony and Coy had then rolled her body up in carpet padding. They carried their burden up the stairs and out into the darkness, placing it in the trunk of Christine's car.

When Tug was through talking, the investigators decided it was finally time to go have a talk with Coy. Maybe a little time in the penitentiary had loosened his ties to Tony Emery.

Ron Coy was released from prison on parole about the same time they indicted Tug Emery. Detective Strong had seen him around Maryville, which worried him because there was always the possibility that he might go after witnesses.

Armed with what Tug had told them, Strong and Lt. Ron Christian decided to go rattle Coy's cage. Coy was short, squat, and all muscle with a quick temper. Strong had pulled him over once the year the before for a traffic infraction. When he tried to hand the five-dollar ticket to Coy, the younger man went into a rage. He jumped up and down and was practically spitting as he yelled at the officer.

This time, he managed to keep his emotions in check when Strong sat him down. "You know we indicted Tug," Strong said. "And we're going to go after Tony."

Coy nodded and replied, "I figured that."

"Well, this is your opportunity to do the right thing," Strong continued. "I believe you were involved, and you need to come forward and tell your side of the story and take what deals you can. Whoever comes through that door first is the one in a position to deal."

Coy denied he was involved, but he said he wanted a few days to think over what had been said. Several days later, he called Strong and said he would talk about what he knew, but he wanted to speak to an attorney first.

The feds were only too happy to find him a public defender. Then they arranged a meeting in Kansas City in the same office where Tug Emery had spilled the beans.

The air in the room was tense. Ron Coy hated the police and had never cooperated before. He wasn't happy about it now.

"I don't know where the body's at," Coy began, lighting up a cigarette. "But I knew he wanted to kill her because she worked for the cops."

Coy said Tony had let the business go to his head. He thought no one could touch him, even after Coy warned him about Christine Elkins being a snitch. Tony wouldn't listen.

Still, when Tony started talking about killing Christine, Coy said he didn't want any part of it. However, he was aware she was going to be murdered, and when he saw the rental truck at Tony's, he knew enough to stay away.

"How'd you know that?" Strong asked.

Coy shrugged. He had a sixth sense about such things, he said, and it was "just something I felt." He went out of his way that day to be with other people and not be seen with Tony.

He had had a similar feeling the night in Denver when they were arrested for the methamphetamine deal with Jay-Dub Watts. "I knew those guys were cops," but again Tony wouldn't listen.

The interview was turned back to the time period when Christine was murdered. Coy said he didn't see Tony until the next day at the car wash. Emery told him, "The problem is gone."

Coy smoked one cigarette after another as he talked. He couldn't be sure, but he believed that Tony and Tug had disposed of the body—"and maybe one other guy." The investigators at first thought the "other guy" he was talking about was Bobby Miller, but Coy soon cleared up that mistake.

This third man was named Dan Clayton, the brother of Tony's

then-girlfriend, Mia. Again, Coy said, it was only a theory, but he had seen Dan Clayton in Emery's sports car one day and was surprised to learn his friend had given the car to the other man. Surprised and angry because Coy had wanted the car himself and had once offered $20,000, Coy said he believed that Emery must have given Clayton the car as a reward for helping dispose of the body.

Coy ended his interview by saying he was "ninety-nine-percent sure" where the body was located. The Missouri River. He said he had deduced that because Tony had told him that Christine was "catfish food." Again, he called upon his "mystical powers" and drew them a crude map that showed the Missouri River and a boat ramp.

After he left, Schmitz told Strong that he thought that Coy was a "lying piece of shit." He didn't believe in the convict's sixth sense or mysticism. Neither Tug Emery nor Bobby Miller had put him in the house on the night of Christine's murder, but if he was the dark figure in the truck parked down the street, maybe he had helped after Miller left.

They were satisfied for now. Coy said he would go before the grand jury and tell the jurors what he knew. In exchange, he wanted to be allowed to move to Texas where he had a job waiting; so they would have to talk to his parole officer to get it approved. The investigators had no problem with that—with Coy out of town, they wouldn't have to worry about him intimidating their witnesses, and they would still know where to find him.

The investigators couldn't help but clap each other on the shoulder. They were so close. Tug Emery was giving up his cousin; they had corroborating witnesses in Bobby Miller and Jay-dub. And now, for the first time since Tug Emery talked about the quarries, they had a lead on what had become of Christine's body. If they could just find her, they were convinced Tony Emery would at last take a long, hard fall.

The only problem was, the Missouri was a big, muddy river with strong currents, and prone to massive floods. Even if Coy's map took them to the spot where Christine's car had been rolled in, there was no telling where it was now, or how to find it.

Schmitz and Strong went to see Tug Emery and mentioned the name Dan Clayton. The convict thought a moment before saying he thought he'd heard the name from Tony. . . . In fact, now that he'd been reminded, he recalled that maybe Tony, Coy, *and* this Clayton fellow had something to do with getting rid of the body and the car. He remembered Tony telling him they had used sticks to hold down the accelerator and secure the steering wheel. And once, when he was picked up at the Kansas City airport by Tony, his cousin had pointed out an exit off the interstate toward the Missouri and indicated that they had taken the body in that direction. He only *thought* that a rock quarry had been mentioned.

Actually, it was not the first time the police had heard the name Dan Clayton. He had come up early in the investigation as someone who bought small quantities of meth from Tony. But he was considered a minor character—not associated with the death or disappearance of Christine—and there was no followup.

Now, Clayton became priority number one. The next day, Schmitz and Strong were on their way to find him. Clayton lived on a farm about 45 miles south of Maryville. It was a remote area of farms with a confusing spiderweb of dirt roads. One such road led to Clayton's old farmhouse. When they got there, only Clayton's wife was home. Her husband was working as a carpet layer and she didn't know when he would be back. She said she thought some other law enforcement people had already been by recently to talk to him. She didn't know about what.

The law officers said they would be back in the evening. They returned that night and found Clayton, just a good ol' boy, country friendly. The night was hot as they stood out in the drive and told Clayton what they were doing.

Clayton look puzzled. "The feds have already talked to me," he said.

"What?" Schmitz asked.

Clayton dug a couple of business cards out of his wallet. The cards belonged to the federal public defenders representing Tug Emery.

The investigator didn't know if the attorneys had posed as federal law officers or if Clayton was just confused. Between the "other feds" and now Schmitz and Strong, Clayton was plenty nervous. They told him he had nothing to worry about if he didn't participate in Christine's murder or help dispose of the body. "You didn't, did you?" Schmitz asked.

"No," Clayton drawled slowly as if not quite sure. "At least, I don't think so."

"What do you mean, you don't think?"

"Well, you ready to hear a story?" Clayton asked, as if getting ready to tell a campfire ghost tale.

A long time ago, Clayton began, some friends had been out at his place for a party. Sometime after midnight they all left, but then he noticed the headlights of two vehicles turn down the long road to his house. He figured that one of his guests had forgotten something, and so he was surprised when he recognized Ron Coy driving the pickup in the lead and then Tony Emery driving the sedan that followed.

The two men got out of their vehicles and walked over to where Clayton was standing, nervously wondering what they wanted. Tony was his sister's boyfriend, but he had no idea why Emery and Coy would drive all this way to visit him in the middle of the night. Unless it was something bad.

Emery, however, was really friendly. He asked if they could have some gasoline for the sedan, which he said was running on empty. He knew that Clayton, like most farmers, stored gasoline on his property for his farm equipment. He didn't need much, Emery said; the car wasn't going to go far. He then fetched the gasoline himself. Next, he wanted to know a good place to run the car off into the Missouri River. He was thinking of a boat ramp Clayton had once taken him to on an outing with his sister.

Clayton told Emery that he was talking about the Nodaway Island access ramp. He started to explain how to get there from the farm, but it was complicated.

Emery decided he wanted Clayton to show him the way. "Stay off the highway," he said, "and don't speed. We don't want no cops pulling us over."

Clayton found himself leading a caravan along the dirt back roads toward the river. He figured the sedan was a stolen car, and Emery wanted to get rid of it. He was not inclined to ask questions. "You just did what Tony said," he told Schmitz and Strong.

About a quarter mile from the boat access ramp, Emery waved him over to the side of the road. "He said he could find it from there," Clayton said, "but he wanted me to wait. He said he'd be about twenty minutes."

It was a little longer than that, but at last the pickup reappeared with Coy and Emery. The sedan was gone. Emery got into Clayton's car. "Coy and I can't be seen together," he said. "I need a ride to Maryville."

Clayton drove Emery back to town and didn't get back home until just before sunup. When he arrived, he said, he walked over by the gasoline storage barrels and noticed a can of chewing tobacco; inside was a quantity of methamphetamine, apparently a gift. A month later, Tony sold him the sports car he had admired for $4,000, much below its real worth. He had also hired him to lay carpet at several homes he owned, paying him well.

Clayton said he had been wondering what all the fuss was about lately. Tug's attorneys weren't the only ones who had been out to see him in recent days. Ron Coy, whom he hadn't seen since that night, had come by, too. Clayton said he wasn't home when Coy stopped— just his wife and sisters, who said he had seemed "real nervous."

With good reason, the two investigators thought; if true, at the very least Coy could be charged with accessory to murder. But he wasn't their focus at the moment.

The next day, Schmitz and Strong found the boat ramp. They never would have believed it. A boat ramp? In the middle of nowhere?

Schmitz would have liked to strangle Coy. All those years, the bitter winters and sultry summer days spent looking in rock quarries. "And the numbskull tells us to look for a boat ramp."

Strong agreed with the sentiment. Who would have guessed that Emery would drive so far with a body in the trunk of a car he didn't own? He had certainly been taking a chance, but there again was further proof of the hoodlum's arrogance.

Their gut feeling was that Clayton was being honest and wasn't the sort to have knowingly participated in a murder. There were a lot of people who were frightened of Tony Emery and would have done what they were told without asking too many questions.

Schmitz had been at the point of demanding that they go forward with the prosecution of Tony Emery whether or not they ever found Christine's body. It had never been done in federal court, but he had found some state cases that had been successfully prosecuted. He was inclined to say the hell with it, if for no other reason than because people had told him it couldn't be done.

At last, Green had agreed to try. He wasn't very confident of their chances of success, but he would give it a shot. Now it was Schmitz who was willing to wait a little longer. Having Christine's body, or at least her car if nothing remained of her, would make the case that much stronger.

They believed that they knew where Christine's car, and presumably Christine, had gone into the Missouri. But what were the chances they could find the car, much less Christine's remains, seven years later? They both recalled the massive flooding in 1993, when a section of the mighty river normally 300 or 400 yards across had flooded its banks until it was a mile wide.

Schmitz and Strong met in Kansas City with representatives of the U.S. Coast Guard, which has law enforcement jurisdiction over the nation's navigable waterways; the U.S. Army Corps of Engineers, which is responsible for keeping those waterways navigable; and the Missouri State Water Patrol, which covers local law enforcement on the state's rivers and was the agency that supplied underwater specialist Dennis Randle.

The news wasn't as bad as they thought it might be. The Corps of Engineers representative said the car might not have moved too far. It was likely the car moved downstream until it settled in some low spot, he said, after which silt and mud probably held it in place even during flood stages.

After the meeting, Mike Schmitz felt better about their chances of locating the car. Randy Strong, however, was unconvinced. The Corps of Engineers couldn't say for sure that the car hadn't first floated and then drifted along the bottom for some distance. Schmitz had seen the Missouri when it flooded: whole uprooted trees rushing downstream on its swift brown waters; buildings floating along like toy models; and cars swept into the torrent, never to be seen again.

Hell, they didn't know for sure that the Nodaway Island boat access ramp was where Elkins and her car had gone in. Emery might not have trusted Clayton, or changed his mind and chosen another spot; and after so many years, Clayton wasn't sure if the night Emery and Coy visited was the night Christine disappeared.

Strong wasn't much more reassured when Schmitz called and told him that he might have found someone who could help them with their search. The ATF agent explained that he had been trying to find a magnetometer like the one they had used on the rock quarries—

and someone who knew how to work it. Buying a magnetometer would cost far more than the ATF would spend. The Coast Guard and the Navy, as well as some private firms that used them for such things as locating underwater cables, had the equipment, but it was either unavailable or too expensive.

However, Schmitz had reached an investigator with the Navy's criminal investigations bureau named Mike Maloney. He had said he would check around. A couple of days later, Maloney had called him back with an odd question.

"You ever hear of the Pig People?"

During his initial conversation with Schmitz, Clark Davenport didn't ask much about the case itself, but he had plenty of other questions. A magnetometer probably had the highest probability for success, he reasoned, though he would want to run the case by his fellow NecroSearch members for their input. But they, and he, would need to know more. Magnetometers weren't magic wands, and NecroSearch didn't jump at every opportunity.

"What's the year, make, and model of the car?" Davenport asked.

"It's a 1983 Oldsmobile Cutlass Supreme two-door," Schmitz replied.

"What about the lighting? Was the suspect familiar with the area? How fast is the water moving? What's the depth?"

Davenport wasn't trying to put the agent on the spot. These were the sorts of questions he was going to hear from his colleagues, but it was a test of sorts. NecroSearch had a limited budget. They had kept it going on small research grants and donations—some from grateful families of victims and agencies they had helped—but there was never much in the kitty. Often they had to beg, borrow, and, only half-jokingly, contemplate stealing the high-priced equipment they sometimes needed in the field. If NecroSearch members were going to invest their resources in an investigation, they at least wanted to know that the requesting agency had put in the time.

Schmitz was good. He knew the answers to a lot of the questions. "Guess I got some homework," he replied for those he didn't.

Good answer, Davenport thought; this was the sort of investigator NecroSearch liked to work with—the sort who wouldn't let ego get in the way. "I'd like to fax you our standard questionnaire," he said. "It's more for terrestrial cases than aquatic, because that's what most of our cases are, but it might help you think about some of the possibilities."

Davenport hung up. A car in a major river could be tough. He had done some aquatic work in the Gulf of St. Lawrence and the Gulf of Mexico, but that had been mapping the shape of the bottom—not trying to find a specific object.

Usually, NecroSearch preferred that the investigating agencies present their cases in person at one of the monthly meetings. That way they could ask their questions directly and get a feel for the investigators. But Schmitz was running out of time. If they didn't find the car, they were going to go ahead and indict Tony. He had a lot to put together in the meantime.

So Davenport took Schmitz's place. As usual, the group had a lot of questions. What time of night? What were the weather conditions? What about lighting? meteorologist Ed Pearl asked. After midnight, a summer night, hot and muggy but otherwise clear, Davenport said, checking the questionnaire that Schmitz had returned to him. No moon; just a little light from a nearby farmhouse that would have allowed the men to see what they were doing, but not so bright that they would have feared discovery.

Someone wanted to know if the car windows were up or down. "They don't know," Davenport answered.

Al Nelson asked if anyone had tried putting dogs in boats to pass over the river.

Someone else wondered what would be left of a body after so long a period underwater. France replied that it might depend on whether it had been wrapped in some sort of material, and on what that material might have been.

"What about wrapped in carpet padding?" Davenport said, consulting the questionnaire.

"It might slow the process up and hold her together," was the reply.

Davenport had questions of his own. How much did the car weigh? What percentage of the body was comprised of iron? How long would it float?

Fellow geophysicist Al Bieber had a list, too. "What's the river channel like? Can you get flow records? Has there been a major flood since . . . what'd you say, nineteen-ninety? How much sediment?"

Davenport smiled. Little did Bieber, the newest member of the group, know, he was setting himself up for a little trip to Missouri. Al now lived in Steamboat Springs, Colorado, a ski town in the mountains, but he had spent most of his career peering beneath the surface of water with remote-sensing equipment. Not only did he have the expertise, Davenport thought; Al had some great toys, such as side-scanning sonar, a magnetometer that could be towed behind a boat, and a video camera that could be lowered into the water.

Davenport didn't have the answers to everyone's questions, including his own. He would have to get back to Schmitz, probably put heads together with some of the agencies, such as the Corps of Engineers and the Coast Guard, that the agent had mentioned, as well as do some research on his own. He was pleased when the group accepted the case and Al Bieber volunteered to be part of the team.

If Mike Schmitz had seemed reticent in their first conversation, he got over it quickly. Whatever Davenport and Bieber needed, he found or he put them in touch with someone who could answer their questions.

At the agent's request, the Corps of Engineers sent the flow records for the Missouri River in the area around the Nodaway boat access ramp. They also sent maps that the corps creates for all the rivers in its jurisdiction, each depicting mile-long segments of the river.

Davenport talked to the engineers and learned that the Missouri was what the corps called a "self-scouring" channel. That meant it had been engineered to stay free of a lot of sedimentation and debris such as logs and stumps. The river wasn't very deep in the area of the boat ramp—only 20 to 30 feet, according to the engineers. But it flowed at a swift 8 miles per hour and was 1,000 feet across in that area. A lot of water to cover.

As they looked over the reports, Davenport and Bieber considered which technology might work best. Initially, Bieber suggested side-scanning sonar. Essentially, the sonar equipment is dragged behind a boat like a water-skier and takes photographs of the bottom—much as a photographer in an airplane photographs the countryside below. However, they discarded the sonar idea when they learned that the river was so shallow: As in an aircraft flying too close to the ground, that depth wouldn't allow the sonar to get much of a picture.

The NecroSearch investigators settled on the magnetometer as the best technology for the problem at hand, but for that they would need to know more about the car itself. The pair began calling General Motors with their questions about the car. They were passed from one department to another until at last they reached an engineer who said he could help. Davenport imagined him as some low-level flunky stuck away in a cubicle without much to do, which may have explained his eagerness to get them their answers after they explained what they were trying to accomplish. "And what I don't know, I'll find out," he assured them.

Actually, it was surprising how much information the engineer had at his fingertips. He quickly got them the weight of the car and the weight of the engine. It wasn't long before the engineer came up with the percentage of iron in the steel that made up the body—an important factor when using a magnetometer, because of its reactions to ferrous materials.

"Have you ever done any testing to see how long the car would float with or without its windows up?" Davenport asked.

The engineer seemed deflated by the unexpected question. "No," he apologized. But he was soon happily theorizing with them about the possibilities.

At last, the two geophysicists felt they were ready to go to Missouri. They would have to rent the magnetometer. The Corps of Engineers promised to provide a Global Positioning System, or GPS, to give the precise location of any anomalies, as well as nonmagnetic aluminum boats. The Missouri State Water Patrol would send its divers, including Dennis Randle, and keep river traffic away from the search area, assisted by the Coast Guard, who would also provide the dive platform and support.

To be honest, Schmitz thought NecroSearch was a shot in the dark. At first, he had put them on about the same level as psychics—maybe a little more sophisticated, but unproven nevertheless. The geophysicist obviously knew what he was talking about, but even he couldn't offer any guarantees that they'd find anything.

Strong thought that the concept of NecroSearch sounded interesting. But he, too, didn't see how they were going to locate a car in a big, muddy river. They weren't the only ones with doubts: the director of the ATF in the Kansas City office let Schmitz know that if the agency was shelling out money, this NecroSearch thing had better work.

There were also concerns about the risk. The water of the Missouri was so filled with sediment that a diver wouldn't be able to see his own hand in front of his face; and it would also be dark at the bottom. There were the huge branches—sometimes whole trees—mostly submerged and hard to spot, that tumbled down the river. But Randle and the other divers were willing to take the risk if someone could point them in the right direction.

On July 26, Schmitz met Davenport and Bieber at the airport. He hadn't really known what to expect from the moment he decided to call the dubiously nicknamed "Pig People," and still didn't. Bieber was a small, quiet man, friendly but reserved. Davenport was tall and gregarious.

Schmitz's doubts had begun to fade when Davenport started firing off his questions during their first few conversations. He believed that between the ATF and the Maryville and Nodaway departments, the case had been investigated as thoroughly as any he had ever heard of—no stone had been left unturned. But when the geophysicist asked his questions, he realized that there was still a lot he didn't know.

Davenport came off as educated and believable. One of the things Schmitz had immediately liked about him was that, unlike some psychics he had come across, the NecroSearch investigator didn't profess to work miracles.

"What we've got can tell you where to look," Davenport said, giving the oft-repeated caveat, "but I don't know of any technology in the world that can find a body."

The difficulty when looking for a clandestine grave, whether it was in a big field or a big river, was where to start, Davenport added. "We hope to be able to show you where we would start."

To Davenport, Schmitz looked as tough as he sounded, like a former football coach—the sort of guy they would have had to drag off the field. He also sensed that the agent wasn't putting a lot of emphasis on whether they were successful or not. However, when they went to the hotel to be debriefed, they met Schmitz's director, who looked them over and told them in no uncertain terms, "This better work." Davenport and Bieber looked at each other. Usually the agency asked for guarantees before they agreed to bring NecroSearch on board. There were no such guarantees, but they decided to keep their mouths shut.

Besides, if any case had a chance of succeeding, it was this one. Schmitz, and the Maryville cop who they understood had been the other half of the team, Randy Strong, had done their homework. They had narrowed the possibilities down as far as they were capable. Now they had assembled an impressive group of people and equipment, including the Corps of Engineers, the water patrol, volunteers from all sorts of agencies, and the U.S. Coast Guard, which, they were told, would have a cutter anchored offshore.

The next morning, Schmitz arrived at the hotel to drive the NecroSearch investigators to the river, where the rest of the response team was convening. A large tent had been set up on the shore as a command post. A U.S. Coast Guard cutter stood offshore to render whatever assistance was necessary.

It was a sunny day, already in the seventies and humid. The boat ramp, a popular spot for fisherman, had been sealed off, upsetting the locals. The Coast Guard and river patrol were ready to direct boaters and the barge traffic on the river away from the areas being searched.

Davenport and Bieber climbed into the boat that would be towing the magnetometer, while two young men loaned by the Corps of Engineers worked the GPS. While more than willing, they didn't know much about the equipment, and Bieber, who was familiar with it, had to assist them. Unfortunately, about noon the GPS stopped working. However Bieber had brought a range finder, which by "shooting" three sites along the shore every few minutes and then figuring the distance and angles, gave them a fairly accurate idea of their position on the river. All day long NecroSearch investigators cruised back and forth across each area they had sectioned off using the maps supplied by the corps. They stopped only to eat lunch and get a drink before climbing back into the boat to continue their work in the blazing sun. If the men on shore had any lingering doubts about the professionalism and dedication of the NecroSearch team, it evaporated as they watched Davenport and Bieber work in the muggy air.

They didn't stop working even after they called it a day on the river. Instead, they went back to the "command center" room at the hotel and went over the data, identifying spots where the magnetometer indicated a significant change in the magnetic field on the bottom of the river.

Here the information they had gathered from the engineer at General Motors came into play. They had particularly concerned themselves with the weight and amount of iron in the engine. The body of the car may well have rusted out, but the engine—which also represented the greatest mass of metal—would take longer. With the information they had, they were able to rule out changes in the magnetic field that weren't large enough to be a car engine.

By doing so, they were able to map out a half-dozen anomaly possibilities. However, the equipment couldn't tell them if the magnetic field change was caused by a piece of scrap metal or a car—or what kind of car, for that matter. After talking it over with Schmitz, Strong, and the other agencies, the NecroSearch scientists said they wanted to go back out again in the morning to verify that day's findings and, hopefully, get the GPS working for more accurate positions of the anomalies.

The next morning the GPS worked fine. But after just a short while in the water, the magnetometer went dead. Again, it was Bieber, and his toys, who came to the rescue. He just happened to have brought along a gradiometer, which, while not as accurate, could also measure the change in the magnetic field while hooked to the bow of the boat. Soon the team was back in business.

It was late in the afternoon before they all got together back at the hotel. Pizza and beer was ordered in while Davenport and Bieber finished plotting the anomalies on the map. When they finished late that night, everyone assembled to be briefed on what they had found. There were seven anomalies that fit the profile of what they were searching for: a magnetic disturbance large enough to be a car, downriver from the boat ramp. They also prioritized the anomalies according to the intensity of the disturbance and the degree to which they seemed to fit the size and shape of a vehicle.

Schmitz drove Davenport and Bieber to the airport early the next morning. As they shook hands, Davenport told the agent, "You're going to find her."

The scientist sounded so convinced that Schmitz wanted to believe him. He had been impressed with the NecroSearch investigators' knowledge and how hard they had worked, but there had been so many disappointments and false leads that he didn't want to get his hopes up.

Schmitz laughed and said, "We'll see."

It was a gray morning and mist hung over the river and the landing when Schmitz arrived back at the boat ramp. The divers were there, ready to get started. Randle, the "old man" of the group, seemed skeptical. He had been in the river here before on another case, "and we didn't find jack." But then, they didn't have a map showing anomalies with the precision of the Global Positioning System satellite.

A decision was reached to head out to Anomaly Number Two on the priority list because it was closest to the boat ramp. In fact, it was almost directly in front of the ramp. The divers reached it and indeed, it was a car—a Jeep with a boat trailer still attached.

Anomaly Number One was going to be harder to reach. It was about 75 feet from the shore and almost 100 yards downriver. The Coast Guard cutter maneuvered over the spot and dropped a 1,000-pound weight with a cable and buoy attached. The idea was that the divers could hang on to the cable to reach the bottom. However, the current was so strong that even the large buoy was dragged under.

The divers returned to shore, where they strapped on so much extra weight that they could hardly walk. These brave men then slowly tromped down the boat ramp in pairs and into the murky Missouri.

The first two sets of divers couldn't find the anomaly and returned empty-handed. Then Randle went in. "Never send boys to do a man's job," he said, joking with Schmitz, who was on a boat in the river and in contact with the divers through radio sets in their headgear.

Schmitz knew that even with the GPS they were going to need some luck. Randle had told him that the divers could pass within a foot of a car and not see it.

Luck was with Randle this day. He had been under for some time when his voice came over the radio: "Mike, I think we got a two-door!"

"Can you grab anything off it?" Schmitz asked, trying not to get too excited.

Randle radioed back that he had some pieces of trim. He was moving back to the rear of the car. He reached the trunk.

"Is it open or closed?" Schmitz asked, holding his breath. If the trunk was open, and it was Christine's car, there probably wouldn't be anything left.

"It's closed," Randle said. "I got the license plate. I'm coming up."

On shore, Randy Strong ran down to the water's edge with a video camera. The tape was rolling when Randle's arm came out of the water "like the Lady of the Lake holding Excalibur," he would recall later. Then Randle's head appeared, as well as his other hand as he struggled to hold the trim up with the plate.

In the boat with Schmitz was Bob Seiple of the Maryville PD. He knew his cars, and though the plate was backward, he could tell by the way it had been attached to the car that it came off an Oldsmobile matching the year of Christine's car. Still, there was that terrible moment before Randle flipped the plate over so it could be read by the men in the boat.

"B-six-E-six-five-two!" Schmitz yelled. "He's got it! He's got it!" It was all he could do to stop himself from leaping in the water to hug Randle. As it was, Strong worried that his friend was going to tip the boat over with his exuberance.

The men in the boat picked up Randle and his precious cargo. Schmitz looked at his watch—almost 1:00 P.M. He figured there had been enough time and placed a call on his cellular telephone. There was one person, representing a group of people, who he felt deserved to hear the news first.

Back in Colorado, Clark Davenport had only been home for an hour when the telephone rang. He had regretted telling Schmitz "You're going to find her," as soon as the words left his mouth. He liked the agent, knew how hard he worked and how much he cared about this case, and had wanted to say something encouraging. But there were no certainties, and as a scientist, he had had no business guaranteeing they would find anything. Yet there he was, spouting off like a psychic.

He was surprised now to hear Schmitz's voice on the telephone. "Clark, I'm standing here on the dive boat, and I've just been handed a license plate. It's the one we need. Thanks, and I'll talk to you later."

* * *

The news of the find spread quickly. There had been perhaps twenty or thirty people at the boat ramp that morning. By 2:00 P.M., when the tow truck arrived, there were more than 200 law enforcement officers from the highway patrol, sheriff's office, Maryville PD, and the ATF office in Kansas City—and U.S. Attorney Green. The area was soon crawling with the media as well.

Still, it wasn't until nearly 7:00 P.M. before the car was hauled out of the water. The divers had worked carefully to make sure no important evidence was lost, placing thick rubber straps over the trunk to make sure it didn't open and lose everything just when it seemed victory was at hand. Amazingly, Dennis Randle told Mike Schmitz and Randy Strong, the Oldsmobile had come to rest on top of another vehicle, which may have accounted for why Davenport had noted such an intense change in the magnetic field, earning it the highest priority.

A colonel of the state highway patrol was all for checking out the other anomalies and, if they were cars, pulling them out of the river. There was no telling what other mysteries might be solved—maybe other murders, he contended. But they would have to wait for another day; this investigation was moving on to the Maryville Police Department garage.

Under the bright lights, a crime-scene team loaned by the Kansas City Police Department began the excavation of the car. They opened the trunk, which was filled with sand and mud. Using garden trowels, they carefully removed the debris. There, wrapped in carpet padding, along with the remains of a shirt and pants and bra, they found the bones of an adult human female.

The crime-scene team finished removing the remains and other bits of evidence from the trunk at midnight and decided to return the next day to search the car's interior. It remained to be proved that the bones belonged to Christine Elkins, but no one doubted it.

The next day, the excavation team got to work again. The interior was filled with sand and silt packed to the top of the dashboard. Digging down, they found the keys still in the ignition, turned to the "on" position. They located a perfume bottle of the type Christine was known to have used, her house keys, and two small socks that had once belonged to a little boy whose mother had disappeared one night. The sticks used to hold the steering wheel straight and the gas pedal down—the sticks Tug Emery had told them about—were still there, held in place and preserved by the sediment.

That evening, Randy Strong went to visit Christine Elkins's son Steven. By coincidence, her mother and father had been in town visiting their other daughter, and they had already been told the news. But Strong wanted to see the boy in person.

Steven had actually been over to Strong's house before visiting his daughter, and the detective knew he was growing up to be a fine young man. His grandparents had done a good job raising him. Still, the detective knew, even after Steven had been told what the police believed had happened to his mother, there was always that lingering doubt.

Now, he would know the truth, and that to Strong was almost more important than being able to bring Tony Emery down for Christine's murder. "We found your mom," he told the boy as his grandparents hovered behind him. "It's like we thought; she's dead. . . . There's a lot we still have to do to get the man who killed her, but I thought it was important that you know that she didn't abandon you."

Steven tried hard to keep his composure. He was only seven when his mother disappeared that night. He hardly remembered her face, though he remembered her love. His eyes filled with tears and his lips trembled. But he didn't cry; after all, he had been told what he had been waiting seven years to hear. His mom hadn't wanted to leave him. It wasn't her fault.

That same evening, Schmitz placed a second call to Colorado. This wasn't over, not until Tony Emery was either looking at life without parole or the death penalty, but he could see the end. One more time, he knew whom he had to thank for putting the final nail in Emery's coffin.

The telephone rang several times at Davenport's home, but no one answered. This time, it was his turn to leave a message, and he didn't care if he sounded like he was about to cry. "We did it, you SOB, we did it."

The skull found in the trunk of the car had been shattered into several fragments. It was pieced together by a forensic anthropologist who said the victim, a female, had been struck from behind and the right front part of her skull had been crushed. The findings matched what Tug Emery had told them. Unfortunately, Christine Elkins's dental records had been lost, so the skull could not be identified by that means.

However, Christine had once suffered a broken tailbone, and the full-body X ray that had been taken following that accident had been preserved. It, according to the anthropologist, matched the mended tailbone as well as other areas on the bones found in the car. He added that the remains were those of an adult female of approximately Christine's age when she disappeared; a woman who had borne at least one child. There was no doubt in his mind that the remains belonged to Christine Elkins.

In October 1997, Schmitz told Strong that there was one more thing he wanted to do. He had never met Tony Emery face to face, "and I want to go introduce myself."

They drove to the penitentiary in Springfield, Missouri, where Tony Emery was brought into the interview room. He was sullen and trying to play the tough guy still. He figured they wanted to talk about working out a deal.

Schmitz sat down and leaned forward until his face was just a couple of feet from his longtime adversary. "I'm Mike Schmitz with the Bureau of Alcohol, Tobacco and Firearms," he said. "I believe you know Sergeant Strong."

When the suspect didn't respond, the agent scooted even closer. "I needed to put a face to Tony Emery," he said. "And I just wanted you to know that you're next. We're finished with this investigation."

Emery sneered. This was all part of the game. They blustered; he would bluster back. "I ain't talkin' without an attorney."

Schmitz held up his hand. "You don't understand," he growled. "We're not here to talk to you. I just wanted you to know: you're next."

A few days later, Tony Emery was indicted for the murder of a federal informant. Christine Elkins.

Less than a year later, back in Colorado as a NecroSearch meeting began, Clark Davenport announced, "I just got a call from Mike Schmitz with ATF in Kansas City. Tony Emery was convicted of murder."

The jurors had been shown the pictures of Christine Elkins's car being pulled from the river, and they were shown her remains. Combined with the testimony of Tug Emery, Bobby Miller, and J. W. Watts, it had taken them only fifty minutes to come back with the verdict. Christine's family had been in tears, and, Schmitz had admitted, so were he, Mark James, and Randy Strong. Tony Emery would now be spending the rest of his life in prison. "Couldn't have done it without you," Schmitz had told Davenport.

The other members quietly congratulated Davenport. They were proud of him and Bieber, and proud that NecroSearch had contributed once again to the cause of justice. But there was no joy. A young woman had died over a drug deal, leaving two sons to wonder if she had simply walked away from them.

VII

THE ROMANOV CASE

February 1998, Yekaterinburg, Russia

The slight woman in the gray turtleneck and dark blazer picked up the leg bone of Dr. Evgeny Botkin, the last physician for the last czar, and sniffed. Her Russian hosts couldn't have looked more shocked than if she had started gnawing on the royal femur of Czar Nicholas II, which lay near at hand.

Noticing the expressions, a mixture of disgust and horror, Diane France thought she had better explain. She said she had seen adipocere, the whitish, soaplike substance that sometimes develops on bones when a body decomposes under cool, damp conditions. She was merely trying to determine the consistency of the adipocere and to detect if it had any odor. If she could smell something, then bloodhounds would easily pick up the scent.

Actually, she thought that it was pretty amazing that there was any adipocere at all after so much time had passed. For nearly eighty years the bone had been lying in a clandestine grave in the Ural Mountains, along with those of the czar, the rest of the Romanov family, and their faithful servants, all brutally murdered by the Bolsheviks in 1918.

The killers' secret burial ground had remained undiscovered until 1978, when a retired geologist named Alexander Avdonin, fellow geologist Mikhail Kachurov, and Geli Ryabov, a national police officer, filmmaker, and writer of detective thrillers, formed a team secretly dedicated to locating the remains of the Romanovs. Neither covert monarchists nor communists, they were willing to risk imprisonment, perhaps death, for the sake of *pravda,* the truth, and to give the royal family a burial reflective of their place in Russian history.

After first removing three skulls from a pit grave, Avdonin and Ryabov later returned them out of fear of discovery, to await a day when the political climate in their country might change. The change came with the concept of *glasnost,* or openness, and the dismantling of the Soviet Union.

In July 1991, Avdonin returned to the burial site—a large meadow 30 kilometers from Yekaterinburg, the city where the royal family was slaughtered in the basement of a house. He brought with him a team that included police officials, detectives, submachine-gun-toting cops, epidemiologists, an archaeology professor, and Avdonin's wife, Galina.

The site was excavated. Bones and skulls, many in pieces, were carefully removed, and a preliminary attempt was made to assemble them anatomically to see how many bodies there were. The excavation crew knew that the bodies needed to be identified, a monumental task. In addition to the gunshot and bayonet wounds, heavy blows, probably from rifle butts, had smashed all facial characteristics, including demolishing the jaws of the victims. Nevertheless, on July 17, 1991, the governor of the region announced the discovery to the press. The bones, he said, in "great probability" had once belonged to the royal family and their servants.

But there was a problem. There were only nine skeletons: four adult males—accounting for Nicholas, Botkin, the footman, and the cook—and five adult or near-adult females. If these were the royal party, then 13-year-old Alexis, the son of the czar, and one of the females were missing. But which one?

American and British scientists used DNA to determine that the remains were indeed those of the Romanovs and their faithful servants. And, they said, the missing female was one of the Romanovs.

The Russian experts studied the bones and decided that the missing female was 19-year-old Maria. But in 1992, Bill Maples, the director of the C. A. Pound Human Identification Laboratory at the University of Florida in Gainesville and one of the world's most respected forensic anthropologists, looked at the remains and reached a different conclusion. He believed that the missing girl was 17-year-old Anastasia.

The Russians didn't appreciate Maples's conclusion, as it kept alive the memory of a horrible and embarrassing episode in their country's history. The Soviets could never quite get past the rumors that at least one of the royal children had survived the massacre.

Over the years, several impostors had laid claim to the Romanov name, throne, and fortune. One in particular, Anna Anderson, had even convinced some members of the Romanov clan who had escaped the revolutionaries that she was Anastasia. Her authenticity was disputed after her death by DNA tests, though her claim continued to have supporters among the exiled Russian community who chose not to believe the science. Worse for the Soviets, Hollywood had embraced the legend of Anastasia's survival in several movies.

None of the experts who examined the remains, including Maples, believed that any of the family could have survived such a vicious attack. They could see the evidence of the bullets, bayonets, and the acid poured on the remains to disfigure them. The assassination of the royal family had been brutally efficient.

The Soviets were gone now, but that didn't mean the bitterness had disappeared. Any two Russians could be expected to argue over whether the czar was a villain or a martyr, and whether the deaths of Nicholas II and his family were justifiable execution or cold-blooded murder.

Six years after Maples's trip to Yekaterinburg, the Russian government was planning a big state funeral for late July 1998, the eightieth anniversary of the murders, so they could officially lay to rest the Romanov family and close the casket lid on that dark night. But nothing was certain, including the funeral. The Russian Orthodox Church refused to recognize the remains as those of the Romanovs, who had been sainted, and threatened to boycott the proceedings.

If it had become public, Maples's contention would only perpetuate the legend and the bitterness that had divided the country for most of the twentieth century. The Russian government, and Avdonin, accepted their own experts' version of the truth. They hoped that the bones of the missing children might be found before the funeral, to wrap up any loose ends. That's why they had invited NecroSearch International to Yekaterinburg.

Diane France knew nothing of the controversy over the remains. She knew and respected Bill Maples, but had never talked to him about his trips to Russia. She and geologist/computer whiz Jim Reed were merely on a scouting mission for NecroSearch. As the Necro-Search representatives, they were there to work out an agreement with the Russians to look for the missing Romanov children, along with forensic anthropologist Tony Falsetti from the University of Florida, and Peter Sarandinaki, a naturalized American sea captain.

Sarandinaki's family had belonged to the Russian aristocracy and had escaped from Russia with little more than what they could carry. His great-grandfather was the White Russian general who tried, but arrived too late, to save the czar and his family. His grandfather was a White Russian who helped bring what were believed to be the last remains of the murdered family, including Czarina Alexandra's severed finger, to western Europe, where they were turned over to the Russian Orthodox Church Abroad and kept in hiding. Sarandinaki had grown up listening to the stories of his brave ancestors and their loyalty to the czar.

The sea captain contacted the anthropologist Tony Falsetti, and the two men had become friends. When Sarandinaki learned that two members of the royal family were missing, it seemed to him that it was his duty to help find those remains. This led to his meeting with Avdonin, who also wanted to pursue locating the last of the Romanovs.

Talk of a state funeral for the Romanovs made it more imperative to Sarandinaki that every effort be made to step up the search for the Romanov children. However, by 1997 Bill Maples's health was failing. He had a brain tumor and had retired, handing over the C. A. Pound Laboratory to his protégé, Falsetti, who also inherited Maples's enthusiasm for the project.

"How do we find the rest of 'em?" Sarandinaki asked Falsetti.

"The people you need are called NecroSearch," Falsetti replied, briefly describing the group. "A good friend and colleague of mine, Diane France, is a member. If you'd like, I'll contact her for you."

The conversation led to a meeting with France in New York, where she was attending the annual meeting of the American Academy of Forensic Sciences, of which she was a fellow. Sarandinaki explained his predicament and asked if she could help.

"I can't speak for NecroSearch," France replied. "It's a group decision, but I'll take it back to them and see what they say."

The group invited Sarandinaki and Falsetti to present their case at a meeting in November 1997. They made their pitch, but there was some reticence on the part of some NecroSearch members.

John Lindemann had worked in Russia and warned that they could be getting themselves "into real hot water. . . . It may even be dangerous."

Despite the passage of time and the reforms sweeping across the former Soviet Union, he knew that the mere mention of the Romanovs still raised volatile emotions. There might be people who wouldn't like Americans stirring the ashes of this part of Russia's past, he said. "We may find ourselves right in the middle of a political and historical frying pan. So if we do become involved, we better do it with our eyes wide open."

Davenport echoed Lindemann's concerns about the politics and added a few of his own. One was that it was not a law enforcement case and therefore, technically, a violation of the group's charter. More than that, he said, he saw it as a quagmire.

Having worked in Soviet-bloc countries, he said they would probably be hindered by a lack of information. "Maps will be difficult to get, and aerial photographs probably impossible. And they may or may not tell us everything we need to know.

"Sure, it's an interesting historical problem, but I don't think it's something we need to be involved in," he argued. If individual members wanted to go on their own, that was one thing, but he had strong reservations about taking this on as an official NecroSearch project.

France had her own concerns about the project, especially after listening to Lindemann discuss the potential dangers. The Russian mob was powerful and might see profit in the sale of "holy relics"; they would have to make sure the Russians provided security.

But she couldn't help but think the risk was worth the potential gain. Not only would the identification process be incredibly interesting and of historical significance, but what a challenge for NecroSearch, which would reap the publicity if they could find evidence of two children who had disappeared—possibly thrown down a mine shaft and then burned—eighty years earlier! It was an incredible story, and she had already made her mind up that if the group didn't want to go, she would go alone.

She didn't have to worry about that. Lindemann was considered one of the level heads in the group, and even the most enthusiastic members were sobered by his words. However, in true NecroSearch fashion, having issued his warning, the geologist had added, "But God, it would be a whole hell of a lot of fun, and frankly, I'd like to be involved." With Davenport still grumbling, the others voted to take the project on.

The decision got the ball rolling, but there wasn't much time. The state funeral was planned for the summer of 1998, and there was an ocean of red tape to get through. That included negotiating with the Obretenyie Foundation, a fund-raising "recovery" foundation created by Avdonin, and with the Russian government over the number of NecroSearch investigators that would be allowed to participate, and who would pay.

NecroSearch wanted to bring fifteen members, including scientists and criminalists, to cover every conceivable sort of expertise they might need. Despite the concerns expressed at the meeting, France had no problem getting volunteers, many of whom came up with imaginative reasons why they should be in on the list.

One of those who expressed an interest without much hope of being chosen was Dick Hopkins. A history buff, "Hoppy" wanted to go, and there might not be another chance for such a trip, for he was seriously ill with cancer. But he also knew that some of the others had more valuable expertise.

He was surprised when France announced that she had chosen him to be the fifteenth person on her list. Not one to tolerate sympathy because of his illness, he had demanded to know why. She told him it was because they would need a photographer—crime scene photography was one of his strengths—and maybe an investigator. If there was one among them whose powers of observation could have matched the legendary Sherlock Holmes, it was Dick.

Gratefully he had accepted the appointment, but with each day that went by, the cancer was gaining. Still, even when it was clear to France that Hopkins's health would not allow him to make the trip, she refused to replace him. She swore she would keep him on the list "forever" if it would give him something to hang on to for a little longer.

In the meantime, Sarandinaki scrambled to find the money, without much luck. They needed on the order of $100,000 to transport the team and the necessary equipment, some of which had to be rented, and the decomp dogs. The Russians weren't going to chip in much, and a couple of potential agreements with television programs fell through.

It looked as though the project was dead until Sarandinaki called France in January. "We have enough for four people to go," he said. "I'm going. Tony's going. I want you to go. So pick one other person from NecroSearch."

France knew that a lot of people would be disappointed. Personally, she felt the worst for Dick. Even if he had been healthy, he would have been the first to say someone else should go, but now there would be no reason for him to pretend to make plans.

It didn't take long for France to make her choice: Jim Reed. He was a geologist and could speak intelligently about the use of geophysical equipment. Avdonin was also a geologist, so the two men would share a common interest or "language." She was certain Reed would impress the Russians with his computer programs that could assimilate disparate data—from geophysical readouts to botany reports to whatever the dogs came up with—and create a database for prioritizing search sites.

Coupled with her expertise in forensic anthropology and archaeology, France thought that as a team they would give a good representation of what NecroSearch could accomplish. If everything went well, the Russians would be impressed enough to bring the full team over. But as much as anything else, France chose Reed because he was so easy-going and had an unfailing sense of humor, even in tight situations.

"Say, Jim, what are you doing in two weeks?" France asked when she called him out of the blue.

"Why?" Reed replied suspiciously. NecroSearch members had a way of getting each other into sticky situations—whether scrambling down an abandoned mine shaft, crawling on hands and knees through thick vegetation, or digging for hours for what might be a "goopy" body or nothing at all.

"Want to go to Russia?" France asked.

There was silence on the other end, and France thought she was about to be turned down. "Hell, yeah, I want to go," he said to dispel that notion.

"Don't you need to ask your wife?"

"Are you kidding? She'll understand."

* * *

The Russians were in a hurry. The funeral was fast approaching, but for the members of NecroSearch, another funeral superseded the burial of the Romanovs.

On January 31, 1998, Dick Hopkins lost his fight with cancer. His funeral was attended by several hundred people including family members, law enforcement officials and officers, and every member of NecroSearch International.

At the services he was remembered for his professionalism as well as his sense of humor, even if he was sometimes the brunt of the joke—as in Davenport's recollection of Hopkins parking his car over the buried explosives. The most poignant remarks were left to his friend and partner of 30 years, Jack Swanburg.

"I don't know if we worked together on a thousand cases, or if that was two thousand cases or five thousand cases," Swanburg said. "I do know that many times we would be working several parts of a crime scene, and with no visual or oral communication between us, he would know what I was doing and I would know what he was doing.

"His work was slow and deliberate, and accurate. He had great patience with anything he was doing, but his pace was almost like he synchronized with a different clock from the rest of us."

There were many nods in the crowd, then laughter as Swanburg recalled how former Sheriff Roy Vogt, who had hired both of them, once observed, "It's hard to believe that Dick Hopkins was the product of the fastest of two hundred fifty thousand sperm."

Swanburg paused and cleared his throat. In a long career he had seen the face of death many times, witnessed its effect on the living over and over. Many of the faces he could see in front of him had chosen, like him, to deal with it for their entire careers. Yet it was always different when death took someone they loved. Despite all Hopkins's renown for taking his time, his friend added, "I'll never understand why he was in such a hurry to leave us. We'll miss him a lot."

It was only a few days later that Diane France and Jim Reed left for Russia with heavy hearts. France had received more bad news: Bill Maples had also died.

The first stop on their journey was Helsinki, Finland. The two NecroSearch investigators were walking downtown with Sarandinaki and Falsetti when Reed spotted a poster for the feature presentation at a movie theater. The film was the just-released feature-length cartoon *Anastasia*.

After the sadness of the past days, coming upon the film in a foreign city seemed like a good omen, and France and Reed happily posed for a photograph in front of the marquee. But they knew the story was fantasy; according to the Russians, Anastasia's remains had been found with those of her parents. They had been told that they would be looking for Alexis and Marie.

The group flew into Moscow. After a few hours' layover, they caught a flight to Yekaterinburg, where they arrived at 2:00 A.M.

Russia in February was just what France expected: 35 degrees below zero and bleak. They got to the hotel, one that catered to foreign visitors, only to find that there was no heat in the rooms. For $300 a night, they had a foam pad on a wooden bed frame to sleep on and ice on the windows so thick they couldn't see out.

France tried to take a bath to warm up, but it was almost a half hour before warm water got through the cold pipes of the hotel and up to her fourth-floor room. Even then it was only tepid. She ended up putting on every bit of clothing she had—including her dress clothes and blazer—to try to stay warm in bed.

In the morning, she walked out of her room just as Sarandinaki was coming out of his. "Were you cold last night?" she asked.

"God, yes," he replied. "I thought I was freezing to death."

They quickly made their way down to the hotel lobby, where Reed and Falsetti met them for the drive over to Avdonin's house. Avdonin would then take them to the mortuary.

The plan was to look at the bones—more a polite gesture by the Russians than to an invitation for their opinions—and then drive to the site where the remains had been discovered. They arrived at the mortuary and walked up a flight of stairs to a narrow hallway. An armed soldier stood guard next to a locked door, a reminder to the NecroSearch investigators that this wasn't just an interesting historical puzzle.

Inside the room, Avdonin proudly invited France to look over his discovery. However, his face fell like a bloodhound's when France picked up Dr. Botkin's femur and gave it a sniff. He didn't smile again until she had replaced the doctor's leg and explained her actions. The presence of adipocere was an important factor to bring up when she reported back to NecroSearch. Although she hadn't detected an odor, the dogs they used had much better noses, she said.

France moved on to look over the remains of the Romanovs, picking up the skull of Nicholas II, leaning over the bones of Alexandra and their two eldest daughters, Olga and Tatiana. She noted that the bones bore the telltale signs of bullets, knife wounds, and what looked like acid burns. Many of the skulls, she saw, had been reconstructed from fragments.

Finally, she walked over to the steel table on which, her hosts said, were the bones of Anastasia. It wasn't necessary this time to make a box to store her emotions. Eighty years was a long time; there were no grieving family members counting on her; and there wasn't that immediacy she felt with a more recent murder victim. Even so, noting the wounds, she couldn't help but feel sorrow over the fear and pain this girl had suffered.

The anthropologist took off her wire-rimmed glasses and picked up the skull. Only the skullcap, down to the ridge beneath the eyebrows, had survived intact; the rest had been reconstructed from dozens of fragments.

After a moment, her polite curiosity turned to concern. The teeth didn't seem right for a girl Anastasia's age—they were too well developed, as though of a somewhat older person.

France looked quickly at the growth plates of "Anastasia's" other bones.

The skeleton of a fetus does not begin with bone, but with cartilage. Gradually, in a fetus, then a baby, a child, and a teenager, bone grows out from primary growth centers in the middle of a long bone, and from secondary growth centers on the ends. Primary and secondary centers grow toward each other until the cartilage between them, which has also continued to grow, though at a slower rate, is gone and they fuse. The place where the growing bone meets the cartilage is known as a growth plate.

Different bones meet and cease to grow at different stages in the life of an individual. Somewhere in the mid- to late teens, the remaining cartilage between the growth centers disappears; when all of the growth centers have met, growth ceases and you have an adult.

By studying the stage of bone growth in individuals whose ages at death were known, anthropologists were able to come up with a range of probabilities for determining the age of an unknown person. However, this is a statistical range and not an absolute; an individual may fall outside the norm. On the far end of the spectrum: if the growth centers met too soon, an individual would stop growing at an early age—a dwarf. If they met too late, the cartilage would continue to grow between the growth plates, creating a giant.

In the Yekaterinburg mortuary, France thought "Anastasia's" bones were more consistent with a woman of her sister Marie's age. Marie was 19 and 4 months; most of her growth centers would have met and fused, as these had. With Anastasia, the anthropologist would have expected to see more cartilage between the growth plates, as well as less-developed dentition. Like any good scientist, she knew there were exceptions to the rule. But considering there were two viable options as to whom the bones could have belonged to—Anastasia or Marie—she wondered how the Russians had reached their conclusion.

Avdonin and his wife were busy talking to Sarandinaki. France quickly pulled Falsetti and Reed aside. "I'm not convinced that this is Anastasia," she said quietly. Turning to her fellow anthropologist, she asked, "Does this look like a seventeen-year-old to you?"

Falsetti shook his head. "Maples didn't think so, either," he said. "He thought these were more consistent with Marie."

This was the first France had heard that Maples had reached a different conclusion than that of the Russian scientists. Now she was in a quandary. It was not their mission to question the identifications made by the Russians. They were there to work out a deal to bring NecroSearch in to find two missing children, whoever they turned out to be.

After talking it over with Reed, they decided to keep quiet for the time being. Although it didn't seem likely to Diane France, the Russian experts might have been right about the identification. Maybe they had other evidence she didn't know about. If not, and Necro-Search could locate the bones of the missing sister, they would stand a better chance of proving France's theory by comparing them to the bones the Russians already had.

"Okay," France agreed, "as long as we don't have to sign anything that says these are the remains of Anastasia to the exclusion of Marie."

* * *

The plan worked fine, at first. They left the mortuary for the next part of their tour. They drove past the spot where the house in which the family was murdered had stood. It had been torn down in 1978 by then-governor and future Russian President Boris Yeltsin when the Soviet secret police complained it had become a pilgrimage site for covert monarchists. There was now a small plaque on the building that had replaced the house, noting the historical significance of the site but little else.

The group next headed for where the remains had been found by Avdonin and his colleagues. It took almost two hours to get out of Yekaterinburg due to traffic congestion. Then they drove an hour into the countryside of pine forests and open fields, which, blanketed by several feet of snow and bitterly cold despite the blue skies, looked right out of the movie *Dr. Zhivago*.

The road turned into an isolated track through the snow to their destination. Although the church had still not accepted the remains as authentic, a simple wooden Russian Orthodox cross had been erected at the site. The NecroSearch investigators noted that the translation of the Russian name for the area was "Pig's Meadow." It seemed an appropriate place to start for the Pig People.

One of the main reasons for going to the site was to gauge the obstacles to a successful search. The NecroSearch investigators immediately noted one: big power lines and the presence of nearby railroad tracks that could throw off some types of geophysical equipment. They would have to take that into account.

They were also trying to get the lay of the land—determine what areas might have been considered as potential burial sites by the killers nearly 80 years earlier. Avdonin told them that there was a large bog area nearby that had been much the same in 1918—an easy place to dig a grave if for some reason the killers had buried two bodies apart from the others.

On the way back to Yekaterinburg, the NecroSearch investigators talked about the possibilities. The dogs could cover a large area with their sensitive noses, particularly if adipocere remained on the bones. They concurred that the best place for the team to start would be a nearby mine, where the murdered family had first been hidden. Perhaps, they thought, the killers had missed two bodies in the dark of the mine tunnel. Some historical accounts contended that the two smallest bodies had been burned near the mine. If so, maybe the fire pits could be located and excavated. Reed noted that if the bonfire was large enough, it could have altered the natural magnetic orientation of rocks in the area. That change could be detected, he said, by a proton magnetometer.

With his wife and Sarandinaki interpreting, Avdonin listened to their conversation and was impressed enough to suggest that they find a way to launch the full-scale NecroSearch investigation. They should do it before the state funeral in July, he said, so that all the remains of the family could be reunited and this chapter of Russian history closed.

The NecroSearch investigators were excited when they got back to their hotel that evening, but they quickly got a reminder of what country they were in.

The first thing the Americans noticed was that they all now had space heaters in their rooms. "They must be mind-readers," France laughed. Later that night, in the hotel bar, a friendly Russian woman pointed out that the arrival of the space heaters wasn't so mysterious.

"You said in the hallway that you were cold this morning, right?" the woman asked. They agreed they had talked about it. "Well, you must know that the rooms have been bugged since this place was built, so of course they knew you were cold."

None of the Americans had even considered the possibility that everything they said in the room—and maybe anywhere—was reaching someone else's ears. It was a sobering thought.

The next day, the plan to keep their suspicions about the bones to themselves fell apart when they met with the Russians to work out a memorandum of agreement. The Obretenyie Foundation was prepared to pay the expenses and provide security for a larger NecroSearch team, Avdonin said. All France and Reed had to do was sign on the dotted line that NecroSearch would provide equipment and expertise.

The problem was the opening line of the contract, which stated: "This is a memorandum of agreement between the Obretenyie

Foundation, the University of Florida, and NecroSearch International to search for and identify the remains of Alexis and Marie."

France, Reed, and Falsetti looked at each other. "We cannot sign the document the way it is written," France said. "We are not convinced that the remains are those of Anastasia."

When her remarks were interpreted, Avdonin turned beet red. "Marie and Alexis are missing!" he yelled in Russian. "Not Anastasia!"

Shocked at the sudden outburst, France tried to answer as calmly as she could. She asked if he knew how his experts had reached such an incontrovertible conclusion.

"Photographic superimposition!" he shouted.

The admission only worried France more. Photographic superimposition was a useful tool in forensic anthropology, but hardly one to have been so adamant about. Even with an undamaged skull, the margin for error was too great for a positive identification. The skull the Russians claimed was Anastasia's had been pieced together like a jig-saw puzzle with pieces still missing. France and Falsetti, who had backed her supposition in the face of the Russian's tirade, said they would be happy to reconsider if they could see the photographic superimposition themselves. And any other proof.

"It's in Moscow," Avdonin answered in a huff. "Surely, you will be allowed to gain access to the study."

"Fine, but we can't sign this document until then," France said. "Or we can make it more generic—"

The Russian again hit the roof. "Who are you to question all these other scientists?" he yelled. Eighty, no, a hundred Russian experts had all reached the same conclusion: the bones belonged to Anastasia.

At times, Avdonin's wife, Galina, who was serving as interpreter, would go on in English much longer than her husband had spoken, and they suspected she was adding her own two cents as well. She would apologize one minute for her husband's rudeness, and the next, add some invective of her own. Or wail, as her spouse turned shades of red and purple, "See what you're doing to my poor husband," who now claimed that 200 scientists "worldwide" agreed with the Russian experts.

Embarrassed for his friend, Sarandinaki was at a loss what to do. He liked Avdonin, although he, too, found him to be a bit brusque, even rude, around other people. He attributed it to the old man's having been raised under the Soviet system, where the strong survived and the weak were ground under. He knew why Avdonin was so upset. The burial of the royal family was teetering on the edge of disaster—the church still wouldn't recognize the remains as real, and now the Russian government, namely Yeltsin, was threatening to stay away from the funeral as well. A challenge to the authenticity of the Russian experts' findings might push the whole thing over.

But Sarandinaki liked France and Reed, too. They were real professionals and, he suspected, probably knew what they were talking about. And if Falsetti agreed with them . . . He cared about the truth—Russian Orthodox believers would want to know over whose bones they were praying—but at this moment, he didn't care who was right. The remains of two children he felt responsible for were out there somewhere, and he hoped something could be done to salvage this agreement.

Looking out the window as Avdonin continued to harangue her, France thought the windblown, snowy landscape looked a lot like Colorado, and she began to wish she were home. What did it really matter if she signed the paper?

Reed gave her a nudge and indicated she should look at his laptop computer screen. All during the nearly 4-hour harangue by Avdonin, Reed typed away, mostly jokes to keep her spirits up. Now, as she watched, he typed a single word.

Pravda. Russian for "truth." She smiled at her colleague and nodded.

In the end, NecroSearch International was not invited back to Russia to look for the remains of the missing Romanov children. Avdonin decided to continue his search with Sarandinaki and Russian experts.

In July 1998, the Russians went ahead with the burial ceremony. For weeks before the event, the Russian Orthodox Church and the government squabbled. The government had organized the burial as a day of national celebration. But the church was still refusing to recognize the remains as anything except "victims of the revolution" and not the royal family. Not because of any evidence to the contrary, but because the church-in-exile continued to contend that the entire family had been burned, and only those few pieces they had hidden survived. The government accused the church of ignoring science and went ahead and buried what it said were the remains of Nicholas II, Alexandra, Olga, Tatiana, and Anastasia.

Diane France found the government's accusations ironic. As far as she was concerned, the Russian government was just as guilty of ignoring science as the church.

AFTERWORD

As of the writing of this final chapter in February 2001, Necro-Search International has participated in more than 150 cases. Their travels have taken them to six countries and thirty states.

If imitation is the sincerest form of flattery, then NecroSearch should be blushing. Their successes, as well as their efforts at networking to bring local experts in other places together to assist the police, has led to other scientists from varying disciplines working together to find clandestine graves. A similar group was formed in England by one of NecroSearch's admirers from Scotland Yard, and the first NecroSearch International "overseas branch" was created in Australia, where the new group was given permission to use the name for the grand total of one dollar.

Sometimes when talking to NecroSearch members, it is the disappointments they recall more than the successes. No one has ever been held accountable for the three men murdered out at the former McCormick Ranch on the plains of eastern Colorado, the case that got CBI agent Tom Griffin wondering if there was a better way. The female found on Windy Point hasn't been identified, much less her killer caught.

Then there are those they couldn't find: Julie Cunningham, who paid with her life for offering to help Ted Bundy; the bodies of the couple alleged to have been murdered by drug dealers and stuffed into drums, in the case that brought Kim Castellano and Clark Davenport together. Those and many others, all still missing.

Through the end of the millenium, NecroSearch cases continued to pile up across the country. A family—the parents and their two children—who disappeared in October 1982 from their home near Los Angeles. A missing one-year-old girl whose mother was discovered murdered and floating in a Michigan lake. A young woman who disappeared from Piqua, Ohio. A woman thought to have been buried by her husband in a sandy gulch south of Denver. Those who commit evil run the gamut: from a former Navy officer thought to have buried his wife in the woods near the base housing, to a hulking suspected serial killer in a tiny northern Sierra Nevada town, believed to have abducted, murdered, and disposed of a 28-year-old woman and a 15-year-old girl a year apart.

Without the bodies there may never be a prosecution. But these killers had better not rest easy. There is no statute of limitations on murder, and there is NecroSearch, as Roy Melanson, Gene Keidel, Thomas Luther, Jill Coit, Michael Backus, Jim and Bonnie Taylor, Randy Bird, Mark Prieur and Tony Emery know all too well. It doesn't sound like a lot of names out of 150 cases, but without NecroSearch, in large or small part, they might have gotten away with murder.

There have also been successes that brought closure if not convictions. In 1998, Clark Davenport and Al Bieber repeated their Missouri River triumph by locating a truck and its driver in an Oregon river. This time, though, their work proved that the man, suspected of child molestation, couldn't have committed the crime. In the summer of 1999, a NecroSearch team found the remains of a young man who had written a suicide note and then wandered away from his home near Cripple Creek, Colorado, during a blizzard.

Not every success brought closure. The family of Lois Kleber returned to the area of her grave identified by NecroSearch, though only a few tiny remains had been found. They were unwilling to have a burial service until they had located more of their mother's remains. The family found several bones and hoped, but Diane France identified the bones as nonhuman. The Kleber family's grief seemed to have no end. However, about a year after the NecroSearch excavation, a fire swept across part of Grouse Mountain. A forest service employee, who knew about the search on the mountain for Lois, was looking for hot spots when he saw something unusual in a burned clump of bushes about 200 yards downhill from the grave. It was the skull of an adult human female. DNA tests were still pending as of the writing of this book.

Many of the detectives who contact NecroSearch for help, often skeptically, stay in touch. They don't hesitate to recommend the group to colleagues. Meanwhile, NecroSearch grows and changes. The debate between those who believe that they should be doing more research at Project PIG and those who favor fieldwork continues. However, the consensus now seems to be that there are enough members favoring one or the other that both objectives can be met.

New members are added as needed. They are even considering adding, of all things, a "forensic backhoe operator," though, as Jack Swanburg says, it will be someone who could remove the dirt off a dime. Tom Adair recently asked to rejoin the group and was welcomed with open arms.

NecroSearch has also experienced its losses. In 1997, Becky the bloodhound died. During her career, she helped catch eighteen murderers who were convicted, two of them since her death. And Dick Hopkins is missed each time they sit down to a meeting or go out in the field.

There have been other changes. Clark Davenport has started a for-profit company called Geoforensics to handle non-law enforcement cases that NecroSearch, by its charter, can't take on. Such requests may come from family members of victims or other interested parties.

Diane France continues to run the Human Identification Laboratory at Colorado State University. As one of the first acts in her new role as president of NecroSearch, she actively promoted open, no-risk discussions about the stress of dealing with violent death and ways to decrease the effects. She is also championing the same sort of discussions in the state and federal mass fatality response teams to which she belongs, including helping create a manual for the Department of Justice on how to respond to such incidents, part of which will deal with the psychological impact on the response teams. She also finds some release in her business, France Casting. There she and a small team make casts of bones and other mammalian anatomy for courts, colleges, and museums. There seems to be nothing more effective at taking her mind off violent death than piecing together a gorilla skeleton.

After the World Trade Center was attacked and destroyed on September 11, 2001, Diane France and Jack Swanburg, were asked to prepare to leave for New York to assist with identifying the human remains of the more than 6,000 victims. France through anthropological techniques, and Swanburg through fingerprint identification.

Their services were requested in their roles as members of the U.S.

Department of Human Services Disaster Mortuary Operational Response Team (DMORT). They and several other members of the Colorado Human Body Identification team, including Arapahoe County coroner Dr. Michael Doberson, were on standby as of the last week of September. They'd been told that they soon would be called to relieve teams already on the scene.

So why do they do it? Simple. Just ask the families of Michele Wallace, Diane Keidel, Cher Elder, Lois Kleber, Ike Hampton, Gerry Boggs, Heather Ikard, Heather Dawn Church, and Christine Elkins. No one could replace the lives lost, but neither were their loved ones left wondering what had happened to them. There is no statute of limitations on grief, and the truth *does* matter.

ACKNOWLEDGMENTS

The author would like to thank the members of NecroSearch International for their assistance without which this book would not have been possible. In particular, I would like to express my appreciation to NecroSearch members Jack Swanburg, Clark Davenport, Al Nelson, Tom Griffin, Diane France, Cecilia Travis, Vicki Trammell, John Lindemann, and Kim Castellano . . . dragonslayers come in many forms. Tax-deductible donations and public inquiries can be made by writing: NecroSearch International, 5686 S. Count Place, Littleton, CO 80120. I would also like to thank the law enforcement officers and district attorneys who cooperated in the making of this book, especially those involved in the cases outlined on these pages: Kathy Young, Ed Reynolds, Scott Richardson, Scott Buckley, and Mike Schmitz. NecroSearch would like to add their thanks and appreciation to Sheriff Patrick J. Sullivan of Arapahoe County and Sheriff Steve Zotos of Douglas County for their support. As always, I owe much to my agent, Mike Hamilburg, and his consigliere, Joanie Kern, Kensington Editor-in-Chief, Paul Dinas, and my gem of an editor at Kensington, Karen Haas, all for putting up with me. Thanks to Patty Calhoun at *Westword* for the freedom and dealing with the headaches I cause. My thanks and love to my number one publicist, Mom, and her assistant, Dad, as well as Marie Torrisi and Dick Torrisi. And lastly, but only on this page, my love and thanks to my wife, Carla, and my children for bringing light and love to balance against these dark tales.

INDEX